GORDON PAPE'S

1996 BUYER'S GUIDE

TO

Mutual Funds

D1413446

Also by Gordon Pape

INVESTMENT ADVICE
Building Wealth in the '90s
Low-Risk Investing in the '90s
Retiring Wealthy
Gordon Pape's 1996 Buyer's Guide to RRSPs

CONSUMER ADVICE
Gordon Pape's 1996 Car Value Guide

HUMOUR
The $50,000 Stove Handle

FICTION
(With Tony Aspler)
Chain Reaction
The Scorpion Sanction
The Music Wars

NON-FICTION
(With Donna Gabeline and Dane Lanken)
Montreal at the Crossroads

GORDON PAPE'S
1996
BUYER'S GUIDE
TO
Mutual Funds

Prentice Hall Canada Inc.
Scarborough, Ontario

Canadian Cataloguing in Publication Data

The National Library of Canada has catalogued this
publication as follows:

Pape, Gordon, 1936–
    Gordon Pape's ... buyer's guide to mutual funds

1993–
Annual.
Continues: Pape, Gordon, 1936–
Gordon Pape's ... guide to mutual funds.
ISSN 1193-9729
ISBN 0–13–399643–3 (1996)

1. Mutual funds – Canada – Handbooks, manuals, etc.
I. Title.

HG4530.P3   332.63'27   C93–030840–9

Prentice-Hall, Inc., Englewood Cliffs, New Jersey
Prentice-Hall International (UK) Limited, London
Prentice-Hall of Australia, Tty. Limited, Sydney
Prentice-Hall Hispanoamericana, S.A., Mexico City
Prentice-Hall of India Private Limited, New Delhi
Prentice-Hall of Japan, Inc., Tokyo
Simon & Schuster Asia Private Limited, Singapore
Editora Prentice-Hall do Brasil, Rio de Janeiro

ISBN: 0-13-399643-3

Production Coordinator: Anita Boyle-Evans
Cover Design: David Sohembri
Cover Image: J. Fitz Maurice
Page Layout: Gail Ferriera Ng-A-Kiel

1 2 3 4 5   K   00 99 98 97 96

Printed and bound in Canada

Contents

Introduction *1*

The Year Ahead *5*

Picking the Right Load Option —
   A Special Report *10*

Taxes *18*

Tax-Advantaged Funds *28*

Real Estate Funds *32*

Choosing a Dividend Income Fund *37*

Labour-Sponsored Funds *41*

Asset Allocation Services —
   How Good Are They? *50*

Assessing Emerging Markets Funds —
   A Special Report *61*

The Bank Funds — A Special Report *69*

The Roller-Coaster Funds — A Special Report *78*

Up-and-Coming Funds — A Special Report *93*

Selecting the Right Portfolio *102*

Fund Families *110*

THE TOP FUND GROUPS *151*

THE ENVELOPE, PLEASE! *165*

GORDON PAPE'S RATINGS 1996 169

How to Use the Mutual Fund Ratings *170*

Canadian Equity Funds (General) *176*

Canadian Equity Funds (Sector) *221*

U.S. Equity Funds *229*

International and Global Equity Funds *245*

Americas Equity Funds *262*

Far East Equity Funds *267*

European Equity Funds *273*

Emerging Markets Equity Funds   *277*

Dividend Income Funds   *280*

Canadian Bond Funds   *289*

Canadian Mortgage Funds   *309*

International Bond Funds   *316*

Canadian Balanced and Asset Allocation
  Funds   *322*

U.S. and International Balanced and
  Asset Allocation Funds   *351*

Specialty Funds   *356*

Canadian Money Market Funds   *360*

International Money Market Funds   *379*

FUNDLISTS   *384*

Fund Index   *414*

Subject Index   *432*

GORDON PAPE'S

1996 BUYER'S GUIDE

TO

Mutual Funds

Prentice Hall Canada Inc.
Scarborough, Ontario

Introduction

I f you've been a regular purchaser of my annual *Buyer's Guide to Mutual Funds*, you'll find some major changes in this year's edition.

Over the past five years, this *Guide* has expanded considerably, reflecting the rapid growth in Canada's mutual fund industry. But the basic format that I used in creating the original *Guide* in 1991 has remained unchanged. Readers seemed to find it useful and helpful in making their mutual fund investing decisions so, operating on the "If-it-ain't-broke-don't-fix-it" principal, I left well enough alone. The ratings were expanded and updated every year, of course, and special reports were added to explain changes in this dynamic industry. But the core of the *Guide* remained essentially the same. ■

Until now, that is. After five editions, I felt it was time to give the *Guide* an overhaul, in an effort to make it even more valuable to you as an investor. The ratings are still the heart of the *Guide*, of course. But this year you'll also find a number of new features, designed to help you make more informed purchase decisions.

Here's a brief summary of some of the highlights.

A look at the year ahead. Forecasting is an imperfect art, at best. But to manage your mutual funds wisely, you should have at least some insight into what economic and political developments are likely to affect your investments over the next 12 months. I'm not always right (who is?), but my track record here is pretty good. In the 1995 edition, for example, I said that economic conditions suggested good returns from equity funds during the year, which turned out to be right on.

In the past, these forecasts have been included in the ratings sections. However, several readers have told me that they would prefer to have this information in a separate chapter, so they could get a full overview of what appears to be ahead. As a result, I've written a new chapter, titled "The Year Ahead," which immediately follows this introduction. I hope you'll find it helpful in planning your mutual fund strategy for 1996.

The 1996 Mutual Fund Awards. Who's best, who's worst, who's up, who's down, who's in line for special recognition. You'll find them all in the "Awards" chapter.

Ratings. To help you spot the top funds quickly, we've added a new feature this year — all $$$ and $$$$ funds will be shown in green. As well, we've rearranged the categories so that they better reflect the many changes that have taken place in the mutual funds marketplace.

The FundLists. Which are the 10 funds you absolutely must own? What are the best funds for an RRSP? Which 10 funds are on the way up — and which are on the way down? What are the five best funds for tax-advantaged income? You'll find all these answers and more in a new feature at the back of the book called "FundLists" — 43 mutual fund lists covering just about every aspect of fund investing you can imagine.

Fund families. We've reorganized the list of funds in each group so you can now see at a glance how all the funds offered by a company are rated.

Index. Over the years, many readers have asked that an index be included in this *Guide*. This year, we've done it. You'll find it at the back.

Special Reports. There are five of them in this edition. "Picking the Right Load Option" will help you decide between front-end load, back-end load, and no-load options. "Emerging Markets Funds" looks at what's happening in these up-and-down markets and what funds are performing best. "The Bank Funds" analyzes how the big no-load groups are performing compared to the competition. "Roller-Coaster Funds" examines some of Canada's most volatile mutual funds from a risk/return perspective. Finally, the "Up-and-Coming Funds" looks at new mutual funds that should fare well but that haven't been around long enough to earn a formal rating.

To make way for all this new information while keeping the *Guide* to a manageable size, we've had to drop some material that had been included in previous editions. Most of this relates to mutual fund fundamentals — definitions, types of funds, risk and volatility, reading a prospectus, the role of the manager, setting objectives, portfolio strategies, etc. If you're just getting into mutual funds for the first time and would like this basic information, watch for my next book, *Getting Started in Mutual Funds,* to be published by Prentice Hall Canada in spring 1996.

To buyers of this *Guide*, we're pleased to make a special offer for my newsletter, *Gordon Pape's Mutual Funds Update*. This newsletter is intended to keep serious mutual fund investors up-to-date on where the best profit opportunities can be found during the period between editions of this *Guide*. It includes model portfolios, which are updated regularly, changes in mutual fund ratings, analyses of trends in the fund industry, reports on hot new funds, danger signals, and a lot more. To get the special offer, just fill out and return the card you'll find in this book.

In conclusion, I'd like to thank the many people who helped make this edition possible. They include Paul Gratias of the Private Client Services Group of the chartered accounting firm of Ernst & Young, who supplied the tax tables; Deborah Pape and Wanda Ottewell, who spent many hours researching the material; and Kendrew Pape, who assisted me in the writing of several chapters. Thanks also to the people in the mutual funds industry who answered our many questions with patience and good humour.

I hope you enjoy this new edition of the *Buyer's Guide to Mutual Funds*, and that you'll find the changes to be helpful. If you have any comments or suggestions, I'm always happy to receive them. Just drop me a note care of Prentice Hall Canada, 1870 Birchmount Road, Scarborough, Ontario M1P 2J7.

GORDON PAPE
Toronto, Ontario

The Year Ahead

When they write the history of mutual funds in Canada, 1994 will not go down as a banner year. The manager of almost any fund that broke even over the 12 months was a hero to his/her unit-holders. Bond funds, stock funds, mortgage funds, real estate funds — everyone took it on the chin. As a group, only money market funds prospered

Not surprisingly, some investors lost confidence in mutual funds, especially those who had been lured by the huge returns of 1993. Many of the so-called "GIC refugees" returned to their instinctive home when interest rates began to rise and stock and bond markets started to tumble. ■

But those who held on through the dark days of '94 were rewarded when the markets turned around in '95 and set new records in the first half of the year. The improvement took place almost across the board — only a few sectors, such as emerging markets generally and Latin America in particular, were trouble spots.

North American stocks were especially strong. According to *The Financial Post,* the average broadly based Canadian equity fund returned 8.6 percent from

January to June, 1995. Some did far better. Six-month returns of 15 percent and higher were not uncommon as the markets steamed ahead, buoyed by falling interest rates.

U.S. stocks were even stronger. The Dow hit record highs and U.S. equity funds went along for the ride. According to *The Financial Post,* the average U.S. stock fund gained 13.2 percent in the first half of '95, with many up 15 percent and more.

If you bought last year's edition of this *Guide* and acted on my recommendations, you should have profited from these developments. Last year I wrote in the introduction to the Canadian Equity Funds section: "The economic recovery seems strong and sustainable, not just here but in the United States as well. That bodes well for stock prices. If we resolve our political problems and make some reasonable effort at deficit control, the Canadian stock market could zoom ahead again in '95."

Well, zoom it did, with healthy profits across the board. But that's history. What comes next?

Normally, after a strong move such as we experienced in the first half of '95, stock markets pause to catch their breath. That's precisely what happened in 1994, after the market explosion of '93. I expect we'll see the same phenomenon again in late '95 or early '96. Exactly how stock markets will be affected will depend on three key factors:

1) The strength of the economy. If North American growth can be sustained at a reasonable pace, the markets could have more life in this cycle. As this is written, in August 1995, there appears a good possibility that will happen. All indications are that the U.S. Federal Reserve Board has achieved that economic Nirvana, the "soft landing," opening the way to continued economic growth at a manageable pace, without strong inflationary pressures. If this is indeed the case, there is nothing to stop stock markets from posting more gains in 1996, albeit at a more modest pace.

   Stock market movements in the mid-'80s, which the mid-'90s have mirrored to a startling degree thus far, offer some important clues. Look at the table that follows, showing total returns from the TSE 300 Index.

Year	Return	Year	Return
1983	35.49%	1993	32.55%
1984	- 2.39%	1994	-0.18%
1985	25.07%	1995 (6 mo.)	8.75%
1986	8.95%	1996	?

As you can see, the TSE continued to rise in calendar 1986, but at a much more restrained pace than in the previous year. We could see a repetition of that pattern in 1996, if all goes well. But be prepared for some market jitters along the way — that's typical as a growth cycle appears to be approaching its end.

2) Interest rates. Higher rates are the bane of stock prices, as we saw in early '94. Keep a close eye on what the Federal Reserve Board does in the U.S. and how the Canadian dollar performs. Those two indicators will tell you where the Bank of Canada is going.

3) Quebec. The Quebec referendum, scheduled for Oct. 30, will have a major impact on the direction of Canadian stocks in the coming months. If the "No" side carries the day, the effect will be positive and markets should react strongly. If the "Yes" side wins, it will usher in a period of uncertainty and confusion that will likely push stock prices down.

Generally, at this point in the business cycle, discretion is warranted. You should consider some selective profit-taking in your North American equity funds and add to cash reserves as we move deeper into 1996. Quality becomes all the more important in times like these. If Quebec votes "No," the Canadian stock market could outperform Wall Street in the year ahead.

Moving over to fixed income securities, I also suggest caution. After taking a hammering in '94, bond markets snapped back smartly in the first half of '95, propelled by a slowing North American economy and a U.S. Federal Reserve Board decision in July to cut rates.

Canadian bond funds gained an average of 9.6 percent

7

in the first six months of '95, according to *The Financial Post*. Many did much better, with gains in the 12 percent plus range.

The comeback in the market was much stronger than I anticipated when I wrote in last year's *Guide* that bond prices would likely continue to be volatile. But I don't expect '95's first half bond rally to continue, although a "No" vote in Quebec could produce a major rally over the rest. A resurgence in economic growth plus uncertainties about Quebec could both act as catalysts to push interest rates higher over the fall of '95 and into '96.

As we approach the later phases of a growth cycle, inflation inevitably starts to rear its head, and that has an upsetting effect on bond markets. Long-term bonds are especially vulnerable to price declines in these conditions. While I don't anticipate a bond market drop of the magnitude we saw in early '94, some dips in bond fund unit values are likely as we move through '96.

If these short-term movements worry you, switch some of your fixed income assets into short-term bond funds, mortgage funds, and money market funds, all of which will be less vulnerable to interest rate changes. However, if you're a long-term investor or holding these funds in an RRSP, you may wish to ride out any temporary storms. Market movements will even out over time (bond values will shoot up again when the next recession arrives) and in the interim you'll continue to collect interest on your holdings.

Interest rates, which fell in the first half of '95 in response to slowing economic growth, will probably begin to firm again late in the year and in '96 if the economic recovery does resume as anticipated. While this will be bad news for bond funds, it will be good news for investors in money market funds, which should produce higher returns.

Overseas, look for some recovery in the Far East, where most markets had an off year in 1995. Japan, which has been in a deep funk in recent years, should start to show some signs of life again. Aggressive investors who can live with the risk may wish to add a Japan fund to their holdings. More risk-averse investors should choose a broadly based Far East fund that invests throughout the region, including Japan.

Europe's economic recovery started to gather some strength in 1995 and European equity funds benefitted accordingly. Growth should continue on the continent and I look for European funds to continue to perform modestly well.

Emerging markets funds were battered in '94 and continued to hurt in '95 as investors, shell-shocked by the peso devaluation, rushed to pull their money out. But the reality is that emerging nations still have much greater growth potential than the developed countries and returns from well-managed emerging markets funds should reflect that. These areas of the world can be very volatile so don't overextend yourself, but a small portion of your assets invested in a good emerging markets fund, especially when prices are weak, should pay some nice returns over time.

All in all, the year ahead appears to promise modest rewards in many areas, but prudence is required. Don't be greedy, and be prepared to take some profits at appropriate times. Hold your gains in money market funds, where yields should be improving, until a clearer picture emerges of where the North American economy is going and what lies in store for Canada after the referendum.

Picking The Right Load Option

— A SPECIAL REPORT

There's a revolution brewing in the mutual funds industry, and it's going to complicate your life. Some of the major players are changing the way they market their products, and the impact could be as far-reaching as the switch to back-end load funds was in the 1980s. ∎

At stake is the heated battle for market share in this rapidly growing industry. In the early '90s, no-load funds offered by financial institutions and fund-by-phone marketers like Altamira steadily eroded the position of traditional fund companies that sell units through brokers and financial planners on a commission basis.

That situation temporarily changed in 1994 and early 1995, as some new investors fled no-load funds, frightened by dropping unit values as stock and bond markets took it on the chin. A major contributing factor to that flight was that the no-load funds had no one to hold the hands of nervous investors — a role filled by brokers and planners for the load fund groups.

But that situation could turn around as markets rebound. Many of the load fund companies interpreted the gains made by their no-load competitors in the early '90s as a shot across their bow, and have resolved to ensure it doesn't happen again.

They're fighting back by invading the competition's turf. Their strategy: to offer no-load (or sometimes low-load) sales options of their own as one of the ways to buy their fund units.

Spectrum Bullock and AGF are two of the major companies that have moved in this direction.

AGF made the switch in late 1994, moving to three classes of fund units after receiving shareholder approval at a series of special meetings. Here's the structure that's now in place:

A shares: These are sold on a front-end load basis, with a maximum commission of 6 percent. They can be redeemed at any time, without a fee. For equity funds, a base management fee of 2 percent plus expenses is deducted from fund assets before units are valued. The management fee for fixed income and money market funds is somewhat less.

B shares: These are sold on a back-end load basis. No commission is payable when they're purchased. But if units are sold within eight years, a redemption fee applies (maximum 5.5 percent). The basic management fee for equity units is 2.5 percent. These units can be converted to A shares without cost after nine years, which means they would then benefit from the reduced management charge.

C shares: Here's the big change. These units are sold without sales commissions of any kind. The basic management fee for equity funds is 2.5 percent, for as long as you hold the units.

So when you buy AGF funds, you have to decide among three purchase options. Which should you choose?

The immediate reaction of many people is to buy the C shares — the no-load option. After all, if you can avoid paying sales commissions, why not?

Because it could end up costing you money, that's why not. The no-load option won't always be the best choice, with AGF or any of the other companies that offer their fund units in this way.

Let's look at some math. To work out the following calculations, I've used my new software program, called *Gordon Pape's Mutual Funds Analyzer*.

(This is just one of the many functions it performs; the program also allows you to compare the performance of all Canadian mutual funds using any criteria you wish, and to set up and monitor your own personal funds portfolio.)

Back to AGF. Let's assume you have $10,000 to invest and you're trying to decide between the A, B, and C shares of one of the AGF equity funds. The rate of return before management fees in each case is 10 percent.

We'll assume you pay a 4 percent front-end load for the A shares, and a redemption fee on the B shares, where applicable, based on your original purchase price. There is, of course, no commission either way on the C shares.

The basic management fee on the A shares will be 2 percent. On the other two, it will be 2.5 percent. There will be taxes and other expenses, but let's confine ourselves only to the difference in the basic management fee for this exercise. The management fee charges shown include the loss of income from your portfolio over time as a result of compounding. Here's a look at the final value of your investment under various scenarios.

Scenario 1 — Short-term hold.   Here we'll assume you only hold your units for three years, then sell. This is what happens.

	Load Charge	Redemption Fee	Management Fees	Total Charges	End Value
A	$400	$0	$817	$1,217	$12,093
B	0	500	887	1,387	11,923
C	0	0	887	887	12,423

In this case, the no-load option is your best choice, although the difference in the end value between it and the 4 percent front-end load is relatively small (although if you paid a higher front-end commission the difference would be more pronounced). The back-end load (B units) is clearly the worst option.

Scenario 2 — Mid-term hold.   Here we'll assume you hold your units for five years, then sell. This is what happens.

	Load Charge	Redemption Fee	Management Fees	Total Charges	End Value
A	$400	$0	$1,600	$2,000	$14,106
B	0	400	1,749	2,149	13,956
C	0	0	1,749	1,749	14,356

The no-load option is still the best choice, but the gap is narrowing. The back-end load option still ends up last.

Scenario 3 — Longer-term hold.   Now we'll take a look at the impact if you hold your units for 10 years, then sell. We'll assume you exercise the option to convert B shares to A units after nine years, thus benefitting from the lower management fee.

	Load Charge	Redemption Fee	Management Fees	Total Charges	End Value
A	$400	$0	$4,812	$5,212	$20,726
B	0	0	5,223	5,223	20,714
C	0	0	5,327	5,327	20,610

Now the picture changes. The front-end load units produce the best end result, because enough years have passed for the initial sales commission to be more than compensated for by the reduced management charge. The no-load option is now the worst performer.

Scenario 4 — Extended-term hold.   Here we'll look at the result if you hold your units for 20 years. Again, we'll assume you convert B units to A units after nine years.

	Load Charge	Redemption Fee	Management Fees	Total Charges	End Value
A	$400	$0	$22,130	$22,530	$44,745
B	0	0	22,555	22,555	44,720
C	0	0	24,768	24,768	42,749

Now the long-term effect of the higher management fees really starts to show. The end value of the A units is $2,000 more than the value of the C (no-load) units. The higher management fee has eaten a big chunk of your profits.

The message is clear. You have to give careful thought to the sales option you select, keeping in mind how long you expect to hold on to your units. Of course, that's difficult to predict, but consider your own investment personality. If you're the kind of person who tends to be impatient and to trade frequently, it's unlikely you'll keep your units for more than a few years. If you think that five years is a long time in investment terms, choose the C shares.

On the other hand, if you are a strong believer in the buy and hold school of investing, the A shares will be your choice. As we've seen, it's better to pay a sales commission up front and get the benefit of a lower management fee if you intend to keep your shares for 10 years or more.

It's interesting to note that the B units don't come out in first place under any of the above scenarios. This won't always be the case, as we'll see in a moment. But since most mutual fund investors who pay a sales commission choose a deferred-load option, this is an important point to keep in mind — and it gives you an idea of just how significant this new marketing revolution may be.

Now let's take a look at another fund group that also offers A, B, and C shares, Spectrum Bullock.

Under their system, A shares (front-end load) carry a 2 percent annual management fee, B shares (back-end load) have a 2.25 percent charge, and C shares (no load) are assessed 2.5 percent.

In this situation, the back-end load (B) units will emerge as the best choice under certain conditions. Spectrum Bullock's vice-president of investments, Karen Bleasby, kindly prepared an analysis for me of the most efficient purchase option, based on your anticipated holding period and the front-end load you're being asked to pay on the A shares. Here are her recommendations:

Holding Period Up to Year	1%	2%	3%	4%	5-6%
1	C	C	C	C	C
2	C	C	C	C	C
3	A	C	C	C	C
4	A	C	C	C	C
5	A	A	C	C	C
6	A	B	B	B	B
7	A	B	B	B	B
8	A	B	B	B	B
9	A	A	B	B	B
10	A	A	B	B	B
11	A	A	B	B	B
12	A	A	B	B	B
13	A	A	A	B	B
14	A	A	A	B	B
15	A	A	A	B	B
16	A	A	A	B	B
17	A	A	A	B	B
18	A	A	A	A	B
19	A	A	A	A	B
20	A	A	A	A	B

Is it any wonder investors are confused by this proliferation of purchase options?

Recommended action: If you're faced with multiple purchase choices with any fund company, use my *Mutual Funds Analyzer* software program to compare options or ask your sales representative to give you an analysis like the one prepared by Spectrum Bullock. Then you'll be able to decide which commission/management fee structure works best for you.

As if trying to choose between A, B, and C purchase options wasn't complicated enough, there's another new angle to the mutual funds buying game that could cost the unwary a lot of money.

It's the negotiable deferred sales charge, a purchase option that's, fortunately, still rare but, unfortunately, spreading. Some of the companies that have adopted this approach are Elliott & Page, Global Strategy, BPI, Sagit, and Admax Regent. If you purchase any of their funds on a back-end load basis, make sure you clearly understand exactly what's going on.

The negotiable back-end load is an extension of the practice that's applied to front-end sales commissions for years. Mutual fund companies set the range of the commission that can be charged. In the past, it was typically 0 to 9 percent on a front-end load basis; more recently some companies have trimmed the range to 0 to 5 percent.

In most cases, the actual amount paid is negotiated between the purchaser and the sales representative. (There are a few situations where the commission is fixed. This is usually the case where organizations employ their own sales forces — Investors Group is an example.) Where commissions are negotiable, the normal practice is that the higher the commission the seller can persuade you to part with, the greater the payment he/she receives on the sale.

This practice is in contrast to standard commission policies in the brokerage industry, where rates are fixed on the basis of the number of shares traded and/or the dollar value of the trade. The mutual fund commission structure creates an adversarial relationship between the client and sales person — it's in the vendor's interest to get the investor to pay as much as possible, while it's in the buyer's interest to negotiate the lowest possible commission.

However, the practice as it relates to front-end loads has been around so long it's unlikely to be changed. What disturbs me is the extension of this adversarial approach to back-end loads, a sales option that buyers are not used to negotiating.

Until recently, when you bought a fund on a back-end load (deferred sales charge) basis you knew the redemption schedule was fixed. Usually the percentage you pay declines over time until it reaches zero after a certain number of years.

Most companies still use a fixed redemption fee schedule. But others now have a range of fees and you, the buyer, have to negotiate what you'll pay.

To illustrate, here are the redemption fee schedules currently allowed by Elliott & Page. At the bottom is the amount of the payout the sales person receives, depending on which schedule he/she can get you to accept.

ELLIOTT & PAGE
DEFERRED LOAD CHARGE SCHEDULE

Year	I	II	III	IV	V
1	6.0%	5.0%	4.0%	3.0%	2.0%
2	5.5%	4.5%	3.5%	2.5%	1.5%
3	5.0%	4.0%	3.0%	2.0%	1.0%
4	4.5%	3.5%	2.5%	1.5%	1.0%
5	4.0%	3.0%	2.0%	1.0%	1.0%
6	3.5%	2.5%	1.5%	1.0%	1.0%
7	0	0	0	0	0
Seller's Payment	5.0%	4.0%	3.0%	2.0%	1.0%

Take a close look at this table and then ask yourself, as an investor, which back-end load structure you want. Number V, of course. Now put yourself in the sales person's place and see which structure you'd prefer. Surprise — Number I, which offers a 5 percent payout instead of the meagre 1 percent on Number V.

Now ask yourself how likely it is that the sales rep is going to lead you through these five structures in detail and then ask which you prefer. What's far more likely to happen is that you'll be told something like: "Right, back-end load. That'll be 6 percent in the first year, declining to zero after six years, okay?"

Your answer should *not* be an automatic okay. With all back-end load purchases now, the correct response is: "Are there other redemption schedule options and, if so, please explain them to me." You'll also find details in the fund's prospectus, which you should read carefully before making any commitment.

As always, it's buyer beware.

Taxes

With Canadian tax rates at back-breaking levels, one of the most important criteria in selecting a mutual funds portfolio is the amount of money you'll end up with in your pocket at the end of the day. Surprisingly, many investors give little or no consideration to the tax consequences of their actions until it's too late to do much about it.

You're liable for taxes on any profits you make from your mutual fund investments, whether you receive the money directly, in the form of a cheque from the mutual fund company, or indirectly, by having any distributions reinvested in additional fund units. But there are several ways to reduce the tax burden, if you know how. ■

The easiest way to cut taxes is to hold your mutual fund investments in some sort of tax shelter, such as a registered retirement savings plan (RRSP) or a registered retirement income fund (RRIF). Most Canadian mutual funds are eligible for such treatment, either without restriction or under the foreign content rules (no more than 20 percent of the book value of your RRSP or RRIF can consist of foreign investments).

If you can't tax shelter your mutual fund investments,

there are other ways to reduce Revenue Canada's bite by selecting your investments wisely. The corporate structure of the mutual fund you purchase will also have an effect on the taxes you pay so you should be aware of what it is (most investors never bother to check).

There are two types of mutual fund structures:

Mutual fund trusts. This is the most common. A mutual fund trust will distribute all the income it takes in to unit-holders in the form it received the money, so that the fund itself does not have to pay any taxes. This means any capital gains earned by the fund come to you as such, as do dividends, interest, rental income, etc. You'll receive a T3 slip from the fund each year, showing the origin of all income distributed to you. For example, you may have received $1,000 from a fund last year, of which $500 represented your share of its total realized capital gains, $300 your share of dividends from taxable Canadian companies, and $200 your share of interest earned by the fund. Each of these individual amounts will be shown in a box on the T3 form and each must be declared separately on your tax return at the appropriate line.

Mutual fund corporations. In this case, the fund itself is taxable on the income it receives from all sources. Once all taxes have been paid, the fund declares a dividend for distribution to shareholders. This means any income you receive from the fund (except for capital gains, which are treated separately) is in the form of a dividend from a taxable Canadian corporation, and is therefore eligible for the dividend tax credit. It doesn't matter whether the fund originally received the income in the form of interest, foreign dividends, or whatever — in your hands, it's all the same. The net result probably won't be any tax saving, since the fund has already paid appropriate taxes on the income before distributing the profits to shareholders. But it greatly simplifies the tax reporting of your income.

Now, here's a rundown of the types of profits your mutual funds may generate and the tax implications of each. As you'll see, in some cases the treatment will be different depending on whether the fund is structured as a trust or a corporation.

Capital gains. Whenever you sell units in a mutual fund for a higher price than you originally paid, you've made a capital gain. However, the amount subject to tax will be affected by several factors. These include:

LOAD CHARGES — If you paid a commission to purchase the fund, this amount can be added to your purchase price for tax purposes, producing a higher "adjusted cost base."

DISPOSITION COSTS — Any expenses associated with the sale of your units, such as a redemption fee, can be subtracted from the proceeds of the sale before calculating the tax owed.

REINVESTED DISTRIBUTIONS — If you have directed that distributions from the fund be used to purchase additional units, these amounts can be added to the adjusted cost base.

Here's how some of these costs would affect your tax payable. Suppose, for example, you bought 100 shares in a no-load fund for $10 each (total $1,000) and later sold them for $15 each (total $1,500). You would have a taxable capital gain of $500. However, if you paid a front-end load of 5 percent, you would add $50 to the amount of your original investment, producing an adjusted cost base of $1,050 and reducing the capital gain to $450. If you were charged a $25 fee for closing your account, you would subtract this from the gross proceeds of the sale, reducing the net amount to $1,475 and the amount subject to tax to $425.

Note that you must sell or otherwise dispose of your units (such as by contributing them to a self-directed RRSP or exchanging them for units in another fund) to trigger the tax liability. Unrealized capital gains are not taxed. The first 25 percent of any capital gain is free; the balance is added to your income and taxed accordingly.

Capital gains distributions. Even if you don't sell your fund units, you may be credited with capital gains for tax purposes if the fund distributes some of the profits it makes from the sale of securities to unit-holders. These will be indicated in Box 21 of the T3 slip. These capital gains are treated the same way for tax purposes as those explained above.

Dividends (Canadian). Any dividends from taxable Canadian corporations that are distributed to you must be declared for tax purposes. However, you'll be allowed to claim the dividend tax credit in connection with these payments, thus reducing the tax impact. If your fund is a trust, you'll find the actual amount of dividends credited to you in Box 23 of the T3 slip. The taxable amount of dividends eligible for the dividend tax credit appears in Box 32 and the amount of dividend tax credit you can claim will be shown in Box 39.

Dividends (foreign). If your mutual fund is a corporation, you don't have to concern yourself with this type of income. All the tax implications will be dealt with at the corporate level before distributions are made. If your fund is a trust, it's a different story. Any dividends from foreign sources will be shown separately on your T3 slip, as will any tax withheld at source. Taxes withheld by another country may be eligible for a foreign tax credit on your Canadian return. Dividends from foreign corporations are not eligible for the dividend tax credit.

Interest. Any interest income credited to you by a mutual fund trust will be shown in Box 26 of the T3 slip, headed "Other Income." This income will be subject to tax at your marginal rate (the rate you pay on the last dollar you earn) and is not eligible for any special tax treatment.

Rental income. If you own units in a real estate fund (either closed- or open-end), some of the income you receive may be from rents. This income is eligible for special treatment because capital cost allowance (CCA) may be used to shelter part or all of it from tax. The mutual fund company will normally make the necessary calculations on your behalf. However, you should be aware that any tax advantages gained in this way may be partially offset when you sell your units in the fund. Ask for full details from the mutual fund company before investing.

You'll pay tax at different rates depending on the type of distribution you receive from the mutual fund company. The applicable tax rates in all brackets for dividends, interest, and non-exempt capital gains are below. They were prepared by Paul Gratias of the Private Client Services group of the firm Ernst & Young, chartered accountants, and are reproduced here with permission.

All rates assume the investment income is being earned on top of a base salary. They include federal and provincial income taxes, surtaxes, and provincial tax reductions. The basic personal tax credit is allowed for in the calculation.

Tax on capital gains, when applicable, is only paid on 75 percent of the total gain. The rates shown below take that into account and represent the effective rate for the full capital gain.

Dividend rates apply to the actual amount of dividends received from taxable Canadian corporations, not the grossed-up amount.

1995 MARGINAL TAX RATES

BRITISH COLUMBIA

Taxable Income	Interest	Dividends	Capital Gains
$6,457 to $29,590	26.43%	7.13%	19.82%
29,591 to 53,292	40.43%	24.62%	30.32%
53,293 to 59,179	44.53%	27.11%	33.39%
59,180 to 62,192	49.66%	33.54%	37.25%
62,193 to 78,201	51.11%	34.52%	38.33%
78,202 and up	54.16%	36.57%	40.62%

ALBERTA

Taxable Income	Interest	Dividends	Capital Gains
$6,457 to $9,545	17.51%	4.72%	13.14%
9,546 to 16,507*	29.86%	8.79%	22.40%
16,508 to 29,590	25.74%	7.43%	19.30%
29,591 to 44,050	39.11%	24.14%	29.33%
44,051 to 59,179	40.06%	24.71%	30.05%
59,180 to 62,192	44.62%	30.42%	33.47%
62,193 and up	46.07%	31.40%	34.55%

SASKATCHEWAN

Taxable Income	Interest	Dividends	Capital Gains
$6,457 to $6,957	17.51%	4.72%	13.13%
6,958 to 9,999	27.42%	9.51%	20.56%
10,000 to 13,999*	33.01%	16.24%	24.76%
14,000 to 19,500	28.05%	9.74%	21.04%
19,501 to 29,590	29.06%	9.99%	21.80%
29,591 to 39,203	43.28%	27.77%	32.46%
39,204 to 59,179	45.53%	29.33%	34.15%
59,180 to 62,192	50.50%	35.54%	37.87%
62,193 and up	51.95%	36.51%	38.96%

MANITOBA

Taxable Income	Interest	Dividends	Capital Gains
$6,457 to $7,793	17.51%	4.72%	13.13%
7,794 to 21,499*	30.35%	12.10%	22.76%
21,500 to 29,590	28.34%	9.60%	21.26%
29,591 to 29,999	42.30%	27.04%	31.73%
30,000 to 59,179	44.30%	29.54%	33.23%
59,180 to 62,192	48.95%	35.35%	36.71%
62,193 and up	50.40%	36.33%	37.80%

ONTARIO

Taxable Income	Interest	Dividends	Capital Gains
$6,457 to $8,535	17.51%	4.72%	13.13%
8,536 to 9,574*	47.11%	12.70%	35.31%
9,575 to 29,590	27.36%	7.38%	20.52%
29,591 to 50,937	41.86%	25.49%	31.40%
50,938 to 59,179	44.88%	27.33%	33.67%
59,180 to 62,192	50.05%	33.80%	37.54%
62,193 to 66,651	51.50%	34.78%	38.63%
66,652 and up	53.19%	35.92%	39.89%

QUEBEC

Taxable Income	Interest	Dividends	Capital Gains
$6,457 to $7,315	14.70%	3.96%	11.03%
7,316 to 13,999	33.70%	16.63%	25.28%
14,000 to 22,999	35.70%	19.13%	26.78%
23,000 to 29,590	37.70%	21.63%	28.28%
29,591 to 30,999	45.49%	31.36%	34.12%
31,000 to 49,999	46.64%	32.24%	34.98%
50,000 to 52,625	47.69%	33.55%	35.77%
52,626 to 59,179	48.89%	34.50%	36.67%
59,180 to 62,192	51.49%	37.74%	38.62%
62,193 and up	52.94%	38.72%	39.71%

NOVA SCOTIA

Taxable Income	Interest	Dividends	Capital Gains
$6,457 to $29,590	27.63%	7.45%	20.72%
29,591 to 59,179	42.25%	25.73%	31.69%
59,180 to 62,192	47.13%	31.82%	35.34%
62,193 to 77,042	48.58%	32.80%	36.43%
77,043 and up	50.30%	33.97%	37.73%

NEW BRUNSWICK

Taxable Income	Interest	Dividends	Capital Gains
$6,457 to $29,590	28.39%	7.65%	21.29%
29,591 to 59,179	43.42%	26.44%	32.57%
59,180 to 62,192	48.43%	32.70%	36.32%
62,193 to 91,824	49.88%	33.68%	37.41%
91,825 and up	51.36%	34.69%	38.52%

PRINCE EDWARD ISLAND

Taxable Income	Interest	Dividends	Capital Gains
$6,457 to $29,590	27.62%	7.45%	20.72%
29,591 to 59,179	42.25%	25.73%	31.69%
59,180 to 62,192	47.13%	31.82%	35.34%
62,193 to 91,531	48.58%	32.80%	36.43%
91,532 and up	50.30%	33.97%	37.73%

NEWFOUNDLAND

Taxable Income	Interest	Dividends	Capital Gains
$6,457 to $29,590	29.24%	7.88%	21.93%
29,591 to 59,179	44.72%	27.23%	33.54%
59,180 to 62,192	49.88%	33.68%	37.41%
62,193 and up	51.33%	34.66%	38.50%

NORTHWEST TERRITORIES

Taxable Income	Interest	Dividends	Capital Gains
$6,457 to $29,590	25.16%	6.78%	18.87%
29,591 to 59,179	38.48%	23.43%	28.86%
59,180 to 62,192	42.92%	28.98%	32.19%
62,193 and up	44.37%	29.96%	33.28%

YUKON TERRITORY

Taxable Income	Interest	Dividends	Capital Gains
$6,457 to $29,590	26.01%	7.01%	19.51%
29,591 to 59,179	39.78%	24.23%	29.84%
59,180 to 60,467	44.37%	29.96%	33.28%
60,468 to 62,192	45.10%	30.45%	33.82%
62,193 and up	46.55%	31.43%	34.91%

* Higher marginal income tax bracket results from the recapture of provincial tax reductions allowed at lower levels of income.

There are a few more important tax considerations to remember when buying mutual funds:

Make sure your registered and non-registered portfolios are structured so you pay the least possible tax. As a general rule, you should hold fixed income and money market mutual funds (those which are designed to generate interest) inside a registered plan, such as an RRSP or RRIF. That's because interest income is taxed at the highest rate, as you can see from the preceding tables. Keep equity, dividend, and real estate funds outside the registered plan, since profits earned by these types of funds are taxed more favourably (see next section). If your money is being professionally managed, check to see these basic tax guidelines are being observed. I recently came across a case where an Edmonton investment house had replicated exactly the same portfolio in a client's registered and non-registered account. As a result, the customer was paying several thousand dollars a year in unnecessary taxes.

Remember that switching from one fund to another may trigger a tax liability. Revenue Canada takes the position that a switch is the same as a sale. If you've made a capital gain on the fund you're leaving, that profit will be subject to tax at the capital gains rate when you file your next return. Obviously, this won't apply if the switch takes place within an RRSP or RRIF. A few fund groups offer "umbrella" funds, which allow you to switch from one "section" of the fund to another without triggering a capital gain. AGF, C.I., and GT Global use this approach for some of their funds. However, the tax-deferral is only temporary. When you eventually sell your units in the umbrella fund, taxes will have to be paid.

Buying funds at year-end may cause tax problems. Many funds make an annual profit distribution at year-end to unit-holders of record on December 31. If you buy into the fund a few days before, you'll receive the same payment as someone who has owned it all year. Sounds great? It's not. As Midland Walwyn financial advisor Stanley Tepner pointed out in *The Globe and Mail* recently, you end up paying tax on money you didn't earn. Here's how. Suppose you own 1,000 fund units that you just bought. They are valued at $10 each on December 31. The total value of your investment therefore equals $10,000. The fund manager declares a $1 distribution. You receive a cheque for $1,000. Because this is an open-end fund, the net asset value of the units is adjusted to $9, reflecting the distribution payment. You still have $10,000 in assets — only now you have to pay tax on $1,000 of that amount. You're out of pocket several hundred dollars, just because you bought in at the wrong time. The solution? Buy new units after the first of the year or choose funds that make distributions more frequently, thereby minimizing this effect.

Tax-Advantaged Funds

There are a number of ways to use mutual funds tax-effectively outside registered plans, but you'll need to give careful consideration to the type of securities they invest in and use some well-planned strategies.

The starting point is understanding that a buck is not a buck when it comes to investment income. Our weird and wacky tax system treats every type of investment income differently, resulting in huge variations in after-tax return depending on the source of the money. ■

Here's a quick rundown on the four types of investment income you can earn and how each is treated for tax purposes by Revenue Canada.

Interest income: Much of our money is in interest-bearing investments, such as GICs, money market funds, fixed income funds, Canada Savings Bonds, and deposit accounts. All the interest you earn on these investments is taxed at your marginal rate — the tax rate that applies on the last dollar you earn. So if you're in a 40 percent tax bracket, you'll send Revenue Canada $40 out of every $100 in interest you receive. This is the only form of investment income for which no beneficial tax treatment is available.

Dividends: Dividends paid by taxable Canadian corporations qualify for a special tax break, known as the dividend tax credit. The formula for calculating the credit is somewhat complicated (needlessly so). You first "gross up" the dividends you receive by multiplying the actual amount by 1.25. This is the total you declare as income. Then multiply the result by 13.33 percent to get the dividend tax credit. This is subtracted from your federal tax owing.

For example, if you received $1,000 in dividends, the calculation would look like this:

$$\text{GROSS-UP} = \$1,000 \times 1.25 = \$1,250$$
$$\text{DIVIDEND TAX CREDIT} = \$1,250 \times 13.33\% = \$166.63$$

The credit is subtracted from your actual tax owing. The net effect is to make dividends one of the most tax-effective ways to receive investment income.

Capital gains: As long as the lifetime $100,000 capital gains exemption was in force (the Liberals ended it in the February 1994 budget), this was the most tax-effective way to earn investment income in Canada. Even without the exemption, capital gains still receive favourable tax treatment, however. Only 75 percent of your profit is included in income for tax purposes. The other 25 percent is, in effect, free. So although capital gains don't look quite as good as before from an after-tax point of view, they should still be one of your main investment priorities.

Rental income: Revenue from income properties is eligible for a wide range of tax write-offs that reduce the net amount on which you must pay tax. One of the most important of these deductions is capital cost allowance (CCA), a bookkeeping concept intended to compensate property owners for the depreciation in value of their buildings, furnishings, and equipment. Many sophisticated tax shelters have been built on the ingenious use of CCA, but ordinary investors can benefit from it too.

All these complex tax rules mean that you must earn many more dollars in interest income than in dividends, capital gains, or rental income to end up with the same after-tax return. The ratios will vary depending on your tax bracket and where you live. A top-bracket Ontario taxpayer, for example, would need to earn $1.37 in interest income to generate the same after-tax return as $1 in dividends. In the case of capital gains, $1.28 in interest would be needed to produce the same return after tax as $1 in capital gains.

Armed with this knowledge about the tax treatment of investment income, how can you take advantage of it?

A good first step is to take a look at your mutual funds portfolio to see if you should be making some changes to improve your after-tax return. The tax tables in the section titled Taxes will help.

If you have a large percentage of your holdings in money market funds, mortgage funds, or bond funds, you're paying tax on most of your investment earnings at your top marginal rate.

When interest rates are high, as they were in 1990 and again in 1994, these funds may perform better for you, even on an after-tax basis.

But when rates are low, as they were from 1991–93 and again in mid-1995, look at alternatives. You may find you can keep more cash in your pocket through some judicious switching of assets.

Obviously, any well-managed fund that generates a significant part of its return in the form of a capital gain is worth considering. But this suggests putting large amounts of money into equity funds, a tactic that makes some investors nervous — and not without reason.

There are alternatives, however. Two types of mutual funds offer some clear-cut tax advantages, sometimes (but not always) with less risk than ordinary equity funds. If you're looking for a bigger after-tax bang for your investment dollar, they're worth considering.

These are dividend income funds and real estate funds. Both come with some built-in tax advantages. Plus, dividend funds usually have less volatility than you'd normally find in a regular equity fund.

However, there are also some disadvantages you need to be aware of before investing.

The two sections that follow are designed to help you decide whether either of these tax-advantaged types of mutual funds is right for you. Dividend funds will especially appeal to those seeking alternatives to GICs. Real estate funds could be considered by investors looking for steady tax-free income, but only if you're willing to take the risks associated with volatile property values.

You'll find individual ratings for both types of funds at the back of this *Guide*.

Real Estate Funds

This has been a tough decade for real estate investors. The recession of the early '90s battered property values in most parts of the country, and a turnaround has been slow in coming.

Mid-city office buildings suffered the most. Vacancy rates, even for prime space, were running upwards of 20 percent in many areas at the nadir. Desperate property managers were cutting rates and doing deals — "anything's better than having the space sit empty," as one put it. ■

The office space disaster had three root causes:

1) Overbuilding during the roaring '80s, when it seemed like the bubble would never burst.

2) Downsizing by many companies hard hit by the recession.

3) A growing trend towards working from home, which is likely to continue as electronic technology becomes increasingly more sophisticated.

But the real estate bust didn't stop there. Industrial and retail properties were also hit hard, as were residential values in many cities, especially in southern Ontario.

Investors in real estate mutual funds were caught squarely in the middle of this crash. Real estate funds invest in commercial real estate properties, such as shopping centres, office buildings, and medical centres. Many saw the value of their assets fall dramatically in the early '90s as the market value of many properties fell and hard-pressed tenants either defaulted on their leases or demanded, and often got, a renegotiation of the terms.

The resulting squeeze put tremendous pressure on Canada's fledgling real estate mutual fund industry. As a result, some funds were wound up, while some that survived were forced to temporarily suspend redemptions.

The rationale for closing the redemption window to nervous investors who wanted to pull out their money was that the cash demands would have forced fund managers to sell properties at fire-sale prices. This would clearly have been detrimental to those who left their assets in a fund in the hope the property market would eventually turn back up.

But the no-redemption policy created problems for people who genuinely needed access to their money. As a result, some funds resorted to an imaginative longer-term solution to deal with the problem.

This was the conversion of three previously open-end real estate funds into closed-end Real Estate Investment Trusts (REITs).

The three are RealFund (formerly FirstCity RealFund), Canadian Real Estate Investment Trust (formerly Metfin Real Estate Growth Fund), and Riocan Real Estate Investment Trust (formerly Counsel Real Estate Fund). All now trade on the Toronto Stock Exchange, the first such securities to be offered in Canada (although REITs have been sold in the U.S. for years, where they represent a $40 billion industry).

The assets of the new REITs were exactly the same as those of the old mutual funds — a diversified portfolio of office, commercial, and industrial buildings located across Canada. The main difference between the old and new structures is valuation and liquidity.

When the old open-end funds converted to REITs, it meant the funds' treasuries would no longer redeem units at their net asset value. But the move enabled investors who wanted to cash out to sell their units on the TSE at the current market price.

The disadvantage is that closed-end funds usually trade at a discount to their book value. In July 1995, for example, units in RealFund were trading in the $12 to $12.50 range, well below the fund's book value of about $16.

But real estate funds, either closed- or open-end, aren't without their benefits. The most important is the tax-advantaged income they generate.

Part of the return on a real estate fund comes from rental income. Some or all of this money is tax-sheltered by the fund managers through capital cost allowance (CCA). This means the rental income portion of your annual distribution is received in your hands tax-free, in whole or in part. This is a tax break unique to real estate mutual funds.

RealFund, for example, made distributions to shareholders in 1994 of $1.08 a unit, 91 percent of which was received on a tax-deferred basis. Based on a market price of $10.50 in mid-1994, that represented a return of 10.3 percent, most of which wasn't subject to tax. Not bad. The fund's managers estimate that final distributions for 1995 will be higher, at $1.24 a unit.

Higher returns, of course, should increase the share value.

One word of caution, however. Rental income is not tax-free — just tax-deferred. If you decide to sell your units, you will have to repay some — but most certainly not all — of your tax savings. In the case of a REIT, your tax base will be adjusted for capital gains purposes by the amount of tax-free distributions you receive. To illustrate, suppose you pay $10 for a REIT unit and receive $1 in tax-free distributions. Your cost base will be reduced to $9 when determining your capital gains liability. If the value of a unit has increased to $12 when you sell, you'll pay tax at the capital gains rate on $3 profit, not $2 as it might appear at first glance. Of course, if the price has fallen to $9 or below, you'll have no capital gains liability, although the amount you can claim as a capital loss will be reduced.

Of course, the way to avoid repaying any of your tax-deferred income is never to sell. As long as you retain your units, you enjoy the full tax benefits. If you hold them until you die, your estate can worry about capital gains liability.

Before you make a decision on buying a REIT, look at the alternatives available and compare the probable returns on an after-tax basis. Also consider interest rate movements. The price of REITs is interest-rate sensitive; when rates rise REIT prices tend to decline.

For an open-end real estate fund, and there are still a few around, the analysis is more straightforward, since units are bought and redeemed at the current net asset value. In this case, find out the projected distributions for the current year, and ask what proportion of that amount is expected to be received tax-deferred. You should then be able to determine whether units in the fund are attractive from a tax-advantaged income point of view.

Remember, the great benefit of real estate funds is the tax-sheltered rental income they generate. If you hold them in an RRSP or RRIF, even though they're eligible for such plans, you'll lose that advantage. So keep them outside your registered portfolio.

Finally, a word of warning. Some investors in REITs have not been getting the tax breaks they deserve. Last spring, some *MoneyLetter* readers called me to say the tax treatment of their income distributions from RealFund and Counsel REITs was screwed up by their brokerage firms.

The story was substantially the same in all cases. The shares were held in street name (effectively in the name of the brokerage house) and distributions went directly to the brokerage firms, which credited them to the clients' accounts. When tax documentation was forwarded in February, it showed the REIT distributions as dividends.

This meant they were taxed at an incorrect, higher rate. If the distributions were large, the extra tax bill could be substantial. Here's an illustration, based on holdings of 1,000 shares in each of RealFund and Counsel REITs and the top marginal tax rate in Ontario. Counsel paid $0.86 a unit in distributions in 1994, 14 percent of which was taxable. RealFund distributed $1.08 per unit, 9.24 percent of which was taxable.

TAX PAYABLE

	Income (1,000 shares)	Taxed as dividends	Taxed correctly
Counsel REIT	$860.00	$308.91	$64.04
RealFund REIT	1,080.00	387.94	53.08

As you can see, taxing the distributions as dividends resulted in a much higher tax bill. Both RealFund and Counsel confirm they received complaints from shareholders about this problem. Both firms alerted senior officers at the large brokerage houses to the situation, but as one RealFund spokesperson commented: "REITs are still very new and many people in the brokerage firms aren't aware of how to treat the income."

Compounding the problem was the fact that RealFund didn't send out its 1994 tax information until the first week of March 1995 (they legally have until March 31), at which point the brokerage firms had mailed out tax forms to clients.

So if you received distributions from any real estate mutual fund or REIT in the past few years, check your documentation to see how the income was treated for tax purposes. If there appears to have been an error (most likely showing the distributions as dividends), contact your broker, explain the situation, and ask for a correct T-3 form to be sent to you. Mail it to Revenue Canada with a covering letter, asking that your return be amended. Be sure to include your social insurance number.

Choosing a
Dividend Income
Fund

D uring the early '40s, soldiers and their loved

ones suffered from the GI Blues. During the

early '90s, investors suffered from the GIC Blues.

Over and over, I heard the same question: "What

should I do with my maturing GICs?" With five-year

rates below 6 percent at one stage, there was real con-

cern among investors, especially retirees, about the loss

of income. ■

For example, in July 1990, a five-year GIC from a major
bank paid an annual rate of return of 12 percent. If you
renewed that GIC for a similar term five years later, in
July 1995, your return would have dropped to 6.625 percent. Five years earlier, you received $120 a year for
every $1,000 invested; in 1995 your return was $66.25 a
year, or only slightly more than half what it had been.

GIC issuers rationalized that, with inflation at low levels, the "real" return in their certificates was still high.
But by mid-1995 inflation was making a modest comeback, puncturing that balloon. In any event, the argu-
ment was cold comfort for those relying heavily on GICs

to fund their retirement. No one could find a supermarket that had cut prices in half to compensate.

So people have been searching for alternatives. The logical place to start is the forgotten form of investment income — dividends.

Dividend income funds were originally conceived as a way to take maximum advantage of the dividend tax credit. Until a few years ago, the portfolios of these funds consisted mainly of preferred shares, selected to provide the highest possible after-tax yield consistent with safety.

But times, and tax laws, change. The federal government introduced legislation making preferred shares less attractive and lowering the value of the dividend tax credit. Dividend funds floundered for a time, then struck out in a new direction.

You'll still find a few that continue to invest mainly in preferreds. But many now have the bulk of their portfolios invested in high-yielding common stock, especially bank, utility, and pipeline issues.

The result has been to convert some dividend funds into high-yielding blue-chip funds, tailored for conservative investors who want a low-risk presence in the stock market.

The tax advantage of these funds is two-fold — good dividend yields that benefit from the reduced but still valuable dividend tax credit, and capital gains potential in a rising stock market.

Now that the $100,000 lifetime capital gains exemption is history, dividends are the most tax-effective way to receive investment income. In fact, if you have no other source of income, you could receive about $23,000 in dividends a year without paying any taxes at all.

To find the approximate interest rate equivalent of a dividend-paying investment, multiply the dividend rate by 1.3. The result will be the interest rate you need to receive to get the same after-tax return. (This factor will vary slightly depending on your tax bracket and where you live, but it will give you a general idea of the tax impact on each form of investment income.)

There are many common and preferred shares with attractive dividend yields, but the easiest way to invest in them is through dividend income mutual funds.

These have long been the outcasts of the mutual funds industry — under-promoted, under-utilized, and generally misunderstood. But, properly used, they are an excellent way to overcome the GIC blues and to make up, on an after-tax basis, some of the interest income you've lost.

However, you have to know what you're doing. Here's a shopper's guide you can use if this type of mutual fund is of interest to you.

Look beyond the raw returns. Dividend income funds have what appear to be unattractive rates of return when compared to other types of mutual funds. But that can be misleading. When you invest in a dividend fund, your primary concern should be the annual yield. Capital gains and interest income are fine, but not critical in this case. You want to maximize use of the dividend tax credit, so don't get sidetracked. Ask hard questions about what the fund is currently yielding in dividend payments, after management fees are deducted. The yield may vary from month to month, depending on the market value of the securities in the fund, so also request a monthly analysis of dividend payments to investors over the past year. This will help you determine how consistent the fund payouts have been.

Check out the portfolio. Many so-called dividend funds are really misnamed balanced funds. Some contain a high percentage of interest-bearing securities, which are not eligible for the dividend tax credit. Others try to juice up their returns through capital gains, sometimes to the extent of adding lower-yielding common stocks to the portfolio. The most efficient dividend income funds are those that invest with the single purpose of maximizing the effect of the dividend tax credit. This is best done through a portfolio that consists almost entirely of preferred shares and high-yielding common stocks.

Check out the safety factor. If you're looking for a substitute for GICs, you want a high degree of safety. See if the manager's policies reflect this. One thing to look for is a fund that will not invest in any preferreds with less than a P-2 safety rating (preferred shares are rated for safety in the same way as bonds: P-1 is safest, P-2 next, and so on).

Ask about distributions. Many people require regular income from their investments. If cash flow is a concern, find out how frequently distributions are made. Monthly payments are the most convenient. If distributions aren't made at least quarterly, the fund may not be suitable for your needs. Note: some funds, such as the Guardian Preferred Dividend Fund, offer a fixed monthly dividend payment. This is helpful if you need a guaranteed income flow.

Don't put fund units in an RRSP or RRIF. Most dividend funds sold in Canada are fully eligible for RRSPs and RRIFs. But if you put units in a registered plan, you'll negate their main purpose — to allow you to use the dividend tax credit.

There are now over 20 dividend funds available. Some fit the above criteria nicely, others don't. If you want more guidance as to which I think are most suitable, check out the ratings section on "Dividend Income Funds" at the back of this *Guide*.

Labour-Sponsored Funds

During RRSP season, millions of Canadians will receive flyers or see advertisements promoting a special type of mutual fund that offers big tax savings. They're called labour-sponsored venture capital funds, and lately they've been multiplying like bunnies.

These funds were originally conceived as a way of channelling investment money into new businesses, creating jobs in the process. In the 1988 budget, the federal government announced a tax break for investors in these funds, and sweetened the pot again in 1992. ∎

The numbers tell you quickly just how sweet this particular pot has become. If you're in a high tax bracket, these deals can almost seem too good to be true. After all tax credits and deductions are taken into account, an investment of $5,000 by a taxpayer with a 53.2 percent marginal rate (the highest rate in Ontario) could actually end up costing only $340. It's almost as if *they* were paying *you*!

But these tax-advantaged funds aren't just for the rich. Even middle-income taxpayers can make good use of them. For example, the net cost of a $5,000 investment in a labour-sponsored fund to a New Brunswick resident with taxable income of $35,000 can be as low as $829.

How are these remarkable tax savings achieved? Let's take a closer look. We'll use Working Ventures as an example, since it has the widest national distribution.

All investors receive a federal labour-sponsored fund tax credit, which is 20 percent of the amount paid for units, to a maximum of $5,000 a year. So the maximum federal credit is $1,000 annually (20% x $5,000), which is deducted directly from your federal tax payable.

As well, residents of Ontario, Prince Edward Island, New Brunswick, Nova Scotia, and Saskatchewan receive comparable provincial tax credits. In the first four, the annual maximum provincial credit is $1,000, calculated in the same way as the federal credit. In Saskatchewan, the maximum provincial credit is $700 (20 percent of $3,500). Residents of Quebec, Manitoba, and B.C. don't get a provincial credit for the Working Ventures Fund, but they receive one for their provincially sponsored funds. Alberta and Newfoundland offer no provincial credits.

Apart from the federal and provincial tax credits, a further tax deduction is available by contributing units to an RRSP. But keep this in perspective. You can claim an RRSP deduction for *any* eligible investment. The only *extra* tax break you get for a labour-sponsored fund is the federal tax credit and provincial tax credits where they apply.

For the record, though, here's the math that applies if you do contribute the units to an RRSP. This example illustrates the situation of a Nova Scotia or P.E.I. resident with a 50.3 percent marginal tax rate who invests $5,000.

Investment in Working Ventures	$5,000
RRSP tax deduction	−2,515
Federal tax credit	−1,000
Provincial tax credit	−1,000
Net cost for investment in Working Ventures	485
Total tax savings	$4,515

Tax savings of this magnitude have attracted a lot of attention in recent years, and resulted in a lot of business for this new type of mutual fund. For example, the Working Ventures Canadian Fund was launched in March 1990. As of mid-1995, it was approaching $500 million in assets under management. That's a remarkable growth rate in five years.

And Working Ventures isn't even the largest of its type. Quebec's Solidarity Fund, the first of the labour-sponsored funds in this country, has more than $1 billion in assets and is one of that province's economic powerhouses.

The obvious popularity of these funds has attracted a host of new players to the field. During the 1995 RRSP season, about a dozen new labour funds appeared, most of them marketed exclusively in Ontario, at least at the outset. Some of the more successful new entries will gradually appear in other provinces.

Here's a rundown of the funds that were available as of mid-1995.

Canadian Medical Discoveries Fund. Invests in leading-edge medical technology, with the idea of developing Canadian discoveries here at home. Manager is MDS Ventures, which already runs three health-care related funds worth $200 million. The fund boasts a blue-ribbon investment committee, which is well experienced in searching out new ventures. Initially sold only in Ontario but is now in the process of expanding into other provinces. Did relatively well in its first season, attracting $14.5 million during January–February 1995.

Capital Alliance Ventures Inc. Goal is to invest in high-tech companies in Ottawa's Silicon Valley. Fund president is L. Richard Charlebois, a former v.p. of Noranda Enterprises.

Covington Fund Inc. This fund boasts a solid management group, headed by Grant Brown, a veteran of the venture capital field. The investment strategy is to put 25 to 30 percent of assets into mid-size companies undergoing restructuring or in need of recapitalization, 15 to 20 percent in small companies with high growth potential, and 30 to 35 percent into debt issues of larger, relatively stable companies for yield and early return of capital. The balance will be in cash reserves. There's no restriction on the type of company that can be selected.

Crocus Fund. Manitoba's provincial fund, sold exclusively in that province. Set up three years ago, now has an asset base of about $13 million. The managers recently completed their first investment, a Winnipeg-based software firm called Infocorp Computer Solutions that trades on the Vancouver Stock Exchange. Has done reasonably well for investors so far; net asset value in early 1995 was $10.71, compared to an original issue price of $10 in January 1993.

DGC Entertainment Ventures Corp.   This one is sponsored by The Directors Guild of Canada (can you believe that earns them a labour-sponsored fund designation?). The main goal is to invest in movies and TV programs, but money will also be directed to such leading-edge fields as virtual reality, CD-ROM, laser imaging, and cellular vision. Adding to the allure is an advisory council and board of directors that reads like a who's who of Canadian entertainment. A few names, selected at random: Norman Jewison, Gordon Pinsent, Ivan Fecan, Douglas Leiterman, David Cronenberg, Daryl Duke. All heady stuff if you're a film buff. But whether all this will translate into profits for investors is a huge question mark. The entertainment industry is, by definition, high risk. It's not a place for small investors, especially RRSP investors. Launched in January 1994 with much fanfare, but had a disappointing debut, raising only $1.8 million. Did slightly better during the 1995 season, adding $2.5 million in new business. Sold only in Ontario.

Enterprise Fund.   This Ottawa-based fund focuses on companies in the technology and manufacturing sectors, with special emphasis on firms whose shares are already publicly traded or will be within two years. In this way, the managers hope to get around one of the major problems facing labour-sponsored funds: how to fairly evaluate the assets in their portfolios. Investment advisor is Venture Asset Management. One of that company's principals is Austin Beutel, a well-known money manager who was co-founder of Beutel Goodman & Company. One of the first marketing pieces for this fund offered some useful thoughts for all prospective labour fund investors: "Beyond the tax savings, what will the investment performance of these funds look like and where do they fit, if anywhere, in a carefully constructed asset allocation process?"

First Ontario Fund.   This is the closest thing to an "ethical" labour-sponsored fund. Its mandate requires the fund managers to consider such criteria as a company commitment to employment equity, pay equity, a healthy workplace, and environmentally responsible business practices when making an investment decision. As well, firms with military or tobacco connections are expressly excluded from the portfolio. The key personnel are mainly from the trade union movement (CEO and president is Ken Delaney, research director of the United Steelworkers).

Integrated Growth Fund. An example of the risks associated with this type of fund. Launched during the 1994 RRSP season, it attracted a fair amount of interest because of its manager, Premier Capital Management, a firm with five years of experience in the merchant banking business. Premier's stated goal was to invest in established firms with $5-$10 million in annual sales that want to expand their operations, rather than putting money into higher-risk start-up ventures. This was supposed to limit the downside risk, while increasing the odds of picking winners. Unfortunately, the plan hasn't worked so far. The fund made one very bad investment, which resulted in heavy losses. As a result, the value of an original $10 unit had tumbled to $7.86 by the end of May 1995 — a loss of 21.4 percent.

Solidarity Fund. The oldest and the largest of the venture capital funds, with assets of about $1 billion. Run by the Quebec Federation of Labour. Unlike other labour-sponsored funds, units are sold only by the fund itself. Available only in Quebec.

Sportfund. Here's one for the jocks. This fund invests in companies with a connection to the sports industry — anything from the manufacture and distribution of sporting equipment to sports medicine. Its Advisory Council includes some big-name sports figures of the past, such as Ernie Whitt (baseball), Franco Harris (football), and Darryl Sittler (hockey). President Joel Albin (a former Bank of Montreal v.p.) is a no-nonsense guy, who stresses the importance of sound investments and the need to gear expenses to results. As a result, the manager's guaranteed compensation is the lowest of all the new funds, at 2 percent (although, as with all other funds, there are generous performance incentives built in). Had a disappointing launch in 1995, taking in only $3.4 million.

Trillium Growth Capital Inc. Mandate is to invest in Ontario-based growth industries. The fund is run by Richard Kinlough, president of Ontario Corporate Funding Inc., a subsidiary of Canadian Corporate Funding Ltd., which has been in the merchant banking business since 1979 (Grant Brown of the Covington Fund also comes from this firm). Kinlough will diversify investments across a range of industries, with no more than 25 percent of assets in any one sector. There's a cap of 20 percent on investments in early-stage companies, which are normally higher risk.

VenGrowth Investment Fund Ltd. VenGrowth is a proven venture capital manager. The company has invested $70 million on behalf of pension funds, insurance companies, and family foundations over the past 12 years, so the managers know the field. The team is headed by Earl Storie, a former president of TD Capital Group. Distributor is BPI, the company that became a major player with the acquisition of the Bolton Tremblay funds last year. This was the most successful of the new 1995 launches, raising almost $30 million.

Working Opportunity Fund. British Columbia's provincial fund, open only to residents of that province. Has about $80 million in assets. Many of its investments are with high-tech firms. Has been around long enough to establish a performance record; average annual return for the three years ending May 31, 1995, was 1.7 percent. This reflects the fact that most assets were held in short-term notes during that time.

Working Ventures Canadian Fund. Working Ventures is sponsored by the Canadian Federation of Labour (which is not affiliated with the Canadian Labour Congress, in case you're worried that Bob White is going to be looking after your money). The objective of the fund is to invest in small and medium-sized Canadian companies with high growth potential. A blue-ribbon board of directors advises on investment strategy, but the real work is done by the fund's professionals. This was the first fund to be sold nationwide. It's raised plenty of money; the main problem has been finding places to invest it. Average annual rate of return for the five years to May 31: 4.8 percent.

As you can see, there's a lot of choice. But should you invest? Here are some things to consider.

Lock-in period. Once you purchase your units, you're stuck with them for at least five years in most cases (even longer in the case of the three provincially sponsored funds). If you redeem sooner, you'll be required to repay your tax credits, plus a redemption charge. However, you can get out early without having to repay your tax savings under certain circumstances, including retiring or turning 65. As a result, many people in their sixties are buying units, pocketing the tax savings, and then cashing in a year or two later.

Above-average risk. These funds invest in venture capital situations — typically companies just starting out or in an early growth phase. That means a higher risk of a company running into severe financial problems or even going belly-up. Investors in the Integrated Growth Fund have already had such an experience.

High fees. It costs more to find good quality venture deals. Those expenses come off the top and reduce investor returns.

Slow profitability. Most venture capital deals take at least three years to come to fruition. Five years is more the average. For a fund that's just starting, you'll be lucky if the unit value doesn't fall in the first year because of start-up costs.

Uncertain future. None of these funds has been around long enough to establish a meaningful track record. Even Working Ventures, which has a five-year record, has only invested a small portion of its assets in venture capital situations. The rest of the money is in short-term notes.

RRSP suitability. Most of these funds are actively promoted as an RRSP investment — indeed, only by contributing units to a retirement plan could you get the maximum tax advantage. Investors have responded accordingly — 92 percent of Working Ventures' outstanding units was in RRSPs in mid-1995. However, most financial advisors recommend conservative investments for retirement plans — which these funds, by definition, are not. If they only form a small portion of RRSP assets, their above-average risk is not a serious concern. But if they represent a significant part of your retirement capital, you could be storing up trouble for the future.

Those are the potential problems. But there are some offsetting advantages.

One arises from a recent change in federal tax rules. Until now, individuals had to purchase units outside their RRSP, then contribute them to the plan to obtain that part of the tax deduction. This procedure was administratively awkward. So changes were made to the tax laws, which came into effect for the first time in the 1995 RRSP season. These amendments make it possible for RRSPs to directly buy units in labour-sponsored funds and obtain the tax credits.

The implications of this are precedent-setting. Never before has it been possible to use assets already in an RRSP, which produced a tax deduction when they were contributed, to generate another tax break. Now you can use your RRSP money in this way by investing up to $5,000 worth of already existing RRSP assets in units of a labour-sponsored fund. When you do this, you'll receive the applicable federal and provincial tax credits *outside your plan!* And this isn't a one-time offer; you can do it every year. (If you live in a province that has its own labour-sponsored fund you should ask for the relevant information about it from a sales person.)

Another advantage, not available in all provinces, is the ability to diversify. Until 1995, there wasn't a lot of choice available. But now investors in several provinces can put together a portfolio of several labour-sponsored funds, thereby reducing risk. Ontario residents have by far the largest selection, but more funds are extending their marketing into other provinces as well.

With this diversification comes improved performance prospects. Some of the new funds appear to have excellent long-term investment potential, on the basis of their mandate and personnel. It's impossible to predict at this stage which will do best, but I like the prospects for the Canadian Medical Discoveries Fund, the Covington Fund, and the VenGrowth Investment Fund. Among the older funds, Working Ventures is my top choice.

If you decide to invest in one of these funds and put the units in an RRSP, I recommend that you calculate your tax savings and invest that amount outside your registered plan. A solid mutual fund with strong capital gains potential is a good choice. This puts your tax savings to work and provides an offsetting investment in the event your labour-sponsored funds don't do well.

Another option is to hold the fund units outside a retirement plan, at least for now. You won't get the tax break for contributing units to your RRSP by doing this. But at least you won't be putting what could be a speculative asset into your plan. If the fund performs well, you can always contribute the units to your RRSP in the future and claim the additional tax saving then.

By keeping fund units outside your RRSP, any profits will be eligible for the reduced capital gains tax rate and losses can be written off against other gains. Plus, you'll get a tax break you won't receive by contributing the units to an RRSP: the federal and provincial credits won't reduce your cost base for capital gains purposes. That means you'll keep more of anything you make. Just remember, you have to wait at least five years to collect.

Asset Allocation Services

— How Good Are They?

Money managers have long been aware of the value of asset mix, or asset allocation, in portfolio management. Some believe it is the single most important factor in improving investment returns.

Fortune magazine reported a few years ago that a study done in the U.S. concluded that "allocation between classes of assets accounted for...93 percent of the difference in returns between various portfolios. Selection of particular assets within classes accounted for no more than 7 percent." ∎

I'm a believer in asset mix, but I'm not sure I'd go that far. Junk is junk, no matter how it's allocated.

But assuming you stick with quality investments, a well-planned asset mix strategy will, over time, improve your return and offer a higher degree of safety by reducing your exposure to asset groups that are likely to carry a greater degree of risk during a particular period.

Mutual fund managers have been practising this for years. Most (although not all) managers of balanced funds use a form of asset allocation to determine their portfolio mix, although the degree of sophistication involved in the process varies considerably — some use up-to-the-minute computer modelling techniques, others fly more or less by the seat of their pants. This is not to say that the computerized methods are better, by the way. I'm simply pointing out that asset allocation strategies can mean very different things, depending on who's running the show.

There are two ways to employ an asset mix strategy in your own mutual funds portfolio. You can do it yourself, or you can pay someone else to do it for you.

Do-it-yourself asset allocation. Toronto Dominion offers what they call a "TD Wealth Allocation Model" through Green Line that you can use to build your own personal asset allocation program. You're asked to answer questions covering four key subjects (age, when money needed, personal income, risk tolerance). The results are self-scored and determine the most suitable asset mix for your needs. Choices are safety of principal, income, income and moderate growth, balanced growth, and aggressive growth, with variations for registered and non-registered plans. You then receive recommendations for a customized portfolio. You can follow those suggestions or select any mutual funds you want for your mix.

The plan is self-regulating, which means setting it up and monitoring it is left entirely to you. There is no automatic rebalancing — TD suggests that you review your portfolio at least once a year to readjust the mix. There are no fees; minimum investment is $100 per fund and non-registered portfolios require a minimum of $2,000 to start.

The main drawback of this plan is that it places all the responsibility on the individual investor. If you have good self-discipline, you might be able to make it work for you. Otherwise, try another route.

Several complex, computer-driven asset allocation programs are now available to individual investors at a reasonable cost. These programs analyze a number of economic trends and then determine an appropriate asset weighting based on the results.

There are two key factors that differentiate these programs. One is the assumptions used and the built-in biases of the programmers — some plans take a conservative approach, others are more aggressive. The second is your investment personality — your risk tolerance, income needs, etc. Some programs give this a heavy weighting, others ignore it entirely.

If you want to hire someone to do your asset allocation for you, there are three ways to go about it.

Asset allocation mutual funds.   These are individual
mutual funds that reposition their portfolios periodically
according to the dictates of the management team or a
computer model. The 20/20 Group is the leader here
with several asset allocation funds, some of which have
turned in solid returns. One example: the American
Tactical Asset Allocation Fund which uses a computer-
driven model developed by Wells Fargo, one of the pio-
neers in this field. It was one of Canada's top-performing
international balanced funds for the five-year period to
June 30, 1995, with an average annual return of 13.3
percent. Even more impressive is the fact that this fund's
performance was better than the average pure U.S. equity fund over that term. These results indicate the Wells
Fargo model really works, making this fund a good
choice for investors wishing to use asset allocation principles for U.S. investing.

Another company that uses an asset allocation
approach is Dynamic. Their Partners Fund, which
employs the expertise of the management team to determine allocations, has been one of the best-performing
balanced funds in recent years, with a five-year average
annual compound rate of return to June 30, 1995, of
14.8 percent.

The success of the original Partners Fund prompted
Dynamic to give it a sibling, the Dynamic Global
Partners Fund, which concentrates on overseas markets,
with a target of 60 percent stocks, 40 percent bonds. It
turned in a below-average performance in its first year.

Another major player in asset allocation funds is
Royal Trust, which offers three choices under the
"Advantage" label. The Advantage Balanced Fund aims
for a more-or-less even mix of stocks and bonds. The
Advantage Income Fund puts the emphasis on fixed
income securities, with stocks representing only 15 to 30
percent of the portfolio. The Advantage Growth Fund
swings the other way, focusing more heavily on equities
(60 to 80 percent of the portfolio). Which does best
short-term depends on prevailing economic conditions
at the time, but over the long haul (five years) the
Income Fund has been the winner.

The growing interest in asset allocation funds has
prompted other companies to jump on the bandwagon.

Fidelity offers the Fidelity Asset Manager Fund, run by Robert Beckwitt, who handles five Fidelity funds in the U.S. This is an international fund, although the majority of the portfolio is normally composed of U.S. securities. Its investment parameters are fairly conservative: the fund can never have more than 60 percent of its portfolio in stocks. The "normal" mix (although asset allocation funds rarely are positioned at the norm) is 40 percent in each of stocks and bonds and 20 percent in money market securities. It has not been a shining star thus far, with a one-year return of 2.6 percent, below average for this category. Fidelity has also launched a Canadian Asset Allocation Fund; initial results are very promising, with a 14.6 percent gain in the six months to June 30.

Other fund companies getting into asset allocation include Mackenzie Financial, Templeton, and Investors Group.

Non-personalized asset allocation services. Three Canadian mutual fund companies offer an asset allocation service that is tied strictly to changes in economic and market conditions, with no reference to investor goals.

AGF, the first into the field, offers two options: a Canadian Asset Allocation Service and a U.S. Asset Allocation Service. Both use a computer model developed by Paine Webber in the U.S. This model evaluates over 20 years of relative returns in stocks, bonds, and cash and projects anticipated rates of return based on this and other data.

The Paine Webber model has been used successfully in the U.S. for several years, consistently producing returns superior to the performance of the Standard and Poor's 500 Index. But it has a major flaw as far as its use for the Canadian Asset Allocation Service is concerned: it has not been modified in any way to reflect differences in Canadian returns and their timing. Over the long term, this shouldn't be a major problem, according to AGF, but short-term results may be affected.

The Canadian Asset Allocation Service has been available since June 1990. It redistributes assets among the AGF Canadian Equity Fund, the AGF Canadian Bond Fund, and the AGF Money Market Account on the basis of projected rates of return for each group. As of mid-July 1995, the weighting was, in my view, completely out of touch with market reality: 23 percent in stocks, at a time when share prices were making a big move, 19 percent in bonds, again during a period of growth in the bond market, and 58 percent in money market instruments, during a period when short-term interest rates were falling. This weighting was in marked contrast to the positioning of the Royal Trust asset allocation portfolio (see below). The divergence of the two computer programs speaks volumes about how different variables and assumptions can produce completely different results.

The computer program isn't the only factor to consider. Returns will also be affected (although, the theory goes, to a lesser degree) by the relative performance of the underlying mutual funds that make up the asset allocation plan.

The AGF Canadian Equity Fund, for example, has historically been a chronic underperformer. Its 10-year average annual rate of return to June 30, 1995, was a weak 5.5 percent (the average Canadian equity fund returned 8.3 percent over that time). Recent results have not been much better.

The Canadian Bond Fund and the Money Market Account have fared better, with generally above-average returns

Your return will depend on what kind of fee arrangement you negotiate with your sales person. You can be charged anything from nothing to 2 percent for each switch carried out at the instructions of the computer program. Here are the annual rates of return to June 30, 1995, based on the applicable switching fee:

Switching fee	1 year	2 years	3 years
2%	10.5%	5.0%	8.9%
1%	11.1%	5.6%	9.5%
0	11.7%	6.2%	10.1%

As a benchmark, here are the returns for the average Canadian balanced fund for those time frames, as reported by *The Globe and Mail Report on Business*: one year, 12.5 percent; two years, 6.9 percent; three years, 9.9 percent. The three-year results suggest you'll do marginally better by using the AGF service, but only if you can negotiate a zero switch fee. Otherwise, the average balanced fund is a better choice.

AGF's U.S. Asset Allocation Service started in December 1992. It uses only two funds, the AGF American Growth Fund and the AGF U.S. Income Fund. The Growth Fund is a consistently good performer with a long track record; the Income Fund is relatively new and has not done much to date. Asset distribution as of mid-1995 was 19 percent in the Growth Fund, 81 percent in the Income Fund — again, very strange in view of the fact the Dow was setting one record after another during that period. A maximum switch fee of 1 percent applies.

This service has not been around long enough to establish any meaningful track record, but the one-year return to June 30, 1995, was 7.8 percent. Compare that to the return of the Talvest U.S. Diversified Fund (+10.3 percent) or the 20/20 American Tactical Asset Allocation Fund (+17.6 percent).

Minimum investment in the AGF plans is $1,000.

Royal Trust was the second major mutual fund group to offer asset allocation. In this case, four funds are used: the Royal Trust Canadian Equity Fund, the Royal Canadian Small Cap Fund (limited to no more than 10 percent of the total stock component), the Royal Trust Bond Fund, and the Royal Trust Canadian Money Market Fund. The Equity Fund has a somewhat better record than its AGF counterpart, the Bond Fund is slightly worse (but still above average for the category), and AGF has the Money Market edge. The Small Cap Fund, the wild card here, has been something of a bomb, although it's performed better recently.

Royal Trust also uses a U.S.-originated computer model, this one created by Banker's Trust of New York. However, the program has been modified to reflect the Canadian economic environment and is now administered by Polaris Capital Management of New York. As of mid-1995, the mix was 53 percent bonds, 47 percent stocks, and no cash — far more realistic than the AGF weightings given the circumstances at that time.

Performance has been unspectacular. Return for the year ending June 30, 1995, was 7.5 percent. Over two years, the service showed an annual compound gain of 3.3 percent; three-year average annual compound rate of return was 6.4 percent. All three of Royal Trust's Advantage funds, which use similar principles but include more funds, did appreciably better.

The annual cost of the Royal Trust service is an administration fee of 1 percent of the value of your assets in the plan. Minimum investment is $10,000.

Two Quebec-based asset allocation services have appeared recently. One was launched in mid-1993 by Quebec-based Trust Prêt et Revenu. It's called Multifund and involves switches among five of the company's funds, based on the assessments of the fund managers. There's no cost for each switch, but there's an annual administration fee of 0.5 percent. You need a minimum investment of $10,000 to participate.

The second was started by Desjardins Trust in early 1995. It created three new funds for the plan: a Diversified Secure Fund, which takes a conservative approach; a Diversified Moderate Fund, which has a balanced portfolio; and a Diversified Audacious Fund (that's the official English name, believe it or not!), which emphasizes stocks. Minimum investment is $50,000.

Personalized asset allocation services. Some brokerage firms and mutual fund companies have recently taken the asset allocation concept to a new level by offering personalized service. This involves face-to-face meetings and the completion of a detailed questionnaire designed to define a client's investment profile and pinpoint an appropriate asset allocation formula.

There are a number of variations on this theme, but a quick look at some of the more highly publicized programs will give you an idea of how they work.

Midland Walwyn's Compass (for Comprehensive Asset Management) plan is a broker-driven program. It involves the completion of a lengthy questionnaire (31 items) to determine such matters as your assets, income needs, retirement savings requirements, risk/return profile, etc. That information is then used to identify a strategic asset allocation approach based on five possible profiles: maximum income, income and growth, balanced, growth, and maximum growth.

The mutual funds used to implement the plan can be selected from the universe of load funds (with a few exceptions) on the basis of decisions made between you and the broker. Or you can use Midland's no-load Atlas and Hercules funds if you prefer.

The plan is centrally administered and reweightings are periodically recommended, but they aren't done automatically — that's left to the discretion of the broker and the client. Cost is a basic $200 annual fee (negotiable) plus sales commissions on funds purchased. Minimum investment is $25,000.

Because the mix of mutual funds will be different in each plan, it's impossible to track the relative efficiency of Compass relative to using a balanced fund or doing it yourself.

Mackenzie Financial's STAR (for Strategic Asset Allocation) program was designed by Gordon Garmaise, of Garmaise Investment Technologies, an expert in asset allocation. It also starts with a lengthy questionnaire, developed with input from behavioural scientists, which attempts to identify an investor's needs and risk tolerance. It's kind of fun to complete, with questions asking you to spin a wheel of fortune and wanting your reaction to going on a completely unplanned trip. The totals lead to one of four broad asset allocation categories: conservative income and growth, balanced growth and income, long-term growth (that's where my score put me), and maximum long-term growth.

Once the scoring is done, your needs are matched to one of 10 portfolios, all of which use only Mackenzie Financial funds. Four portfolios are for RRSPs, four for non-registered plans and two are based on 100 percent foreign content (calculated in either Canadian or U.S. dollars, your choice). Rebalancing is done automatically but is kept to a minimum to avoid taxes (see below) and transaction fees. In order for a switch to occur, there has to be a 10 percent variance from the recommended asset mix. That's a lot — Royal Trust rebalances at 5 percent, for example. So don't expect a lot of movement in the make-up of your portfolio.

Cost of the program is a low 0.1 percent of the value of your assets, with a minimum charge of $25 a year and a maximum of $100 — those fees are tax-deductible. You also pay normal sales commissions and switching fees up to 2 percent (negotiable). Minimum investment is $2,500. This cost structure makes STAR one of the best asset allocation bargains around. Because of the costs involved in computer programming, Midland Walwyn was the only major brokerage firm administering the plan in-house as of mid-1995. Other brokers and financial planners will make it available to you, but all the paperwork will originate from Mackenzie.

It's possible to track the results of the various STAR portfolios, although technically they're not supposed to be published (at least for promotional purposes) because of securities commission rules. The program hasn't been around long enough for any meaningful returns, having been launched in early January 1995. To the end of June, however, the non-registered conservative income and growth plan was the best performer, with a healthy 9.9 percent gain. Funds used in this plan are Universal World Income RRSP (25 percent), Industrial Bond (19 percent), Ivy Mortgage (16 percent), Ivy Foreign Equity (14 percent), Ivy Canadian (10 percent), Industrial Growth (10 percent), and Universal World Precious Metals (6 percent).

Worst performer over that time (somewhat surprisingly) was the 100 percent foreign content version of the maximum long-term growth plan (Canadian dollar option), which returned just 3.9 percent. Interestingly, the U.S. dollar version of the same fund returned 6.4 percent. Mackenzie says the differential is purely a reflection of currency movements, but those results make it clear that careful thought needs to be given to the selection of your currency base.

AGF also offers a personalized asset allocation plan for those who aren't satisfied with the regular Canadian and U.S. programs. It's called AGF MAP (for Maximum Asset Plan). Like STAR, it involves completing a questionnaire to determine your risk tolerance level. Based on the results, your financial advisor then recommends a portfolio of five to seven AGF funds that combines the highest potential returns with the risk level you're prepared to accept. You are not required to accept the recommendations, however; the percentages and even the funds can be adjusted if you wish. Portfolio recommendations are updated periodically, but not automatically implemented. Minimum investment is $10,000.

Drawbacks of this plan are the lack of automatic adjustments, lack of comparative monitoring since the portfolio can be changed from that recommended, and reliance on the AGF funds, some of which have been indifferent performers.

Several financial institutions, including TD Bank and Royal Trust, also offer personalized allocation services for high-end clients. Minimum investment is usually $50,000 to $100,000.

If you're interested in exploring asset allocation services further, here are five key points to consider:

The underlying computer model: As the divergence between the AGF and Royal Trust programs in bond/stock ratios indicates, your asset mix may vary considerably from one computer model to another. Ask some hard questions about how aggressive the program is (could you end up 100 percent in stocks?) before you make a commitment.

Costs: They can be considerable, depending on which route you select. With the 20/20, BPI, and Dynamic funds, you pay sales commission (or back-end load) only. In the case of AGF, the funds themselves carry a sales charge (either front- or back-end), and you'll pay up to 2 percent a year on top of that. Royal Trust's funds are no load, but a 1 percent annual fee applies for the asset allocation service. The Compass and STAR services will each require a sales commission for the basic fund purchase, plus their annual fees.

Taxes: Every time assets are switched from one mutual fund to another in any of the plans, there is a "deemed disposition" for tax purposes (unless you're operating within an RRSP or RRIF). This means you are liable for tax at the capital gains rate on any profits. Asset allocation mutual funds aren't affected in this way, because the switches take place inside the individual funds. But in the case of the services, where assets are moved from one fund to another, taxes will apply on any profits. So if you're considering one of the services, ask how often switches normally occur (STAR attempts to keep them to a minimum). This should be an important factor in your decision, because of the tax implications of frequent switches.

The underlying funds: Asset allocation is a powerful tool, but you need to give careful consideration to the strength of the underlying funds that make up the core of the program. Mediocre funds will, by definition, produce mediocre returns. Consider the alternatives carefully before making a decision.

Wrap accounts: This chapter only looks at asset allocation options that use widely available mutual funds. If you have a lot of money to invest, you may want to explore the "wrap accounts" offered by brokerage firms (Richardson Greenshields' Sovereign plan is an example). These also employ asset allocation principles, but your money is invested in pooled funds, run by selected managers. Costs, although they may seem high at first glance, are tax-deductible and no additional sales commissions are charged. Consult your broker for more information.

   Some companies have also developed asset allocation software for use by their representatives or by brokers in servicing wealthy clients. These programs are designed to help a sales person create a completely personalized mix for an investor. Examples include the Talvest Asset Allocation Plan and the TD Trust Navigator. Since each individual's plan will be different, there is no way to monitor the effectiveness of these programs.

Recommendations: The standard AGF and Royal Trust services are too limited in scope to be of more than marginal value. The restriction to a few funds (only two in the case of the AGF U.S. plan) limits diversification and does not allow for foreign content in a Canadian program. Royal Trust clients would be better off using one or more of the company's Advantage funds. All have a much better return than the Asset Allocation Service. Plus the Advantage funds don't charge an asset management fee, offer greater diversification, and don't trigger a taxable event with every switch. If you have $100,000 to invest, ask about RT's Personal Asset Management (PAM) program.

Of the three asset allocation services offered by mutual fund companies, Mackenzie Financial's STAR program is the winner by a wide margin. The plan offers personalization, a broad range of funds for proper diversification, registered and non-registered packages, automatic rebalancing, a much stronger fund base than AGF or Royal Trust, and a reasonable price tag.

For maximum flexibility, Midland Walwyn's Compass plan is the best choice. However, the program has some drawbacks that need to be seriously considered. For example, Compass will generate portfolio reweighting recommendations, but doesn't automatically implement them. That decision is left to the discretion of you and your broker, which can result in inaction, especially if you're travelling for long periods. As well, there's no way to track how well (or how badly) the Compass recommendations are doing because so much will depend on the performance of the individual mutual funds selected to implement the weightings. That leaves the investor in the dark as to whether the extra cost is actually paying off, or whether a good balanced fund would perform just as well.

My choice: Mackenzie Financial's STAR — a well-conceived, high-quality, low-cost asset allocation program. The industry leader at this time.

Assessing Emerging Markets Funds

— A SPECIAL REPORT

How quickly things change in the mutual funds business! A couple of years ago, emerging markets funds were the hottest items on the shelf. Billions of Canadian and U.S. dollars poured in to what had been previously regarded as underdeveloped, Third World countries filled with starving peasants — the kind of places to which we sent wheat, not our savings. These were nations where the birth rate was too high, food production too low, and hope for the future non-existent. ■

Well, guess what? Somewhere along the way, many of these countries acquired hope, and a lot more. Suddenly, economists were telling us these were the areas of greatest growth potential, the places where our money should be if we wanted to achieve above-average returns. China, Malaysia, Turkey, the Philippines, Mexico, Brazil, Hungary, India, Pakistan — all unexpectedly found themselves the recipients of huge amounts of western capital.

The predictable happened. Large amounts of cash flowing into small, unsophisticated stock markets sent share prices soaring. Emerging markets mutual funds rode the upward wave, scoring big gains, especially in 1993. Investors in the Templeton Emerging Markets Fund saw unit values shoot up 82.8 percent in that one year alone. The Green Line Emerging Markets Fund was up 70 percent. C.I. Emerging Markets Fund leaped 65 percent.

Some of the region-specific funds did even better. Hyperion Asian Trust more than doubled in '93, gaining 117 percent. Investors Pacific International advanced 88.1 percent. AGF Asian Growth was up 87 percent. Fidelity Far East was close behind, at 86.4 percent.

Heady days! But then came 1994 and the inevitable correction. As stock markets in developing countries around the world reacted to this artificial share value inflation, most of the big winners became big losers, with some funds dropping more than 20 percent in value. Frightened investors bailed out left and right. The first half of 1995 wasn't much better, as the Mexican peso devaluation severely damaged investor confidence in emerging markets and led to a flight to quality as money poured back into more stable environments in North America and Europe.

So is that the story? A bubble that has now burst, a temporary fad?

Not by a long shot. The original case for investing in emerging markets still stands — these are the countries that will lead the world in growth as we move into the 21st century. But the past couple of years have reminded us about the dangers of speculative excess. These markets are still fragile and cannot absorb billions of dollars in new money within a short time. While profit potential is excellent, the dangers of future artificial price run-ups remain.

Normally, I recommend a long-term approach to mutual fund investing. But there are certain types of funds I classify as "opportunity funds." These are situations where you are most likely to maximize returns by buying in when prices are down and switching your assets elsewhere after a big run-up. Natural resource funds fall into this category. So do emerging markets funds.

Of course, investing in mutual funds in this way isn't

for everyone. It requires market timing and a willingness to take positions when everyone else is dripping pessimism. If that's not your thing, there are three ways you can handle emerging markets funds:

1) Tuck them away for 10 years and forget about them.
2) Use a dollar-cost averaging approach to reduce risk.
3) Ignore them.

I see late 1995 and 1996 as a good time to get back into these funds, or take a position for the first time if you haven't been there before. Share values are down. Investors are much more realistic about the prospects for these countries. The amount of new money pouring in has slowed. Meanwhile, growth in many of these nations continues strong. It all adds up to a combination that could send these markets moving forward again.

If you're prepared to risk some of your money (not more than 10 percent of your investable assets, please), here's a rundown of the funds I think have the best prospects. If you wish to limit your risk, stick with the broadly based emerging markets funds, which allow the managers to invest anywhere in the world.

If you plan to use some market timing and you experience a big run-up in unit values, don't be afraid to take some profits. These funds tend to be volatile, so ride the crests and get out before the next trough. Within each group, the funds are listed in my order of preference.

WORLDWIDE FUNDS

Templeton Emerging Markets Fund.   You'll never go far wrong by choosing the Templeton organization for an international fund. Their Emerging Markets Fund, run by Dr. Mark Mobius, is one of the best. Yes, it had down years in 1992, 1994, and the first half of 1995. But the losses were modest, and more than offset by the big gain of 1993. This fund offers a proven, value-oriented stock selection approach, solid management, excellent diversification, and a broad mixture of large and small cap companies. Promising areas as of mid-'95 were Turkey and Latin America. Looking farther ahead, the Templeton organization sees great potential in Russia (it has set up an office in Moscow) and India. Three-year average annual rate of return to June 30, '95, was 15.7 percent. If you want an emerging markets fund as a long-term hold, this is the one I'd recommend.

Fidelity Emerging Markets Portfolio Fund. This is a brand new fund, launched in December 1994, that has made a very impressive debut. It's jointly run by two of Fidelity's Boston-based managers, Richard Hazlewood (who also handles the U.S. clone of this fund) and Patti Satterthwaite (whose responsibilities include the Fidelity's Canadian and U.S. Latin America funds). This fund turned in an impressive 17.1 percent gain in the first half of '95, during a period when many other emerging markets funds were losing money. Reason: the managers made a big bet on Malaysia, investing almost a third of their portfolio in that country. Malaysia was one of the better-performing emerging markets in the first half of the year — its stock market advanced 13.3 percent in U.S. dollar terms from January 1 to July 20. The fact the managers stayed out of India, where markets have experienced tough sledding, also helped. It's not likely the managers can keep the returns coming at that early pace, but Fidelity is a sound organization and this figures to be one of the better EM funds over the long term. This is one of the smallest of the Fidelity funds, with only $6 million in assets at mid-year. It should grow significantly in size as investors move back into emerging markets.

Everest Emerging Markets Fund. Another new entry, this is a no-load fund offered by Canada Trust but managed out of the U.S. by Montgomery Asset Management of San Francisco. This is a fund for those who want to limit risk by broad diversification. When it's fully invested, the portfolio will consist of as many as 250 stocks, spread across more than 20 countries. Here again, initial results are very encouraging, with a 9.1 percent gain between April and July 1995. The Everest group is showing a great deal of initiative in expanding its range of offerings and this could turn out to be one of the winners.

Green Line Emerging Markets Fund. This fund had the good fortune to debut in November 1992, just as the run-up in emerging markets stocks was commencing. Green Line's managers were rewarded for their foresight with a 70 percent return in '93, a performance that, not surprisingly, attracted tens of millions of dollars in new investments. The fund has struggled since, with a 5 percent loss in 1994 and an 11.1 percent drop in the first half of 1995, but was showing definite signs of recovery at mid-year. The managers are Morgan Stanley Asset Management of New York, considered to be among the world's leading experts on developing markets. The portfolio is well diversified, with Brazil being the country of choice in mid-'95, making up 18 percent of the portfolio. The fund also had a 4 percent weighting in Russia, a country that fascinates but frightens many EM managers. This is an excellent choice for no-load investors, especially if you're already a TD Bank client.

Guardian Emerging Markets Fund. You could have done a lot worse than to put a few bucks into this fund when it was launched in late July 1994 at $10 a unit. One year later, the units were valued at $10.88, for an 8.8 percent gain. That was during a time when many EM funds were losing ground, which says something about the investment acumen of London-based Kleinwort Guardian Overseas Ltd., who run the show. Heaviest country concentration in mid-'95 was in Korea, which made up almost a quarter of the portfolio. Management strategy is to overweight countries with larger capitalization (which reduces the risk of speculative run-ups) and good economic forecasts. The fund holds between 100 and 150 stocks, providing good diversification.

REGIONAL FUNDS

AGF Asian Growth Fund "A". This is a solid performer that has stood up very well to the recent turmoil in Asian markets. The fund gained 12 percent in the year ending June 30, 1995, while the average Far East fund was losing 5.7 percent. Three-year record averages out to a 23.5 percent annual return. The managers seek to identify those markets with the best growth potential and then select stocks within the chosen areas using a fundamental, bottom-up approach. As of mid-1995, about a third of the portfolio was invested in Hong Kong, with other significant holdings in Malaysia, Singapore, and Thailand. Holdings in Korea were being reduced because of concerns over inflation. This is a good choice for investors seeking a well-balanced Far East fund.

Fidelity Far East Fund.   This is another solid fund that held its ground well in the face of some tough Asian markets, gaining 9 percent for the year to June 30, 1995. Its longer-term record is also good, averaging 20.6 percent a year over the past three years. As of mid-1995, manager K.C. Lee was betting heavily on Hong Kong, with over half the portfolio concentrated in that market, predominantly in large corporations. There were no holdings in the Indian market, which the manager feels is higher risk.

C.I. Pacific Fund.   This has the distinction of being the top-performing mutual fund in Canada over the past decade, with an average annual return of 18.9 percent. Recent numbers have not been as good, however; the fund lost 3.7 percent in the year ending June 30, 1995. Still, that was better than average for this category. The portfolio is very well diversified with just about every country in Asia that has a stock market represented, including Vietnam which is just putting a toe into the lake of capitalism. Some of the newer Far East funds appear to be catching up and even passing this perennial leader, but it's still one of the better bets in this region.

Investors Pacific International.   If you're an Investors Group client who doesn't have some of this in your portfolio, you're missing a good bet. This is a sound, well-diversified fund — and, unlike many funds in this group, one of the prime objectives is to minimize risk. Last year was just so-so (gain of 4.5 percent to June 30, 1995), but any profit is better than a loss in tough times. Three-year return averages 20.7 percent annually.

Hyperion Asian Fund.   One of the older Asian funds and a solid performer with a five-year average annual rate of return of 13.4 percent to June 30, 1995. The managers invest primarily in well-established companies, although they will look at smaller firms with unusual growth potential. This is primarily a value fund, with the managers focusing on stocks that are deemed to be underpriced.

Trimark Indo-Pacific Fund.   My top choice among the new Far East funds, partly because of the Trimark name. This is a company that hasn't disappointed investors yet and, hopefully, this fund will continue that tradition. Despite the name, holdings in India are small, although Hong Kong-based manager Robert Lloyd George felt at mid-year there were some good buying opportunities in the sub-continent. Main concentration was in Hong Kong, with over a quarter of the portfolio. This fund got off to a promising start, with a 6.6 percent gain in the first half of '95.

Trimark—The Americas Fund. Okay, I'm cheating a bit here. But I'm nervous about Latin America and this is one way to get exposure to that hot-and-cold market without risking the house. A large chunk of this portfolio (42.9 percent at mid-year) is in the U.S., where manager Richard Whiting invests in "emerging companies," particularly those with some sort of technological edge. The rest of the fund is in blue-chip Latin American stocks, well diversified over several countries. This mix allowed the fund to escape the full impact of the devaluation of the Mexican peso. It lost only 2.2 percent in the first half of 1995, compared to declines of 15 percent and more for most other Latin funds. For investors who prefer to hedge their bets.

SINGLE-COUNTRY FUNDS

AGF China Focus Fund "A". Playing the emerging markets game through a single country fund is rather like going to the race track and betting the bundle on a long-shot. If the nag comes in, you win big. Otherwise, it's a hitch-hike home. Fortunately, AGF has found a way around this problem. This is a China fund, yes. But no, it's not really. The fund's mandate is to invest in "companies that will benefit from the economic development and growth opportunities of the People's Republic of China." That's a pretty broad directive. Canadian companies with big China contracts could be made to fit — and they have been! As a result, what we have here is a fund that's quite broadly diversified internationally. Hong Kong shares are the largest single component of the portfolio (about 30 percent). Investments within China only account for 10 percent of the holdings. The fund got off to a slow start, losing 4.2 percent in the year to June 30, 1995. But if you want a China fund that lays off some of the risk elsewhere, this should be a good choice.

Regent Korea Fund.   The AGF China fund may not be
a true single-country fund, but this one is — and a small
country it is, too. Admax Regent, which owns this fund,
makes no effort to dilute it; they're a licensed foreign
investor in Korea so they buy their shares directly on the
Seoul exchange. To add to your concerns, the Korean
market can be quite volatile, and then there's always that
little matter of the folks up north, who make bellicose
noises with disturbing frequency. This is definitely not a
fund for worriers. Still, it has a bright manager, Peter
Everington of Regent Capital Management, Hong Kong.
And it's been rather exciting to be a unit-holder for the
past couple of years — the fund was up 26.1 percent in
1993 and added another 31.3 percent in 1994. It gave
some of those gains back in the first half of 1995, however, with a 16 percent drop. This is one of those funds
I'd be in and out of, depending on which way the winds
were blowing. Buy when Korea is out of favour and sell
when the Seoul market is on a roll.

The Bank Funds

—A Special Report

The big chartered banks control a large chunk of the mutual fund business, but lately they've been struggling to maintain market share. Poor stock and bond markets in 1994, combined with rising interest rates, prompted thousands of Canadians to pull their money out of mutual funds and go back into GICs. The banks were the big losers, with billions of dollars drained away (although a lot of that money just moved from one counter to another). The net result: the big five banks saw their market share of fund assets under management drop from 28 percent in April 1994 to just over 22 percent in April 1995. ∎

There are several theories about why the bank funds were hit so hard. They include:

The "GIC refugees" went home. When interest rates tumbled in the early '90s, shocked GIC investors looked around for alternatives. Mutual funds were hot, so they took a fling. Many got in just as the big profits of '93 were petering out, just in time for the slump of '94. After watching the value of their fund units slip for several months, they decided that low GIC returns were better than mutual fund losses and cashed in.

Lack of credible investment advice. It's significant that while the bank funds were losing ground, most of the big load-fund groups were adding market share, including Trimark and Mackenzie Financial. The reason most often given for this phenomenon is that the load funds provided hand-holding in a difficult time. The broker or financial planner who sold the units was in a position to talk to investors, advise them about what was happening, and explain the value of taking a longer view. The banks could offer no such solace. In many cases, their mutual fund sales representatives have had only basic training and lack the experience and credibility to counsel investors. So when the going got rough, worried investors had no one to turn to for guidance. As a result, they pulled out.

Poor performance. The banks have traditionally offered solid, if dull, fixed income funds. Their bond funds, mortgage funds, and money market funds have provided steady returns with minimal risk. The fact they are no-load and convenient to buy makes them obvious choices for investors looking for a slightly better return than GICs provide, with marginally more risk.

But on the equity fund side, the banks had little to offer. This may come as a surprise, but prior to 1987, only Royal Bank offered a Canadian stock fund (RoyFund Equity). The Bank of Montreal didn't get around to setting up a managed Canadian stock fund until 1994 (although it had an index fund prior to that).

Until recently, most of the banks have continued to sit on their duffs, either because they didn't think the mutual fund business was significant or because they believed it would fall into their hands by default. Only Toronto Dominion aggressively moved to expand its mutual fund offerings and bring in top managers.

(Royal Trust did the same when it was an independent company. Now Royal Bank will reap the benefits of the solid mutual funds lineup established under the direction of former president Paul Starita and his second-in-command, Simon Lewis, who has since assumed the presidency of the Royal funds.)

The rush is now on to catch up, but Green Line and the Royal Funds have established such a big lead that the other banks are going to have their work cut out for them. And it's not just Royal and TD who are the targets. The fact is that all the banks are behind the best of the independent fund companies when it comes to the quality of their equity funds.

For evidence, take a look at the following table. It shows how the bank equity funds stack up against other major fund companies in terms of performance for the 12 months to June 30, 1995. Only funds with at least a one-year track record are included. Bank groups are in bold face. The Royal funds include both Royal Trust and RoyFunds, which are in the process of being integrated.

Fund Group	Equity Funds	% in top quartile	% in top 10%
Fidelity	8	50%	25%
PH&N	8	50%	13%
Trimark	6	33%	33%
TD Green Line	**12**	**33%**	**17%**
Mackenzie	19	26%	16%
Scotia Funds*	**5**	**20%**	**0**
Altamira	11	18%	9%
Royal	**13**	**15%**	**8%**
Investors	14	14%	7%
First Canadian	**6**	**0**	**0**
CIBC	**5**	**0**	**0**

*Does not reflect merger with Montreal Trust funds, which took effect Oct. 1, 1995.

Clearly, if you're looking for a high-performance equity fund, the odds are you won't find it at your bank. Two of the bank groups, Green Line and Royal, have some quality stock fund offerings. But for the rest, Scotia, Bank of Montreal, and CIBC between them place only one of 16 funds in the top 25 percent of performers in their respective categories. (Although Scotia Funds will look much better as a result of the recent merger with Montreal Trust's Excelsior Funds.)

And even though Green Line and Royal Funds have some good equity offerings, if growth is your main goal the odds are that you'll do better by investing your money with Fidelity, Trimark, or Phillips, Hager & North.

That may gradually change, however. Some of the new bank funds are doing well. Green Line's Science and

Technology Fund, for example, got off to an amazing start with a gain of 70.1 percent for the year to June 30. The Royal Funds hope to emulate that success with their new Life Science and Technology Fund, which was launched in July 1995.

But while there are a few bright spots, there are also many examples of weak performances among bank equity funds. A few examples:

CIBC Canadian Equity. Its five-year average annual compound rate of return to June 30, 1995, was just 3.5 percent. That earned it a ranking of number 132 out of the 135 Canadian equity funds surveyed by the Southam Information and Technology Group over that period.

Green Line Blue Chip Equity. Five-year average annual return: 5.1 percent. Ranking: 121.

First Canadian Equity Index Fund. Five-year average annual return: 6.2 percent. Ranking: 103.

RoyFund Equity. Five-year average annual return: 6.7 percent. Ranking: 98.

Green Line Canadian Index. Five-year average annual return: 6.9 percent. Ranking: 95.

The best-performing — *the best!* — bank Canadian stock fund with at least a five-year record is Green Line's Canadian Equity Fund. And it only managed a 7.3 percent average annual gain, good for a number 86 ranking. That means it didn't even come close to being in the top 50 percent of all Canadian stock funds during that time.

To underline the point, the average Canadian equity fund in the Southam survey had an annual gain of 9.2 percent during the five years to June 30. Not one bank fund even approached the average.

Apart from the occasional shooting star such as the Green Line Science and Technology Fund, many of the newer bank offerings have also been disappointments. One example: the recent move of most of the banks into small cap funds. Here's how they've fared:

Royal Canadian Small Cap Fund (previously the Royal Trust Canadian Special Growth Fund). Gain for the year ending June 30, 1995, was a paltry 0.6 percent. That ranked it number 179 out of 195 funds in the Canadian Equity category as reported by Southam.

RoyFund Canadian Growth, which gained 1 percent for the period (rank #177).

Bank of Montreal's First Canadian Special Growth Fund, up 2.1 percent for the period (rank #175).

CIBC Capital Appreciation Fund, up 5.7 percent

(#159). This is not strictly a small cap fund, but the mandate does permit extensive investments in that area.

Granted, it was a tough year for small cap funds generally, but some funds that specialize in this area managed to pay big returns to investors. Examples: United Canadian Growth (+20.6 percent), Talvest New Economy (+15 percent), Special Opportunities (+12.1 percent), BPI Canadian Small Companies Fund (+10.8 percent), Hyperion Aurora (+9.1 percent).

The main problem seems to be that the banks have not been good at choosing equity fund managers. While other companies have been buying the top talent available, both in Canada and internationally, most of the banks have appeared reticent to make similar moves.

Royal Trust brought in star managers like New York's Martin Zweig when the company was independent, and that aggressive approach is now being carried into their new Royal Bank alliance. Green Line has also reached for outside help and the other banks are starting to see merit in this idea. But it's going to take time to build a solid stable of managers and some credible performance results.

So be very selective in your choice of bank equity funds. Choose a group with a wide range of offerings. This gives you more diversity and the ability to switch assets from a weak fund to a better-performing one at the appropriate time. Here's how I rate the groups right now.

1) Royal Funds.   They offer a good mix of conservative and aggressive funds with some solid performers. Former Royal Trust funds dominate this group and bring variety and a solid performance record to the table. The addition of some of the better RoyFunds (such as the RoyFund Balanced Fund) to the mix increases its strength and diversity. Best of the bunch at the present time.

Some Royal funds to look at especially closely:

Royal Trust American Stock Fund/RoyFund U.S. Equity Fund.   The Royal Trust fund is one of the oldest of the bank-owned U.S. equity funds, dating back 30 years. It has a solid long-term record (average annual compound rate of return of 12.3 percent for the decade ending June 30, 1995) and a good management team. Manager is James Young. This fund will be merged in 1996 with the RoyFund U.S. Equity Fund, another solid performer that's also managed by Young.

His style is to limit his portfolios to between 50 and 60 mid-size companies, with sales of between US$500 million and $5 billion annually. Favourite sectors are technology, manufacturing, consumer products, financial, and energy.

Comments Young: "They may not be all that well-known, but we find we get the best combination of value and growth prospects in this group. They tend to be solid, but not flashy, companies that build their businesses and deliver the goods year in, year out. We like companies whose track record indicates they can grow earnings at a pace stronger than general economic growth. We have a longer-term focus so the weightings haven't changed much, although when a stock reaches our targeted valuation we sell it."

Royal European Growth Fund. If you're looking for a no-load way to get into Europe, you won't do better than this fund. Return for the two years to May 31 was 18 percent, making this the top-performing European fund available in Canada over that time. As of mid-1995, just under 30 percent of the portfolio was invested in U.K. companies, after some profit-taking in that country. Other major holdings were in France (14.4 percent) and the Netherlands (11.3 percent).

The fund is managed by Michael Levy of Banker's Trust, the company's leading international equity strategist.

Royal Energy Fund. This is a volatile fund that's suited only for more aggressive investors. I definitely do not recommend it for retirees. Because it's highly specialized, it will do spectacularly well when energy issues are in favour and smell out the joint when they're not. A recent history of the fund's performance tells the story:

Year	Return
1989	+37.5%
1990	- 6.8%
1991	-12.4%
1992	+37.1%
1993	+45.6%
1994	- 7.1%
1995 (6 months)	+ 6.2%

Real boom or bust stuff! So timing is critical — hold it during growth periods, but get out before the next recession hits.

Manager Gordon Zive took over this fund in October 1994. His approach is to focus on companies with sound management, above-average growth potential, and low exploration and operating costs. The fund maintains a relatively balanced exposure to both crude oil and natural gas. During 1995, Zive's emphasis was on more senior producers, as opposed to higher-risk junior companies.

Zweig Strategic Growth Fund. This fund is managed by U.S. investment guru Martin Zweig. It invests in smaller companies with above-average growth potential. Normally, small cap funds are considered higher risk, but Zweig has developed some unique risk-management techniques designed to keep losses to a minimum during rough times. The fund hasn't been around long enough to test his methods over the long term, but an encouraging sign was the fact it managed a gain of 3.7 percent in 1994, a year when many U.S. equity funds, especially small caps, were recording losses (Bullock American, for example, was down 9.4 percent). Three-year returns to June 30, 1995, show an average annual compound rate of return of 16.5 percent, well above average for U.S. funds generally.

Zweig stresses that, despite the small cap orientation, this is a defensive fund, suitable for conservative investors. "If people are looking for an aggressive fund, it's not ours," he says.

2) TD Green Line. The Toronto Dominion funds earn the number two spot because of their range of products, solid performance, and aggressive addition of new offerings. Green Line's six bond funds (two international, four Canadian) each fills a specific investor need and all are respectable performers. Ditto the two money market and mortgage funds.

The equity funds are a mixed bag, however. Green Line has enjoyed outstanding success with its new Science and Technology Fund, and the new North American Growth Fund is also off to a promising start. But some of the other international funds look weak and the four Canadian equity funds, while not terrible by any means, haven't been particularly impressive.

But don't sell this group short. They've made tremendous strides in the past few years and if Royal Bank hadn't acquired the Royal Trust funds in their takeover, this would be the number one bank group today.

3) Scotia Excelsior Funds.   The merger of Scotia Funds with the Montreal Trust Excelsior Funds, which became official Oct. 1, 1995, catapulted this bank family into the number three spot and created a power to be reckoned with. Prior to the merger, the Scotia family had some decent fixed income funds but, with the exception of the CanAm Growth Fund, the equity side was unimpressive. Folding in the Montreal Trust funds (which Scotia already owned) changed the entire picture. This group now offers a sold lineup. The Canadian Growth Fund, which was the old Montreal Trust Excelsior Equity Fund, is a reliable performer and retains the same management team. It earns a $$$ rating this year. Other strong additions that originated with Montreal Trust are the Scotia Excelsior International Fund ($$$), the Scotia Excelsior Dividend Fund ($$$), and the Scotia Excelsior Total Return Fund ($$$). This group is now in a position to challenge Royal and Green Line for the leadership among the bank fund groups in terms of quality and performance; however it does not yet have the diversification of the other two.

4) First Canadian Funds.   The third place bank group, Bank of Montreal's First Canadian Funds, is a long way behind Royal, Scotia, and Green Line. The group offers good variety, with some well-established fixed income funds (including the highly rated First Canadian Mortgage Fund) and 11 equity funds. But most of the stock funds are brand new (nine have been launched since 1993) and performance has been spotty. Best so far have been the U.S. Growth Fund (+22.8 percent for the year ending June 30, 1995), the NAFTA Advantage Fund (+8.2 percent for the first half of '95), and the Far East Growth Fund (+5.9 percent for the six months to June 30, bucking a general down trend among Far East funds). This group is showing promise, however, and may move up in the rankings if the new funds turn out well.

5) CIBC Funds.   CIBC has been trying to refurbish its mutual fund image with the launch of several new equity funds in recent years. But performance so far has generally been weak. As noted earlier, the Canadian Equity Fund has been a perennially disappointing entry. The Global Equity Fund has also been a below-average performer. The group's fixed income funds are much the better bet, with both the Canadian Bond Fund and the Mortgage Fund turning in good long-term results.

CIBC has also been having trouble at the top. The new CEO of CIBC Securities, Keith Sjogren, announced in July he was quitting, just months after taking over from the retiring John Vivash. Whoever takes the job next will have their work cut out for them.

Recommendation: Even if you don't bank there, Royal, Toronto Dominion, or Scotiabank should be your choice if you have a substantial amount to invest in mutual funds and growth is one of your main objectives. But the reality is that even the best of the bank groups still fall well short of mutual fund companies like Trimark, Fidelity, and PH&N when it comes to equity funds.

If you're going to keep virtually all your assets in fixed income and/or money market funds, there's not much to choose among the groups from a performance point of view, although TD Green Line offers the widest product selection.

The Roller-Coaster Funds

— A SPECIAL REPORT

T he conventional wisdom is that mutual fund volatility is a bad thing. Funds that rise and fall sharply in value give investors nervous stomachs, sleepless nights, and poor returns.

But that's not necessarily the case — or at least the poor returns part isn't. Some roller-coaster funds have rewarded investors handsomely, although it's possible they've been responsible for a few ulcers in the process. ■

Take the Marathon Equity Fund, an aggressive fund that specializes in small cap stocks. It has a volatility rating of seven on a scale of 10, according to the Southam Information & Technology Group. (By way of comparison, the staid Trimark Canadian Fund rates a four.) But over the five years to June 30, 1995, Marathon Equity was the number one performing Canadian equity fund with an average annual compound rate of return of 29.6 percent.

If you'd invested money when the fund was first created, back in 1986, there would have been several occasions when you would have been tempted to bail out, however, and other times when you might have felt more than a twinge of concern. Here's a year-by-year look at how it has performed:

MARATHON EQUITY FUND

Year	Return
1987	-31.4%
1988	+19.7%
1989	+27.0%
1990	-14.5%
1991	+12.9%
1992	+ 32.2%
1993	+102.9%
1994	-6.7%
1995 (6 mo.)	+ 38.2%

Heart-stopping stuff, especially if you were an early investor and saw the value of your holdings drop by 31 percent in 1987. But that's the way these funds are.

Let's look at another example, the small Multiple Opportunities Fund. It's an unrepentant speculator's fund, dealing exclusively in junior stocks traded on the free-for-all Vancouver Stock Exchange. It has a volatility rating of 10 — meaning it's right at the top of the scale. Mutual funds don't come in any more explosive packages than this.

And how has it done? Just managed to rank number three among Canadian equity funds for the five years to June 30, with an average annual return of 24.1 percent. Like Marathon Equity, there have been a lot of peaks and valleys along the way, however. Here's a look at its year-by-year track record:

MULTIPLE OPPORTUNITIES FUND

Year	Return
1986	+45.6%
1987	+17.5%
1988	-37.5%
1989	+20.2%
1990	-10.9%
1991	- 6.4%
1992	+ 9.0%
1993	+159.2%
1994	- 15.3%
1995 (6 mo.)	+ 54.1%

Again, pretty exciting stuff, as long as you have the nerves to ride through the sometimes precipitous dips.

So maybe highly volatile funds aren't so bad after all? Unfortunately, there are some bummers in this league too. Consider the sad example of the Cambridge Special Equity Fund, a growth-oriented fund run by Sagit Management of Vancouver. It had an incredible year in 1993, with an almost unbelievable gain of 146.9 percent. But the rest of the story is nowhere near as happy. Here's what it's done:

CAMBRIDGE SPECIAL EQUITY

Year	Return
1988	+14.9%
1989	+20.3%
1990	-34.7%
1991	- 2.2%
1992	- 26.6%
1993	+146.9%
1994	- 20.3%
1995 (6 mo.)	-4.7%

Except for the huge advance in 1993, this decade has been a wipeout for this fund. If you'd invested $10,000 in it at the start of 1990, your money would have shrunk to $8,791 at the end of June 1995, even with the great 1993 profit factored in.

Clearly, high volatility funds can be either good or bad — in the same way as any other type of fund can. So if you're something of a gambler, how can you pick the winners from the losers? Well, there are no guarantees, but here's a rundown of Canada's most volatile mutual funds that may help you make the right decision. Only funds with a volatility rating of seven or greater are listed. This means only funds that have been in existence at least three years, since it takes at least that long to determine volatility. The volatility ratings are calculated by the Southam Information & Technology Group. The high–low range shows the difference in percentage points between a fund's best year and worst year. The higher the number, the greater the peaks and valleys.

BROADLY BASED EQUITY FUNDS

Normally, you don't expect a broadly based equity fund to be included in the high volatility class. That's because the diversification of the portfolio tends to keep returns on a more even keel. Highly volatile funds are usually found among those that invest in specific sectors of the economy or in rapidly growing regions of the world. But there are exceptions to this rule. Let's look at some.

Cambridge Special Equity Fund. Volatility rating: 10. Best year: +145.9 percent (1993). Worst year: -34.7 percent (1990). High-low range: 181.6. Run by Sagit Management of Vancouver, a company that has a lot of funds in this section. Does that tell you something about their management style? This fund focuses on small cap and start-up companies. Emphasis is on stocks with strong growth potential, selling at a discount to book value. As we've already seen, returns fluctuate wildly. You may luck in and hit a hugely successful year. More likely, though, you won't.
    Success probability: Low.

Dynamic Canadian Growth Fund. Volatility rating: 7. Best year: +100.1 percent (1993). Worst year: -18.8 percent (1987). High-low range: 118.9. I was somewhat surprised to find this one turning up in the high-volatility group. It's not a sector fund and doesn't even specialize in small cap stocks. But here it is nonetheless, and with a new manager since former string-puller Jonathan Baird left Dynamic in mid-1995. His replacement is another Jonathan, Goodman. Since Goodman is more of a resources expert, this fund's direction is being adjusted to reflect that. Management style will therefore be even more aggressive than in the past and the make-up of the fund will change as well. Who knows where that will lead. For that reason, be wary of the good five-year track record because in this case the past is most definitely not indicative of the future.
    Success probability: Unknown.

Marathon Equity Fund. Volatility rating: 7. Best year: +102.9 percent (1993). Worst year: -31.4 percent (1987). High-low range: 134.3. This fund has recently changed managers, which is always a cause for some concern — particularly when the fund has been doing extremely well. New person at the top is Wayne Dean, whose style is consistent with the way the fund has been run in the past. The fund has scored some big gains recently, thanks in part to a large holding in Diamond Fields, the Voisey Bay play that has turned huge profits for investors. But the portfolio make-up has been moving away from resources and into the industrial sector, which is usually more stable. The key here is whether the new manager can maintain the momentum.

Success probability: Medium.

Multiple Opportunities Fund. Volatility rating: 10. Best year: +159.2 percent (1993). Worst year: -37.5 percent (1988). High-low range: 196.7. This is the speculator's delight. It's a fund that gambles on start-ups, good stories, and holes in the ground, and does so without apology and with great success. If you're a B.C. resident, you don't have to go to Vegas to play the tables; this fund will do the job just as nicely. The managers buy and sell junior issues traded on the Vancouver Stock Exchange and they've turned out to be right more often than not. Still, when things go bad, they can be dazzlingly bad. Fortunately, that doesn't happen too often. Although this fund is technically sold only in B.C., you might be able to acquire it if you live elsewhere. Ask your broker.

Success probability: High.

Trans-Canada Pension Fund. Volatility rating: 9. Best year: +62.6 percent (1993). Worst year: -15.4 percent (1992). High-low range: 78.0. Now this really doesn't make sense. A fund with the word "pension" in the name, showing up among the high-rollers? Must be a mistake, right? Well, no. Perhaps when I tell you this is another entry from the Sagit stable all this will make more sense. Sagit's managers seem to revel in running highly volatile funds and this is one more example. Stocks are mainly small to mid-cap. The fund holds some fixed income securities to reduce risk; as of mid-1995 about a quarter of the portfolio was in bonds and T-bills. Long-term results have been okay — 10-year average annual return was 8.2 percent. Fund was also turning out some good numbers in mid-1995. This might be a choice for aggressive investors who want their risk tempered a bit.

Success probability: Medium.

RESOURCE FUNDS

Canada's natural resource industry is highly cyclical. Companies in forestry, mining, energy, etc., usually have their best results during periods when the economy is booming. When recession takes over, these companies do poorly, with the bigger ones susceptible to huge losses. Stock prices suffer accordingly.

Mutual funds that invest in this sector follow similar patterns. They tend to generate big returns at times when the economy is strong and suffer declines in unit values during other periods. Shrewd investors trade them like resource stocks, getting in during times of recession when the prices are cheap and selling as they approach cyclical highs.

AGF Canadian Resources. Volatility rating: 7. Best year: +67.7 percent (1993). Worst year: -12.1 percent (1994). High-low range: 79.8. Specializes in small to medium-sized resource companies. Willing to take big bets on sectors that are felt to be undervalued. In mid-1995, for example, the oil and gas sector comprised 40 percent of the portfolio as the managers took advantage of historically low p/e multiples to add to their holdings. Main risk management technique is good diversification. Performance results have been so-so.

Success probability: Medium.

All-Canadian Resources. Volatility rating: 8. Best year: +82.7 percent (1993). Worst year: -28.8 percent (1990). High-low range: 111.5. This is a tiny fund, with only $5 million in assets. The managers have the latitude to invest throughout the resource sector, but the emphasis recently has been on precious metals, where they feel the best opportunities lie. No risk reduction strategies are used, beyond building cash reserves if resource stocks appear poised for a downturn. Recent returns haven't been bad, although longer-term results are weak.

Success probability: Medium.

BPI Canadian Resource. Volatility rating: 7. Best year: +51.5 percent (1993). Worst year: -13.5 percent (1994). High-low range: 65.0. Manager Fred Dalley uses a bottom-up, value-oriented style in selecting stocks for this fund. Has recently taken a more balanced approach with no extreme sector bets, a strategy that tends to reduce overall risk. Results over the past couple of years have been below average, although returns have improved recently.

Success probability: Medium.

Cambridge Resource Fund. Volatility rating: 9. Best year: +85.3 percent (1993). Worst year: -27.8 percent (1990). High-low range: 113.1. This fund focuses on smaller companies in the resource field. The managers, the Sagit company of Vancouver, use a bottom-up stock selection strategy, focusing on companies with long-term high growth potential that represent good value for the money. No special risk management techniques are employed. Although the fund shows long-term profits (average annual gain of 6.7 percent over the decade to June 30, 1995), results have not been as good as those of some of the other leading resource funds.

Success probability: Low.

Dominion Equity Resource. Volatility rating: 10. Best year: +79.7 percent (1993). Worst year: -36.9 percent (1988). High-low range: 116.6. This Calgary-based fund specializes in the oil and gas sector. Fund invests in a range of energy companies from small junior companies to the giants of the industry. Manager Ron Coleman and members of the fund's board have worked as executives in the oil patch and should know it well. Selection emphasis is on companies with good management, strong balance sheets, good drilling prospects, and quality reserves. Long-term results haven't been bad (five-year average annual rate of return of 10.6 percent), but fund has been a downer recently because of skidding stock values in the energy sector. If you expect the oil patch to recover, this might be a worthwhile short-term speculation.

Success probability: Medium.

Prudential Natural Resource Fund. Volatility rating: 7. Best year: +78.3 percent (1993). Worst year: -7.9 percent (1990). High-low range: 86.2. Although the volatility rating brings this one into the roller-coaster funds category, risk-averse investors should take note of the fact that this fund's worst year since its launch in early 1988 was a 7.9 percent loss in 1990. For a natural resource fund, that's very good — many broadly based, lower-volatility funds have had much worse down years. The fund managers attempt to reduce risk by balancing the portfolio over all the key sectors in the resource field: precious metals, energy, forest products, and base metals. They also make maximum use of the 20 percent foreign content allowance. Results have been very good; the fund has an average annual return of 21.4 percent over the five-year period to June 30, 1995. However, lead manager Veronika Hirsch left Prudential in the fall of 1995, which could have a negative impact on results.

Success probability: Medium.

Royal Trust Energy Fund. Volatility rating: 7. Best year: +45.6 percent (1993). Worst year: -11.5 percent (1986). High-low range: 57.1. The historic record of this fund shows it to have one of the best high-low variations of any entry in this group. Offsetting that is the fact its one-year peak is the second lowest of any fund discussed in this section. This is a no-load fund that specializes in the Canadian energy sector, which means it only has a universe of about 100-125 companies to choose from. New manager Gordon Zive (who took over in fall 1994) doesn't use any particular risk reduction strategies, pointing out that there's really nowhere to go except cash if energy stocks turn down. Long-term performance is fair; average annual compound rate of return over the past decade is 8.2 percent.

Success probability: Medium.

Universal Canadian Resource Fund. Volatility rating: 8. Best year: +89.2 percent (1993). Worst year: -19.9 percent (1990). High-low range: 109.1. This fund uses a sector rotation style of portfolio management, zeroing in on areas of the resource industry that are expected to outperform. In mid-'95, for example, almost half the portfolio was in oil and gas, 26 percent in mines and metals, and 19 percent in the forestry sector. Risk is reduced by diversifying the fund across several sectors and by holding senior companies in the portfolio as well as juniors. Long-term track record is pretty good, but the big bet on the sluggish energy sector has hurt recent results, although in mid-'95 some action was becoming evident.

Success probability: Medium.

PRECIOUS METALS FUNDS

Funds in this group specialize in gold and gold stocks, but they may also hold other precious metals assets, such as silver, platinum, and diamonds. As a rule, however, fund values tend to reflect what's happening to the price of gold; when the yellow metal is strong, so are these funds.

Dynamic Precious Metals Fund.   Volatility rating: 7. Best year: +96.2 percent (1993). Worst year: -18.8 percent (1988). High-low range: 115.0. This is the largest precious metals fund in Canada and, until recently, one of the better performers. It lagged behind most of its competitors in the past year, however. As of mid-1995, almost a third of the portfolio was invested in gold bullion and platinum, neither of which was doing much of anything. Manager Jonathan Goodman does not use any particular risk-management strategies.
    Success probability: Medium.

Goldfund.   Volatility rating: 8. Best year: +115.4 percent (1993). Worst year: -29.7 percent (1988). High-low range: 145.1. Small fund with respectable results. Average annual compound rate of return for the five years to June 30, 1995, was 12.6 percent. Manager Robert McEwen blends senior and junior companies in the portfolio for better balance and risk reduction. Will move to as high as 40 percent cash if conditions warrant.
    Success probability: Medium.

Prudential Precious Metals Fund.   Volatility rating: 7. Best year: +97.7 percent (1993). Worst year: -19.1 percent (1990). High-low range: 116.8. This fund uses a growth-oriented, bottom-up approach to stock selection (which means looking first at a company's fundamentals). Emphasis is on stocks rather than bullion because they tend to outperform in most conditions. Focus is small cap companies (the big players are too expensive, the managers feel). No specific risk management techniques; Prudential recommends that investors have no more than 10 percent of their assets here. Decent track record; five-year average annual return of 12 percent. Was managed by Veronika Hirsch, who moved to AGF in September, 1995. It might be wise to see how the new manager does before investing.
    Success probability: Medium.

Royal Precious Metals Fund.   Volatility rating: 7. Best year: +44.0 percent (1993). Worst year: -7.7 percent

(1991). High-low range: 51.7. Good no-load precious metals fund; displays a more consistent high-low profile than most of the other funds in this group. Was the top precious metals fund in Canada for the year ending June 30, 1995, with a big 34.1 percent gain. That came as something of a surprise because there was nothing in the fund's previous history to suggest that kind of result; the managers credit the performance to good stock selection (Goldcorp, Kinross, and Bre-X shares did especially well).

Success probability: Medium.

FAR EAST FUNDS

If you want to invest internationally, the Far East is the region that has provided the most action, good and bad, over the years (the Latin American funds haven't been around long enough to establish a volatility rating). This is a region of stunning highs and dismaying lows, and many investors have experienced both in recent years. Let's have a look.

AGF Asian Growth Fund. Volatility rating: 7. Best year: +87.0 percent (1993). Worst year: -6.5 percent (1994). High-low range: 93.5. This is a bottom-up fund that seeks out value opportunities throughout Asia. Portfolio is diversified among several countries, with Hong Kong, Malaysia, the Philippines, and Singapore the major geographic concentrations in mid-1995. Infrastructure and consumer companies are currently favoured. No specific risk-reduction strategies. Good results: three-year average annual rate of return to mid-1995 was an excellent 23.5 percent.

Success probability: High.

AGF Japan Fund. Volatility rating: 7. Best year: +53.1 percent (1986). Worst year: -20.4 percent (1990). High-low range: 73.5. This fund focuses on blue-chip Japanese stocks, using a series of intensive screens to make selections. Current emphasis is on infrastructure and export sectors with the managers looking to profit from any decline in the international value of the yen. No active risk management; currency risk a special concern. Good long-term record but has taken a clobbering recently.

Success probability: Medium.

C.I. Pacific Fund.   Volatility rating: 7. Best year: +91.7 percent (1993). Worst year: -15.5 percent (1990). High-low range: 107.2. Invests in larger companies across Asia. Portfolio is well diversified to keep risk at manageable levels. This is one of the few broadly based Far East funds that can invest in Japan, although exposure there as of mid-1995 was just 10 percent. Excellent long-term record; average annual return of 18.9 percent over the past decade makes this the number one international fund in Canada over that period.
   Success probability: High.

Cambridge Pacific.   Volatility rating: 7. Best year: +61.6 percent (1993). Worst year: -50 percent (1988). High-low range: 111.6. Talk about gut-wrenching — how about that 50 percent drop in 1988! I wonder how many shell-shocked investors were still around in 1989. Things didn't get quite as bad in 1994, but a 25.6 percent loss that year must have caused more than a few sleepless nights. Managers use a bottom-up investment style and invest in a broad range of companies from small operations to blue chips. Biggest geographic concentration in mid-1995 was in China, with 26 percent of the portfolio. Five-year average annual return was a ho-hum 6.7 percent.
   Success probability: Low.

Fidelity Far East Fund.   Volatility rating: 7. Best year: +86.4 percent (1993). Worst year: -16.7 percent (1994). High-low range: 103.1. Manager K.C. Lee focuses on mid-size to large companies throughout the Far East, except Japan, which is excluded from this fund's mandate. He uses a bottom-up approach for selecting funds and maintains a well-diversified portfolio. Lee was taking a big bet on Hong Kong in mid-1995, with over half his portfolio invested there. He's more cautious about China, which he sees as a very illiquid market. Returns have been good; fund averaged 20.6 percent a year for the three years to June 30, 1995.
   Success probability: High.

Hyperion Asian Trust.   Volatility rating: 9. Best year: +117 percent (1993). Worst year: -20.1 percent (1994). High-low range: 137.1. This is a value-oriented fund that invests primarily in established companies throughout Asia, although it will consider new companies with high growth potential. Major geographic concentration in mid-1995 was in Hong Kong, Malaysia, Thailand, and Singapore. Returns have been above average for Far East funds as a group.

Success probability: High.

Investors Japanese Growth Fund. Volatility rating: 7. Best year: +61.5 percent (1986). Worst year: -27.1 percent (1990). High-low range: 88.6. One of the oldest Japan funds sold in Canada (started in 1971). Had many glory years in the '70s and '80s before the collapse of the Nikkei Index. Has taken a beating recently, however, along with other Japan funds. Manager Collin Abraham takes a value approach to stock selection, looking carefully at such factors as book value, p/e ratios, and the like. He makes an effort to minimize risk, an approach that causes the fund to lag behind during roaring bull markets but limits losses when the Japanese market is down.

Success probability: Medium.

Royal Japanese Stock Fund. Volatility rating: 7. Best year: +63.5 percent (1986). Worst year: -28.4 percent (1990). High-low range: 91.9. Although this is not an index fund, the managers do try to reflect the broad weightings of the Japanese stock market. Stock-picking style is bottom-up. No active risk-management strategies, like currency hedging. Performance has not been very impressive.

Success probability: Low.

Investors Pacific International Fund. Volatility rating: 7. Best year: +88.1 percent (1993). Worst year: -6.7 percent (1994). High-low range: 94.8. This is a relatively new fund (launched in June 1990) that has established a fine track record to date. Low point (-6.7 percent in 1994) is among the best of the high-volatility funds. Well-diversified portfolio reduces risk. Manager Jeremy Higgs uses a bottom-up, value-oriented approach to stock selection. Fund does not invest in Japan. As with other Investors funds, philosophy is to limit risk to the extent possible. That means this fund won't soar to great heights, but neither should it suffer heavy losses.

Success probability: High.

NEWCOMERS

Several potentially volatile funds have been launched recently that invest in derivatives and/or commodities. These are designed for well-heeled investors who are prepared to take risks to achieve potentially high returns. None of these funds has been around long enough to establish a track record or a formal volatility rating, so I haven't attempted to assess their likely degree of success. Nor is their inclusion here to be considered an endorsement of any kind. They are listed for information purposes only.

Contrarian Strategy Futures Limited Partnership. This Vancouver-based operation is a continuous limited partnership offering with a high entry-level price tag (US$20,000 for B.C. residents, US$120,000 in Ontario, CAN$97,000 in Alberta). This is a pure derivatives fund; investments are in commodities futures, currencies futures, and stock indices. The managers employ defensive strategies to control risk, such as placing a limit of 1 to 2 percent of capital on any given trade. As you might expect from the fund's name, the investing philosophy is contrarian — sell into rising markets and buy into falling ones. One-year return to June 30, 1995, was an unexciting 8.3 percent. For information, call 1-800-665-1158.

Friedberg Currency Fund. This fund is available as a continuous offering limited partnership through the Toronto-based Friedberg Mercantile Group. Its guiding light is the secretive and highly influential Albert Friedberg, regarded as one of the world's leading currency experts. This fund is not for the faint of heart. It is highly speculative, investing in currency futures, forward markets, and options. If the managers get their calls right, returns can be huge. If they're wrong, well.... Because of this, the prospectus stresses that this is a fund only for those who can afford to lose part or all of their investment (minimum required is $5,000). Although the fund has only been offered to the general public since November 1994, a look at the results of Friedberg's private managed accounts currency trading program, on which the fund is based, will give you an idea of the kind of volatility to expect. I've used an original investment of $10,000 to show you where you would have stood at the end of each year.

FRIEDBERG CURRENCY ONLY TRADING PROGRAM

Year	Return	Value of Original $10,000
1986	117.6%	$21,760
1987	47.2%	32,030
1988	- 34.0%	21,140
1989	3.3%	21,838
1990	291.4%	85,474
1991	- 39.5%	51,712
1992	- 13.0%	44,989
1993	35.8%	61,095
1994	29.4%	79,057
1995	16.1% (6 mo.)	91,785

The numbers look great. But remember, it all depends on when you started. If you were drawn in by the big profits of 1990 and invested $10,000 on January 1, 1991, your total profit as of June 30, 1995, would only have been $738 — not a great return over 4 1/2 years. Call Friedberg Mercantile Group at 1-800-461-2700 for more information.

20/20 Managed Futures Fund. This new fund from the Oakville, Ont.-based 20/20 Group was launched in March 1995. Run by John Di Tomasso, the fund invests in commodities markets, an area in which the manager has a high degree of expertise (he parlayed $225,000 into $3 million during the 1987 stock market crash). Although this may seem like high-risk territory at first glance, the fund is structured in such a way as to minimize the downside. About 80 percent of the assets are in T-bills, which provide stability and limit risk. All margins are fully covered by the T-bill holdings. And unrealized profits are never used to pyramid winning positions. 20/20 contends that these safeguards make the fund suitable for RRSPs, for which it's 100 percent eligible. The idea is that holding units in a registered plan will provide an additional measure of diversification, since commodity price movements have little correlation with stock and bond market fluctuations. I suggest you wait until the fund has proven this to be the case before putting any of your retirement money into it. It's very early days yet, but a 3 percent decline in unit value during June 1995 is a big move for a single month and may be an indicator that this fund could turn out to be more volatile than 20/20 expects. You can only buy units through major brokerage firms with a commodities trading department. Minimum investment is $2,000.

Up-and-Coming Funds

— A SPECIAL REPORT

O ne of the main criteria for inclusion in my mutual fund ratings is a three-year performance record. That's no guarantee a fund will continue to display the same pattern in the future, but at least it provides some insight into how well the manager is doing relative to his/her peers.

One of the drawbacks of my three-year rule, however, is that it doesn't permit an assessment of the new funds that show unusual promise. So in this edition of the *Guide*, I'm adding this chapter on exciting new funds, which I expect will become a regular feature of this book. ■

There's no particular criteria for including a fund in this section, beyond my belief that it stands a good chance of being one of the stars of the future. If you decide to invest in any of them at this stage, use discretion. Remember that these funds, while they display great potential, are unproven. Also, many of these are sector funds that will normally show greater volatility than a more broadly based stock fund. So don't go overboard!

Admax Global Health Sciences Fund. This fund invests internationally in companies in the businesses of health care, medical equipment, pharmaceuticals, biotechnology, and related industries — a can't-miss growth sector given current demographic trends.

Initial timing was bad — the fund appeared right in the midst of Bill Clinton's 1992 presidential campaign while he and Hillary were busy savaging the health care industry and driving down share values of pharmaceutical giants like Merck.

But the fund quickly righted itself, helped by the rebound in health care stocks when it became apparent the Clintons' grandiose plans for a national health care system in the U.S. were going nowhere. This was one of the hottest funds in Canada during the year to June 30, 1995, with a gain of 41.4 percent. Despite those impressive numbers, investors still haven't discovered this gem; the fund had only $15 million under management in mid-'95. The managers, Invesco Trust of Denver, use a sector rotation approach. They currently favour the health care delivery sector, which represents about half the portfolio. Since, they expect the Canadian dollar to rally against the U.S. dollar over the next year, so they've hedged about 45 percent of the fund's U.S. dollar exposure to protect currency gains.

In mid-'95, the managers were slowly increasing their portfolio weighting in the high-potential but tricky biotechnology sector, zeroing in on companies with strong technology platforms and sufficient cash to fund product development.

Bissett Multinational Fund. The small Calgary-based firm of Bissett & Associates has come up with a unique approach to the problem of reducing international investment risk.

This fund invests exclusively in dividend-paying multinational European and North American companies that trade on the New York Stock Exchange. Company principal David Bissett, who has half a million dollars of his own money in the fund, says the rationale is to enable investors to get worldwide exposure through multinational companies at prices that are truly reflective of the North American context.

The result is a conservative portfolio that gained a healthy 15.2 percent during the year to July 31, 1995. Some of the holdings include Motorola, Unilever,

Polygram, Thomson Corp., and Northern Telecom. As of mid-year, the portfolio consisted of 51 companies, of which 49 had recently announced significant dividend increases in the 8 to 15 percent range.

The fund was originally available only to "sophisticated" investors (meaning people with a lot of money). However, it was opened to all investors in August 1995.

GT Global Infrastructure Class.   GT is a U.S. company that recently entered the Canadian market. This fund, managed out of San Francisco by David Sherry and Michael Mahoney, focuses on infrastructure companies in such fields as energy, transportation, and communications. The portfolio is well diversified internationally and includes a number of key stocks in emerging markets, such as Siam Cement in Thailand.

Companies in the infrastructure field figure to do very well as emerging nations seek to upgrade their highways, airports, shipping facilities, and power production systems. India, for example, expects to triple the number of phone lines in the country in the next few years.

But this isn't just another take on an emerging markets fund. Investments will be made in developed countries as well. For example, the U.S. is expected to spend billions in the next decade repairing and upgrading the interstate highway system, 40 percent of which is in a state of decay.

Like most of the funds in this chapter, this one hasn't had time to jell. But initial results are promising, with a gain of 5.3 percent for the first half of '95.

GT Global Telecommunications Class.   Another GT entry, managed by the same duo as the Infrastructure Fund. This one concentrates on the telecommunications business, with the goal of making big profits for investors from the fact that over half the world's population has never made a phone call — and would like to! The fund will invest in companies that are geared to supply those services, as well as in firms on the leading edge of new telecommunications technology.

It will be fascinating to see which of Canada's two new promising telecommunications funds (see the United fund, below) emerges as the winner over time. This one scored a very respectable 11.4 percent gain in the first half of '95 — but United did even better. Still, it's early days.

Green Line Science and Technology Fund. This was the top-performing fund in Canada over the past year, with a gain of over 70 percent for the year ending June 30. It's an international fund that invests, as you might guess, in science and technology issues. About two-thirds of its assets are currently in the U.S., which enabled investors to benefit from the run-up in U.S. technology stocks in early '95. Some of the fund's key holdings are Vodafone Group PLC (UK), 4.7 percent of the portfolio; Adobe Systems, 3.6 percent; and Xilinx Inc., 3.4 percent.

If you got in on this one early (and very few people did), you've had a helluva ride until now. If you didn't, you're probably tempted to get on board as soon as possible. A word of warning in either case: nice though it would be, this fund is not going to return 70 percent, or anything like it, every year. Technology stocks are historically highly volatile, and this fund is likely to be the same. A big gain could just as easily be followed by a large loss. In anticipation of that possibility, in mid-'95 the managers were focusing on defensive securities with a proprietary edge that would stand up well to any shake-up in the technology sector. Plus, they'd trimmed back the electronics portion of the portfolio by about 10 percent because it seemed to be vulnerable to a market downturn.

Science and technology is certainly a good place to have some of your money long-term. But don't invest here if you're liable to panic at the first sign of a correction and pull out. This is a fund for aggressive investors who are prepared to take a long-term view. If you want to reduce the risk factor, use a dollar-cost averaging strategy.

Global Strategy Canadian Small Cap Fund. When John Sartz was running the Bolton Tremblay Small Cap Fund, it was one of the best of its kind in the country. Launched in 1987, it had a slow start and took a beating in 1990, when stock markets everywhere slumped. But after that, it took off, gaining 26.5 percent in '91, 16.7 percent in '92, and an impressive 38.1 percent in '93. The fund had an average annual return of 11.6 percent for the five-year period ending May 31, 1994, just before it was taken over by BPI, along with the rest of the Bolton Tremblay funds. There aren't many small cap funds in Canada, but those impressive results put Sartz's entry at the top of the list over that period.

Sartz left the manager's job when ownership of the fund changed hands, although he remains a vice-president of Bolton Tremblay Inc., which continues to operate as an investment management company. Now he has resurfaced as manager of the new Global Strategy Canadian Small Cap Fund, which was launched in January 1995.

This fund will be worth watching. Sartz's approach to running a small cap fund is quite different from that of other managers. He avoids the Vancouver and Alberta stock exchanges — usually happy hunting grounds for small cap investors. He won't invest in mining stocks or gold shares either, so you won't find any hole-in-the-ground speculatives here. Rather, he looks for small companies with solid fundamentals, preferably those that no one else has ever heard of. He does all his own research and he takes a long-term approach.

Some investors have been unhappy with the recent performance of Global Strategy's funds and have been looking for ways to exit without paying a fortune in redemption fees. Switching some assets into the new Sartz fund may be a solution. With a little patience, there could be some pleasant surprises down the road.

The fund made a respectable showing in its early days, gaining 6.3 percent for the first half of '95. Some key stock holdings as of mid-year: Shaw Industries A, Richland Petro SP warrants, Harris Steel Group B, Bolistic Energy, and Ensign Resource Service Group — all companies with good 12-month earnings, solid value, and strong growth potential.

Interestingly, Sartz's old fund, now called BPI Canadian Small Companies Fund, outperformed his new entry with a 10.4 percent gain for the first six months of '95. We'll see how they compare over the long haul!

Talvest New Economy Fund. In 1992, economist Nuala Beck wrote a best-selling book entitled *Shifting Gears*. In it, she postulated that our economy is passing through a transition phase every bit as significant as the Industrial Revolution of the 19th century. She believes we are entering a new knowledge economy, which will be driven by what she calls "four engines": computers and semi-conductors; health and medical; communications and telecommunications; and instrumentation.

Why, that sounds like it might be a formula for a new mutual fund! Eureka — Talvest has done it!

The New Economy Fund has been set up to invest in companies that are poised to benefit from the fundamental changes we are experiencing — assuming Ms. Beck is correct, of course. That means this fund should be ideally suited for anyone structuring a portfolio with the 21st century in mind.

The fund is managed by Richard Campbell, who uses a bottom-up approach to stock selection — that means his starting point is a company's fundamentals. He intends to keep the portfolio relatively small (30 to 40 stocks), with an emphasis on medium-sized companies. At least 60 percent of the portfolio is in New Economy stocks. U.S. stocks form a minimum of 10 percent of the holdings, but the fund is RRSP/RRIF-eligible.

Some key holdings in mid-'95: Allelix Biopharmaceuticals (3.3 percent of the portfolio), a high-quality biotechnology company with a strong research base; Hemosol (3.3 percent), which recently announced a strategic alliance with a German company, Fresenius, to develop and market a red blood cell substitute; Xillix (3.4 percent, a different company from Xilinx in the Green Line Science and Technology portfolio), which sells lung imaging systems able to detect early signs of lung cancer; Corel (4.3 percent), which dominates Windows-based illustration graphics with 50–60 percent of the market share; Newbridge (4.8 percent), a pioneer and leader in the development of asynchronous transfer mode (ATM) switches that allow transmission of voice, data, image, and video over computer and telephone networks; BCE Mobile (3.6 percent), whose wireless marketplace is predicted to be one of the faster-growing segments of the telecommunications sector; Pallet Pallet (2.6 percent), a single-product company driven by qualified management with exceptional vision.

So far, the fund and Ms. Beck's theories are looking pretty good. Gain for the year ending June 30 was a solid 15 percent.

Trimark Advantage Bond Fund.   New bond funds normally rank up there with cutting the grass on the excitement scale, but this one is an exception. It invests in "high yield" corporate bonds. That's a polite euphemism for junk bonds, securities of below-average quality that pay above-average returns.

Normally, you'd expect such a fund to be higher risk. But data released by Trimark suggests that, in reality, high-yield bonds did better than supposedly more conservative issues in '94, due to less sensitivity to interest rate movements.

Trimark's strengths have historically been in the equities field — their three bond funds are all relatively new. But this is a company that hasn't taken a false step yet, so you have to give them the benefit of a doubt. Early results from this one have been very impressive; the fund gained 12.5 percent in the first half of '95.

Manager Patrick Farmer, who came over from Crown Life in 1993, searches for value in bonds that may be overlooked because of low or non-existent credit ratings. He especially likes situations where an improvement in a company's financial position may result in a credit upgrading. He also balances the portfolio with higher-quality, investment grade bonds for liquidity and reduced risk. In fact, as of mid-1995, some 60 percent of the holdings were in government securities.

Despite that, I can't bring myself to recommend this fund for conservative fixed income portfolios — at least, not until it has been around for a while longer. But if you're willing to accept a higher level of risk in a bond fund, it's worth a look. Trimark is one of the best fund groups in the country. If anyone can make a fund like this work in Canada, it's them.

Trimark Indo-Pacific Fund. Well, why not? Every other Canadian fund company has a foothold in the Far East — why should Trimark be any different?

Well, perhaps because they've never done anything like this before. There's a strong tendency to suggest they should stick to what they know best. Still, with half the world's population and exploding economic growth, the lure of Asia is overwhelming.

Trimark reached outside its own organization for the first time for a manager in this case, hiring Hong Kong-based Lloyd George Management to assume responsibility for the fund (and to safeguard Trimark's cherished reputation). Results so far have been everything Trimark could have hoped for. This was one of the top-performing Far East funds in the first half of '95, with a gain of 6.6 percent. If that seems modest, consider that the average for all Far East funds during that period, as reported by *The Financial Post*, was minus 4.7 percent.

Although India figures prominently in the fund's name, investments in that country were minor as of mid-

'95. The majority (30 percent) of the portfolio was in Hong Kong, with other sizeable holdings in Thailand, Malaysia, and Singapore.

Investing in the Far East for the rest of this decade figures to be equivalent to attending a lot of wild parties — there'll be some great excitement, but there'll be a lot of hangovers too. But when all is said and done, I expect this fund to be way up there on the leader board.

United Global Telecommunications Fund. This was the first telecommunications fund to set up in Canada (it beat GT by a few months). The managers, Curt McLeod and Sandra Shrewsbury, focus on companies they believe will benefit from the boom in personal communications services. This is not a Bell Canada, AT&T, and Telefonos de Mexico fund. It aggressively invests in firms involved in the development of computer hardware and software, as well as entertainment and media companies. That means it will be much more volatile than a plain old phone company fund — and also potentially more profitable. Some key holdings as of mid-'95 were Paging Network Inc., the largest and fastest growing wireless messaging company in the U.S.; DSC Communications, a major supplier of telecommunications equipment; VLSI Technology Inc., a well-diversified semiconductor company; Fuji Software, a medium-sized software company with strength in communications products; DDI Ltd., a small Japanese company in the rapidly growing cellular market; and Broderbund Software Inc.

Results so far have been very impressive — the fund gained 21.8 percent in the year ending June 30. This is an international fund, so it counts as foreign content in an RRSP/RRIF.

Universal Growth Fund. Why, you may wonder, does Mackenzie Financial need to add yet another fund to its already overflowing stable? Apparently because they had the chance to sign on Bill Kanko as manager. Maybe you've never heard of Kanko, but he's well known in the mutual funds industry. He spent a decade with the Trimark organization, absorbing the highly disciplined investment techniques used there and playing an important role in the success of some of their key funds. Now he's soloing, running his own investment management company.

Mackenzie saw the opportunity and snapped up his services for this fund. Although it's international, the emphasis will be on U.S. growth stocks and the number of holdings in the portfolio will be limited. His target is no more than 25 stocks. Kanko's approach is to look for a winning combination of strong management, good cash flow, and growth opportunities. Three of his early stock selections: Rubbermaid, Electronic Arts, and McGraw-Hill, a company he feels has been under-managed for the last decade but should turn around with new people at the top.

Another ex-Trimark manager, Dina DeGeer, has joined Kanko and will work with him on this fund and the Universal Canadian Growth Fund, which you should keep an eye on.

This fund has no track record to speak of yet, but I expect it to do well. It's foreign content for RRSP/RRIF purposes.

Selecting the Right Portfolio

Putting together the right mutual fund portfolio for your specific needs is not easy. There are several factors that need to be considered: your age, investment goals, risk acceptance level, whether the portfolio is in a registered plan, income requirements, and more. You also have to consider which funds are readily available to you; the whole mutual fund universe won't be. For example, if you're not a client of Investors Group, you won't be able to include any of their offerings in your mix.

One way around the dilemma is to use a mutual fund asset allocation service, as explained in the earlier section on that subject. There are several problems involved with that course, however. There are extra costs involved, the funds offered by the service may not meet your specific needs, and the performance level of some of the programs has been mediocre at best. ■

I believe that the best way to ensure you have the right blend of funds is to do it yourself, using appropriate asset mix principles. Unfortunately, many people who take this approach end up cobbling together mutual fund portfolios that aren't right for their goals, usually because they don't pay close attention to what they're doing.

To help get you on the right track, I've constructed a selection of sample fund portfolios that are suitable for investors at different stages of life and with varying objectives.

For illustration purposes, I've listed some sample funds for each portfolio. In selecting these, I've avoided any with initial entrance requirements of more than $1,000, because I wanted to show that it's possible to have adequate diversification, even with a relatively small amount of money.

Please keep in mind these are sample portfolios only. There are many other funds that would fit nicely into the various categories, so don't assume that the ones listed below are the only possible choices, or even the best ones.

Also note that the portfolio mix was suitable for the economic conditions that existed at the time this edition of the *Guide* was put together (August 1995). As conditions change, the mix would have to be modified for optimum results.

AGGRESSIVE GROWTH

This portfolio is suitable for investors who wish to maximize medium to long-term growth potential. It is most appropriate for people under 50 who are prepared to accept an above-average degree of risk.

International money market (5%) — Altamira Short-Term Global Income, Global Strategy Diversified Savings

Canadian equity (20%) — Altamira Equity, Trimark Canadian, United Canadian Growth

International equity (20%) — Cundill Value, Trimark Fund, Templeton Growth

U.S. equity (15%) — Altamira Select American, Fidelity Growth America, RoyFund U.S. Equity

Far East equity (15%) — C.I. Pacific, Fidelity Japanese Growth

European equity (5%) — Fidelity European Growth, Royal European Growth

Canadian bond (15%) — Altamira Income, Talvest Bond

International bond (5%) — Talvest Foreign Pay, Royal Trust International Bond

Comments: This portfolio is more heavily weighted to stocks (75 percent) than I would normally advise, but it is designed for an aggressive investor. A fifth of the holdings are in the Canadian stock market, which should continue to perform well over the coming year, as long as the Quebec situation doesn't cause it to come unglued. The balance of the equity holdings are well diversified internationally. I have increased the percentage in the Far East, as I expect we'll see some rebound in '96 from the doldrums those markets have experienced. International money market funds and bond funds provide some protection against downward moves in the Canadian dollar if the Quebec referendum turns up a yes vote.

CONSERVATIVE GROWTH

This portfolio is designed for investors who want some growth potential while keeping risk relatively low. Those over 50 might find this one especially suitable. It's worthy of note that all the funds I mentioned in this segment in last year's edition were profitable in the 12 months to July 31, 1995. That's the key to a conservative fund — keep risk to a minimum.

U.S. money market (5%) — AGF U.S. Dollar Money Market, United U.S. Dollar Money Market

Canadian money market (10%) — First Canadian Money Market, RoyFund Canadian T-Bill

Canadian equity (20%) — Altamira Equity, Trimark Canadian, United Canadian Equity

International equity (20%) — Templeton Growth, Trimark Fund

Balanced (20%) — Altamira Growth and Income, Dynamic Partners

Canadian bond (20%) — Altamira Income, Talvest Bond

International bond (5%) — Talvest Foreign Pay, Royal Trust International Bond

Comments: This portfolio takes a more balanced approach, but the emphasis is still on growth. As a result, the total equity component will be about 50 percent — the exact percentage depends on the composition of the balanced funds you select. This year I've added Canadian money market funds to the list, replacing international money funds. That's because I think the Canadian dollar will strengthen in 1996 — but the outcome of the Quebec referendum will play a critical role in that, so keep a close watch on the situation and adjust your mix if appropriate.

INCOME

This portfolio is for those who wish to maximize income while keeping risk to a minimum. It would be especially suitable for retired people, outside a RRIF. Despite the low-risk nature of this portfolio, the unit value of several of the listed funds was hard hit in the first half of 1994 because of a sudden, sharp rise in interest rates. In such conditions, it's essential that income investors keep their cool and not sell their funds at a loss. That was demonstrated by the fact that the funds on this portfolio list snapped back well in the second half of '94 and the first half of '95, more than recovering their earlier losses. Remember, the key advantage of this portfolio is steady income. Keep your eye on that and forget about market fluctuations.

Canadian money market (15%) — First Canadian Money Market, RoyFund Canadian T-Bill

U.S. money market (5%) — AGF U.S. Dollar Money Market, United U.S. Dollar Money Market

Dividend (25%) — Dynamic Dividend Fund, Scotia Excelsior Dividend

Canadian equity (5%) — Trimark Canadian, 20/20 Dividend

International equity (5%) — Templeton Growth, Trimark Fund

Balanced (15%) — Dynamic Partners, Industrial Mortgage Securities

Canadian bond (10%) — Altamira Income, Talvest Bond

Mortgage (15%) — CIBC Mortgage, First Canadian Mortgage

International bond (5%) — Talvest Foreign Pay, Royal Trust International Bond

Comments: This portfolio offers a combination of safety, income, and some modest growth potential. A significant portion of the income will benefit from the dividend tax credit, thus improving after-tax returns. The inclusion of the 20/20 Dividend Fund in the Canadian equity listing is not an oversight. Despite the name, I don't regard this as a true dividend fund (see the review in the "Choosing Dividend Income Funds" chapter for an explanation). However, as a conservatively managed Canadian stock fund, it is very suitable for this portfolio.

> **SPECIAL NOTE:** Because I've limited my selections to funds requiring no more than a $1,000 initial investment, several good money market funds have been left out. I've also excluded money market funds with a load charge. However, if you can find a dealer who'll provide a quality money market fund, such as the Guardian Short-Term Money Fund, on a no-load basis, take it.

RRSP

The following portfolio is designed for self-directed RRSPs. It assumes the investor does not have a non-registered portfolio (if so, equities would be held outside the RRSP).

Canadian money market (10%) — First Canadian Money Market, RoyFund Canadian T-Bill

International money market (5%) — Altamira Short-Term Global Income, Global Strategy Diversified Savings

U.S. money market (5%) — Green Line U.S. Money Market, RoyFund U.S. Dollar Money Market Fund

Canadian equity (15%) — Altamira Equity, Trimark RSP Equity

International equity (10%) — Templeton Growth, Trimark Fund

Balanced (15%) — Dynamic Partners, Industrial Mortgage Securities

Canadian bond (20%) — Altamira Income, Talvest Bond

Mortgage (5%) — CIBC Mortgage, First Canadian Mortgage

International bond (10%) — Dynamic Global Bond, Royal Trust International Bond

Comments: This is a well-balanced blend, with some growth potential but low risk and diversified enough for today's complex investing environment. The U.S. money market, international money market, and international bond funds listed here are all fully RRSP-eligible, so they won't cut into your 20 percent foreign content allowance.

RRIFS

The following portfolio is suitable for registered retirement income funds, where the main objectives are safety and liquidity.

Canadian money market (10%) — First Canadian Money Market, RoyFund Canadian T-Bill

U.S. money market (10%) — Green Line U.S. Money Market, RoyFund U.S. Dollar Money Market Fund

Canadian equity (10%) — Altamira Capital Growth, Trimark RSP Equity

International equity (5%) — Templeton Growth, Trimark Fund

Balanced (15%) — Dynamic Partners, Industrial Mortgage Securities

Mortgage (20%) — CIBC Mortgage, First Canadian Mortgage

Canadian bond (25%) — Altamira Income, Talvest Bond

International bond (5%) — Dynamic Global Bond, Royal Trust International Bond

Comments: This portfolio will generate strong cash flow for RRIF investors, and I have made no distribution changes since last year beyond shifting a 5 percent weighting from international bonds to Canadian bonds. The portfolio also contains some growth potential, as a hedge against inflation. As well, there is some international exposure to avoid being overly vulnerable if the Canadian dollar declines — whether that happens will depend in large part on the outcome of the Quebec referendum. The U.S. and international money funds and the international bond funds mentioned are all fully RRIF-eligible and will not count against your foreign content.

SHORT TERM

This final portfolio is intended for people who are saving for a relatively short-term goal (perhaps buying a home). The goals are a higher return than from a GIC, with good liquidity and low risk. Note, however, that low risk does not mean no risk. During times when interest rates are rising sharply, the unit value of bond and mortgage funds will fall, as happened in early 1994. If you are unfortunate enough to have to cash in your portfolio at precisely that time, you may suffer a capital loss. This portfolio will be held outside an RRSP.

Canadian money market (20%) — First Canadian Money Market, RoyFund Canadian T-Bill

U.S. money market (10%) — Green Line U.S. Money Market, RoyFund U.S. Dollar Money Market Fund

Canadian equity (10%) — Trimark Canadian, 20/20 Dividend

International equity (5%) — Templeton Growth, Trimark Fund

Balanced (10%) — Dynamic Partners, Industrial Mortgage Securities

Mortgage (25%) — CIBC Mortgage, First Canadian Mortgage

Canadian bond (15%) — Dynamic Income Fund, Scotia Defensive Income Fund

International bond (5%) — Dynamic Global Bond, Royal Trust International Bond

Comments: More than half the assets (55 percent) are in the most conservative types of mutual funds: money market and mortgage. Another 20 percent is in bonds. A relatively small proportion of the portfolio is exposed to the stock market, because of stock volatility. This reduces the return on this portfolio, but ensures the money is available when needed in a few years.

None of these sample portfolios may be exactly right for your own situation, but they may help get you moving in the right direction. Certainly, the worst mistake you can make in mutual fund investing is to have too much of your money tied up in one type of asset — especially if that particular asset category is out of favour at the time.

Fund Families

These are the main mutual fund families available to the general public in Canada. I've included only those companies that offer one or more funds in at least four of the five key categories: money market, fixed income, balanced, Canadian equity, and international equity (including U.S.). Load charges will sometimes vary within a group, so inquire about the specific fund in which you're interested. Where switching charges are stated in terms of a maximum (e.g., 2 percent maximum), you can negotiate the fee with your broker or mutual fund sales person. Obviously, you should try to pay as little as possible.

To make these listings more user-friendly this year, the funds within each group are listed according to the ratings they've received in this edition. So you can pick out the top funds within each family at a glance. Funds listed as "NR" are not rated because they haven't been in existence long enough to establish a three-year track record. ∎

All 800 numbers shown are, of course, toll free.

ADMAX REGENT GROUP

NUMBER OF FUNDS:	13
ASSETS UNDER MANAGEMENT:	$220.8 MILLION
LOAD CHARGE:	FRONT: MAXIMUM 9%; BACK: MAXIMUM 7%
SWITCHING CHARGE:	4 FREE TRANSFERS PER YEAR, $25 THEREAFTER
WHERE SOLD:	ACROSS CANADA
PHONE NUMBER:	1-800-667-2369
FUNDS IN GROUP:	$$$$ — NONE
	$$$ — NONE
	$$ — AMERICAN SELECT GROWTH, REGENT INTERNATIONAL, REGENT KOREA, REGENT TIGER, REGENT WORLD INCOME
	$ — ADMAX CANADIAN PERFORMANCE, CANADIAN SELECT GROWTH
	NR — ADMAX ASSET ALLOCATION, ADMAX CASH PERFORMANCE, ADMAX GLOBAL HEALTH SCIENCES, REGENT DRAGON 888, REGENT EUROPA PERFORMANCE, REGENT NIPPON
COMMENTS:	ADMAX HAS INTRODUCED A NO-LOAD PURCHASE OPTION THIS YEAR. THEY ARE ALSO ONE OF THE FUND GROUPS WITH A NEGOTIABLE BACK-END LOAD. BE SURE TO GET FULL DETAILS BEFORE BUYING. THIS GROUP'S BEST PERFORMER RIGHT NOW IS THE GLOBAL HEALTH SCIENCES FUND.

AGF GROUP

NUMBER OF FUNDS:	20
ASSETS UNDER MANAGEMENT:	$4.3 BILLION
LOAD CHARGE:	3 OPTIONS ARE AVAILABLE ON MOST FUNDS
	OPTION A — FRONT: MAXIMUM 6% (EXCEPT ON MONEY MARKET FUND WHERE THE MAXIMUM IS 2%)
	OPTION B — BACK: MAXIMUM 5.5%
	OPTION C — NO LOAD
SWITCHING CHARGE:	2% MAXIMUM
WHERE SOLD:	ACROSS CANADA
PHONE NUMBER:	1-800-268-8583
FUNDS IN GROUP:	$$$$ — NONE
	$$$ — AMERICAN GROWTH, CANADIAN BOND, GROWTH EQUITY, JAPAN, ASIAN GROWTH
	$$ — CANADIAN RESOURCES, GLOBAL

GOVERNMENT BOND, MONEY MARKET,
SPECIAL FUND, STRATEGIC INCOME,
U.S.$ MONEY MARKET

$ — CANADIAN EQUITY, GROWTH AND INCOME,
HIGH INCOME

NR — CHINA FOCUS, EUROPEAN GROWTH,
INTERNATIONAL SHORT-TERM INCOME,
RESOURCE CAPITAL, U.S. INCOME,
WORLD EQUITY

COMMENTS: A SOLID ORGANIZATION WITH A GOOD MIX OF FUNDS.
PERFORMANCE CAN BE SPOTTY, HOWEVER. ONE OF THE
FEW FUND COMPANIES WITH AN ASSET ALLOCATION
SERVICE (ACTUALLY, THREE OF THEM).

AIC GROUP

NUMBER OF FUNDS:	6
ASSETS UNDER MANAGEMENT:	$239 MILLION
LOAD CHARGE:	FRONT: MAXIMUM 6%; BACK: MAXIMUM 5.5%
SWITCHING CHARGE:	NONE
WHERE SOLD:	ACROSS CANADA
PHONE NUMBER:	1-800-263-2144
FUNDS IN GROUP:	$$$$ — NONE
	$$$ — ADVANTAGE FUND, VALUE FUND
	$$ — NONE
	$ — NONE
	NR — DIVERSIFIED CANADA, EMERGING MARKETS, MONEY MARKET, WORLD EQUITY
COMMENTS:	GROWING COMPANY. FOUR OF THE FUNDS ARE BRAND-NEW, SO TOO SOON TO JUDGE. THE TWO THAT HAVE BEEN AROUND A WHILE ARE GOOD PERFORMERS AND WORTH A LOOK.

ALTAMIRA INVESTMENT SERVICES

NUMBER OF FUNDS:	22
ASSETS UNDER MANAGEMENT:	$5.5 BILLION
LOAD CHARGE:	NONE
SWITCHING CHARGE:	NONE
WHERE SOLD:	ACROSS CANADA
PHONE NUMBER:	(416) 413-5359 OR 1-800-263-2824
FUNDS IN GROUP:	$$$$ — EQUITY, GROWTH AND INCOME, INCOME
	$$$ — BOND, CAPITAL GROWTH, SELECT AMERICAN
	$$ — ALTAFUND INVESTMENT CORPORATION, BALANCED, RESOURCE, SHORT-TERM GLOBAL INCOME

$ — Global Diversified, Special Growth

NR — Asia Pacific, Dividend, European Equity, Global Bond, Global Discovery, Japanese Opportunity, North American Recovery, Precious and Strategic Metal, Short-Term Government Bond, U.S. Larger Company

COMMENTS: The pioneer in mutual funds by telephone. An aggressive company, which has thrived on a combination of high performance, good marketing, and no load charges. However, the performance of some funds has shown signs of slipping, so you have to be selective.

AMI PRIVATE CAPITAL FUNDS

NUMBER OF FUNDS:	4
ASSETS UNDER MANAGEMENT:	$11 MILLION
LOAD CHARGE:	NONE, IF PURCHASED FROM MANAGER
SWITCHING CHARGE:	NONE
WHERE SOLD:	B.C., Ontario, Quebec, Nova Scotia
PHONE NUMBER:	(416) 865-3006
FUNDS IN GROUP:	$$$$ — None
	$$$ — Money Market
	$$ — Equity, Income, Optimix
	$ — None
	NR — None
COMMENTS:	A small, Toronto-based company. Best performers have been the bond and money market funds. You'll need a lot of money to get in; minimum investment is $50,000.

APEX FUNDS

NUMBER OF FUNDS:	6
ASSETS UNDER MANAGEMENT:	$125 MILLION
LOAD CHARGE:	Front: maximum 4%; back: maximum 6%
SWITCHING CHARGE:	NONE
WHERE SOLD:	Across Canada except Quebec and New Brunswick
PHONE NUMBER:	(604) 737-9107
FUNDS IN GROUP:	$$$$ — None
	$$$ — None
	$$ — None
	$ — None
	NR — Asian Pacific, Balanced Allocation,

EQUITY GROWTH, FIXED INCOME, MONEY
MARKET, MORTGAGE

COMMENTS: THIS IS A NEW GROUP OF SEGREGATED FUNDS FROM
SEABOARD LIFE.

ATLAS FUNDS

NUMBER OF FUNDS: 18
ASSETS UNDER
MANAGEMENT: $331 MILLION
LOAD CHARGE: NONE
SWITCHING CHARGE: NONE
WHERE SOLD: ACROSS CANADA
PHONE NUMBER: 1-800-268-8697
FUNDS IN GROUP: $$$$ — NONE
$$$ — NONE
$$ — AMERICAN GROWTH, CANADIAN BOND,
CANADIAN GROWTH, CANADIAN MONEY
MARKET, CANADIAN T-BILL, GLOBAL
EQUITY, U.S. MONEY MARKET
$ — CANADIAN BALANCED
NR — AMERICAN BALANCED, AMERICAN EMERGING
VALUE, AMERICAN OPPORTUNITY, AMERICAN
VALUE, CANADIAN DIVERSIFIED, CANADIAN
EMERGING GROWTH, CANADIAN EMERGING
VALUE, CANADIAN VALUE, HIGH-YIELD
BOND, MANAGED FUTURES
COMMENTS: THE FINSCO FUNDS WERE PURCHASED BY MIDLAND
WALWYN ON DECEMBER 31, 1993. THE NAME OF THE
FAMILY WAS CHANGED TO ATLAS IN JULY 1994. NOT
JUST THE NAME CHANGED, HOWEVER. THE COMMISSION
STRUCTURE WAS ALSO OVERHAULED AND THE FUNDS ARE
NOW SOLD ON A NO-LOAD BASIS.

BPI CAPITAL

NUMBER OF FUNDS: 17
ASSETS UNDER
MANAGEMENT: $1.2 BILLION
LOAD CHARGE: MONEY MARKET — NONE
CANADIAN BOND — FRONT: MAXIMUM 5%;
BACK: MAXIMUM 5%
ALL OTHER FUNDS — FRONT: MAXIMUM 9%;
BACK: MAXIMUM 9%
SWITCHING CHARGE: 2% MAXIMUM
WHERE SOLD: ACROSS CANADA EXCEPT QUEBEC

PHONE NUMBER:	1-800-263-2427
FUNDS IN GROUP:	$$$$ — NONE
	$$$ — AMERICAN SMALL COMPANIES, GLOBAL BALANCED RSP
	$$ — AMERICAN EQUITY VALUE, CANADIAN EQUITY VALUE, CANADIAN RESOURCE, CANADIAN SMALL COMPANIES, GLOBAL EQUITY, INCOME, INTERNATIONAL EQUITY, T-BILL
	$ — CANADIAN BALANCED, CANADIAN BOND
	NR — GLOBAL OPPORTUNITIES, GLOBAL REAL ESTATE SECURITIES, GLOBAL RSP BOND, SMALL COMPANIES, NORTH AMERICAN BALANCED RSP

COMMENTS: THIS SMALL PLAYER SHOCKED THE MUTUAL FUND WORLD IN MID-'94 BY SWALLOWING THE HUGE BOLTON TREMBLAY FAMILY. A COMPLETE REORGANIZATION SAW THE DEPARTURE OF MOST OF BT'S MANAGEMENT TEAM. SOME OF THE NEW FUNDS THAT HAVE EMERGED LOOK PRETTY GOOD, ESPECIALLY THE ONES RUN BY LAZARD FRERES OF NEW YORK.

BANK OF MONTREAL

NUMBER OF FUNDS:	18
ASSETS UNDER MANAGEMENT:	$4.3 BILLION
LOAD CHARGE:	NONE
SWITCHING CHARGE:	NONE
WHERE SOLD:	ACROSS CANADA
PHONE NUMBER:	1-800-665-7700
FUNDS IN GROUP:	$$$$ — MORTGAGE
	$$$ — BOND
	$$ — MONEY MARKET
	$ — ASSET ALLOCATION, EQUITY INDEX
	NR — DIVIDEND INCOME, EMERGING MARKETS, EUROPEAN GROWTH, FAR EAST, GROWTH, INTERNATIONAL BOND, INTERNATIONAL GROWTH, JAPANESE GROWTH, NAFTA ADVANTAGE, RESOURCE, SPECIAL GROWTH, T-BILL, U.S. GROWTH

COMMENTS: THE MORTGAGE FUND IS PARTICULARLY GOOD HERE, HAVING MOVED UP TO $$$$ STATUS THIS YEAR. THIS GROUP IS AGGRESSIVELY EXPANDING TO COMPETE WITH THE OTHER BANK MUTUAL FUNDS, AS THE NUMBER OF UNRATED FUNDS INDICATES. ALL FUNDS GO UNDER THE NAME FIRST CANADIAN.

BEUTEL GOODMAN FUNDS

NUMBER OF FUNDS:	7
ASSETS UNDER MANAGEMENT:	$88 MILLION
LOAD CHARGE:	NONE, IF BOUGHT DIRECTLY FROM MANAGER; OTHERWISE, FRONT: MAXIMUM 4%
SWITCHING CHARGE:	NONE
WHERE SOLD:	ONTARIO DIRECTLY, OTHERWISE THROUGH A BROKER
PHONE NUMBER:	1-800-461-4551
FUNDS IN GROUP:	$$$$ — NONE
	$$$ — AMERICAN EQUITY, MONEY MARKET
	$$ — BALANCED, CANADIAN EQUITY, INCOME
	$ — NONE
	NR — INTERNATIONAL EQUITY, SMALL CAP
COMMENTS:	RELATIVELY NEW TO THE MUTUAL FUNDS INDUSTRY, BUT THIS COMPANY HAS BEEN IN THE PENSION FUND MANAGEMENT BUSINESS FOR MANY YEARS. THE AMERICAN EQUITY FUND IS ESPECIALLY WORTH A LOOK.

BISSETT FUNDS

NUMBER OF FUNDS:	8
ASSETS UNDER MANAGEMENT:	$50 MILLION
LOAD CHARGE:	NONE
SWITCHING CHARGE:	NONE
WHERE SOLD:	CAN SOLICIT IN ALBERTA ONLY; HOWEVER, OTHER PROVINCES CAN PURCHASE
PHONE NUMBER:	(403) 266-4664
FUNDS IN GROUP:	$$$$ — NONE
	$$$ — BOND, CANADIAN EQUITY, MONEY MARKET, RETIREMENT
	$$ — AMERICAN EQUITY, SMALL CAP
	$ — DIVIDEND INCOME
	NR — MULTINATIONAL GROWTH
COMMENTS:	A SMALL, CALGARY-BASED COMPANY, OFFERING SOME GOOD QUALITY FUNDS.

CANADA LIFE ASSURANCE CO.

NUMBER OF FUNDS:	6
ASSETS UNDER MANAGEMENT:	$1.5 BILLION
LOAD CHARGE:	BACK: MAXIMUM 4.5%
SWITCHING CHARGE:	4 FREE TRANSFERS PER YEAR, $20 THEREAFTER
WHERE SOLD:	ACROSS CANADA
PHONE NUMBER:	1-800-387-4447

Funds in group:	$$$$ — **None**
	$$$ — **U.S. and International Equity**
	$$ — **Canadian Equity, Managed**
	$ — **Fixed Income, Money Market**
	NR — **International Bond**
Comments:	A family of segregated funds. The U.S. and International Equity Fund has been the best performer over time.

CANADIAN IMPERIAL BANK OF COMMERCE

Number of funds:	17
Assets under management:	$5.6 billion
Load charge:	None
Switching charge:	None
Where sold:	Across Canada
Phone number:	1-800-465-FUND or 1-800-980-FUND
Funds in group:	$$$$ — **None**
	$$$ — **Mortgage Investment, Premium Canadian T-Bill**
	$$ — **Balanced Income & Growth, Canadian Bond, Equity Income, U.S. Money Market**
	$ — **Canadian Equity, Canadian T-Bill, Capital Appreciation, Global Equity, Money Market, U.S. Equity**
	NR — **Canadian Income, Canadian Resources, Far East Prosperity, Global Bond, Japanese Equity**
Comments:	CIBC has been aggressively expanding its mutual fund operation and is now one of the larger bank operations. The family is well diversified, but some of the equity funds continue to be indifferent performers. The core strength is still the fixed income funds.

CANADIAN INTERNATIONAL GROUP

Number of funds:	20
Assets under management:	$4.6 billion
Load charge:	Money Market — front: maximum 2%; back: maximum 4.75%
	All other funds — front: maximum 5%; back: maximum 4.75%
Switching charge:	2% maximum

WHERE SOLD:	ACROSS CANADA
PHONE NUMBER:	1-800-563-5181
FUNDS IN GROUP:	$$$$ — NONE
	$$$ — GLOBAL, MONEY MARKET, PACIFIC, SECTOR
	$$ — NONE
	$ — EMERGING MARKETS, EUROPEAN
	NR — AMERICAN, CANADIAN BALANCED, CANADIAN BOND, CANADIAN GROWTH, CANADIAN INCOME, EMERGING ASIAN, GLOBAL BOND, GLOBAL EQUITY, INTERNATIONAL BALANCED, INTERNATIONAL BALANCED RSP, LATIN AMERICAN, NEW WORLD INCOME, U.S. MONEY MARKET, WORLD BOND
COMMENTS:	AN AGGRESSIVE, FAST-GROWING ORGANIZATION THAT HAS STAKED OUT A POSITION AS ONE OF THE LEADING MARKETERS OF INTERNATIONAL FUNDS. C.I. PACIFIC IS ONE OF MY FAVOURITES. BECAUSE THIS IS SUCH A YOUNG FIRM, MANY OF THEIR FUNDS ARE STILL TOO NEW TO BE RATED.

CLEAN ENVIRONMENT FUNDS

NUMBER OF FUNDS:	4
ASSETS UNDER MANAGEMENT:	$55.5 MILLION
LOAD CHARGE:	FRONT: MAXIMUM 9%; BACK: MAXIMUM 4.5%
SWITCHING CHARGE:	2% MAXIMUM
WHERE SOLD:	ACROSS CANADA EXCEPT QUEBEC
PHONE NUMBER:	1-800-461-4570
FUNDS IN GROUP:	$$$$ — NONE
	$$$ — BALANCED, EQUITY
	$$ — NONE
	$ — NONE
	NR — INCOME, INTERNATIONAL EQUITY
COMMENTS:	FROM A PERFORMANCE PERSPECTIVE, THIS IS THE MOST PROMISING OF THE "SOCIALLY RESPONSIBLE" FUND ORGANIZATIONS. TWO OF THEIR FUNDS ENJOY $$$ STATUS. WORTH YOUR ATTENTION.

COLONIA LIFE FUNDS

NUMBER OF FUNDS:	5
ASSETS UNDER MANAGEMENT:	$26 MILLION
LOAD CHARGE:	MONEY MARKET — NO LOAD
	ALL OTHER FUNDS — BACK: MAXIMUM 6%, OR NO-LOAD OPTION

SWITCHING CHARGE:	2 FREE TRANSFERS PER YEAR, $50 THEREAFTER
WHERE SOLD:	ACROSS CANADA
PHONE NUMBER:	(416) 960-3601 OR 1-800-461-1086
FUNDS IN GROUP:	$$$$ — NONE
	$$$ — BOND
	$$ — MONEY MARKET
	$ — EQUITY, MORTGAGE
	NR — SPECIAL GROWTH
COMMENTS:	A SMALL FAMILY OF SEGREGATED FUNDS FROM COLONIA LIFE. BOND FUND IS THE BEST PERFORMER.

CONCORDE FUNDS

NUMBER OF FUNDS:	7
ASSETS UNDER MANAGEMENT:	$30 MILLION
LOAD CHARGE:	FRONT: MAXIMUM 9%; BACK: MAXIMUM 6%
SWITCHING CHARGE:	2 FREE TRANSFERS PER YEAR, $25 THEREAFTER
WHERE SOLD:	ONTARIO AND QUEBEC
PHONE NUMBER:	(418) 694-0000 OR 1-800-363-0598
FUNDS IN GROUP:	$$$$ — NONE
	$$$ — NONE
	$$ — GROWTH, MONEY MARKET, MORTGAGE
	$ — INCOME
	NR — BALANCED, DIVIDEND, INTERNATIONAL
COMMENTS:	A QUEBEC-BASED COMPANY. NONE OF THEIR FUNDS HAS SHOWN MUCH THAT'S EXCITING TO DATE.

CORNERSTONE FUNDS

NUMBER OF FUNDS:	6
ASSETS UNDER MANAGEMENT:	$220 MILLION
LOAD CHARGE:	NONE
SWITCHING CHARGE:	NONE
WHERE SOLD:	ALBERTA, B.C., MANITOBA, ONTARIO, SASKATCHEWAN
PHONE NUMBER:	1-800-387-0869
FUNDS IN GROUP:	$$$$ — NONE
	$$$ — NONE
	$$ — BALANCED, BOND, CANADIAN GROWTH, GLOBAL, GOVERNMENT MONEY, U.S.
	$ — NONE
	NR — NONE
COMMENTS:	THE FUTURE OF THIS FUND FAMILY IS UP IN THE AIR, SINCE THE SPONSORING COMPANY, NORTH AMERICAN TRUST, IS UP FOR SALE. WAS PURCHASED BY LAURENTIAN BANK IN FALL, 1995.

DESJARDINS FUNDS

NUMBER OF FUNDS:	12
ASSETS UNDER MANAGEMENT:	$776 MILLION
LOAD CHARGE:	NONE
SWITCHING CHARGE:	NONE
WHERE SOLD:	ONTARIO AND QUEBEC
PHONE NUMBER:	(514) 286-5839 OR 1-800-361-2680
FUNDS IN GROUP:	$$$$ — NONE
	$$$ — INTERNATIONAL
	$$ — BALANCED, BOND, ENVIRONMENT, MONEY MARKET, MORTGAGE
	$ — EQUITY
	NR — AUDACIOUS, DIVIDEND, GROWTH, MODERATE, SECURE
COMMENTS:	LARGE, QUEBEC-BASED ORGANIZATION. FUNDS ARE SOLD THROUGH DESJARDINS TRUST.

DYNAMIC FUNDS MANAGEMENT

NUMBER OF FUNDS:	19
ASSETS UNDER MANAGEMENT:	$2.9 BILLION
LOAD CHARGE:	MONEY MARKET AND GOVERNMENT INCOME — FRONT: MAXIMUM 2%; BACK: MAXIMUM 6%
	INCOME — FRONT: MAXIMUM 5%; BACK: MAXIMUM 6%
	EQUITY — FRONT: MAXIMUM 9%; BACK: MAXIMUM 6%
SWITCHING CHARGE:	2% MAXIMUM
WHERE SOLD:	ACROSS CANADA
PHONE NUMBER:	1-800-268-8186
FUNDS IN GROUP:	$$$$ — NONE
	$$$ — DIVIDEND, DIVIDEND GROWTH, GLOBAL BOND, INCOME, INTERNATIONAL, PARTNERS
	$$ — CANADIAN GROWTH, FUND OF CANADA, MANAGED PORTFOLIO, MONEY MARKET
	$ — AMERICAN, GLOBAL GREEN, PRECIOUS METALS
	NR — EUROPE, FAR EAST, GLOBAL PARTNERS, GLOBAL REAL ESTATE, GLOBAL RESOURCES, GOVERNMENT INCOME
COMMENTS:	THERE ARE A NUMBER OF VERY ATTRACTIVE ENTRIES IN THIS OFTEN-OVERLOOKED GROUP. THE PARTNERS FUND HAS BEEN ESPECIALLY OUTSTANDING IN RECENT YEARS.

ELLIOTT & PAGE INVESTMENT MANAGEMENT

NUMBER OF FUNDS:	11
ASSETS UNDER MANAGEMENT:	$722 MILLION
LOAD CHARGE:	MONEY FUND — FRONT: MAXIMUM 1.5%
	T-BILL — BACK: MAXIMUM 6%
	ALL OTHER FUNDS — FRONT: MAXIMUM 9%; BACK: MAXIMUM 6%
SWITCHING CHARGE:	2% MAXIMUM
WHERE SOLD:	ACROSS CANADA
PHONE NUMBER:	1-800-363-6647
FUNDS IN GROUP:	$$$$ — NONE
	$$$ — BALANCED, MONEY
	$$ — AMERICAN GROWTH, BOND, EQUITY
	$ — NONE
	NR — ASIAN GROWTH, EMERGING MARKET, GLOBAL BALANCED, GLOBAL BOND, GLOBAL EQUITY, T-BILL
COMMENTS:	GOOD DIVERSIFICATION, WITH A MONEY MARKET FUND THAT'S CONSISTENTLY ONE OF THE BEST IN THE COUNTRY. E&P IS ONE OF THE COMPANIES WITH A NEGOTIABLE BACK-END LOAD SCHEDULE, SO BE SURE TO GET FULL DETAILS BEFORE YOU BUY.

EMPIRE FUNDS

NUMBER OF FUNDS:	8
ASSETS UNDER MANAGEMENT:	$649 MILLION
LOAD CHARGE:	MONEY MARKET — NO LOAD
	PREMIER EQUITY — FRONT: MAXIMUM 5%
	ASSET ALLOCATION, ELITE EQUITY, AND FOREIGN CURRENCY
	CANADIAN BOND — BACK: MAXIMUM 5%
	ALL OTHER FUNDS — FRONT: MAXIMUM 5%; BACK: MAXIMUM 5%
SWITCHING CHARGE:	4 FREE TRANSFERS PER YEAR, $50 THEREAFTER
WHERE SOLD:	ACROSS CANADA
PHONE NUMBER:	(613) 548-1881
FUNDS IN GROUP:	$$$$ — NONE
	$$$ — INTERNATIONAL GROWTH
	$$ — BOND, EQUITY GROWTH #3, PREMIER EQUITY
	$ — ELITE EQUITY, MONEY MARKET
	NR — ASSET ALLOCATION, FOREIGN CURRENCY CANADIAN BOND

COMMENTS: SOLID GROUP OF LIFE INSURANCE SEGREGATED FUNDS. THE INTERNATIONAL FUND IS THE BEST BET.

EQUITABLE LIFE FUNDS

NUMBER OF FUNDS: 8

ASSETS UNDER MANAGEMENT: $89.4 MILLION

LOAD CHARGE: SEGREGATED COMMON STOCK AND ACCUMULATIVE INCOME — FRONT: MAXIMUM 5%
ALL OTHER FUNDS — BACK: MAXIMUM 5%

SWITCHING CHARGE: NONE

WHERE SOLD: ACROSS CANADA EXCEPT QUEBEC

PHONE NUMBER: (519) 886-5110 OR 1-800-265-8878

FUNDS IN GROUP:
$$$$ — NONE
$$$ — ACCUMULATIVE INCOME
$$ — SEGREGATED COMMON STOCK
$ — NONE
NR — ASSET ALLOCATION, CANADIAN BOND, CANADIAN STOCK, INTERNATIONAL, MONEY MARKET, MORTGAGE

COMMENTS: EQUITABLE LIFE RECENTLY LAUNCHED A NEW SERIES OF FUNDS. THEY HAVEN'T BEEN AROUND LONG ENOUGH TO EARN A RATING YET.

ETHICAL FUNDS

NUMBER OF FUNDS: 8

ASSETS UNDER MANAGEMENT: $396 MILLION

LOAD CHARGE: NONE, IF PURCHASED THROUGH CREDIT UNION BRANCHES. OTHERWISE, MONEY MARKET — FRONT: MAXIMUM 2%; BACK: MAXIMUM 4.5%
SPECIAL EQUITY,
PACIFIC RIM,
GLOBAL BOND — STRICTLY NO LOAD
ALL OTHER FUNDS — FRONT: MAXIMUM 5%;
BACK: MAXIMUM 4.5%

SWITCHING CHARGE: NONE THROUGH CREDIT UNION; OTHERWISE, MAXIMUM 2% EXCEPT ON SPECIAL EQUITY, PACIFIC RIM, AND GLOBAL BOND, WHICH HAVE NO SWITCHING FEES.

WHERE SOLD: ACROSS CANADA EXCEPT QUEBEC

PHONE NUMBER: 1-800-267-5019

FUNDS IN GROUP:
$$$$ — NONE
$$$ — NONE
$$ — BALANCED, GROWTH, INCOME, MONEY MARKET, NORTH AMERICAN EQUITY

> NR — GLOBAL BOND, PACIFIC RIM, SPECIAL EQUITY

COMMENTS:	ETHICAL GROWTH FUND, THE FIRST SOCIALLY RESPONSIBLE FUND IN CANADA, IS NOW PART OF THIS GROUP, WHICH IS EXPANDING INTO INTERNATIONAL TERRITORY. BEST CHOICE FOR INVESTORS SEEKING BROAD DIVERSIFICATION IN AN ETHICAL PORTFOLIO.

EVEREST FUNDS

NUMBER OF FUNDS:	15
ASSETS UNDER MANAGEMENT:	$4.1 BILLION
LOAD CHARGE:	NONE
SWITCHING CHARGE:	NONE
WHERE SOLD:	ACROSS CANADA
PHONE NUMBER:	1-800-668-8888
FUNDS IN GROUP:	$$$$ — NONE
	$$$ — MORTGAGE
	$$ — BALANCED, BOND, INTERNATIONAL EQUITY, MONEY MARKET, NORTH AMERICAN, SPECIAL EQUITY, STOCK
	$ — U.S. EQUITY
	NR — AMERIGROWTH, ASIAGROWTH, DIVIDEND INCOME, EMERGING MARKETS, EUROGROWTH, INTERNATIONAL BOND
COMMENTS:	A DECENT FINANCIAL INSTITUTION FAMILY, SOLD THROUGH CANADA TRUST. AMERIGROWTH, ASIAGROWTH AND EUROGROWTH ARE FOREIGN FUNDS THAT ARE FULLY RRSP-ELIGIBLE.

FIDELITY FUNDS

NUMBER OF FUNDS:	20
ASSETS UNDER MANAGEMENT:	$5.9 BILLION
LOAD CHARGE:	MONEY MARKET AND SHORT TERM ASSET — FRONT: MAXIMUM 2%
	INCOME AND CAPITAL BUILDER — FRONT: MAXIMUM 4%; BACK: MAXIMUM 6%
	EQUITY, NORTH AMERICAN EQUITY, AND ASSET MANAGER — FRONT: MAXIMUM 5%; BACK: MAXIMUM 6%
SWITCHING CHARGE:	2% MAXIMUM
WHERE SOLD:	ACROSS CANADA

PHONE NUMBER:	**1-800-263-4077**
FUNDS IN GROUP:	**$$$$ — NONE**
	$$$ — EUROPEAN GROWTH, FAR EAST, GROWTH, INTERNATIONAL PORTFOLIO
	$$ — CANADIAN BOND, CANADIAN SHORT-TERM ASSET, CAPITAL BUILDER
	$ — GROWTH & INCOME
	NR — ASSET MANAGER, CANADIAN ASSET ALLOCATION, CANADIAN GROWTH COMPANY, CANADIAN INCOME, EMERGING MARKETS BOND, EMERGING MARKETS PORTFOLIO, GLOBAL BOND, JAPANESE GROWTH, LATIN AMERICA, NORTH AMERICAN INCOME, SMALL CAP AMERICA, U.S. MONEY MARKET
COMMENTS:	THE FAST-GROWING CANADIAN SUBSIDIARY OF THE GIANT BOSTON-BASED FIDELITY GROUP. THE INTERNATIONAL FUNDS ARE WELL WORTH YOUR ATTENTION; THE CANADIAN ENTRIES LEAVE A LOT TO BE DESIRED.

GBC GROUP

NUMBER OF FUNDS:	5
ASSETS UNDER MANAGEMENT:	$261 MILLION
LOAD CHARGE:	NONE, IF PURCHASED FROM MANAGER; OTHERWISE, FRONT: MAXIMUM 3%
SWITCHING CHARGE:	NONE
WHERE SOLD:	ACROSS CANADA
PHONE NUMBER:	1-800-668-7383
FUNDS IN GROUP:	$$$$ — NONE
	$$$ — CANADIAN BOND, CANADIAN GROWTH, MONEY MARKET
	$$ — NORTH AMERICAN GROWTH
	$ — INTERNATIONAL GROWTH
	NR — NONE
COMMENTS:	SMALL GROUP WHOSE FUNDS HAVE GENERALLY BEEN VERY GOOD PERFORMERS (EXCEPT FOR THE INTERNATIONAL FUND, WHICH SHOULD BE AVOIDED). UNFORTUNATELY, YOU MUST HAVE AT LEAST $100,000 TO INVEST IN ORDER TO BE INVITED TO THE PARTY.

G.T. FUNDS

NUMBER OF FUNDS:	9
ASSETS UNDER MANAGEMENT:	$97.4 MILLION

LOAD CHARGE:	FRONT: MAXIMUM 5%; BACK: MAXIMUM 5%
SWITCHING CHARGE:	NONE
WHERE SOLD:	ACROSS CANADA
PHONE NUMBER:	1-800-588-5684 (ENGLISH SERVICE)
	1-800-588-5689 (FRENCH SERVICE)
	1-800-588-2890 (CANTONESE SERVICE)
FUNDS IN GROUP:	$$$$ — NONE
	$$$ — NONE
	$$ — NONE
	$ — NONE
	NR — AMERICA GROWTH, CANADA WORLDWIDE RSP, GLOBAL GROWTH AND INCOME, GLOBAL INFRASTRUCTURE, GLOBAL NATURAL RESOURCES, GLOBAL STRATEGIC INCOME, GLOBAL TELECOMMUNICATIONS, LATIN AMERICA GROWTH, PACIFIC GROWTH
COMMENTS:	ANOTHER U.S. GROUP TRYING TO INVADE THE CANADIAN MARKET. SOME OF THE SECTOR FUNDS (INFRASTRUCTURE, TELECOMMUNICATIONS) LOOK PROMISING. ALL ARE TOO NEW TO RATE.

GENERAL TRUST INVESTMENT FUNDS

NUMBER OF FUNDS:	8
ASSETS UNDER MANAGEMENT:	$242 MILLION
LOAD CHARGE:	NONE
SWITCHING CHARGE:	NONE
WHERE SOLD:	QUEBEC
PHONE NUMBER:	(514) 871-7562 OR 1-800-309-0145
FUNDS IN GROUP:	$$$$ — NONE
	$$$ — MORTGAGE
	$$ — BOND, GROWTH, INTERNATIONAL, MONEY MARKET, U.S. EQUITY
	$ — BALANCED, CANADIAN EQUITY
	NR — NONE
COMMENTS:	WELL-DIVERSIFIED NO-LOAD GROUP, SOLD THROUGH GENERAL TRUST BRANCHES IN QUEBEC ONLY.

GLOBAL STRATEGY FUNDS

NUMBER OF FUNDS:	29
ASSETS UNDER MANAGEMENT:	$3.1 BILLION
LOAD CHARGE:	FRONT: MAXIMUM 9%; BACK: MAXIMUM 5.6%
SWITCHING CHARGE:	9% MAXIMUM
WHERE SOLD:	ACROSS CANADA

PHONE NUMBER: 1-800-387-1229

FUNDS IN GROUP: $$$$ — NONE

$$$ — DIVERSIFIED ST INCOME, INCOME PLUS

$$ — EUROPE PLUS, T-BILL SAVINGS, U.S. SAVINGS

$ — CANADA GROWTH, DIVERSIFIED AMERICAS, DIVERSIFIED BOND, DIVERSIFIED GROWTH, JAPAN, REAL ESTATE SECURITIES, WORLD BOND, WORLD EQUITY

NR — ASIA, BOND, CANADIAN SMALL CAP, DIVERSIFIED ASIA, DIVERSIFIED EUROPE, DIVERSIFIED FOREIGN BOND, DIVERSIFIED GOLD PLUS, DIVERSIFIED JAPAN PLUS, DIVERSIFIED LATIN AMERICA, DIVERSIFIED WORLD EQUITY, FOREIGN BOND, LATIN AMERICA, U.S. EQUITY, U.S. GROWTH, WORLD BALANCED, WORLD EMERGING COMPANIES

COMMENTS: THIS CHRONICALLY UNDER-PERFORMING GROUP HAS BEEN UNDERGOING A MAJOR OVERHAUL, INCLUDING MERGERS, NEW LAUNCHES, A MULTI-MANAGER APPROACH, AND JUST ABOUT ANYTHING ELSE THEY THINK CAN TURN THINGS AROUND. WE'LL SEE.

GREAT WEST LIFE

NUMBER OF FUNDS: 13

ASSETS UNDER MANAGEMENT: $3.6 BILLION

LOAD CHARGE: OPTIONAL BACK-END LOAD: MAXIMUM 4.5%

SWITCHING CHARGE: NONE

WHERE SOLD: ACROSS CANADA

PHONE NUMBER: 1-800-665-0551

FUNDS IN GROUP: $$$$ — NONE

$$$ — EQUITY/BOND

$$ — CANADIAN EQUITY, DIVERSIFIED RS

$ — CANADIAN BOND, EQUITY INDEX INVESTMENT, MONEY MARKET, MORTGAGE, REAL ESTATE INVESTMENT

NR — GOVERNMENT BOND, INCOME, INTERNATIONAL BOND, INTERNATIONAL EQUITY, U.S. EQUITY

COMMENTS: RESPECTABLE GROUP OF SEGREGATED FUNDS, BUT NOTHING EXCITING. THE REAL ESTATE FUND HAS BEEN EXPERIENCING TOUGH TIMES, TO THE POINT THAT THE COMPANY NO LONGER REPORTS ITS RESULTS IN THE

MONTHLY MUTUAL FUND SURVEYS CARRIED BY THE
BUSINESS PRESS.

GUARDIAN GROUP

NUMBER OF FUNDS:	14
ASSETS UNDER MANAGEMENT:	$981 MILLION
LOAD CHARGE:	MONEY MARKET — FRONT: MAXIMUM 2%; BACK: MAXIMUM 6% INCOME — FRONT: MAXIMUM 5%; BACK: MAXIMUM 6% ALL OTHER FUNDS — FRONT: MAXIMUM 9%; BACK: MAXIMUM 6%
SWITCHING CHARGE:	2% MAXIMUM
WHERE SOLD:	ACROSS CANADA
PHONE NUMBER:	(416) 947-4025 OR 1-800-668-7327
FUNDS IN GROUP:	$$$$ — NONE $$$ — AMERICAN EQUITY, CANADIAN BALANCED, CANADIAN MONEY MARKET $$ — CANADIAN INCOME, GLOBAL EQUITY, GROWTH EQUITY, INTERNATIONAL INCOME, PREFERRED DIVIDEND, U.S. MONEY MARKET $ — ENTERPRISE, INTERNATIONAL BALANCED NR — ASIA PACIFIC, EMERGING MARKETS, FOREIGN INCOME
COMMENTS:	AN OFTEN OVERLOOKED GROUP WITH SOME DECENT FUNDS ON OFFER.

HERCULES FUNDS

NUMBER OF FUNDS:	11
ASSETS UNDER MANAGEMENT:	$191 MILLION
LOAD CHARGE:	NONE
SWITCHING CHARGE:	NONE
WHERE SOLD:	ACROSS CANADA
PHONE NUMBER:	1-800-567-4525
FUNDS IN GROUP:	$$$$ — NONE $$$ — NONE $$ — NONE $ — NONE NR — EMERGING MARKETS DEBT, EMERGING MARKETS DEBT U.S.$, EUROPEAN VALUE, GLOBAL SHORT-TERM, LATIN AMERICAN, MONEY MARKET, MONEY MARKET U.S.$,

NAFTA Value, Pacific Basin Value, World Bond, World Bond U.S.$

Comments:	A new fund group under the sponsorship of Midland Walwyn in Canada (it's also sold in the U.S.). All the funds are too new to be rated.

HODGSON ROBERTON LAING FUNDS

Number of funds:	5
Assets under management:	$132 million
Load charge:	None
Switching charge:	None
Where sold:	Across Canada
Phone number:	1-800-268-9622
Funds in group:	$$$$ — Instant $$
	$$$ — None
	$$ — Bond
	$ — Balanced, Canadian
	NR — Overseas Growth
Comments:	The Instant $$ Fund is the star here. It's one of the best money market choices around.

HONGKONG BANK FUNDS

Number of funds:	12
Assets under management:	$340 million
Load charge:	None
Switching charge:	None
Where sold:	Across Canada except P.E.I.
Phone number:	1-800-830-8888
Funds in group:	$$$$ — None
	$$$ — None
	$$ — Balanced, Equity, Money Market
	$ — None
	NR — Americas, Asian Growth, Canadian Bond, Dividend Income, Emerging Markets, European Growth, Global Bond, Mortgage, Small Cap Growth
Comments:	No-load family, available through Hongkong Bank branches. The company is in the process of aggressively expanding its product line.

IMPERIAL LIFE

NUMBER OF FUNDS:	4
ASSETS UNDER MANAGEMENT:	$116 MILLION
LOAD CHARGE:	FRONT: MAXIMUM 5%
SWITCHING CHARGE:	NONE
WHERE SOLD:	ACROSS CANADA
PHONE NUMBER:	(416) 324-1891
FUNDS IN GROUP:	$$$$ — NONE
	$$$ — NONE
	$$ — CANADIAN EQUITY, NORTH AMERICAN EQUITY
	$ — DIVERSIFIED, MONEY MARKET
	NR — NONE
COMMENTS:	THE CANADIAN EQUITY FUND HAS ONE OF THE BEST 10-YEAR RECORDS IN CANADA, BUT THE NORTH AMERICAN FUND HAS BEEN THE BETTER PERFORMER LATELY.

INDUSTRIAL ALLIANCE FUNDS

NUMBER OF FUNDS:	5
ASSETS UNDER MANAGEMENT:	$512 MILLION
LOAD CHARGE:	BACK: MAXIMUM 5%
SWITCHING CHARGE:	NONE
WHERE SOLD:	ACROSS CANADA
PHONE NUMBER:	(418) 684-5000
FUNDS IN GROUP:	$$$$ — NONE
	$$$ — DIVERSIFIED, STOCKS
	$$ — BOND, MORTGAGE
	$ — MONEY MARKET
	NR — NONE
COMMENTS:	DON'T CONFUSE THESE FUNDS WITH MACKENZIE FINANCIAL'S INDUSTRIAL GROUP. THESE ARE SEGREGATED FUNDS OFFERED BY A QUEBEC-BASED INSURANCE COMPANY.

INVESTORS GROUP

NUMBER OF FUNDS:	26
ASSETS UNDER MANAGEMENT:	$18 BILLION
LOAD CHARGE:	MONEY MARKET — NO LOAD MORTGAGE, GLOBAL BOND, AND GOVERNMENT

	BOND — BACK: MAXIMUM 3%
	ALL OTHER FUNDS — FRONT: MAXIMUM 2.5%;
	BACK: MAXIMUM 3%
SWITCHING CHARGE:	NONE
WHERE SOLD:	ACROSS CANADA
PHONE NUMBER:	CONTACT YOUR REGIONAL OFFICE
FUNDS IN GROUP:	$$$$ — U.S. GROWTH
	$$$ — CANADIAN EQUITY, DIVIDEND, EUROPEAN GROWTH, GROWTH PORTFOLIO, GROWTH PLUS PORTFOLIO, JAPANESE, NORTH AMERICAN GROWTH, PACIFIC INTERNATIONAL, SPECIAL
	$$ — GLOBAL, GOVERNMENT BOND, INCOME PORTFOLIO, MONEY MARKET, MORTGAGE, MUTUAL OF CANADA, REAL PROPERTY, RETIREMENT GROWTH PORTFOLIO, RETIREMENT MUTUAL, SUMMA
	$ — INCOME PLUS PORTFOLIO, RETIREMENT PLUS PORTFOLIO
	NR — ASSET ALLOCATION, CORPORATE BOND, GLOBAL BOND, WORLD GROWTH PORTFOLIO
COMMENTS:	STILL THE LARGEST MUTUAL FUND COMPANY IN CANADA, AND WITH GOOD REASON. OFFERS A WIDE SELECTION OF CONSERVATIVELY MANAGED FUNDS THAT CONSISTENTLY PRODUCE SOLID, IF MOSTLY UNSPECTACULAR, RESULTS. SOLD ONLY BY INVESTORS GROUP REPRESENTATIVES.

JONES HEWARD FUNDS

NUMBER OF FUNDS:	5
ASSETS UNDER MANAGEMENT:	$157 MILLION
LOAD CHARGE:	FRONT: MAXIMUM 9%; BACK: MAXIMUM 5%
SWITCHING CHARGE:	2% MAXIMUM
WHERE SOLD:	ACROSS CANADA
PHONE NUMBER:	(416) 359-5000 OR 1-800-361-1392
FUNDS IN GROUP:	$$$$ — NONE
	$$$ — NONE
	$$ — JONES HEWARD FUND LTD., BOND, CANADIAN BALANCED
	$ — AMERICAN
	NR — MONEY MARKET
COMMENTS:	SMALL GROUP THAT IS NOW OWNED BY BANK OF MONTREAL. SOME OF THEIR FUNDS HAVE EXPERIENCED ROUGH GOING RECENTLY.

LAURENTIAN FUNDS MANAGEMENT

NUMBER OF FUNDS:	14
ASSETS UNDER MANAGEMENT:	$1.7 BILLION
LOAD CHARGE:	MONEY MARKET — NO LOAD ALL OTHER FUNDS — FRONT: MAXIMUM 3%; BACK: MAXIMUM 5.5%
SWITCHING CHARGE:	NONE
WHERE SOLD:	ACROSS CANADA
PHONE NUMBER:	(416) 324-1673
FUNDS IN GROUP:	$$$$ — NONE $$$ — COMMONWEALTH, DIVIDEND, SPECIAL EQUITY $$ — AMERICAN EQUITY, GLOBAL BALANCED, GOVERNMENT BOND, INTERNATIONAL, MONEY MARKET $ — CANADIAN BALANCED, CANADIAN EQUITY, INCOME NR — ASIA PACIFIC, EMERGING MARKETS, EUROPE
COMMENTS:	THERE'S NOTHING OUTSTANDING ABOUT THIS GROUP, BUT SOME OF THE FUNDS ARE QUITE RESPECTABLE.

LEITH WHEELER

NUMBER OF FUNDS:	5
ASSETS UNDER MANAGEMENT:	$26 MILLION
LOAD CHARGE:	NONE
SWITCHING CHARGE:	NONE
WHERE SOLD:	ALBERTA, B.C.
PHONE NUMBER:	(604) 683-3391
FUNDS IN GROUP:	$$$$ — NONE $$$ — BALANCED $$ — NONE $ — NONE NR — CANADIAN EQUITY, FIXED INCOME, MONEY MARKET, U.S. EQUITY
COMMENTS:	SMALL, VANCOUVER-BASED GROUP THAT IS WORKING HARD TO ESTABLISH A FOOTHOLD IN THE CROWDED MUTUAL FUNDS MARKETPLACE. THE BALANCED FUND IS WORTH A LOOK.

LONDON LIFE

NUMBER OF FUNDS:	6
ASSETS UNDER MANAGEMENT:	$2.4 BILLION
LOAD CHARGE:	BACK: MAXIMUM 5%

SWITCHING CHARGE:	NONE
WHERE SOLD:	ACROSS CANADA
PHONE NUMBER:	(519) 432-5281
FUNDS IN GROUP:	$$$$ — NONE
	$$$ — MORTGAGE
	$$ — BOND, CANADIAN EQUITY, DIVERSIFIED, MONEY
	$ — U.S. EQUITY
	NR — NONE
COMMENTS:	SOLID FAMILY OF SEGREGATED FUNDS WITH RESPECTABLE, BUT NOT SENSATIONAL, PERFORMANCE RESULTS. MORTGAGE FUND IS THE STANDOUT.

MACKENZIE FINANCIAL CORPORATION

NUMBER OF FUNDS:	35
ASSETS UNDER MANAGEMENT:	$10.6 BILLION
LOAD CHARGE:	INDUSTRIAL CASH MANAGEMENT AND IVY SHORT-TERM — FRONT: MAXIMUM 2%
	IVY MORTGAGE — FRONT: MAXIMUM 3%; BACK: MAXIMUM 3.3%
	EQUITY, BALANCED, AND INCOME — FRONT: MAXIMUM 5%; BACK: MAXIMUM 5.5%
SWITCHING CHARGE:	2% MAXIMUM
WHERE SOLD:	ACROSS CANADA
PHONE NUMBER:	1-800-387-0615
FUNDS IN GROUP:	UNIVERSAL
	$$$$ — NONE
	$$$ — CANADIAN RESOURCE, U.S. EMERGING GROWTH
	$$ — AMERICAS, WORLD EQUITY, WORLD INCOME RRSP, CANADIAN EQUITY
	$ — NONE
	NR — EUROPEAN OPPORTUNITIES, FAR EAST, GROWTH, JAPAN, U.S. MONEY MARKET, WORLD ASSET ALLOCATION, WORLD BALANCED RRSP, WORLD EMERGING GROWTH, WORLD GROWTH RSP, WORLD PRECIOUS METALS, WORLD TACTICAL BOND
	INDUSTRIAL
	$$$$ — CASH MANAGEMENT
	$$$ — FUTURE
	$$ — AMERICAN, BALANCED, BOND, DIVIDEND, EQUITY, GROWTH, HORIZON, INCOME, MORTGAGE SECURITIES, PENSION, SHORT-TERM

$ — NONE
NR — NONE

IVY
$$$$ — NONE
$$$ — NONE
$$ — ENTERPRISE
$ — NONE
NR — CANADIAN, FOREIGN EQUITY, GROWTH AND
INCOME, MORTGAGE

COMMENTS: THIS IS THE LARGEST FUND ORGANIZATION IN THE
COUNTRY IN TERMS OF THE TOTAL NUMBER OF FUNDS
OFFERED. THEY'VE FINALLY GOTTEN THEIR ACT TOGETHER
BY REORGANIZING THEIR OFFERINGS INTO THREE QUITE
DIFFERENT GROUPS: INDUSTRIAL, IVY, AND UNIVERSAL.
THE LATTER TWO ARE THE MOST EXCITING RIGHT NOW,
WITH LOTS OF NEW OFFERINGS AND SOME GOOD
PERFORMERS.

MANULIFE CABOT FUNDS

NUMBER OF FUNDS: 7
ASSETS UNDER
MANAGEMENT: $29 MILLION
LOAD CHARGE: NONE
SWITCHING CHARGE: NONE
WHERE SOLD: ACROSS CANADA
PHONE NUMBER: 1-800-265-7401
FUNDS IN GROUP: $$$$ — NONE
$$$ — NONE
$$ — NONE
$ — NONE
NR — BLUE CHIP, CANADIAN EQUITY, CANADIAN
GROWTH, DIVERSIFIED BOND, EMERGING
GROWTH, GLOBAL EQUITY, MONEY MARKET

COMMENTS: MANULIFE AGGRESSIVELY EXPANDED ITS FUND
OPERATIONS WITH THE LAUNCH OF THE CABOT GROUP IN
EARLY '94. SEVERAL OF THESE ARE MANAGED BY
ALTAMIRA. ALL ARE TOO NEW TO BE RATED BUT ARE
WORTH WATCHING.

MANULIFE-VISTA FUNDS

NUMBER OF FUNDS: 8
ASSETS UNDER
MANAGEMENT: $1.2 BILLION
LOAD CHARGE: FRONT: MAXIMUM 4%; BACK: MAXIMUM 3.5%
SWITCHING CHARGE: NONE

WHERE SOLD:	ACROSS CANADA
PHONE NUMBER:	(519) 747-7000
FUNDS IN GROUP:	$$$$ — NONE
	$$$ — NONE
	$$ — BOND, CAPITAL GAINS GROWTH, DIVERSIFIED
	$ — EQUITY, SHORT-TERM SECURITIES
	NR — AMERICAN STOCK, GLOBAL BOND, GLOBAL EQUITY
COMMENTS:	THIS IS MANULIFE'S SEGREGATED FUND LINE. THE PURCHASE OPTIONS ON THESE FUNDS LEAVE A LOT TO BE DESIRED, SO TREAD CAREFULLY.

MARITIME LIFE

NUMBER OF FUNDS:	10
ASSETS UNDER MANAGEMENT:	$662 MILLION
LOAD CHARGE:	NONE
SWITCHING CHARGE:	5 FREE TRANSFERS PER YEAR
WHERE SOLD:	ACROSS CANADA
PHONE NUMBER:	(902) 453-4300
FUNDS IN GROUP:	$$$$ — NONE
	$$$ — NONE
	$$ — BALANCED, BOND
	$ — GROWTH, MONEY MARKET
	NR — AMERICAN GROWTH AND INCOME, CANADIAN EQUITY, DIVIDEND INCOME, GLOBAL EQUITY, PACIFIC BASIN EQUITIES, S & P 500
COMMENTS:	THIS HALIFAX-BASED GROUP OF SEGREGATED FUNDS HAS ADOPTED A NEW MULTI-MANAGER APPROACH IN AN EFFORT TO IMPROVE RETURNS. THEY'VE ALSO PURCHASED SOME OF THE FUNDS PREVIOUSLY RUN BY NOW-DEFUNCT CONFEDERATION LIFE.

MAWER INVESTMENT MANAGEMENT

NUMBER OF FUNDS:	9
ASSETS UNDER MANAGEMENT:	$171 MILLION
LOAD CHARGE:	NONE
SWITCHING CHARGE:	NONE
WHERE SOLD:	SOLICIT IN ALBERTA AND SASKATCHEWAN ONLY; HOWEVER, ALL OTHER PROVINCES CAN PURCHASE
PHONE NUMBER:	(403) 267-1989
FUNDS IN GROUP:	$$$$ — NONE

$$$ — NEW CANADA
$$ — CANADIAN BALANCED RETIREMENT SAVINGS,
CANADIAN BOND, CANADIAN DIVERSIFIED
INVESTMENT, CANADIAN EQUITY, CANADIAN
MONEY MARKET, WORLD INVESTMENT
$ — NONE
NR — CANADIAN INCOME, U.S. EQUITY

COMMENTS: CALGARY-BASED COMPANY. FUNDS ARE SMALL, BUT
SOME HAVE TURNED IN VERY GOOD RESULTS. THE
NEW CANADA FUND, A SMALL CAP FUND, HAS BEEN
ESPECIALLY IMPRESSIVE.

MCLEAN BUDDEN FUNDS

NUMBER OF FUNDS:	5
ASSETS UNDER MANAGEMENT:	$39 MILLION
LOAD CHARGE:	NONE
SWITCHING CHARGE:	NONE
WHERE SOLD:	ACROSS CANADA
PHONE NUMBER:	(416) 862-9800
FUNDS IN GROUP:	$$$$ — NONE

$$$ — AMERICAN GROWTH, FIXED INCOME
$$ — BALANCED, EQUITY GROWTH, MONEY
MARKET
$ — NONE
NR — NONE

COMMENTS: MAINLY A PENSION FUND MANAGER, OFFERING SOME
SMALL MUTUAL FUNDS ALMOST AS A SIDELINE. STEADY
PERFORMERS, NOTHING SENSATIONAL.

METROPOLITAN LIFE

NUMBER OF FUNDS:	6
ASSETS UNDER MANAGEMENT:	$114 MILLION
LOAD CHARGE:	BACK: MAXIMUM 2.5%
SWITCHING CHARGE:	MONEY MARKET FUND — 12 FREE TRANSFERS PER YEAR
	ALL OTHER FUNDS — 4 FREE TRANSFERS PER YEAR, $25 THEREAFTER
WHERE SOLD:	ACROSS CANADA
PHONE NUMBER:	(613) 560-6994
FUNDS IN GROUP:	$$$$ — NONE

$$$ — NONE
$$ — NONE
$ — BALANCED, BOND, EQUITY, MONEY MARKET

NR — GROWTH, U.S. EQUITY

COMMENTS: THIS SEGREGATED FUND FAMILY HAS A TRULY UNINSPIRING PERFORMANCE RECORD. SOMEONE NEEDS TO TAKE A CLOSE LOOK AT THESE FUNDS BECAUSE THEY ARE DOING A DISSERVICE TO INVESTORS WITH THEIR BELOW-AVERAGE RETURNS.

MUTUAL INVESTCO INC.

NUMBER OF FUNDS:	16
ASSETS UNDER MANAGEMENT:	$1.2 BILLION
LOAD CHARGE:	MONEY MARKET AND PREMIER FUNDS — NONE ALL OTHER FUNDS — FRONT: MAXIMUM 3.75%
SWITCHING CHARGE:	NONE
WHERE SOLD:	ACROSS CANADA
PHONE NUMBER:	(519) 888-3863
FUNDS IN GROUP:	$$$$ — NONE
	$$$ — NONE
	$$ — AMERIFUND, BOND, MONEY MARKET
	$ — CANADIAN INDEXFUND, DIVERSIFUND 25, DIVERSIFUND 40, DIVERSIFUND 55, EQUIFUND
	NR — PREMIER AMERICAN, PREMIER BLUE CHIP, PREMIER BOND, PREMIER DIVERSIFIED, PREMIER EMERGING MARKETS, PREMIER GROWTH, PREMIER INTERNATIONAL, PREMIER MORTGAGE
COMMENTS:	ALTHOUGH MUTUAL LIFE OWNS THESE FUNDS THROUGH SUBSIDIARY COMPANIES, THEY ARE NOT SEGREGATED FUNDS. PERFORMANCE HAS BEEN SPOTTY; CHECK INDIVIDUAL RATINGS. MUTUAL RECENTLY PURCHASED THE STRATA FUNDS, WHICH ARE TO BE INTEGRATED INTO THIS GROUP.

NATIONAL BANK

NUMBER OF FUNDS:	17
ASSETS UNDER MANAGEMENT:	$1.7 BILLION
LOAD CHARGE:	NONE
SWITCHING CHARGE:	NONE
WHERE SOLD:	ONTARIO, QUEBEC
PHONE NUMBER:	CONTACT YOUR LOCAL BRANCH OFFICE
FUNDS IN GROUP:	INVESNAT $$$$ — NONE

    $$$ — NONE
     $$ — MONEY MARKET, MORTGAGE, SHORT-TERM
          GOVERNMENT BOND, U.S. MONEY MARKET
      $ — CANADIAN EQUITY, RETIREMENT BALANCED
     NR — BLUE CHIP AMERICAN, CORPORATE CASH
          MANAGEMENT, EUROPEAN EQUITY, FAR
          EAST, INTERNATIONAL RSP BOND, JAPANESE
          EQUITY

NATCAN
$$$$ — NONE
 $$$ — NONE
  $$ — TREASURY BILL
   $ — NONE
  NR — AMERICAN EQUITY, CANADIAN BOND,
       CANADIAN EQUITY, DIVIDEND

COMMENTS: THE NEW NATCAN SERIES IS FOR HIGH-ROLLERS ONLY; MINIMUM INVESTMENT IS $50,000. RESULTS SO FAR HAVEN'T BEEN IMPRESSIVE.

NATIONAL LIFE

NUMBER OF FUNDS: 5
ASSETS UNDER
MANAGEMENT: $90 MILLION
LOAD CHARGE: BACK: MAXIMUM 5%
SWITCHING CHARGE: 4 FREE TRANSFERS PER YEAR, $50 THEREAFTER
WHERE SOLD: ACROSS CANADA
PHONE NUMBER: (416) 585-8094
FUNDS IN GROUP: $$$$ — FIXED INCOME
 $$$ — BALANCED, EQUITIES, MONEY MARKET,
       GLOBAL EQUITIES
  $$ — NONE
   $ — NONE
  NR — NONE

COMMENTS: THIS SMALL, UNHERALDED GROUP OF SEGREGATED FUNDS HAS PRODUCED AN OUTSTANDING TRACK RECORD THAT IS WORTHY OF MORE ATTENTION, AND MORE INVESTMENT DOLLARS. IF YOU'RE LOOKING FOR A TOP-NOTCH FAMILY OF LIFE INSURANCE FUNDS, LOOK NO FURTHER.

NATIONAL TRUST

NUMBER OF FUNDS: 11
ASSETS UNDER
MANAGEMENT: $550 MILLION
LOAD CHARGE: NONE

137

SWITCHING CHARGE:	NONE
WHERE SOLD:	ALBERTA, B.C., ONTARIO, MANITOBA, QUEBEC, SASKATCHEWAN
PHONE NUMBER:	1-800-563-4683 OR (416) 361-FUND
FUNDS IN GROUP:	$$$$ — NONE
	$$$ — NONE
	$$ — CANADIAN BOND, MONEY MARKET
	$ — BALANCED, CANADIAN EQUITY
	NR — AMERICAN EQUITY, DIVIDEND, EMERGING MARKETS, INTERNATIONAL EQUITY, INTERNATIONAL RRSP BOND, MORTGAGE, SPECIAL EQUITY
COMMENTS:	UNEXCITING NO-LOAD GROUP. MOVED INTO INTERNATIONAL FUNDS FOR THE FIRST TIME IN MID-'94.

NN FUND MANAGEMENT LTD.

NUMBER OF FUNDS:	10
ASSETS UNDER MANAGEMENT:	$286 MILLION
LOAD CHARGE:	BACK: MAXIMUM 6%
SWITCHING CHARGE:	4 FREE TRANSFERS PER YEAR, $25 THEREAFTER
WHERE SOLD:	ACROSS CANADA
PHONE NUMBER:	(416) 391-2200
FUNDS IN GROUP:	$$$$ — NONE
	$$$ — MONEY MARKET
	$$ — BOND, CANADIAN 35 INDEX, T-BILL
	$ — BALANCED, CANADIAN GROWTH
	NR — CAN-AM, CAN-ASIAN, DIVIDEND, ELITE
COMMENTS:	SEGREGATED INSURANCE COMPANY FUNDS. GENERALLY INDIFFERENT RESULTS SO FAR.

NORTH AMERICAN LIFE

NUMBER OF FUNDS:	8
ASSETS UNDER MANAGEMENT:	$282 MILLION
LOAD CHARGE:	BACK: MAXIMUM 4.5%
SWITCHING CHARGE:	4 FREE TRANSFERS PER YEAR, $25 THEREAFTER
WHERE SOLD:	ACROSS CANADA
PHONE NUMBER:	1-800-668-1503
FUNDS IN GROUP:	$$$$ — NONE
	$$$ — NONE
	$$ — CANADIAN BOND, CANADIAN MONEY MARKET, GLOBAL EQUITY
	$ — CANADIAN DIVERSIFIED, CANADIAN EQUITY
	NR — BALANCED GROWTH, EQUITY GROWTH, U.S. EQUITY

COMMENTS: GLOBAL EQUITY FUND IS THE STANDOUT BY FAR IN THIS
SEGREGATED FUND GROUP.

OPTIMUM FUNDS

NUMBER OF FUNDS:	5
ASSETS UNDER MANAGEMENT:	$19 MILLION
LOAD CHARGE:	NONE
SWITCHING CHARGE:	NONE
WHERE SOLD:	QUEBEC
PHONE NUMBER:	1-800-363-7675
FUNDS IN GROUP:	$$$$ — NONE
	$$$ — NONE
	$$ — BALANCED, BOND, SHORT-TERM
	$ — NONE
	NR — EQUITY, INTERNATIONAL
COMMENTS:	ROUTINE FUND GROUP FROM QUEBEC-BASED COMPANY.

PHILLIPS, HAGER & NORTH

NUMBER OF FUNDS:	12
ASSETS UNDER MANAGEMENT:	$2.8 BILLION
LOAD CHARGE:	NONE
SWITCHING CHARGE:	NONE
WHERE SOLD:	ACROSS CANADA, EXCEPT SASKATCHEWAN
PHONE NUMBER:	1-800-661-6141
FUNDS IN GROUP:	$$$$ — BOND, CANADIAN MONEY MARKET, U.S. EQUITY
	$$$ — BALANCED, DIVIDEND INCOME, U.S.$ MONEY MARKET, VINTAGE
	$$ — CANADIAN EQUITY, RSP/RIF EQUITY
	$ — NONE
	NR — INTERNATIONAL EQUITY, NORTH AMERICAN EQUITY, SHORT-TERM BOND & MORTGAGE
COMMENTS:	HIGHLY RESPECTED VANCOUVER-BASED INVESTMENT HOUSE WITH SOME OUTSTANDING PERFORMERS IN ITS STABLE. MANAGEMENT FEES ARE AMONG THE LOWEST IN THE INDUSTRY. NO LOAD CHARGES. AN EXCELLENT CHOICE FOR CONSERVATIVE, LONG-TERM INVESTORS.

PRUDENTIAL GROUP

NUMBER OF FUNDS:	9
ASSETS UNDER MANAGEMENT:	$400 MILLION

LOAD CHARGE:	MONEY MARKET — NO LOAD
	ALL OTHER FUNDS — FRONT: MAXIMUM 5%
SWITCHING CHARGE:	4 FREE TRANSFERS PER YEAR, $25 THEREAFTER
WHERE SOLD:	ACROSS CANADA EXCEPT THE TERRITORIES
PHONE NUMBER:	1-800-463-6778
FUNDS IN GROUP:	$$$$ — NONE
	$$$ — DIVIDEND, MONEY MARKET, NATURAL RESOURCE
	$$ — DIVERSIFIED INVESTMENT, GROWTH, INCOME, PRECIOUS METALS
	$ — NONE
	NR — AMERICAN EQUITY, GLOBAL EQUITY
COMMENTS:	THERE ARE SOME STRONG PERFORMERS IN THIS OFTEN-OVERLOOKED GROUP. THE DIVIDEND FUND ISN'T REALLY A DIVIDEND FUND, BUT VIEWED AS A SIMPLE STOCK FUND IT'S PRETTY GOOD.

PURSUIT GROUP

NUMBER OF FUNDS:	6
ASSETS UNDER MANAGEMENT:	$43 MILLION
LOAD CHARGE:	NONE
SWITCHING CHARGE:	NONE
WHERE SOLD:	ONTARIO
PHONE NUMBER:	1-800-383-3981
FUNDS IN GROUP:	$$$$ — NONE
	$$$ — MONEY MARKET
	$$ — CANADIAN EQUITY, INCOME
	$ — AMERICAN
	NR — INTERNATIONAL BOND, INTERNATIONAL EQUITY
COMMENTS:	SMALL GROUP, MANAGED BY NIGEL STEPHENS COUNSEL OF NORTH YORK, ONT. NOW MOVING INTO THE INTERNATIONAL ARENA.

ROYAL FUNDS

NUMBER OF FUNDS:	34
ASSETS UNDER MANAGEMENT:	$11.8 BILLION
LOAD CHARGE:	NONE
SWITCHING CHARGE:	NONE
WHERE SOLD:	ACROSS CANADA
PHONE NUMBER:	1-800-463-FUND
FUNDS IN GROUP:	ROYAL

$$$$ — NONE
 $$$ — BALANCED, EUROPEAN GROWTH, JAPANESE
        STOCK, ZWEIG STRATEGIC GROWTH
  $$ — ENERGY, PRECIOUS METALS
   $ — NONE
  NR — ASIAN GROWTH, CANADIAN GROWTH,
        CANADIAN SMALL CAP, INTERNATIONAL
        EQUITY, LATIN AMERICAN, LIFE SCIENCE AND
        TECHNOLOGY, ZWEIG GLOBAL MANAGED
        ASSETS

ROYAL TRUST

$$$$ — AMERICAN STOCK
 $$$ — BOND, INTERNATIONAL BOND
  $$ — ADVANTAGE BALANCED, ADVANTAGE
        GROWTH, ADVANTAGE INCOME, CANADIAN
        MONEY MARKET, $U.S. MONEY MARKET
   $ — CANADIAN STOCK, CANADIAN TREASURY
        BILL, GROWTH AND INCOME, MORTGAGE
  NR — NONE

ROYFUND

$$$$ — NONE
 $$$ — MORTGAGE, U.S. EQUITY
  $$ — BOND, CANADIAN T-BILL, EQUITY, U.S.
        MONEY MARKET
   $ — MONEY MARKET
  NR — DIVIDEND, INTERNATIONAL INCOME

COMMENTS: THIS GROUP CONTINUES TO UNDERGO A MASSIVE OVERHAUL AS THE ROYAL BANK AND ROYAL TRUST FUNDS ARE INTEGRATED. RIGHT NOW, CONFUSION REIGNS — YOU CAN BUY SOME OF THESE FUNDS ONLY AT ROYAL BANK, SOME ONLY AT ROYAL TRUST, AND SOME (THE ONES WITH THE "ROYAL" PREFIX) AT BOTH. EVERYTHING IS SCHEDULED TO BE SORTED OUT BY LATE '96, HOWEVER.

ROYAL LIFE

NUMBER OF FUNDS: 6
ASSETS UNDER MANAGEMENT: $190 MILLION
LOAD CHARGE: BACK: MAXIMUM 4.5%
SWITCHING CHARGE: 4 FREE TRANSFERS PER YEAR, $50 THEREAFTER
WHERE SOLD: ACROSS CANADA
PHONE NUMBER: 1-800-263-1747
FUNDS IN GROUP: $$$$ — NONE

$$$ — NONE
$$ — EQUITY
$ — BALANCED, INCOME
NR — CANADIAN GROWTH, INTERNATIONAL
        EQUITY, MONEY MARKET

COMMENTS: THESE ARE SEGREGATED FUNDS THAT CAN ONLY BE
PURCHASED AS PART OF AN INSURANCE OR ANNUITY
CONTRACT.

SAGIT MANAGEMENT

NUMBER OF FUNDS: 14
ASSETS UNDER
MANAGEMENT: $192 MILLION
LOAD CHARGE: MONEY MARKET — FRONT: MAXIMUM 2%
ALL OTHER FUNDS — FRONT: MAXIMUM 8.75%;
                                BACK: MAXIMUM 7%

SWITCHING CHARGE: 2% MAXIMUM
WHERE SOLD: ACROSS CANADA
PHONE NUMBER: 1-800-663-1003
FUNDS IN GROUP: **CAMBRIDGE**
$$$$ — NONE
$$$ — NONE
$$ — AMERICAS, GLOBAL, PACIFIC
$ — AMERICAN GROWTH, BALANCED, GROWTH,
        RESOURCE, SPECIAL EQUITY
NR — CHINA

TRANS-CANADA
$$$$ — NONE
$$$ — MONEY MARKET
$$ — BOND, INCOME, PENSION
$ — EQUITY
NR — NONE

COMMENTS: THIS VANCOUVER-BASED OPERATION IS CHARACTERIZED
BY AN AGGRESSIVE INVESTMENT STYLE THAT WON'T BE TO
ALL TASTES. WHEN THINGS ARE GOING WELL, THEY CAN
PRODUCE SOME INCREDIBLE RESULTS, AS IN '93. WHEN
THEY ARE GOING BADLY, WATCH OUT. THE LOSSES CAN BE
BRUTAL.

SAVINGS AND INVESTMENT TRUST / PRÊT ET REVENU

NUMBER OF FUNDS: 9
ASSETS UNDER
MANAGEMENT: $257 MILLION
LOAD CHARGE: NONE

SWITCHING CHARGE:	NONE
WHERE SOLD:	ONTARIO AND QUEBEC
PHONE NUMBER:	(613) 241-1221 OR (418) 692-1221
FUNDS IN GROUP:	$$$$ — NONE
	$$$ — NONE
	$$ — AMERICAN, BOND, CANADIAN, MONEY MARKET, MORTGAGE, RETIREMENT AND BALANCED
	$ — NONE
	NR — DIVIDEND, INTERNATIONAL, WORLD BOND
COMMENTS:	SMALL FUND FAMILY SOLD BY QUEBEC-BASED SAVINGS AND INVESTMENT TRUST IN THAT PROVINCE AND EASTERN ONTARIO.

SCEPTRE FUNDS

NUMBER OF FUNDS:	6
ASSETS UNDER MANAGEMENT:	$227 MILLION
LOAD CHARGE:	NONE, IF PURCHASED FROM MANAGER; OTHERWISE FRONT: MAXIMUM 2%
	MONEY MARKET — NO LOAD
SWITCHING CHARGE:	NONE
WHERE SOLD:	ACROSS CANADA
PHONE NUMBER:	(416) 360-4826 OR 1-800-265-1888
FUNDS IN GROUP:	$$$$ — MONEY MARKET
	$$$ — BALANCED, EQUITY, INTERNATIONAL
	$$ — BOND
	$ — NONE
	NR — ASIAN GROWTH
COMMENTS:	MAINLY PENSION FUND MANAGERS. MUTUAL FUND RESULTS HAVE BEEN SOLID, WITH INTERNATIONAL FUND ESPECIALLY GOOD.

SCOTIA EXCELSIOR FUNDS

NUMBER OF FUNDS:	19
ASSETS UNDER MANAGEMENT:	$3.1 BILLION
LOAD CHARGE:	NONE
SWITCHING CHARGE:	NONE
WHERE SOLD:	ACROSS CANADA
PHONE NUMBER:	1-800-268-9269
FUNDS IN GROUP:	$$$$ — NONE
	$$$ — AMERICAN EQUITY GROWTH, CANAM INCOME, CANADIAN GROWTH, DIVIDEND, INTERNATIONAL, MORTGAGE, TOTAL RETURN

$$ — Balanced, Defensive Income, Income, Money Market, T-Bill

$ — Blue Chip

NR — CanAm Growth, Global Bond, Latin American, Pacific Rim, Precious Metals, Premium T-Bill

COMMENTS: This group was strengthened immensely by the merger of the Scotia and Montreal Trust funds in mid-'95. It now contains several very strong entries and is poised to compete as one of the top bank fund groups in the country.

SPECTRUM/BULLOCK FUNDS

NUMBER OF FUNDS: 18
ASSETS UNDER MANAGEMENT: $2.3 billion
LOAD CHARGE: Spectrum Savings — no load
All other funds — Class A front: maximum 6%; Class B back: maximum 6%; Class C: none

SWITCHING CHARGE: 2% maximum
WHERE SOLD: Across Canada
PHONE NUMBER: 1-800-263-1851
FUNDS IN GROUP: SPECTRUM

$$$$ — None
$$$ — Savings
$$ — Cash Reserve, Diversified, Dividend, Government Bond, Interest
$ — Canadian Equity, International Equity
NR — International Bond

BULLOCK

$$$$ — None
$$$ — Growth
$$ — American
$ — Asset Strategy, Canadian Investment
NR — Asian Dynasty, Emerging Market, European Enterprise, Global Bond, Optimax U.S.A.

COMMENTS: Growing in size. Recently introduced new international series with no-load option. The flagship American Bullock fund has been showing strong signs of a turnaround recently, which is great news for investors. Acquired United Funds in 1995; see separate entry.

STANDARD LIFE

NUMBER OF FUNDS:	4 SEGREGATED, 10 MUTUAL
ASSETS UNDER MANAGEMENT:	$171 MILLION
LOAD CHARGE:	SEGREGATED — BACK: MAXIMUM 4.5%
	MUTUAL — BACK: MAXIMUM 5%
SWITCHING CHARGE:	NONE
WHERE SOLD:	ACROSS CANADA
PHONE NUMBER:	1-800-NO LOADS
FUNDS IN GROUP:	SEGREGATED (IDEAL)

$$$$ — NONE
$$$ — BOND
$$ — BALANCED, EQUITY
$ — NONE
NR — MONEY MARKET

MUTUAL
$$$$ — NONE
$$$ — NONE
$$ — NONE
$ — NONE
NR — BALANCED, BOND, CANADIAN DIVIDEND, EQUITY, GROWTH EQUITY, INTERNATIONAL BOND, INTERNATIONAL EQUITY, MONEY MARKET, NATURAL RESOURCE, U.S. EQUITY

COMMENTS:	YOU HAVE TO BE CAREFUL WITH YOUR CHOICES HERE. THE IDEAL FUNDS CAN ONLY BE PURCHASED THROUGH INSURANCE CONTRACTS. THE NEW MUTUAL FUND FAMILY IS MADE UP OF ORDINARY, NON-SEGREGATED FUNDS. THEY ARE ALL TOO NEW TO QUALIFY FOR A RATING.

TALVEST FUNDS

NUMBER OF FUNDS:	15
ASSETS UNDER MANAGEMENT:	$1.2 BILLION
LOAD CHARGE:	MONEY MARKET — FRONT: MAXIMUM 2%
	INCOME — FRONT: MAXIMUM 2%;
	BACK: MAXIMUM 2.5%
	BOND AND FOREIGN PAY — FRONT: MAXIMUM 5%;
	BACK: MAXIMUM 4.5%
	EQUITY AND BALANCED — FRONT: MAXIMUM 5%;
	BACK: MAXIMUM 5.5%
	HYPERION FUNDS — FRONT: MAXIMUM 5.5%;
	BACK: MAXIMUM 6.5%
SWITCHING CHARGE:	2% MAXIMUM

WHERE SOLD:	**ACROSS CANADA**
PHONE NUMBER:	**1-800-268-0081** (SALES)
	1-800-268-8258 (CLIENT SERVICES)
FUNDS IN GROUP:	**TALVEST**

$$$$ — NONE
 $$$ — BOND, MONEY
  $$ — GLOBAL DIVERSIFIED, GROWTH, INCOME, U.S. DIVERSIFIED, U.S. GROWTH
   $ — DIVERSIFIED
  NR — GLOBAL RRSP, NEW ECONOMY

HYPERION

$$$$ — NONE
 $$$ — ASIAN, VALUE-LINE EQUITY
  $$ — EUROPEAN
   $ — NONE
  NR — AURORA

COMMENTS:	TALVEST PURCHASED THE HYPERION FUNDS FROM CIBC IN MID-'95 AND CONTINUES TO OPERATE SOME OF THEM UNDER THAT NAME. THERE WAS NO CHANGE IN THE MANAGEMENT, HOWEVER, AS TALVEST WAS ALREADY RUNNING THE HYPERION FUNDS.

TEMPLETON MANAGEMENT LTD.

NUMBER OF FUNDS:	12
ASSETS UNDER MANAGEMENT:	**$5.4** BILLION
LOAD CHARGE:	TREASURY BILL — NO LOAD
	BALANCED — FRONT: MAXIMUM 6%
	ALL OTHER FUNDS — FRONT: MAXIMUM 6%; BACK: MAXIMUM 6%
SWITCHING CHARGE:	2% MAXIMUM
WHERE SOLD:	DIRECTLY IN ONTARIO, OTHERWISE THROUGH DEALERS AND BROKERS
PHONE NUMBER:	(416) 364-4672 OR 1-800-387-0830
FUNDS IN GROUP:	$$$$ — GROWTH

 $$$ — EMERGING MARKETS, GLOBAL SMALLER COMPANIES, INTERNATIONAL STOCK, TREASURY-BILL
  $$ — BALANCED, CANADIAN BOND, CANADIAN STOCK, GLOBAL BOND
   $ — NONE
  NR — CANADIAN ASSET ALLOCATION, GLOBAL BALANCED, INTERNATIONAL BALANCED

COMMENTS:	INTERNATIONAL FUNDS ARE THE STANDOUT HERE. THE ORIGINAL TEMPLETON GROWTH FUND IS STILL GOING

STRONG AND SHOULD BE PART OF MOST FUND
PORTFOLIOS. THE CANADIAN ENTRIES ARE STARTING TO
SHOW IMPROVEMENT.

TORONTO DOMINION SECURITIES (GREEN LINE)

NUMBER OF FUNDS:	31
ASSETS UNDER MANAGEMENT:	$5.3 BILLION
LOAD CHARGE:	NONE
SWITCHING CHARGE:	NONE
WHERE SOLD:	ACROSS CANADA
PHONE NUMBER:	1-800-268-8166
FUNDS IN GROUP:	$$$$ — NONE
	$$$ — CANADIAN BOND, CANADIAN MONEY MARKET, MORTGAGE, SHORT-TERM INCOME
	$$ — CANADIAN EQUITY, CANADIAN GOVERNMENT BOND, CANADIAN INDEX, CANADIAN T- BILL, MORTGAGE-BACKED, U.S. INDEX, U.S. MONEY MARKET
	$ — BALANCED GROWTH, BALANCED INCOME, BLUE CHIP EQUITY, DIVIDEND INCOME
	NR — ASIAN GROWTH, EMERGING MARKETS, ENERGY, EUROPEAN GROWTH, GLOBAL GOVERNMENT BOND, GLOBAL RSP BOND, GLOBAL SELECT, INTERNATIONAL EQUITY, JAPANESE GROWTH, LATIN AMERICAN GROWTH, NORTH AMERICAN GROWTH, PRECIOUS METALS, REAL RETURN BOND, RESOURCE, SCIENCE AND TECHNOLOGY, VALUE
COMMENTS:	THIS IS A WELL-BALANCED, HIGHLY DIVERSIFIED FUND GROUP THAT IS AGGRESSIVELY EXPANDING ON ALL FRONTS. THERE ARE LOTS OF GOOD CHOICES IN THE LINEUP, BUT A FEW WEAK SPOTS AS WELL. AMONG THE BANK FUND GROUPS, THIS IS ONE OF THE BEST.

TRANSAMERICA'S GROWSAFE FUNDS

NUMBER OF FUNDS:	5
ASSETS UNDER MANAGEMENT:	$20 MILLION
LOAD CHARGE:	BACK: MAXIMUM 5%
SWITCHING CHARGE:	4 FREE TRANSFERS PER YEAR, $100 THEREAFTER
WHERE SOLD:	ACROSS CANADA
PHONE NUMBER:	1-800-387-8879
FUNDS IN GROUP:	$$$$ — NONE

$$$ — NONE
$$ — NONE
$ — NONE
NR — BALANCED, CANADIAN BOND, EQUITY,
INTERNATIONAL BALANCED, MONEY MARKET

COMMENTS: NEW LINE OF SEGREGATED FUNDS FROM TRANSAMERICA
LIFE. THEY HAVEN'T BEEN AROUND LONG ENOUGH TO BE
RATED.

TRIMARK INVESTMENT MANAGEMENT

NUMBER OF FUNDS: 13
ASSETS UNDER
MANAGEMENT: $12.3 BILLION
LOAD CHARGE: CANADIAN, INCOME, AND TRIMARK FUNDS — FRONT:
MAXIMUM 9%
INTEREST FUND — FRONT: MAXIMUM 2%
ALL OTHER FUNDS — FRONT: MAXIMUM 4%;
BACK: MAXIMUM 4.5%

SWITCHING CHARGE: 2% MAXIMUM
WHERE SOLD: ACROSS CANADA
PHONE NUMBER: 1-800-387-9845
FUNDS IN GROUP: $$$$ — CANADIAN, RSP EQUITY, TRIMARK
$$$ — INCOME, INTEREST, SELECT BALANCED, SELECT
GROWTH
$$ — NONE
$ — NONE
NR — ADVANTAGE BOND, AMERICAS, CANADIAN
BOND, GOVERNMENT INCOME,
INDO-PACIFIC, SELECT CANADIAN GROWTH

COMMENTS: THIS IS THE TOP FUND GROUP IN CANADA AT THIS TIME,
WITH ALL SORTS OF SOLID, MONEY-MAKING OPTIONS
FOR INVESTORS. SO IT'S NOT SURPRISING THAT
TRIMARK MOVED PAST MACKENZIE FINANCIAL IN '95 TO
BECOME THE NUMBER TWO COMPANY IN TERMS OF
ASSETS, AFTER INVESTORS GROUP. IF YOU DON'T HAVE
SOME TRIMARK FUNDS IN YOUR PORTFOLIO, YOU'RE
REALLY MISSING OUT. MAIN WEAKNESS IS CONFUSING
PURCHASE OPTIONS: CANADIAN, RSP EQUITY, AND
SELECT CANADIAN GROWTH ARE SIMILAR FUNDS THAT
REQUIRE A HIGH LEVEL OF MATHEMATICAL SKILL TO
CHOOSE AMONG.

20/20 GROUP

NUMBER OF FUNDS:	20
ASSETS UNDER MANAGEMENT:	$2.8 BILLION
LOAD CHARGE:	FRONT: MAXIMUM 9%; BACK: MAXIMUM 6%
SWITCHING CHARGE:	2 FREE TRANSFERS PER YEAR, $25 THEREAFTER
WHERE SOLD:	ACROSS CANADA
PHONE NUMBER:	1-800-268-8690
FUNDS IN GROUP:	$$$$ — NONE
	$$$ — AMERICAN TACTICAL ASSET ALLOCATION, DIVIDEND
	$$ — CANADIAN ASSET ALLOCATION, CANADIAN GROWTH, INTERNATIONAL VALUE, MONEY MARKET, WORLD
	$ — INCOME
	NR — AGGRESSIVE EQUITY, AGGRESSIVE GROWTH, ASIA PACIFIC, EUROPEAN ASSET ALLOCATION, FOREIGN RSP BOND, INDIA, INTERNATIONAL EQUITY ALLOCATION, LATIN AMERICA, MANAGED FUTURES VALUE, MULTIMANAGER EMERGING MARKETS, U.S. SHORT-TERM HIGH YIELD, WORLD BOND
COMMENTS:	THIS GROUP ORIGINALLY TOOK A VERY CONSERVATIVE APPROACH TO FUND MANAGEMENT. BUT THE LAUNCH OF FUNDS LIKE AGGRESSIVE GROWTH, MANAGED BY U.S. SMALL CAP EXPERT RICHARD DRIEHAUS, HAS CHANGED THAT IMAGE. ONE OF THEIR RECENT ENTRIES, THE INDIA FUND, GOT OFF TO AN EXTREMELY POOR START THAT LEFT A BAD TASTE IN INVESTORS' MOUTHS.

UNITED FINANCIAL MANAGEMENT

NUMBER OF FUNDS:	13
ASSETS UNDER MANAGEMENT:	$1.1 BILLION
LOAD CHARGE:	MONEY MARKET AND INTEREST — FRONT: MAXIMUM 2%; BACK: MAXIMUM 5%
	MORTGAGE — FRONT: MAXIMUM 5%; BACK: MAXIMUM 5%
	ALL OTHER FUNDS — FRONT: MAXIMUM 9%; BACK: MAXIMUM 5%
SWITCHING CHARGE:	2% MAXIMUM
WHERE SOLD:	ACROSS CANADA
PHONE NUMBER:	(416) 598-7777 OR 1-800-263-1867
FUNDS IN GROUP:	$$$$ — NONE

$$$ —	AMERICAN GROWTH, CANADIAN EQUITY, CANADIAN GROWTH, CANADIAN INTEREST, CANADIAN PORTFOLIO OF FUNDS
$$ —	AMERICAN EQUITY, CANADIAN BOND, GLOBAL GROWTH, GLOBAL PORTFOLIO OF FUNDS, U.S. DOLLAR MONEY MARKET
$ —	CANADIAN MORTGAGE, GLOBAL EQUITY
NR —	GLOBAL TELECOMMUNICATIONS

COMMENTS: THE UNITED funds WERE PURCHASED BY SPECTRUM BULLOCK IN EARLY '95, ALTHOUGH THEY CONTINUE TO OPERATE UNDER THEIR OWN NAME, AT LEAST FOR NOW. THERE ARE SOME PRETTY GOOD OFFERINGS HERE, INCLUDING THE FUNDS MANAGED BY KIKI DELANEY, AS WELL AS THE AMERICAN GROWTH FUND AND THE NEW GLOBAL TELECOMMUNICATIONS FUND.

WESTBURY LIFE FUNDS

NUMBER OF FUNDS:	4
ASSETS UNDER MANAGEMENT:	$70.7 MILLION
LOAD CHARGE:	NONE
SWITCHING CHARGE:	1 FREE TRANSFER PER YEAR, $25 THEREAFTER
WHERE SOLD:	ACROSS CANADA
PHONE NUMBER:	(905) 528-6766 OR 1-800-263-9241
FUNDS IN GROUP:	$$$$ — NONE
	$$$ — NONE
	$$ — NONE
	$ — BALANCED, BOND, EQUITY GROWTH
	NR — EQUITY INTEREST ACCOUNT
COMMENTS:	SMALL, UNEXCITING FAMILY OF SEGREGATED FUNDS FROM THIS LIFE INSURANCE COMPANY.

THE TOP FUND GROUPS

very mutual fund investor would like to have the top-performing funds in each category in his or her portfolio.

But that isn't always easy, or convenient. ■

If you buy your funds through brokers or mutual fund sales representatives, they may be reluctant to acquire the traditional type of no-load funds on your behalf since they normally receive no commission (the new breed of no-loads now offered by a few companies such as AGF is a different matter).

If you deal with a bank, trust company, or insurance company, you'll only be able to acquire mutual funds sold and managed by that particular organization.

Some big mutual fund companies, such as Investors Group, insist you deal with their own sales people to buy their funds. No outside representatives sell them.

In short, unless you're prepared for the hassle of dealing with a variety of sales organizations, building a diversified portfolio of high-performance mutual funds is tough.

That's why many investors prefer to deal with one or two mutual fund companies in which they have confidence. They don't concern themselves with chasing the number one fund in each category. Rather, they look for solid across-the-board performance, a broad selection of funds, free or low-cost switching, timely reporting, and overall good management.

To help you make the best selection among the many companies out there, I analyze all the mutual fund families in Canada each year and select what I regard as the top three no-load organizations and the best three load companies.

It is never an easy choice. There are about 70 fund families listed in this *Guide*. Among them are many excellent organizations that don't make the top three listings for a variety of reasons — perhaps because they don't offer a wide enough range of funds, perhaps because they're weak in a particular category, perhaps because several of their funds haven't been in existence long enough to establish a dependable track record.

Again this year, in reviewing all the entries, I found that there is no perfect fund group in Canada — even the best have some flaws. But there are many high-quality companies, and more appearing all the time as competition in the industry continues to heat up.

Here are the organizations that win my vote as the best of 1996, and my reasons.

NO-LOAD FUND COMPANIES

1. ALTAMIRA INVESTMENT SERVICES ★★★★

Ever since I began ranking the top fund companies each year, Altamira has finished number one in the no-load category. They've made it again, for the fourth year in a row — but this time just by the skin of their teeth. Phillips, Hager & North is just a fraction behind and, in fact, would be number one by a wide margin if fund performance were the sole criterion used in making this call. But Altamira's broader product range, easy telephone ordering system, and low entry requirements (you can invest for as little as $1,000) tip the balance in their favour. But oh, only so slightly.

Altamira's dominance of this class is slipping because the relative performance of its funds is declining. The table below tells the story. It shows the number of Altamira funds in each quartile for various periods ending June 30, 1995. The first quartile means a fund was among the top 25 percent in its particular category. The second quartile means it was in the top half. Third and fourth quartile scores indicate funds that were below average in performance. The number of funds will differ in each column, reflecting new start-ups along the way. The calculations were done with my new software program, *Gordon Pape's Mutual Fund Analyzer*, which uses data prepared by the Southam Information and Technology Group.

ALTAMIRA PERFORMANCE

Quartile	1 Year	2 Years	3 Years	5 Years	10 Years
1st	4	5	8	7	1
2nd	4	1	1	1	1
3rd	2	2	2	1	0
4th	7	4	1	0	2

Take a close look at the pattern. Over the past five years, seven of nine Altamira funds have finished in the top quartile — an outstanding 78 percent. Only one fund with a five-year record finished in the bottom half of its category.

The three-year pattern shows similar strength. Of the 12 Altamira funds with a three-year record, eight (67 percent) are in the top quartile for their respective categories.

But the two-year and one-year numbers show how performance has slipped relative to the competition. Only 42 percent of the funds make it into the top quartile in the two-year rankings, and half of the total of 12 finished in the bottom 50 percent. Looking at one-year returns, only 24 percent are in the top group, while slightly more than half of the Altamira entries are in the bottom 50 percent.

All this tells you that you must be increasingly selective when you buy any Altamira funds. In the past, it almost didn't matter which ones you picked — they were all among the leaders in their categories. Now, however, there are several weak performers in the Altamira stable and you should try to keep your exposure to those funds to a minimum.

The key funds to include in your Altamira portfolio are the two fixed income entries, Income and Bond, and two stock funds, Capital Growth and Equity. Newcomers worth considering are the European Equity and U.S. Larger Companies funds.

Altamira continues to expand its fund family, with the launch of a Science and Technology Fund and a Speculative High-Yield Bond Fund in late summer 1995. A major service innovation in the past year is a fully self-directed RRSP for clients in Ontario, which allows them to hold mutual funds from other organizations as well.

The company intends to extend this program across the country soon.

You don't need a lot of money to open an Altamira account — the minimum investment is $1,000. Although the funds are no load, you are assessed a one-time set-up fee of $40 when you open an account (the prospectus allows them to charge up to $200 but, fortunately, they've kept the cost well below that).

The company's client communications include a regular newsletter explaining investment strategies and providing useful money management and tax-saving tips. They've also opened an Internet site that provides current information about their funds.

Weak points: The slipping performance numbers must be a cause of concern to Altamira's management and certainly should be to investors. This is the number one issue that has to be addressed if the company hopes to hold on to its top ranking in the future.

Investors should also be aware that Altamira's managers generally have an aggressive style. This is personified by Frank Mersch, the company's best-known manager, who believes in actively trading the shares in his portfolios. There's nothing wrong with this approach — indeed it has been very successful over the years — but it may produce more volatility than some investors are comfortable with.

Summary: Altamira's crown may be slipping but, with careful selection, you can continue to build a portfolio of winning funds from their offerings.

2. PHILLIPS, HAGER & NORTH ★★★★

After almost falling out of the top three a few years ago, Vancouver-based PH&N has regrouped and is now snapping at Altamira's heels for the number one position in this class. The main barrier to top status at this point is the company's high minimum entry fee — unless you're opening an RRSP, you need a minimum of $25,000 to invest in a PH&N fund. That puts this organization out of the reach of many Canadians.

That's a shame, because PH&N's performance record has improved to the point where it now dominates the no-load category. Take a look.

PH&N PERFORMANCE

Quartile	1 Year	2 Years	3 Years	5 Years	10 Years
1st	10	9	6	5	4
2nd	1	3	4	2	1
3rd	3	0	0	1	0
4th	1	1	0	0	0

These are outstanding numbers by any measure. Ten of PH&N's 15 funds made it to the top quartile in the year to June 30, 1995. Only four were in the bottom half. If you trace the record back, you'll see that PH&N has always been well-represented in the top-performing group, but the relative standing over the past three years has been steadily improving.

PH&N's strength rests on several pillars. One is the conservative, long-range approach its managers use. You won't find major changes in investment style for the sake of short-term performance numbers here; this is a company that prides itself on long-term asset building. As a result, you're not likely to see a PH&N fund as the top performer in its category in any given year. What you will see, however, are consistently good results over the long haul.

Another PH&N strength is its low management fees. To put it bluntly, this is not a greedy company. Whichever fund you look at, you'll find its management expenses are among the lowest in the category. With less being taken off the top, that means more profits for investors.

The company's other big strength is its people. PH&N is very selective about the new managers it brings on board. They must not only have all the technical qualifications, but they must also fit in well with the corporate philosophy of conservative, long-term money management.

This is not an organization that adds new funds to its list on an almost monthly basis, as many other companies have been doing recently. As a result, you won't find any "flavour-of-the-month" funds in its lineup. There is no emerging markets fund, no Latin America fund, not even a Far East fund. For some investors, that may be a drawback. For PH&N, it ensures that they keep a tight focus on the things they do best.

If you're planning to build a portfolio of PH&N funds, it's pretty hard to go far wrong. Even the fund that finished in the fourth quartile in last year's returns is a solid holding, depending on your investment goals. It's the Short-Term Bond and Mortgage Fund, which is designed for investors seeking to minimize bond market risk. That type of fund will always under-perform when bond markets are strong, as they were in the first half of 1995. But it will protect your asset base when interest rates rise and bonds run into trouble.

Some of the top PH&N performers you should include in your mix are the Balanced Fund, the Bond Fund, the Canadian Equity Fund, and the Money Market Fund. Add the Dividend Income Fund if tax-advantaged income outside a registered plan is an investment goal.

Really, it's hard to go far wrong here. This is a company every prudent investor should consider.

Weak points: The $25,000 initial investment requirement is the major one. However, you can open an RRSP account with as little as $3,500. The only other weakness in some people's view might be the limited product range on offer.

Summary: If you have the money and are looking for conservative, long-term investment management, this is the place to be.

3. ROYAL FUNDS ★★★

The Royal group holds on to third place in the no-load field this year, but TD's Green Line funds are closing the gap fast and are making a strong bid to break through into the top three. Royal's main problem right now is trying to integrate the massive fund operation that was created when Royal Bank purchased Royal Trust. That merger is still in progress, with the untidy result that some funds in this group can only be purchased at Royal Trust branches (Royal Trust funds), some only at Royal Bank branches (RoyFunds), and some at both (Royal funds).

Hopefully, by next year's edition all this will have been straightened out. For now, however, it's still a dog's breakfast and the funds available to you will depend on where you do your banking business.

Despite this consumer confusion, the Royal funds hold on to the number three spot because of their many high-quality offerings and the wide selection available, whether you're a Royal Bank or Royal Trust client. But this is a fund group where careful selection is extremely important. The performance numbers will explain why.

ROYAL FUNDS PERFORMANCE

Quartile	1 Year	2 Years	3 Years	5 Years	10 Years
1st	3	6	3	0	0
2nd	8	7	5	7	1
3rd	10	8	6	6	4
4th	11	10	9	4	2

As you can see, there are a lot of weak performers in this group. In fact, 21 of the 32 funds in this organization finished in the bottom half of their respective categories in the year ending June 30, 1995. That still leaves 11 pretty decent funds — but you've got to choose with care.

You'll see a similar pattern over the years — several winners, but a lot of losers as well.

The best bets in this organization at present are these:

For Royal Bank customers: RoyFund U.S. Equity, RoyFund Mortgage, RoyFund International Income, RoyFund Equity, and RoyFund Dividend.

For Royal Trust clients: Royal Trust American Stock Fund and Royal Trust International Bond Fund.

Customers of both financial institutions can buy the Royal Zweig Strategic Growth Fund, Royal European Growth Fund, and Royal Precious Metals Fund, all of which have done well.

Even in the midst of integration, this group continues to launch new funds. Three appeared during the summer of 1995: Royal Zweig Global Managed Assets, Royal Life Science and Technology, and Royal Latin American.

All the domestic funds are managed in-house. International portfolio advisors are hired to supervise the foreign funds.

When full integration is complete (expected in fall 1996), this group will have the largest distribution network in Canada, with all funds available in each of the 1,700 branches of Royal Bank and Royal Trust across the country.

Weak points: The slow progress to full integration is a big problem, creating customer confusion and managerial changes as funds are merged (for example, the successful managers of the Royal Trust International Bond Fund were shown the door last fall in a move designed to make an eventual merger with its RoyFund counterpart easier).

Uneven performance is another major problem. The official goal is to consistently have all the Royal funds performing in at least the second quartile, but that's going to take some doing on the basis of historical results.

Summary: There's some genuine quality here, but finding it is rather like wandering through an unfinished house — you have to look very carefully.

Honourable mention: TD Green Line, Scotia Excelsior

LOAD FUNDS

1. TRIMARK INVESTMENT MANAGEMENT ★★★★

There's a new champion in this category this year. Trimark has dethroned Investors Group as the top load fund company in Canada. It has seized the crown for a number of reasons, including:

Consistency. The funds in the Trimark family have been at or near the top of their categories for years.

Returns. Flagship funds like Trimark Canadian and Trimark Fund are among the best in the country.

Growth. Trimark has now passed Mackenzie Financial for number two spot on the assets list. Only Investors Group is larger.

Initiative. The knock against Trimark in the past was that the company didn't offer the range of funds needed for a well-balanced portfolio. That's now changed with the launch of several new targeted funds, including the Indo-Pacific Fund, the Advantage Bond Fund, and the Americas Fund.

Here's a look at how Trimark's funds have done compared to the competition over the years.

TRIMARK PERFORMANCE

Quartile	1 Year	2 Years	3 Years	5 Years	10 Years
1st	4	7	5	6	2
2nd	4	1	2	1	0
3rd	1	0	0	0	0
4th	1	1	0	0	0

You can see the consistency here. No matter how far back you go, most of Trimark's funds are regularly in the top quartile. It's a record that's matched only by Phillips, Hager & North.

As with PH&N, this is a group where it almost doesn't matter which funds you select. You're almost sure to come up with a winner. However, the most consistent performers have been the Trimark Fund, Trimark Income and Growth, Trimark Select Balanced, and Trimark Select Growth. All finished in the top quartile of their respective categories for every time frame measured. Trimark Canadian didn't quite achieve that level, but it's a strong candidate for your portfolio as well.

Among the newer funds, Trimark Indo-Pacific, Trimark Advantage Bond, and Trimark Canadian Bond have all gotten off to a strong start.

The Trimark management style is highly disciplined, which is one of the company's great strengths. The number of securities held in each fund is limited to about 40. This ensures that each company can be properly researched and monitored. It also means that any potential new addition must be clearly shown to offer greater profit potential than the security it will displace.

Stock selection is done on the basis of a detailed, bottom-up approach. Trimark's managers are instructed to view themselves as "business people buying businesses." As a result, they look for the hallmarks of a well-run company in making their evaluations: innovation, growth potential, sound management, and decent value. Unlike an organization like Altamira, these are not active traders. Trimark tends to hold its stocks for a long time, only selling when they feel the price no longer represents good value or if a stock with better potential appears.

Weak points: The only real fault I can find with Trimark is one I've complained about in the past — its dog's breakfast of purchase options. There are three Canadian stock funds, for example, all of which are more or less the same except for the way you buy them. Trimark would be doing the investing public a big favour if it cleaned up this little mess.

Summary: This is a sound, well-run mutual fund company that looks after its clients' money well. It deserves some of your business.

2. INVESTORS GROUP

This was the number one load fund group for three years running, but no more. It has slipped to number two, not because it did anything wrong but because Trimark has been coming on like an express train on several fronts.

But neither Investors Group representatives nor their clients should hang their heads. This is still a fine company, with some first-class funds in its stable. It's just that Trimark has become a little better.

Investors Group's strengths remain what they always were: a broad range of sound, conservatively managed funds. There aren't many stars in this organization. But for people interested in solid, above-average money management, this is a good place to be. Let's take a look at their performance.

INVESTORS GROUP PERFORMANCE

Quartile	1 Year	2 Years	3 Years	5 Years	10 Years
1st	4	6	5	4	4
2nd	10	13	8	4	5
3rd	10	3	6	8	2
4th	5	5	6	2	1

Investors always has several funds in the top quartile. The majority, however, are clustered around the middle, in the second and third quartile. This tells you a lot about this company — a few stellar performers, a lot of middle-of-the-road funds, and a few dogs. You can build a very solid mutual funds portfolio from that mix — as long as you keep the dogs at bay.

This is all consistent with Investors' basic style. The goal they set for their fund managers is to achieve above-average returns with below-average risk. They'll freely acknowledge that this conservative approach will cause them to lag somewhat behind in bull markets — but it will also prevent large losses when markets turn down. Essentially, Investors Group wants to be somewhere in the middle — exactly where they believe a large proportion of Canadians are as well.

The best performers in this group are the U.S. Growth, European Equity, Pacific International, and Canadian Equity Funds. Those that haven't been as consistent historically include the Summa Fund, Japanese Growth Fund, and Mortgage Fund.

This is probably the oldest mutual fund company in Canada, although it wasn't always in that business. Ironically, it actually started in the United States, in Minneapolis, as Investors Syndicate Inc., an investment certificate company. A Canadian office was opened in 1926, and a separate Canadian company, headquartered in Winnipeg, was set up in 1940. The firm didn't actually get into mutual funds until a decade later, with the 1950 launch of Investors Mutual of Canada. The company is now part of Power Financial Corporation, has 94 financial planning centres across the country, and has a sales force of about 3,400. In other words, it's big!

Weak points: When you deal with an Investors Group sales rep, he or she has just one line of products to sell you. Although it's a good line, your options are clearly limited by this. There have been rumours for some time that the company was going to expand its product line by allowing its representatives to sell other funds, but that had not transpired by the time we went to press.

Also, all sales commissions are fixed — there's no negotiation with the sales representative; you pay what's on the card. So even though commissions were reduced a couple of years ago, you may still pay more for an Investors fund than for a similar fund with another organization. As well, you could also be hit with a redemption fee, on top of the sales charge, if you cash in your units within five years.

You may also be subject to a switching charge under certain conditions. If you switch between equity funds, or from one fixed income fund to another, there is no cost. But if you switch from a fixed income fund to an equity fund, you may get dinged. Ask first.

Another concern is that some Investors sales reps can be overly aggressive. Make sure you stay in control of the situation.

Summary: A solid, middle-of-the-road organization. No flash, not much dash, but they're pretty good when it comes to managing your cash.

3. MACKENZIE FINANCIAL CORPORATION   ★★★★

After several years of seemingly aimless growth (acquiring the Sentinel and Universal funds in the process), Mackenzie has finally pulled its act together. The result is a powerhouse organization that offers more than 30 funds in three distinct groups, each with a different management style: the Industrial Group, the Ivy funds, and the Universal funds. Each group has several good performers and, best of all, you can finally switch between them without difficulty.

The Industrial Group is still the core of the organization and remains under the guiding hand of Mackenzie founder Alex Christ. This segment of the company used to suffer from a multiplicity of Canadian equity and balanced funds that were virtually indistinguishable from one another in terms of portfolio content and style. That's all changed, however. Each of the Industrial funds occupies its own market niche, as you'll see if you read the individual reviews for each fund in the ratings section. This has provided investors with more choice and the ability to tailor an investment portfolio more precisely to individual goals.

Mackenzie doesn't like to see a specific management style attributed to each group, but the fact is that the Industrial funds tend to employ a sector rotation strategy. That means the managers will identify those sectors of the economy they think are likely to outperform and then overweight their fund portfolios in those areas. Resource stocks have dominated their thinking in recent years, which is why over half the holdings in most of the Industrial equity funds were in that sector in mid-'95.

The Ivy funds were created to accommodate two people — Gerald Coleman and Jerry Javasky, who left the United funds a few years back to join the Mackenzie organization. They use a value approach to investing, a style that is quite different from that employed by Christ and his team. The Ivy funds are managed on that basis, which is why you'll find their portfolios are quite different from those in the Industrial Group.

The Universal Group grew out of a transaction between Mackenzie and what is now Canadian International.

Mackenzie managed several funds for C.I. (known then as Universal). Through a complex buy-sell arrangement, Mackenzie ended up buying out those funds and the remnants of Universal reorganized into C.I.

The Universal funds were redundancies within the Mackenzie organization for some time, but now they've been given a whole new personality. This is the go-go segment of the Mackenzie empire; the home of high-growth, higher risk funds that invest in some of the world's hottest markets. You'll find most of the company's international funds here, along with a revamped Universal Canadian Fund, which is under the direction of two ex-Trimark managers.

Although Trimark has overtaken Mackenzie for the number two spot in terms of fund assets, it wouldn't surprise me to see Mackenzie retake that position in the next few years. They have far more products than Trimark and the division of the company into three distinctive groups now gives investors a range of purchase options unmatched in the fund industry.

In terms of quality, however, Mackenzie still has a long way to go to overtake Trimark. Here are their performance results.

MACKENZIE PERFORMANCE

Quartile	1 Year	2 Years	3 Years	5 Years	10 Years
1st	7	4	7	0	3
2nd	6	5	5	7	2
3rd	8	6	2	3	3
4th	7	7	2	4	2

Mackenzie's performance is all over the place. There are a number of good funds in the group, but there are a lot of mediocre ones and some downright poor performers. Within the Industrial Group, the Cash Management Fund is clearly the star performer — hardly a compliment to an organization where stock-picking is the main business. Among the equity funds, Industrial Future is the high-flyer right now, because of its emphasis on technology stocks.

The best performances are currently coming from the other two groups. Ivy's Canadian and Foreign Equity funds are looking good so far. So are the new Universal European Opportunity, U.S. Emerging Growth, and World Precious Metals funds.

But there is a lot of chafe mixed in with the Mackenzie wheat. You'll need a good financial advisor to help you find the winners.

Weak points: The multitude of funds is both a blessing and a curse. Yes, you have a lot of choice. But understanding the nuances between several funds with the same general goal can be difficult for many investors. Fortunately, Mackenzie is putting out some excellent literature to assist in the purchase decision.

Performance, especially in the flagship Industrial funds, needs to be significantly improved. The old leaders, Industrial Growth and Industrial Horizon, seem tired and lacklustre these days. They need a fresh dose of energy — and profits.

Summary: Mackenzie has cobbled together an empire of gigantic proportions. Now they need to make the whole thing fly.

Honourable mentions: Fidelity, Dynamic

THE ENVELOPE, PLEASE!

— THE 1996 MUTUAL FUND AWARDS

E ach year after this *Guide* comes out I get

bombarded with questions like:

"What's the best mutual fund of all?"

"What fund should I avoid at all costs?"

"Which group has the lowest costs?"

"Which fund manager bakes the best cookies?" ■

The first three I can answer. The last I have to skate around, by saying something like: "None of them can match my wife's chocolate chips!"

This year, I decided to anticipate all these queries by handing out my prizes for the best (and the worst) of everything associated with mutual funds. Some of the awards that follow are serious, while others are just fun. I intend this to become an annual feature of this *Guide*, so if you'd like to participate, send your nominations to me in care of my publisher, Prentice Hall Canada, 1870 Birchmount Road, Scarborough, Ontario M1P 2J7. You don't have to stick to the categories below; feel free to make up your own. Be sure to include a brief rationale for your nomination. I won't be able to acknowledge your letter personally, but if your nominee does win an award, you'll be given credit in next year's *Guide*.

And now, with a trumpet fanfare, the envelopes, please!

THE BIGGIES

Fund of the Year. Trimark Fund.   This fund has the best 10-year track record of all broadly based international funds, but it's certainly not resting on its laurels. Bob Krimbil and company turned in a solid 20 percent return for the year to June 30, '95, proving once again that this fund deserves all the praise it gets.

Fund Company of the Year. Trimark Investment Management.   They've now shot past Royal and Mackenzie Financial to take the number two spot on the fund company list in terms of assets under management. Combine that with some successful new launches (Indo-Pacific, Advantage Bond) and you have a shoo-in for this award this year.

Manager of the Year. Tim McElvaine.   Most people have never heard of him, but since joining Peter Cundill and Associates in 1991, he's taken the moribund Cundill Security Fund and made it into a star.

Rookie of the Year.   Lots of worthy candidates here, but how can you pass up a fund that roared to a 70 percent gain in its first year? Congratulations to the Green Line Science & Technology Fund.

Comeback of the Year. Altamira Bond Fund.   It was one of the worst performers in this category during the 12 months ending June 30, 1994. Then it did a complete turnaround to finish in the number one spot over the next 12 months, with a gain of almost 25 percent.

THE NOT-QUITE-SO-BIGGIES

The Merger of the Year. Scotia Funds and Montreal Trust.   The lineup that resulted instantly transformed Scotia Excelsior into one of the better no-load fund groups in the country.

Segregated Fund Group of the Year.   To National Life, which very quietly has put together an impressive lineup of consistent, conservatively managed, well-performing funds that should be attracting more investment dollars than they are.

Underrated Fund Group of the Year. Awarded to **Sceptre Funds**, who have a lot of terrific funds and no really bad ones in their lineup. On top of that, they have no load charges.

Reorganization of the Year. This one goes to **Mackenzie Financial**, who finally managed to make some sense out of their stable full of funds and provide investors with some really interesting alternatives, along with an excellent asset allocation program.

THE REST

The Jacques Parizeau Lobster-in-the-Pot Award. To investors in the *20/20 India Fund*. Launched with great publicity in late '94, the fund proceeded to lose 30 percent of its value in the first half of '95. Investors who attempted to escape the plunge were reminded of the fund's unique 10 percent penalty fee on all transfers or redemptions within the first three years! I'm glad it wasn't me.

The Class Act of the Year Honour. To *Altamira Investment Services*, whose "no-load concerts" under the stars with the Canadian Opera Company at Toronto's Harbourfront were one of the highlights of the summer of '95.

The Most Exclusive Mutual Fund Prize. To the *CIBC Premium Canadian T-Bill Fund*, which offers above-average returns to everyone with $250,000 to invest.

The Broker–Client Adversarial Award. To *Elliott & Page, BPI, Admax Regent, Global Strategy, Sagit*, and any other fund company that sanctions a back-end load formula that offers big rewards to those sales people who can persuade their clients to accept the most expensive redemption fee schedule.

Mind Blower of the Year Trophy. To *Global Strategy*, whose dizzying array of mergers, new funds, and multiple purchase options left even some veteran brokers shaking their head in bewilderment.

The "I've Got a Secret" Prize. To *Great-West Life*, who stopped publishing the returns on their Real Estate fund, presumably because they made such gloomy reading for their investors.

The Maybe-We-Should-Take-Another-Look Presentation.
To *Met Life*, who spend a lot of money on promoting their life insurance products but can't seem to generate decent performance out of any of their segregated funds.

The Fund I'd Most Like to Have Invested in 10 Years Ago Prize.   To *C.I. Pacific*, whose average annual rate of return of almost 19 percent for the decade ending June 30, 1995, was far and away the best performance of any mutual fund sold in Canada.

The Fund I'd Least Like to Have Invested in 10 Years Ago Prize.   To *Altamira Global Diversified Fund*, which has managed an average annual return of only 3.4 percent over the past decade.

The Balancing Act Award.   To *Mackenzie Financial's Industrial Group*, which has four balanced funds on offer. They're all slightly different, but you'll need Mackenzie's special Balanced Funds brochure (or this *Guide*) to tell them apart.

The Messiest Fund Group Award.   No contest here. The *Royal Funds*, which are going through a massive integration, win hands down. Everything should be straightened out by this time next year, but right now you can only buy some of these funds at Royal Bank, some at Royal Trust, and some at both. If customers are confused, who can blame them.

The Eat-My-Dust Prize.   To *CIBC Securities*, who are falling way behind in the big bank mutual fund race, both in range of products and performance. They've gone through two presidents in the past year and desperately need someone to take charge and lead them out of the wilderness.

New Fund Group to Watch.   *G.T.*, another American invader that's mining for Canadian dollars with a very attractive lineup of imaginative entries.

The Condolences Prize.   To investors in the tiny, Quebec-based *Exar Realty Fund*, who saw their unit values plunge almost 70 percent in 1994. If that's not a mutual fund record, I'd like to know what is.

Gordon Pape's Ratings 1996

How To Use The Mutual Fund Ratings

The ratings on the pages that follow are designed to help you identify those mutual funds that may be most suitable for your personal investing strategy. They should not be interpreted as buy or sell recommendations! Because of publishing deadlines, these ratings were compiled in August 1995 and use performance results to June 30, 1995. Conditions may have changed significantly since then, so you should consult an investment advisor before making any final decisions. As well, you should obtain a copy of the simplified prospectus (the document that provides all the information about the fund and its management) and study it carefully before going ahead. ■

My ratings take into account a number of factors. These include:

RISK LEVEL — Most investors, me included, prefer lower-risk investments, so this weighs heavily in my ratings. A higher-risk mutual fund, even one that has a good performance record, will generally receive a lower rating than one which may not promise as good a return but which is less risk-prone. But remember, there is no such thing as an absolutely risk-free investment. You can select funds that limit risk, but you can't avoid it entirely. Risk levels are relative within each fund category. Equity funds, for example, are generally higher-risk than fixed income funds. So a medium-risk equity fund will have a higher degree of risk than a medium-risk fixed income fund.

PERFORMANCE RECORD — A fund's past results will weigh heavily in its rating. While previous performance is no guarantee of future success, it's a far better indicator than throwing darts at a board. Because I regard performance records as being vitally important in judging the suitability of mutual funds, no fund which has been in existence for less than three years is included in the ratings. Mutual fund performance ratings are based on results for the period ending June 30, 1995. My information sources include *The Financial Post*, *The Globe and Mail Report on Business*, Southam's *Mutual Fund SourceBook,* and *Gordon Pape's Mutual Fund Analyzer* software program, plus the mutual fund companies themselves. The performance results published by the various financial newspapers will sometimes vary due to slightly different methods of calculating average annual compound rates of return over several years. Where these inconsistencies occur, I've used results supplied by the fund companies.

TREND PATTERN — As a further check, I've taken the recent trend pattern into account. This means that a fund with a strong performance over the past five years would rank higher than one that did well five to 10 years ago but which has tailed off recently. My main source for information on trend performance is the *Mutual Fund SourceBook.*

ECONOMIC CONDITIONS — Certain funds are more suitable under specific economic conditions, such as a climate of low interest rates. My ratings take this into account, based on economic conditions as they were anticipated to develop in summer 1995.

COSTS — High cost will impact negatively on the rating of a particular fund. A low cost earns Brownie points. In cases where a front-end load is charged, assume the fee is negotiable unless the entry specifically states otherwise. Regardless of the posted commission scale, you should not pay more than 4 percent when purchasing a fund with a negotiable fee, even if the amount you're investing is small.

MANAGEMENT — The strength of the fund manager has been taken into account in the ratings, as well as his or her tenure at the fund.

PERSONAL EXPERIENCE — Over the years, I've found that some funds have performed better for me than others. I've tossed these personal preferences into the ratings stew as well; consider them as the X factor if a particular fund ends up with a rating you don't fully understand.

I've attempted to include as many of the more than 1,000 Canadian mutual funds as possible in my ratings. Excluded are those funds with a performance record of less than three years, funds which are open only to a specific group of people (e.g., doctors, teachers), closed-end funds, and a few funds about which I have been unable to obtain adequate information.

Reference in the ratings to "compound average annual rates of return" refers to the amount by which a fund would have grown each year over the period assuming all dividends, interest, and capital gains were reinvested. Thus a fund which is said to have an average annual compound rate of return of 15 percent over 10 years is one in which $1,000 invested a decade ago would have grown at an average annual rate of 15 percent. Taxes are not taken into account in this calculation. Remember, all figures are based on results for the year ending June 30, 1995.

References to rates of return of one year or less refer to simple rates of return — how much your money would have increased in value since you made the investment.

Load charges are not taken into account in any of these calculations since they will vary from one investor to another.

Note that not all mutual funds are sold in every province. Consult a sales representative in your area to determine whether any fund in which you're interested is available. You'll also find information about this in the "Fund Families" section.

Each entry is introduced with a series of symbols. Here's how to interpret them.

OVERALL SUITABILITY

§   Below average. There are better choices
        available.
§§   Average. May produce only mediocre returns or,
        alternatively, may have a higher level of risk
        than is suitable for a conservative investor.
§§§   Above average. Should be seriously considered.
§§§§   Superior. Should consistently perform in the top
        quartile of its category.

RISK LEVEL

⇑   High. Suitable only for investors willing to
        accept an above-average level of risk in
        exchange for potentially higher returns.
⇒   Medium. Some degree of risk involved.
⇓   Low. Among the most conservatively managed
        in its category; relatively low chance of loss.

ASSET TYPE

These ratings are designed to help you allocate each fund for asset mix purposes.

C   Cash or cash equivalent.
FI   Fixed income.
G   Growth.
FI/G   Balanced.
G/FI   Balanced, with a growth bias.

CHARACTERISTICS

Front-end load.
*   Back-end load.
#/*   Optional front- or back-end load.
#/*/No Front-end, back-end, and no-load options.
#&*   Front- and back-end loads applicable.
No   No load fees or broker's commission.

S   Segregated fund of an insurance company.

RSP   Fully eligible for RRSPs and RRIFs, without
        restriction.

£   Foreign property in RRSPs and RRIFs. Limits
        apply.

MUTUAL FUND TYPES

Funds are categorized on the basis of the main type of
security in which they invest. Most funds will hold other
types of assets from time to time, especially Treasury
bills and other short-term notes.

CE   Canadian equity. Invests primarily in stocks of
        Canadian mid-size to large companies or a blend
        of large and small cap stocks.

CSC   Canadian small cap. Invests primarily in stocks
        of smaller Canadian firms.

USE   U.S. equity. Specializes in stocks of larger
        American companies or a combination of small
        and large corporations.

USSC   U.S. small cap. Invests in stocks of smaller U.S.
        firms.

IE   International equity. Invests in international
        stocks from one or several countries.

AE   Americas equity. Invests in stocks from two or
        more countries in North and/or South America.
        May include some U.S. holdings.

FEE   Far East equity. Invests mainly in Asian stocks.

EE   European equity. Invests in European stocks.

EME   Emerging markets equity. Invests in stocks from
        developing countries.

CB   Canadian bond. Invests primarily in Canadian
        dollar bonds and debentures with maturities of
        more than one year.

IB   International bond. Invests in bonds and deben-
        tures denominated in foreign currencies.

M   Mortgage. Invests mainly in residential first
        mortgages.

B/M   Bond/Mortgage. Invests in a combination of
        bonds and residential mortgages and/or mort-
        gage-backed securities.

INC   Income. Emphasis is on generating regular divi-
        dend income.

CBAL   Canadian balanced. Invests in a blend of
        Canadian equities and debt securities.

IBAL	International balanced. Invests in a blend of foreign equities and debt securities.
PM	Precious metals. Invests in gold, precious metals, and shares in mining companies.
D	Derivatives. Invests primarily in futures, options, and other types of derivatives.
RE	Real estate. Invests primarily in commercial real estate.
SEC	Sector. Invests in a specific area of the economy.
CMM	Canadian Money Market. Invests in Canadian short-term debt securities such as Treasury bills.
IMM	International Money Market. Invests in short-term securities denominated in foreign currencies, usually U.S. dollars.
LAB	Labour-sponsored venture capital funds.

Canadian Equity Funds (General)

Canadian stock funds are coming off a good run. And, as I point out in "The Year Ahead" chapter, the good times aren't necessarily over yet — historically, our resource stocks perform best in the final stages of a growth cycle. But 1996 will be a time for caution and for careful fund selection. Stick with high quality; avoid excessively volatile funds in these conditions. ■

RATINGS CHANGES

A total of 28 funds in this category have had their ratings changed since last year's edition. Of those, exactly half are up and half are down.

The big news is the addition of a new $$$$ fund. Trimark RSP Equity, now the largest Canadian stock fund in the country, joins stablemate Trimark Canadian at the top of the heap. That's only fair, because they are essentially two versions of the same fund, with the only real difference being the purchase option.

A total of five funds advance to $$$ status. The big story here is the rise of Cundill Security Fund. This had been an ugly duckling for years, but has blossomed into a magnificent swan under the guidance of Fund Manager of the Year Tim McElvaine.

On the downside, several former $$$ funds have been

demoted to the $$ rank. Included here are several of the equity funds in Mackenzie's Industrial Group, the big Industrial Growth and Industrial Horizon funds among them.

The three funds that received a $$$$ ranking in last year's edition retain their position in '96, although none posted an outstanding year: ABC Fundamental Value Fund, Altamira Equity Fund, and Trimark Canadian Fund.

There are eight new funds in this category this year, as well as several name changes. The most significant changes relate to the Montreal Trust and Scotia Funds, which have been merged under the Scotia Excelsior label.

Among the new funds, the Clean Environment Equity Fund is worth special attention if you're interested in socially responsible investing. It debuts with a $$$ rating.

1996 RATINGS

ABC FUNDAMENTAL VALUE FUND $$$$ ⇒ G NO RSP CE

Not the greatest of years for this go-go fund; gain for the 12 months to June 30, '95, was just 4.7 percent — well below the average for Canadian equity funds during that period. This was in part due to the defensive position taken by manager Irwin Michael, who entered '95 with a large amount of cash in his portfolio. He started to move aggressively back into the market over the winter, however, and returns began to pick up. Michael is a value investor who seeks out bargains — and, at mid-'95, he felt there were still plenty available in the Canadian stock market. Despite the sub-par, one-year return, this fund's average annual performance for the five years to June 30, '95, was over 25 percent — still the best performance of any Canadian equity fund over that period. I'm maintaining the $$$$ rating this year on the strength of those longer-term results. This was a small fund (it had assets of less than $20 million at the start of '94), but the big gains have attracted a lot of money and it's now ballooned to well over $100 million. Minimum initial investment is still $150,000. But even if you have that kind of spare cash, you may not get in. Michael screens all potential investors to be sure they are in accord with his stock selection approach, and refuses to accept money if it represents too large a percentage of a person's net worth. Call (416) 365-9696 for information.

AGF CANADIAN EQUITY FUND $ ⇒ G #/*/NO RSP CE

You can now buy AGF funds on a front-end load (A units), back-end load (B units), or no-load basis (C units). In each case, the annual management fee differs. If you're in for the long term, the front-end load/lower management fee is the best choice, otherwise look at the no-load option. For purposes of historical results, I'll quote A unit numbers throughout this *Guide*. This fund has been a chronic underperformer. Its returns have been consistently below average for this fund category; over the 10 years to June 30, '95, it produced an average annual return of just 5.5 percent. It's hard to show much enthusiasm for this one. Perhaps a change at the top will make a difference; New manager Veronika Hirsch moved from Prudential to take over this fund in September '95.

AGF GROWTH EQUITY FUND $$$ ⇑ G #/*/NO RSP CE

This fund has emerged as a much better choice than the AGF Canadian Equity Fund (above). Over the 10 years to June 30, '95, average annual return was an excellent 10.1 percent, well above average for Canadian equity funds as a group. The managers use an investment technique called sector rotation, targeting those areas of the economy that are expected to outperform the market as a whole and then choosing stocks in those sectors that show strong growth potential. The fund stumbled in '94 with a 16.8 percent loss, but rebounded with a gain of almost 9 percent in the first half of '95. Best performer among AGF Canadian stock funds, but tends to be more volatile as well. Portfolio is extremely large (almost 300 securities) which means good diversification, but all those stocks may be difficult to stay on top of. The assets of the old Corporate Investors Stock Fund were merged into this fund in October '94.

AIC ADVANTAGE FUND $$$ ⇑ G #/* RSP CE

Mutual fund stocks and technology shares are the two keys to the remarkable success of this unusual fund, based in the unlikely city of Hamilton, Ontario. Both areas did very well in the first half of '95, contributing big gains. Manager Jonathan Wellum sunk a big chunk of his assets into Trimark Financial (the fund owns about 5 percent of the shares), and the bet paid off handsomely when Trimark stock rocketed in the first six months of the year. Technology stocks, which also had a big run in early '95, are another main component of the portfolio. Most have done well, but a $1 million investment in Sprint Canada has been a disappointment. But, quibbles aside, the results have been impressive. The fund gained 24.8 percent in the year ending June 30, '95, and had a five-year average annual rate of return of 19.1 percent at that point. Only a handful of Canadian stock funds managed to do better. One word of warning, though: technology and mutual fund stocks tend to get badly beaten up in market downturns. This fund lost 18.6 percent in '90 and 12.9 percent in '94. So don't buy in just when the market is peaking. Wait until there's been a correction and then buy for the long term. Call 1-800-263-2144 for details on how to purchase. Now available in all provinces.

AMI PRIVATE CAPITAL EQUITY FUND $$ ⇒ G NO RSP CE

This fund has a highly diversified portfolio — too much so for my liking. With only $2.2 million in assets, the managers were holding positions in 83 different securities entering '95. That's really spreading yourself thin. Recent returns are about average; the fund gained 11.7 percent for the year ending June 30, '95. No load charges are applied if you purchase directly from the manager (B.C., Ontario, Nova Scotia, and Quebec residents only). Brokers and dealers will charge a sales commission of up to 2 percent, although you might be able to negotiate that. The minimum initial investment has doubled in the past year, to $50,000, which may be spread among several funds in the group (minimum $10,000 per fund). Investors who purchased units of these funds prior to April 1, '94, can still invest under the old guidelines. Formerly the Church Street Equity Fund.

ADMAX CANADIAN PERFORMANCE FUND $ ⇒ G #/*/NO RSP CE

Recent strategy has been to concentrate on export-oriented companies and to increase the emphasis on technology stocks. The result has been some improvement in the performance of this underachiever, with a gain of 10.7 percent for the year ending June 30, '95. However, returns continue to be below average in relation to other funds in this category, so no rating upgrade yet. Note: the Admax funds allow for a negotiable back-end load. If you plan to buy that way, ask to see the full range of options and the dealer sales commissions for each. You'll need that information to negotiate properly. Also, new this year, Admax has a no-load purchase option, which requires you to pay a 0.25 percent annual fee. This may be the best purchase choice if you expect to hold your units less than five years.

ALL-CANADIAN COMPOUND FUND

See entry for All-Canadian CapitalFund.

ALL-CANADIAN CAPITALFUND $$ ⇒ G # RSP CE

It's hard to get a handle on the investment approach of this fund. When it was known as the All-Canadian Dividend Fund, the style was conservative. Then came a shift in strategy, along with a name change, and the fund invested heavily in gold and silver stocks. They represented about a quarter of the portfolio at the beginning of '94. But during that year, the precious metals component was scaled back to just over 15 percent and the fund took on a more balanced look with consumer products the dominant sector. While all this may seem a bit confusing, there's no arguing with the end result. Returns on this fund have been steadily improving, with a solid 16.9 percent gain for the year to June 30, '95. This small fund looks like it is moving towards a higher rating. Available only in Ontario. The All-Canadian Compound Fund is a twin, investing solely in units of the CapitalFund. It is no longer sold. For information, Ontario residents may call (905) 842-8677.

ALTAMIRA CAPITAL GROWTH FUND $$$ ⇒ G NO RSP CE

Altamira now has several Canadian equity funds available, so you have to check carefully to make sure you buy the one that best suits your goals. This one specializes in blue-chip stocks, with an emphasis on those with high dividend yields. So you'll find a lot of familiar names on the portfolio list: Bank of Montreal, Nova, CIBC, Abitibi-Price, BCE, Northern Telecom, etc. Performance has been steadily improving. In fact, over the past couple of years it has outperformed the better-known (and much bigger) Altamira Equity Fund, the company's flagship. Two-year average annual return to June 30, '95, was 10.6 percent, well above average for this category. Better suited to more conservative investors. There are no load charges for the Altamira funds, but there is a small one-time setup fee of $40 when a new account is opened, plus annual trustee fees of $35 for an RRSP/RRIF.

ALTAMIRA EQUITY FUND $$$$ ⇒ G NO RSP CE

This is not the same fund it was during the early '90s, when I began recommending it to readers of this *Guide*. Then it was a small fund that churned out eye-popping returns by zeroing in on high-growth companies and trading them actively. Manager Frank Mersch succeeded in rewarding investors with annual gains of more than 30 percent in four of the five years from 1989 to 1993. Not surprisingly, money poured in and the fund ballooned. It's now pushing $2 billion in assets and the portfolio list reads like a Who's Who of Canadian industry: Bank of Nova Scotia, Seagram, Noranda, Hollinger, Alcan, and the like. A fund of this size, and the increased emphasis on large companies, means the glory days of those 30 percent plus returns are likely gone forever. Which doesn't mean this isn't still a good fund. It's different and, of necessity, more conservative, although Mersch remains an active trader. In '94, the return plunged to a meagre 1.7 percent. But before you allow that to discourage you, consider this: the average Canadian stock fund lost 2.7 percent that year. Altamira Equity's result ranked it number 30 out of 182 funds in this category surveyed by the Southam Information and Technology Group. Not exactly shabby. The 9.4 percent gain in the first half of '95 was also above average, and the fund continued its strong performance through July. The pack is catching up, but this is still a winner and a solid place for your money.

ALTAMIRA SPECIAL GROWTH FUND $ ⇑ G NO RSP CSC

This Altamira entry specializes in emerging growth companies, a tricky and sometimes risky area of investment. It's been a disappointment recently, losing 2.7 percent in the year to June 30, '95. Over two years, the average annual loss is 6.3 percent. Only one small cap fund in Canada did worse during that time. Granted, the small cap market has been weak but many other funds in this category managed substantial gains despite that. Manager Sue Coleman has a lot of stock-picking talent, but she's been struggling with this fund recently. Until she regains her touch, the rating is being dropped to $.

ASSOCIATE INVESTORS LTD. $ ⇒ G NO RSP CE

This is one of the country's older mutual funds, started in '50. It was a solid if unspectacular performer for many years, but has slipped back relative to others in this category. Small blue-chip portfolio. Gained 10.3 percent for the year ending June 30, '95 — not bad, but below the average for Canadian stock funds as a group. Managed by Leon Frazer and Associates. Redemption fee of 1 percent applies when units are cashed within 90 days of purchase, otherwise no load charges. Available in Ontario only.

ATLAS CANADIAN GROWTH FUND $$ ⇒ G NO RSP CE

The Finsco and Jarislowsky Finsco funds were purchased by the brokerage firm of Midland Walwyn at the end of '93. All were renamed in July '94 under the Atlas designation (Midland has another line of funds called Hercules, for those who like classical allusions). This one was formerly the Jarislowsky Finsco Canadian Equity Fund. It was an underperformer in that guise, but initial results under new managers Bissett and Associates of Calgary are promising. I raised the rating a notch in last year's *Guide* on the strength of Bissett's good results with its own funds, and it paid off. The fund gained 13.8 percent for the 12 months to June 30, '95, well above average for this category. The managers invest primarily in larger companies (in fact, this was originally called the Large Cap Canadian Growth Fund). Good first half '95 results can be traced to large holdings in the forestry sector (e.g., Abitibi-Price) and companies that enjoyed big price spurts, like Seagram. Note that all the Atlas funds are no load; previously this was a front-end load fund. This and all the other Atlas funds are available through Midland Walwyn offices, Laurentian Bank, and Financial Concept Group.

BPI CANADIAN EQUITY VALUE FUND $$ ⇒ G #/* RSP CE

Tiny BPI stunned the mutual fund world in '94 by swallowing up one of the giants of the business, Bolton Tremblay. As a result, all the old Bolton Tremblay and Landmark funds disappeared in a top-to-bottom reorganization. Some just had a name change, but most were merged with existing BPI funds to create a new entity. This is one of those cases, spawned from the BT Landmark Canadian Fund and the BPI Canadian Equity Fund. The merged fund is being run by Steven Misener, who was brought into BPI after the BT takeover. He uses a value investing approach, and the portfolio is a mix of large and small companies. Since he's had barely a year on the job, the previous track record of the two merged funds is irrelevant. For the record, results in the first half of '95 were slightly below average, but not enough so to cause concern. This is a wait-and-see situation. Note: along with some other groups, BPI has implemented a negotiable back-end load structure which rewards the sales person on the basis of how large a redemption fee schedule you can be persuaded to accept. Ask to see the complete schedule, and the commission payments attached to it, and then negotiate from there.

BPI CANADIAN SMALL COMPANIES FUND $$ ⇑ G #/* RSP CSC

Previously, this was the BPI Canadian Small Cap Fund and prior to that, the BT Landmark Small Cap Fund. It specializes in small capitalization Canadian stocks, which makes it potentially more volatile than blue-chip funds. So it's not well-suited for conservative investors. This fund was one of the better performers in the old Bolton Tremblay stable, but well-known manager John Sartz no longer runs the show (he has a new fund with Global Strategy). So past results don't count for very much. New manager is Steven Misener, brought into BPI in '94 to beef up the staff after the BT takeover. Initial results have been good; the fund was ahead 12.2 percent for the first half of '95. I've left the rating untouched for now, but if Misener keeps up the pace, it'll move up a notch next year.

BEUTEL GOODMAN CANADIAN EQUITY FUND $$ ⇒ G NO RSP CE

Beutel Goodman is a well-established money management company that earned its reputation in the pension management and investment counselling fields. This is one of a family of funds started in late '90. The managers focus on mid- to large-size companies and emphasize strong fundamentals — firms with low debt, a low price/earnings ratio, and good profit potential. The portfolio is limited to 30 to 40 stocks, a method that enforces a tight discipline. Results so far haven't been bad — but they haven't been very exciting either. Three-year average annual return to June 30, '95, was 11 percent, slightly below average for this category. I think there's a lot of potential here, but it has to translate into more profits before the rating will advance. Note that there's no sales commission if you buy directly from the manager, but you may have to pay up to 4 percent if you purchase units elsewhere. Phone 1-800-461-4551 for information.

BISSETT CANADIAN EQUITY FUND $$$ ⇒ G NO RSP CE

This is a small, Calgary-based fund ($10 million in assets) that's a consistently above-average performer. Stumbled a bit in '94 with a small 2.3 percent loss, but recovered with a nice 10 percent gain in the first half of '95. Portfolio manager Michael Quinn has kept the fund well diversified, with a strong holding of blue-chip stocks plus growth issues. He uses a bottom-up approach to stock selection, with emphasis on a company's fundamentals. This is a solid little fund that's worth more attention than it's received, and I'm raising the rating a notch this year. Minimum investment is $5,000. Sold through the manager at Suite 1120, 500 Fourth Ave. S.W., Calgary, T2P 2V6, phone (403) 266-4664. Can only solicit business in Alberta but can accept purchases from other provinces.

BISSETT SMALL CAP FUND $$ ⇑ G NO RSP CSC

A new entry from the Calgary-based Bissett group, this fund specializes in small Canadian and U.S. companies with a special focus on Western Canada. Had a sensational debut, with a gain of 112.5 percent in '93, its first full year. Came back to earth in '94 with an 8.6 percent loss, but made up that and a little more in the first half of '95. Hard to get a sense of where this one's going, beyond the fact it's been highly volatile so far. Needs more time to shake out.

BULLOCK GROWTH FUND $$$ ⇒ G #/* RSP CSC

A most unusual fund. It targets smaller Canadian companies with better-than-average growth potential, with special emphasis on companies below #100 on the TSE 300 Index. It may also hold up to 20 percent of its assets in units of the Bullock American Fund, although the actual amount has been just 12 percent for the past couple of years. Portfolio is well diversified, with industrial products and communications currently favoured. Results tend to be above average; one-year return to June 30, '95, was 8.3 percent. If you worry about smaller companies and risk, this fund has a lower volatility rating than many others in the small cap category. A major managerial change has just happened here, with the fund taken over on August 1, '95, by the highly respected Kiki Delaney. She was signed up by Spectrum Bullock when they purchased the United funds in spring '95.

CIBC CANADIAN EQUITY FUND $ ⇒ G NO RSP CE

The Bank of Commerce has some decent income funds, but their equity funds lag behind those of their competitors. This is one example. The portfolio looks excellent, with a lot of blue-chip holdings, but the performance has never materialized. Five-year average annual return to June 30, '95, is a meagre 3.5 percent, giving this fund 132nd place out of 135 funds in this category reported by the Southam Information and Technology Group. It pains me to say it because we've banked with CIBC for years, but this fund just isn't cutting it. I can't understand how it's attracted over $360 million in business. Look elsewhere.

CIBC CAPITAL APPRECIATION FUND $ ⇑ G NO RSP CSC

This is a growth-oriented fund that takes a more aggressive approach than the Canadian Equity Fund (above). As a result, it holds more small cap stocks, making it potentially more volatile. It's also a below-average performer, but the average annual three-year returns are substantially better than those of the Equity Fund (12.7 percent versus 7.7 percent). If you must have a CIBC Canadian stock fund, this is the better bet.

CAMBRIDGE GROWTH FUND $ ⇑ G #/* RSP CE

If you study long-term records, this fund looks pretty good. Over the decade to June 30, '95, it produced average annual returns of 11.8 percent. Only one Canadian equity fund did better. But until early '92, the fund was directed by manager Tony Massie, who left the Sagit organization for Global Strategy. Since then, the style of this fund has become much more aggressive, with a lot of junior stocks in the portfolio. That approach paid off big in '93, with a gain of 61.7 percent. But the fund lost 21.3

percent in '94 and struggled to break even in the first half of '95. Sagit's investment approach has become much like that of a major league power hitter — it's out of the park or a strikeout. There's not much middle ground. This isn't my kind of investing, so I'm dropping the rating back two notches this year. But in doing so, I recognize that the home runs will come, and I won't be there. Note that Sagit is one of the fund companies with a negotiable back-end load. Unless you ask, you'll automatically get the most punitive schedule, so do your homework if you plan to buy.

CAMBRIDGE SPECIAL EQUITY FUND $ ⇑ G #/* RSP CSC

Here's another mind-boggling story from Sagit. After three years of losses in a row, including a 26.6 percent drop in '92, investors in this one suddenly won the lottery. The fund gained 146.9 percent in '93. Some of the technology and oil and gas issues took off and bingo! In a small fund, the effect of a few big gainers can be dramatic. Predictably, new investors flooded in — and got hit. The fund dropped 20.3 percent in '94 and a further 4.7 percent in the first half of '95. So, what next? I don't know — which suggests you should be cautious about committing money here. This is for aggressive investors only.

CANADA LIFE CANADIAN
EQUITY S-9 $$ ⇒ G * RSP S CSC

This fund's performance compared to the competition has been slipping in recent years, and in last year's *Guide* I commented that the $$ rating was hanging on by a thread. However, matters have improved a bit; return for the year to June 30, '95, was 12.6 percent. That was slightly above average for Canadian equity funds generally, and substantially better than the results for small to mid-cap funds (this fund focuses on medium and smaller companies). Sold by Canada Life agents and licensed insurance brokers. Redemption fees payable if cashed before seven years. Like all segregated funds, this one carries some guarantees. You'll get a return of at least 75 percent of your contributions at maturity if you hold your units for 10 years. If you die, your estate will receive no less than the full value of your contributions. If the units have gained in value in the meantime, the payouts will, of course, reflect that.

CANADIAN ANAESTHETISTS MUTUAL ACCUMULATING FUND $$ ⇒ G NO RSP CE

The tongue-twister name has been shortened to the acronym CAMAF. That makes it easier to order, but you may want to hold off a while to let the recent changes at the helm take hold. Long-time lead manager Robert J. Bernardo was replaced in 1993 by Laketon Investment Management. Then came an announcement from the directors that Sceptre Investment Counsel, which managed the foreign content part of the portfolio, was turning over the job to Canada Life Investment Management, which has done a superb job with the Canada Life U.S. and International Equity Fund. The immediate impact has been positive; this fund gained an above-average 13.5 percent in the year ending June 30, '95. But more time is needed to assess how well the new team will perform over the long haul, so no change in the rating. Call 1-800-267-4713 for information. Not available in P.E.I.

CANADIAN INVESTMENT FUND $ ⇒ G #/* RSP CE

This is one of the oldest funds in Canada, in existence since '32. The investment style is conservative, with a focus on blue-chip stocks. Many of the companies in the portfolio are household names, like Bell, Seagram, and a bunch of banks. That translates into less risk — but, unfortunately, less profit more often than not. Average annual compound rate of return for the decade ending June 30, '95, was a meagre 5.2 percent, although latest results have been quite a bit better. Very little new money is coming into this fund, and it will likely be folded into one of the other Spectrum funds (probably the Dividend Fund) before long.

CANADIAN PROTECTED FUND $$$ ⇓ G #/* RSP CE

Manager Jean-Pierre Fruchet uses portfolio insurance and market-timing techniques to achieve solid returns while limiting risk. Stated objective is to avoid any down years and to outperform the TSE over two full market cycles. System worked well during market crash year of '87 and kept the fund in the black during the rough markets of '89 and '90. Was the number one performing Canadian equity fund in '90, a year when most funds in this category lost ground, with a gain of 7.9 percent.

Suffered a small loss of 1.5 percent in '94, the first down year in its history — but even that was better than the average Canadian equity fund, which fell 2.7 percent. Over 10 years, returns are slightly above average for Canadian equity funds as a group. The defensive strategy used by Fruchet will tend to underperform when stock markets are strong but will protect investors when markets are falling. So this fund is more suitable to investors who wish to limit risk and are prepared to give up some potential return as a trade-off. This fund is sold through offering memorandum only, which means it's for "sophisticated investors." Minimums to get in are $150,000 for Ontario and Quebec residents, $100,000 for Alberta, New Brunswick, Manitoba, Newfoundland, and Nova Scotia, and $25,000 for B.C. Not sold in the other provinces. You can buy Class A units on a front-end load basis (maximum commission is 5 percent) or Class B units on a back-end load option (maximum 5 percent). Phone (416) 960-4890 for purchase details.

CHOU RRSP FUND $ ⇒ G # RSP CE

Started in '86 as an RRSP-eligible companion to the Chou Associates Fund (see International and Global Funds). Small fund, less than $1 million in assets. Manager Francis Chou seeks to minimize risk, selecting stocks on the basis of solid value. Long-term results are below average and the fund gained only 2.6 percent for the year ending June 30, '95. Phone (416) 299-6749 for purchase details.

CLEAN ENVIRONMENT
EQUITY FUND $$$ ⇒ G #/* RSP CE

If you're trying to find a socially responsible fund for your investment portfolio, look no further. This is it. Managers Robert Swan and Ian Ihnatowyez have built a winner despite their self-imposed restriction to companies that have shown a strong environmental commitment and do not derive a significant portion of their earnings from products that may cause serious health problems. So who makes their list? High-tech companies like Geac and Mitel, manufacturers like Royal Plastics and Toromont, and even some mining firms, like Barrick Gold. Results have been very good; average annual three-year rate of return to June 30, '95, was 15.7 percent. That's good enough to earn this fund a solid $$$ rating in its first appearance in the *Guide*.

COLONIA EQUITY FUND $ ⇒ G * RSP S CE

Small segregated fund offered by Colonia Life, making its debut in the *Guide* this year. Mandate is to invest in large companies with strong growth potential (a bit of a contradiction in terms). Results haven't been good so far; three-year average annual return to June 30, '95, was a weak 5.7 percent. More recent returns have looked better, however. As with all segregated funds, you get some guarantees. In this case, Colonia undertakes to ensure you'll receive at least 100 percent of the amount originally invested five or more years prior to the policy maturity date; 75 percent of the amount within the last five years. If you die, your estate gets a 100 percent guarantee for all money invested. Sold by Colonia representatives.

CONCORDE GROWTH FUND $$ ⇒ G #/* RSP CE

Small stock fund with a growth orientation. Returns not great, but not bad; gained an average of 10.1 percent a year for the three years to June 30, '95. Sold by Concorde Financial Group, Quebec City; call 1-800-363-0598 for purchase details.

CONFED GROWTH FUND

This fund was part of the ill-fated Confederation Life group. It was sold by the receiver to Burgeonvest Ltd. in mid-'95 and plans for its future are still uncertain.

CONFEDERATION LIFE B FUND

Sold to Maritime Life in May '95. Plans for the future are uncertain.

CORNERSTONE CANADIAN
GROWTH FUND $$ ⇒ G NO RSP CE

Has bounced back nicely after going through a rough period. One-year gain to June 30, '95, was a healthy 17.3 percent. This fund uses a sector rotation approach to investing, focusing on areas of the economy where above-average growth is expected. Sold at branches of North American Trust. They were purchased by Laurentian Bank in fall '95, so look for the Cornerstone funds to be Folded into the Laurentian group soon. Not available east of Ontario.

CUNDILL SECURITY FUND $$$ ⇒ G # RSP CE

Long the ugly duckling of the Cundill duo, this has suddenly emerged into a beautiful swan, to the surprise of
almost everyone except perhaps new manager Tim
McElvaine. He's a bottom-up manager who takes a value
investing approach, sniffing out the bargains others have
passed up. This fund has been around since 1979, but
until McElvaine joined the Cundill organization in 1991
it never did much of anything. Since then it has blos-
somed; three-year average annual rate of return to June
30, '95, was a terrific 20.5 percent. Portfolio is kept small
and easily manageable. This Vancouver-based fund is
still not well-known to Canadian investors (total assets
only $13.4 million). It's worth asking your financial advi-
sor about.

DESJARDINS ENVIRONMENT FUND $$ ⇒ G NO RSP CE

Socially responsible entry from the Quebec-based
Desjardins group. The assets are invested primarily in
Canadian companies that make a contribution toward
improving or maintaining the environment. It's always
interesting to see what companies qualify for the portfolio of these funds. Some of the holdings at the start of '95
were Alberta Energy, Noranda Forest, Alcan, Placer
Dome, and Dofasco. Over the past two years, this has
been the best-performing Desjardins Canadian stock
fund. If you're looking for a socially responsible fund,
this is one of the better choices.

DESJARDINS EQUITY FUND $ ⇒ G NO RSP CE

One of the older mutual funds in Canada (launched in
'56). Mandate is growth through investment in larger
companies, although there are some small and mid-cap
stocks in the mix. Long-term results are well below average for this category — five-year average annual return
of only 6.5 percent for the period ending June 30, '95.
Has looked better recently, however. Purchase through
branches of the Quebec-based Desjardins Trust and
Caisses Desjardins.

DYNAMIC CANADIAN GROWTH FUND $$ ⇑ G NO RSP CE

The big news here was the sudden departure of manager
Jonathan Baird in mid-'95, to be replaced by Michael

Sprung, who was recruited by Dynamic from Aetna Capital Management. A change at the top is always cause for concern. On top of that, this fund's recent performance has been decidedly anaemic, in part due to a heavy weighting in the underachieving gas and oil sector. So while past glories are great (this fund gained 100 percent in '93!), today's realities suggest a downgrade until we see where Sprung is heading. Formerly the Allied Canadian Fund.

DYNAMIC FUND OF CANADA $$ ⇒ G #/* RSP CE

This fund has also been hit by the departure of Jonathan Baird from Dynamic (see above). Perhaps new manager Michael Sprung can breathe some life into it; after a long, profitable run this fund has been looking rather tired lately (two-year average annual return to June 30, '95, was a decidedly unimpressive minus 1.5 percent). Like the Canadian Growth Fund, portfolio in mid-'95 was heavily weighted in energy issues — a sector which will eventually come back, but which has been taking its own sweet time. Rating drops a notch this year while the new manager takes hold.

ELLIOTT & PAGE EQUITY FUND $$ ⇒ G #/* RSP CE

The company suffered a major blow in mid-'93 with the departure of highly respected equity manager John Zechner, but new lead manager Nereo Pittico, who took over at the end of '93, is more than filling his shoes. The 12-month gain on this fund to June 30, '95, was 17.5 percent, well above average for the category. The fund uses a sector rotation approach to stock selection, over-weighting the portfolio in areas of the economy the manager thinks will produce above-average returns. Portfolio size is kept small, about 35 – 40 stocks, a discipline I approve of because it forces managers to make tough decisions rather than simply buying any stock that strikes their fancy. As of spring '95, the largest weightings were in the energy and forestry sectors. Because Pittico is still relatively new to this fund, I'm not changing the rating yet, but it's a candidate for an upgrade with one more good year. One point to watch: along with some other fund groups, Elliott & Page has implemented a negotiable back-end load structure which bases the sales person's commission on how high a redemption schedule he/she can persuade you to accept. If you agree to a schedule starting at 6 percent in year one and declining to 3.5 percent in year six, the broker gets a 5 percent payout from E&P. If you negotiate a schedule starting at 2 percent in year one, the broker only gets a 1 percent commission. Clearly, *you* want the lowest schedule possible — and the broker wants you to accept the highest. Buying a mutual fund is getting to be almost as bad as buying a car! Also, if you go for the back-end load, you may be charged a switching fee if you want to move some assets to another E&P fund. If you're going to invest here, I recommend avoiding the back-end load option, unless you can negotiate the lowest schedule. A low front-end load (say, 2 percent) is a better bet.

EMPIRE ELITE EQUITY FUND $\quad$ \$ $\Rightarrow$ G * RSP S CE

Objective here is capital growth, with income secondary. Large, diversified portfolio mixes both small and large cap companies. Results have been slipping in recent years; all multi-year returns are now well below average. As a result, rating is being downgraded. Sold by Empire Life agents and brokers. Note: although the portfolios aren't exactly the same, there is a great deal of similarity between the holdings of this fund and the Empire Premier Fund (below). The difference is in the purchase option and management fee. The Elite funds are back-end load, with a 2.4 percent annual management charge. The Premier funds are front-end load (5 percent for the first \$100,000, declining after that), but have a lower management fee (2.04 percent). If you're investing for the long term, the Premier funds may be the better choice.

EMPIRE EQUITY GROWTH FUND #3 $\quad$ \$\$ $\Rightarrow$ G # RSP S CE

A solid record over many years. No new investors are being accepted at present; only current unit-holders can add to their stake. The portfolio is similar to those of the Elite Equity and Premier funds, but this fund benefits from a lower management expense ratio, which boosts returns. So if you have the option to buy in, it's the best bet of the three.

EMPIRE PREMIER EQUITY FUND $\quad$ \$\$ $\Rightarrow$ G # RSP S CE

Main investment goal is capital appreciation. Portfolio is similar to other Empire equity funds, but a lower management fee gives it an edge over the Elite Fund. For example, this one gained 10.4 percent for the year to

June 30, '95, while the Elite Fund was ahead only 9.6 percent. See purchase comments in Empire Elite Fund entry, above. Name changed from Equity Growth Fund #1 in January '92. Sold by Empire Life reps.

EQUITABLE LIFE SEGREGATED COMMON STOCK FUND — $$ ⇒ G * RSP S CE

Steadily improving results earn an upgrade this year. Can only be purchased with dividends from participating Equitable insurance policies. If you own such a policy, this is worth your consideration.

ETHICAL GROWTH FUND — $$ ⇒ G #/*/NO RSP CE

This was the first mutual fund in Canada to combine conscience with profits by investing in companies that meet specific standards of practice. Originally launched by the Vancouver City Savings Credit Union, it was taken over by the Credit Union Central of Canada in late '92 to form the cornerstone of a new Ethical Funds family. The manager is Alastair Dunn of Connor, Clark, and Lunn. He brings a conservative style to the fund, moving heavily into cash at times of above-average risk. As well, he will not invest in companies in turnaround situations or firms that have made large acquisitions outside their field of expertise. Ethical screens exclude firms involved in military contracts, the tobacco industry, nuclear power, or unfriendly environmental activities. Performance has been generally lacklustre in the '90s, although the fund has looked better lately, with a gain of 17.1 percent for the year to June 30, '95. A viable alternative for those interested in ethical investing. No load charge if purchased through participating credit unions, otherwise you can pay a front-end load of up to 5 percent or a back-end load with a 4.5 percent maximum. Not sold in Quebec.

EVEREST SPECIAL EQUITY FUND — $$ ⇑ G NO RSP CSC

An aggressive fund, specializing in small- and medium-sized Canadian companies with high growth potential. Objective is to outperform the stock market averages. Started slowly but turned in strong performances from '91 – '93. Gain in '93 alone was an impressive 47.1 percent. But hit rough water in '94, dropping 18.5 percent. The first half of '95 saw a return to profitability, but results were below average for this category. That kind of volatility is not unusual in funds of this type. Strictly for investors who aren't afraid of risk. Sold by branches of Canada Trust.

EVEREST STOCK FUND $$ ⇒ G NO RSP CE

More conservative in style than the Special Equity Fund (above). Invests mainly in blue-chip Canadian stocks with a good sprinkling of U.S. and international equities to make up the foreign content portion. Returns have been good, although they have been tailing off lately compared to the competition. Was ahead 9.6 percent for the year ending June 30, '95, well below average for this category. This is a fund for Canada Trust clients who prefer their stock funds to be a little less daring. Formerly known as Everest Growth Fund.

FICADRE STOCK FUND $ ⇒ G * RSP CE

Long-term results are poor, but this fund has been looking better lately, with a solid 16 percent gain for the year to June 30, '95. Portfolio holdings are mainly of the blue-chip variety. Available only in Quebec through Société Nationale de Fiducie. Formerly SNF Stock Fund.

FIDELITY CAPITAL BUILDER FUND $$ ⇒ G #/* RSP CE

This fund has been a disappointment to investors in recent years, and its five-year returns have now slipped to below average for this category. Boston-based manager George Domolky is a value investor who looks for fundamentally strong companies. He's been coming in for some criticism because of the fund's recent poor performance, but he says he's sticking to his guns. Critics have also noted that this is the only Canadian stock fund that's managed from the U.S. (Boston is home base for the giant Fidelity organization), suggesting that may also be part of the problem. Whatever the reasons for the lacklustre returns, Fidelity had better take steps to fix them fast. This fund is holding $600 million in assets and a lot of that money is going to start to drift away unless returns improve. This one started out as a balanced fund but was converted to a Canadian equity fund in '90. Portfolio emphasis in mid-'95 favoured the resource sector. I said last year that this fund would have to do better to maintain its rating. It hasn't, so I'm cutting it to $$ this year. Note: Fidelity now offers three purchase options for its funds: a back-end load and two front-end loads. One front-end load is identified as the "Sales Charge Option"; it carries a maximum commission of 5 percent. The other is called the "Low Sales Charge Option"; in this case the maximum commission is 2 percent. Since there is no difference in your management fee, whichever option you select, I recommend the Low Sales Charge Option if you are going the front-end load route. In fact, there's no plausible reason for using the other one, unless your broker offers you a sweet deal because he likes the commission structure better.

FIRST CANADIAN EQUITY INDEX FUND $ ⇒ G NO RSP CE

Designed to emulate the performance of the TSE 300 Index. Below-average long-term performance. Average annual compound rate of return for 10-year period to June 30, '95, was 6.2 percent; average for this category was 8.3 percent, according to *The Globe and Mail*. A fund managed by a good stock picker is a better bet. Sold by branches of the Bank of Montreal.

GBC CANADIAN GROWTH FUND $$$ ⇒ G NO RSP CSC

This fund, operated by Pembroke Management Ltd., invests in growth situations, focusing mainly on small to mid-size companies. Major holdings in spring '95 included Videotron Group, Franco-Nevada, Geac Computer, and Rogers Communications. Long-term results are good (five-year average annual compound rate of return of 16.1 percent to June 30, '95). However, more recent results have been slightly below average. The minimum required to invest is $100,000, which effectively shuts out most people. No load if purchased directly from the manager. Dealers may charge up to 3 percent. Phone 1-800-668-7383 for more details.

GENERAL TRUST CANADIAN EQUITY FUND $ ⇒ G NO RSP CE

This fund has been going through some very rough times, but the past year has seen some improvement, with an above-average gain of 14.7 percent for the 12 months to June 30, '95. However, longer-term results are still way below average for this category. The mandate of this fund is to invest in large Canadian companies, but there were several small and mid-size stocks on the portfolio list in mid-'95 as well. Until this year, the Growth Fund (below) had been the better choice for General Trust clients, but this fund has outperformed it lately. Sold through General Trust branches in Quebec only. General Trust is now owned by National Bank, so there could be a marriage of these two fund groups in the future. Note: although this is a no-load fund, you'll be assessed a 2 percent fee if you cash in within three months.

GENERAL TRUST GROWTH FUND $$ ⇒ G NO RSP CSC

The mandate is to invest in more growth-oriented stocks than will normally be found in the Canadian Equity Fund. The portfolio may also hold some short-term bonds. Has not been as strong lately as in the recent past; gain for the year to June 30, '95, was just 4.4 percent. Longer-term results are still better than average when compared to Canadian equity funds as a group. Sold in Quebec only by offices of General Trust.

GLOBAL STRATEGY CANADA
GROWTH FUND $ ⇒ G #/* RSP CE

There was a lot of publicity and anticipation when high-profile fund manager Tony Massie left the Vancouver-based Sagit organization a few years ago and hooked up with Global Strategy to launch this fund. Massie had enjoyed great success with Sagit and much was expected of his new entry. So far, unfortunately, things haven't panned out. The new fund has been profitable, all right — three-year average annual return of 9.5 percent to June 30, '95. Trouble is, the average Canadian equity fund gained 12.1 percent during that period, so Massie wasn't even keeping pace. He's looking for better things in the future, but I suggest you await results before plunging in. Portfolio is conservatively managed, but contains a number of small companies in the mix. Still seems to be in the breaking-in stage. Note: Global Strategy is one of the companies that has a negotiable back-end load structure. If you're planning to buy on that basis, ask for all the details from your sales rep.

GREAT-WEST LIFE CANADIAN
EQUITY FUND $$ ⇒ G */NO RSP S CE

A steady performer that consistently provides solid but not spectacular returns. Five-year average annual return to June 30, '95, was a slightly above-average 8.6 percent. The portfolio is deliberately kept small (a style that enforces valuable discipline on fund managers), and focuses on companies with above-average growth potential. One of the better bets among insurance company segregated funds. Note the two purchase options. You can choose to pay no load and be assessed a higher annual management fee. Or you can buy on a back-end load basis (maximum 4.5 percent declining to zero after seven years) and pay a slightly lower management charge. The difference is small (only 0.12 percent a year). But if you're going to invest in a segregated fund it should be for the long haul, so you may as well realize the savings and choose the back-end load. Sold by representatives of Great-West Life.

GREAT-WEST LIFE EQUITY INDEX FUND $ ⇒ G */NO RSP S CE

This fund is designed to mirror the performance of the TSE 300 Index. When the stock market is strong, it will do well. Example: a 29.7 percent gain in '93. But when the market's down, watch out! I prefer a more actively managed fund, such as the companion Canadian Equity Fund (see above), which consistently outperforms this one. Want proof? The average annual rate of return for this fund for the five years to June 30, '95, was just 5.9 percent. The Canadian Equity Fund averaged 8.6 percent. That should tell you where your money works best, but, ironically, this fund has over $200 million more in assets. That suggests that, for some reason, people prefer it. Obviously, they haven't been reading this *Guide*! All Great-West Life funds guarantee you'll get back at least 75 percent of your contributions when your contract matures. See above for purchase details.

GREEN LINE BLUE-CHIP EQUITY FUND $ ⇒ G NO RSP CE

Originally the FutureLink Canadian Growth Fund; taken over by TD Bank and Green Line as part of the purchase of Central Guaranty Trust. The objective of the fund is to invest in blue-chip stocks with good growth potential — which means it should be doing a lot better than it is. The managers, Sceptre Investment, have an excellent reputation in the industry, but results since they took over haven't been very exciting. The fund gained 9.1 percent for the year ending June 30, '95, but that was well below average for Canadian equity funds generally. It's a puzzle why they aren't doing better, but until some flashes of brilliance appear, choose another Green Line fund.

GREEN LINE CANADIAN EQUITY FUND $$ ⇒ G NO RSP CE

Another equity entry from the ever-expanding Green Line family, this one specializing in growth stocks. Ostensibly higher risk but a better performer than the Blue-Chip Equity Fund, although still tends to be below average for this category. Five-year average annual rate of return to June 30, '95, was 7.3 percent. Management is by Knight, Bain, Seath & Holbrook Capital Management, who have been involved with this fund for some time. Sold at branches of the Toronto-Dominion Bank.

GREEN LINE CANADIAN INDEX FUND $$ ⇒ G NO RSP CE

Designed to mirror the stocks which make up the TSE 300 Index. The Canadian Equity Fund (see above) hasn't been great, but this one has been even less impressive over the longer term, although more recent results are better. I'm not thrilled with any of Green Line's Canadian stock funds, but if you have to choose one, make it the Canadian Equity Fund or this. Sold through TD Bank's Green Line Investors Services.

GUARDIAN CANADIAN EQUITY FUND

Merged with Guardian Growth Equity Fund in December '94.

GUARDIAN ENTERPRISE FUND $ ⇒ G #/* RSP CSC

Mandate is to concentrate on small and medium-sized companies with a strong entrepreneurial bent. Long-term results are below average, although things have been picking up recently. Still, if it's a small cap fund you want, there are much better choices. One bit of good news — Guardian has eliminated the 0.623 percent "financing fee" on back-end load purchases, which many investors found annoying and expensive.

GUARDIAN GROWTH EQUITY FUND $$ ⇒ G #/* RSP CE

A growth-oriented fund, with a mandate to invest in medium to large companies. Concentrates on underpriced companies with strong earnings momentum. Long-term results are above average but recent performance has been, to use Guardian's own word, lacklustre. Here's their explanation, from the 1994 annual report: "Your fund experienced lacklustre performance in the latter part of the year due to an underweighting in cyclicals and an overweighting in energy." The managers still hadn't recovered by the first half of '95; performance was well below average for this category. For years this fund was far and away the best performer among Guardian's Canadian equity entries, to the point where I raised the rating last year. It appears I was premature; this year's rating drops back to $$. Previously known as the Guardian Vantage Fund.

HODGSON ROBERTON LAING CANADIAN FUND $ ⇒ G NO RSP CE

The stated investment objective of this fund is dividend income combined with long-term capital growth. However, the portfolio doesn't show much dividend potential. Entering '95, there wasn't a single bank stock on the list and many of the holdings (e.g., Enserv Corp., Extendicare Inc., Future Shop, Wascana Energy) were in companies that pay no dividends at all. So if dividend income is high on your shopping list of priorities, don't look here. Unfortunately, the growth part of the mandate hasn't been much of a success recently either. This fund lost 2.5 percent over the year to June 30, '95, during a period when most Canadian stock funds were rolling up nice profits. Minimum investment to open an HRL account is $2,500, which may be spread among several funds. Buy directly from the manager at 1-800-268-9622. Formerly Waltaine Canadian Fund.

HONGKONG BANK EQUITY FUND $$ ⇒ G NO RSP CE

This was an index fund until the fall of '92; the mandate was changed at that time to make it a fully managed equity fund under the direction of Greg Bay of Vancouver-based M.K. Wong and Associates. The payoff was instant; in '93 the fund gained 49.9 percent as a result of big profits in oil and gas and lumber shares. That was one of the best performances of all Canadian stock funds for the year. Results slipped substantially in '94, however, with a drop of 7.8 percent. The fund got back into the black in the first half of '95, but performance was still weak. Very large portfolio. Canadian securities tend towards small and medium-sized companies. Some big U.S. blue chips have been mixed in for stability. Needs to regain '93 form.

IMPERIAL GROWTH CANADIAN
EQUITY FUND $$ ⇒ G # RSP S CE

This fund is an example of how long-term results can be deceiving. For many years, this was one of the top-performing equity funds in Canada. That's reflected in an average annual compound rate of return of 12.8 percent over the past decade, the best in this category — even beating out such stalwarts as Trimark Canadian. More recent returns have been less impressive, however. While the fund did gain 11.4 percent during the year ending June 30, '95, that was below the average for this category. Portfolio is well-diversified across all sectors, and consists mainly of large and medium-sized corporations. All Imperial Life funds guarantee that you'll receive at least 75 percent of your contributions at maturity, thereby limiting your risk. Hopefully, you'll never have to fall back on that. Sold through Imperial Life and selected insurance brokers across the country. Load charge is 5 percent on the first $15,000, 3.5 percent thereafter.

INDUSTRIAL ALLIANCE
STOCKS FUND $$$ ⇒ G * RSP S CE

Don't confuse this or any other fund with the Industrial Alliance name with the more widely known Industrial group run by Mackenzie Financial. Industrial Alliance is a Quebec City-based insurance company, and this is part of their segregated fund family. Returns on this fund have been better than average. The portfolio is a mix of blue-chip holdings (lots of banks) and smaller growth companies. It's worth considering if you're a client of the company. Phone (416) 684-5000 for information.

INDUSTRIAL EQUITY FUND $$ ⇑ G #/* RSP CSC

Specializes in emerging growth companies. Languished for several years in the early '90s, along with the other Industrial equity funds, but was one of the hottest funds around in '93 with a 72.6 percent return. Managed a small gain in the first half of '94, when most Canadian equity funds were suffering losses. But the past year has been bad news; the fund lost 7.6 percent for the 12 months to June 30, '95. Sure, small cap stocks were out of favour for much of that time, but several competitors in this area managed gains. Main problem appears to have been the heavy emphasis on the natural resource sector (a favourite of Mackenzie's Industrial Group in good times and bad), particularly the languishing energy sector. This segment of the economy should recover and restore some of the fortunes of this fund. But there are better small cap choices out there now.

INDUSTRIAL FUTURE FUND $$$ ⇒ G #/* RSP CE

The portfolio strategy of this fund took a big shift towards high-tech at just the right time. Manager John Rohr was able to ride the technology wave to a solid 20.3 percent gain for the year ending June 30, '95. This isn't a pure technology fund, however; about a third of the portfolio was still in Mackenzie's beloved resource sector in mid-'95. You have to accept more risk than in the companion Industrial Growth and Industrial Horizon Funds if you put any cash here, but the reward has been returns that are way, way better. Example: the five-year average annual rate of return on this fund to June 30, '95, was 10.3 percent. For Horizon it was 7.2 percent; for Growth, 5.9 percent. If you have money invested with Mackenzie, allocate a small chunk of it (5 or 10 percent) here.

INDUSTRIAL GROWTH FUND $$ ⇒ G #/* RSP CE

This is a diversified fund, investing in both small and large cap companies with a focus on the "producer sector." Like other equity funds in the Industrial Group, it was heavily into resource stocks in mid-'95 (about half the portfolio). Long Mackenzie's flagship fund, it now seems somewhat dated in its style, and the long-term results have now fallen below average (10-year average annual rate of return of 8.2 percent). Manager is the legendary Alex Christ, Mackenzie's founder.

INDUSTRIAL HORIZON FUND $$ ⇒ G #/* RSP CE

For a while, there was little to choose between this fund and its stablemate, Industrial Growth. But recently, this has been redefined as a primarily large cap fund, under the direction of manager Neil Lovatt, Mackenzie's vice-chairman. The make-up of the fund is now quite different from that of Growth; of the top 20 holdings in mid-'95, only five were duplicated between the two. However, Horizon continues to reflect the company's interest in (obsession with?) natural resources, which represent about half the portfolio. Recent performance has been substantially better than that of Growth (an 11.7 percent gain for the year to June 30, '95, versus only 7.5 percent for Growth). But Horizon's results have also slipped below the average for this category.

INVESNAT CANADIAN EQUITY FUND $ ⇒ G NO RSP CE

InvesNat is a no-load fund group offered by National Bank of Canada. Stock selection technique for this fund is a bottom-up approach, based on corporate fundamentals. Long-term results have been slightly below average, although things have been brightening lately — the fund gained 15.2 percent in the year to June 30, '95.

INVESTORS CANADIAN
EQUITY FUND $$$ ⇒ G * RSP CE

Well-diversified portfolio, conservative management style under the capable direction of Scott Penman, who has been at the helm for more than a decade. Largest holdings are blue-chip companies, but there is a good mix of growth-oriented small and medium-sized businesses in the portfolio. Respectable track record with solid, above-average returns. Average annual gain for the decade to June 30, '95, was 9.1 percent (industry average was 8.3 percent). Note the unusual commission structure. There is no front-end load if your total investment in all funds exceeds $10,000 (it's 2.5 percent if your holdings are less than that). A redemption charge will apply if you sell before seven years (maximum 3 percent). This means that if you invest less than $10,000, you'll potentially face *both* a front-end and back-end load. The fund is also assessed an annual "service fee" of 0.5 percent on the market value of your investments (this is over and above the normal management fee). If your total assets are between $35,000 and $150,000, you'll receive a partial rebate of this amount. Over $150,000, you get it all back. Sold through Investors Group representatives, who can give you more details of this rather complex payment structure.

INVESTORS RETIREMENT GROWTH
PORTFOLIO $$ ⇒ G * RSP CE

Investors Group offers a number of "portfolio" funds. These invest in units of several Investors funds, to provide more diversification. The composition of this one has changed since last year's *Guide*; it's now composed 30 percent of units in the Canadian Equity Fund, 20 percent Global Fund, and 50 percent Retirement Mutual Fund. Returns over the past five years have been somewhat better than investing everything in the Retirement Fund, but the Canadian Equity Fund is the best of this bunch.

INVESTORS RETIREMENT MUTUAL FUND $$ ⇒ G * RSP CE

This is a huge fund by Canadian standards, with assets of almost $1.9 billion. It's managed by the same team that runs the Canadian Equity Fund. Not surprisingly, the portfolios of the two are very similar. In fact, there's little to distinguish between them apart from a greater emphasis on blue-chip stocks here and the strange fact that, with the single exception of 1994, the Canadian Equity Fund has produced a better return in every year since 1988. On that basis, I know where my money would go!

INVESTORS SUMMA FUND $$ ⇒ G * RSP CE

A "socially responsible" fund; investment policies preclude companies involved in tobacco, alcohol, munitions, pornography, and gambling. Historic results have been below average for this category, although this was the top-performing Investors Canadian stock fund in the year to June 30, '95, with a gain of 10.9 percent. If ethical investing is important to you, choose it by all means. If it's good returns you want, go with the Canadian Equity Fund.

IVY ENTERPRISE FUND $$ ⇒ G #/* RSP CSC

This is the old Mackenzie Equity Fund, with a new name and a new mandate. Manager Jerry Javasky will be focusing on small cap companies in Canada and the U.S. As a result, previous performance is meaningless. It's too soon to know how this will perform, but Javasky has a solid reputation so we'll give it $$ for now and watch.

JONES HEWARD FUND $$ ⇒ G #/* RSP CE

The Jones Heward Group was a wholly owned subsidiary of the brokerage firm of Burns Fry. As a result, it became an add-on to the sale of Burns Fry to Bank of Montreal in

'94. The fund company continues to operate independently, however. Strategy for this fund favours growth-oriented companies, with some conservative holdings, such as the big banks, added for stability. Performance had been on the upswing, but the fund took a big hit in '94, losing 10.3 percent. That put a potential rating increase on hold. Founded in '39 as Group Investment Ltd., making it one of the oldest continuous funds in Canada.

LAURENTIAN CANADIAN
EQUITY FUND $ ⇒ G #/* RSP CE

The mandate here is to invest primarily in medium to large companies. It's a fund designed for conservative investors, but the results leave much to be desired. The 10-year annual return to June 30, '95, is a well below-average 6 percent. Shorter-term results aren't a lot better. Definitely an underachiever in this category. Maximum front-end load is 3 percent; less if you're a big investor ($50,000 or more). Not available in the Territories. Formerly the Viking Canadian Fund.

LAURENTIAN SPECIAL
EQUITY FUND $$$ ⇑ G #/* RSP CSC

A growth-oriented fund; invests in small to medium-sized companies. More suitable for aggressive investors willing to take a little more risk. Results have been much superior to those of the companion Canadian Equity Fund (above) and are above average for this category over the past couple of years. Returns were given a big lift by a large position in Diamond Fields Resources when the stock soared after a big ore find in Labrador. One of the better bets from this fund company. Formerly called the Endurance Canadian Equity Fund.

LONDON LIFE CANADIAN
EQUITY FUND $$ ⇒ G * RSP S CE

This fund focuses on mid-size to large companies represented on the TSE 300 Index. However, it's not your standard insurance company blue-chip portfolio. The style of this one tends to be somewhat more aggressive, with significant holdings in the resource sector. About as average a performer as you'll find. The annual rate of return over the decade to June 30, '95, was 8.3 percent — bang on the average for all Canadian equity funds over that period. Commission policy changed in '93. All front-end load charges have been eliminated (you used to pay up to 5 percent) and replaced by a declining redemption fee. The bad news is that management and administration fees are up. London Life guarantees a death benefit of not less than the total value of your contributions to any of their funds. There's also a maturity guarantee of at least 75 percent of the value of all contributions. Sold by London Life agents.

MACKENZIE EQUITY FUND

See Ivy Enterprise Fund.

MACKENZIE SENTINEL CANADA EQUITY FUND $$\Rightarrow$ G # RSP CE

Mackenzie Financial took over this and the other Sentinel funds in '88. Not actively marketed at present, and will probably be folded into another Mackenzie fund before long. Rating is a reflection of Mackenzie's apparent disinterest in this fund; actual results are pretty good.

MANULIFE VISTAFUND CAPITAL GAINS GROWTH FUND $$\Rightarrow$ G #/* RSP S CE

All Manulife VistaFunds offer two purchase options. Option one involves paying a 4 percent front-end load, in return for which you're charged a reduced management fee (base rate of 1.625 percent). Option two is a back-end load plan, with a much higher management fee (2.375 percent). The track record of this fund, which emphasizes capital gains, shows that the longer you hold the fund, the better option one looks. Overall, results tend to be better than those of the older Equity Fund (see below). Performance has improved significantly recently since management responsibility was assumed by Altamira.

MANULIFE VISTAFUND EQUITY FUND $\Rightarrow$ G #/* RSP S CE

By the standard of most equity funds, the track record of this one is fair, but its returns tend to lag behind the companion Capital Gains Fund. Emphasis is on large-capitalization stocks with above-average earnings potential. If you're investing for the long term (and why else would you buy an insurance company segregated fund?), the front-end load with the lower management fee (option one) is by far the better choice. Managed by Altamira.

MARATHON EQUITY FUND $$$ ⇑ G NO RSP CSC

A high-roller fund that combines above-average volatility with excellent returns. But beware: the man who produced the eye-popping results for investors, Robert Disbrow, left the helm of this fund in the fall of '94, to be replaced by Wayne Deans of Deans Knight Capital Management. In the first six months under the new boss, the fund showed no signs of slackening its pace, with a big 38.2 percent advance. But it sometimes takes a while for a new manager's style to be felt, so we'll have to wait and see. Purchase units directly from Marathon; phone number is 1-800-661-FUND.

MARITIME LIFE GROWTH FUND $ ⇒ G NO RSP S CE

This long-time sub-par performer changed its managerial approach in late '92 and now employs a multi-manager style. This involves dividing the fund into two segments. Segment one approximates the return on the TSE 300 Index (about 60 percent of the portfolio). Segment two is growth oriented. Five managers are involved in the process. So far investors haven't seen a big payoff from the switch; two-year average annual return to June 30, '95, was a meagre 4.1 percent, well below average. But the jury is still out and things started to pick up in '95. If you're considering investing, however, I'd wait a bit for more evidence the new approach really works. Available on a no-load basis since September '93. Sold through insurance agencies that represent Maritime Life.

MAWER CANADIAN EQUITY FUND $$ ⇒ G NO RSP CE

Small entry from Calgary-based company, specializing in shares of medium to large Canadian corporations. Diversified portfolio with a weighting towards resource stocks in mid-'95. Early returns were weak but has performed better recently. Only solicits business in Alberta and Saskatchewan, but anyone can buy in. There's an initial minimum of $25,000, although the company has the discretion to waive that. Call (403) 267-1989 for information.

MAWER NEW CANADA FUND $$$ ⇑ G NO RSP CSC

This Calgary-based fund zeros in on small cap stocks with good growth potential and sound balance sheets. Started slowly but had a dynamite year in '93 with a big 63.9 percent gain. Hasn't done much since then, however, and is in danger of being downgraded if results don't pick up. Original mandate was to invest in all North American issues, but now focuses on Canada. Worth considering by investors who can handle the potentially higher risk. Name changed from Mawer North American Shares Fund in January '94.

MCLEAN BUDDEN EQUITY
GROWTH FUND $$ ⇒ G NO RSP CE

Specializes in shares of large Canadian companies. Conservative investment policy. Small fund, about $5.2 million in assets. Results for the year to June 30, '95, were slightly above average, with a gain of 12.7 percent. Longer-term results are sub-par. No load if purchased directly from the manager. Call (416) 862-9800 for details.

METLIFE MVP EQUITY FUND $ ⇒ G * RSP S CE

Portfolio doesn't look bad but results have been very weak. Average annual return for the five years to June 30, '95, is just 3.7 percent. There are much better choices out there. Sold by MetLife reps and insurance brokers; no redemption fee if held more than four years.

MULTIPLE OPPORTUNITIES FUND $$$ ⇑ G # RSP CSC

A small, roller-coaster fund for the stout-hearted only, but if you have the guts you could be very well rewarded. Invests mainly in junior companies traded on the Vancouver Stock Exchange. Extremely volatile, see "The Roller-Coaster Funds — Special Report" for more details. But this is volatility with a big payoff. This was one of the top-performing equity funds in Canada for the five years to June 30, '95, with an average annual return of 24.1 percent. Gained over 54 percent in the first six months of '95 alone! When this fund is hot, it's *really* hot. On the basis of performance alone, it definitely rates a $$$ rating, so I'm giving it its due. But the high volatility, the small size of the fund (only $6.4 million in assets), the speculative nature of the investments, and the fact it's only available to B.C. residents are serious negatives. Don't put this one in your RRSP, even though it's eligible. Front-end load of up to 6 percent.

MUTUAL CANADIAN INDEXFUND $ ⇒ G # RSP CE

A fund designed to mirror the performance of the TSE 35 Index. When the market rises, it should too. When the markets are weak, so is the performance of this fund. That's the theory anyway; in fact, the fund's performance has actually lagged behind that of the market, in part because of the 2 percent management expense ratio. Average annual return over the five years to June 30, '95, was only 5.7 percent. If you want to play the TSE 35 Index, TIPS are a better bet. Maximum load has been reduced; it's now 3.75 percent, less if you invest over $100,000. Sold by Mutual Investco.

MUTUAL EQUIFUND $ ⇒ G # RSP CE

A managed fund that invests primarily in Canadian common stocks. Also holds American issues. Returns have been well below average. There's really not much to choose between this and the Indexfund; both are poor performers, although the Indexfund tends to have better results.

NAL CANADIAN EQUITY FUND $ ⇒ G * RSP S CE

The emphasis of this fund is on larger, well-established companies, although there are a number of growth stocks in the portfolio. The managers, Elliott & Page (a wholly owned subsidiary of North American Life), use a sector rotation approach, weighting the portfolio towards areas of the economy they think will outperform. Long-term results have been below average; five-year annual return to June 30, '95, was just 6.7 percent. However, performance has improved markedly recently, with a 16.4 percent gain over the past 12 months. Could this be a trend? We'll watch with interest. Redemption fee if sold within five years. Offered by representatives of North American Life.

NN CANADIAN GROWTH FUND $ ⇒ G * RSP S CE

This fund focuses on stocks on the TSE 300 Index, with a healthy measure of smaller growth stocks and U.S. blue chips tossed in. Co-managed by Jones Heward and

Corporate Investment Associates (who run some of the Royal Trust funds). Continues to be an uninspiring performer. Average annual compound rate of return for the decade to June 30, '95, was only 4.5 percent. Recent results aren't much better. Like all NN funds, 75 percent of the money you invest is guaranteed by the company, effectively putting a floor under any potential losses. Sold by representatives of NN Life Insurance.

NN CANADIAN 35 INDEX FUND $$ ⇒ G * RSP S CE

Designed to track the TSE 35 Index. Results have improved significantly over the past year; return for year ending June 30, '95, was 16 percent. Longer-term results are well below average. Neither NN Canadian fund is particularly impressive, but if you must have one this looks like the better bet at this time.

NATIONAL LIFE EQUITIES FUND $$$ ⇒ G * RSP S CE

High-performing insurance company fund that focuses on growth stocks and special situations. Excellent long-term results; average annual rate of return for the decade ending June 30, '95, was 10.3 percent. The consistency of performance is also impressive. The fund had only one losing year in the past decade ('90). Never a world-beater, but solid — perfect for an insurance firm. As with all segregated funds, offers guarantees to protect you on the downside. Get details from representatives of National Life.

NATIONAL TRUST CANADIAN EQUITY FUND $ ⇒ G NO RSP CE

The rating of this fund was cut back last year because of a declining performance trend. There's a modest improvement to report — the fund gained 11.9 percent for the year to June 30, '95. But that was still slightly below average for this category. The portfolio is essentially blue chip in nature, with lots of banks and utilities at the core. Not exciting, but not as risky as some other funds either. Purchase through National Trust branches.

OPTIMUM STOCK FUND $ ⇒ G NO RSP CE

Unimpressive entry, results have been below average. Available in Quebec only. Can be purchased no load through Placements Optimum du St-Laurent, phone 1-800-363-7675. Formerly known as St. Laurent Optimum Stock Fund.

PHILLIPS, HAGER & NORTH
CANADIAN EQUITY FUND $$ ⇒ G NO RSP CE

Long one of the steadiest performers around but went into a sharp decline in the early '90s. Weak results were attributed to an overconcentration on old growth companies that had come to the end of their cycle. PH&N made some changes in its strategy, strengthening the management team and paying more attention to growth sectors like technology. We've started to see the payoff: the fund managed a small 3.9 percent gain in '94 at a time when many competitors were losing money. That was followed with an above-average 8.6 percent gain in the first half of '95. One more good year will see the restoration of a $$$ rating. Minimum initial investment is a hefty $25,000, with subsequent minimum purchases of $5,000. RRSP accounts can be opened with $3,500 if the RRSP is held by PH&N. Order direct from PH&N; phone 1-800-661-6141.

PHILLIPS, HAGER & NORTH
RSP/RIF EQUITY FUND $$ ⇒ G NO RSP CE

Performance pattern is, not unexpectedly, similar to the company's Canadian Fund, so the same comments apply. The portfolios are also similar; the main difference is that a chunk of this fund's holdings are in foreign securities (12.8 percent as of mid-'95), thus providing international diversification. As a result, returns tend to be slightly better than those of companion Canadian Equity Fund.

PHILLIPS, HAGER & NORTH
VINTAGE FUND $$$ ⇒ G NO RSP CSC

This was in the front rank of Canadian equity funds from '89 to '92, dropped off a bit for a while, but is now churning out fine returns once again. This is the most aggressive fund in the Phillips, Hager & North family, specializing in small cap stocks. A portion of the assets (13.5 percent in mid-'95) is invested in international securities. This fund was closed to new subscribers in March '93, so if you aren't already in, it's too late. Current unit-holders are allowed to add to their holdings, however.

PRUDENTIAL GROWTH FUND
CANADA LTD. $$ ⟹ G # RSP CE

This fund is coming off an excellent year (up 22.7 percent for the 12 months to June 30, '95). But let's keep things in perspective. A big chunk of the profit came from a 219,000 share position in Diamond Fields Resources, the company that set out to search for diamonds in Labrador and instead came up with the biggest nickel find since Sudbury. Share values soared and the fund quintupled its million-dollar stake. Next to that, all else paled. It just goes to show that one big bet can have a dramatic effect on a fund's performance numbers. Over the years, this fund has been a so-so performer — not particularly good nor bad. But the big boost from Diamond Fields has helped inflate the longer-term averages as well, to the point where they look pretty outstanding. However, I'm not going to move up the rating on the strength of one great stock pick, especially since lead manager Veronika Hirsch has moved over to AGF. Let's wait and see whether the new manager can sustain this momentum. Maximum sales fee is 5 percent. Sold by Prudential Fund Management; phone 1-800-463-6778 for information.

PURSUIT CANADIAN
EQUITY FUND $$ ⟹ G #/NO RSP CE

This fund is run by Nigel Stephens Counsel Inc. of North York, Ontario, a firm that employs a systematic and highly disciplined approach to stock selection. Results since they took over (the fund had two previous incarnations) have been encouraging; the portfolio gained an average of 11.2 percent a year for the five-year period ending June 30, '95, well above average for this category. However, '94 was rough, with a loss of 4.8 percent. The fund invests in a combination of blue-chip and emerging growth companies, with a strong foreign component. If you buy through a broker or mutual funds sales person, you'll pay a negotiable front-end load of up to 5 percent. Alternatively, you can pay an annual service fee of up to 0.5 percent, or a combination of the two. There is no load fee if you buy direct from the manager. Minimum initial purchase is $10,000. Call (416) 502-9300 for information. Sold only in Ontario.

ROYAL LIFE EQUITY FUND $$ ⇒ G * RSP S CE

This is a value-oriented fund that uses a bottom-up approach for stock selection, emphasizing corporate fundamentals. Conservatively managed, with blue-chip issues favoured. Results have been slightly above average for this category, with a five-year average annual compound rate of return of 9 percent. All Royal Life funds guarantee you won't get back less than you invested on death or at policy maturity, so there's solid downside protection. Sold by Royal Life representatives.

ROYAL TRUST CANADIAN STOCK FUND $ ⇒ G NO RSP CE

This fund offers a large, diverse portfolio that tends towards blue-chip holdings. Long-term results are well below average. 10-year average annual return to June 30, '95, was 6.8 percent, compared to an average for this category of 8.3 percent. More recent results have been slightly better. This fund is slated to be merged with the RoyFund Equity Fund in '96 to form a single Royal Canadian Equity Fund. This one is only available at Royal Trust, but the merged version will be available to both RT and Royal Bank customers.

ROYFUND CANADIAN EQUITY $$ ⇒ G NO RSP CE

This is Royal Bank's blue-chip stock fund. It went through a rough period in the early '90s, but has looked much better recently, with an above-average annual three-year rate of return of 14.4 percent to June 30, '95. This fund will merge with the Royal Trust Canadian Stock Fund around the end of '96 to form a single mega-fund.

SAVINGS AND INVESTMENT TRUST CANADIAN FUND $$ ⇒ G NO RSP CE

Primary mandate is to invest in shares of large Canadian corporations, but smaller companies with high growth potential are also included in the portfolio. Long-term results have been below average, with a 10-year average annual rate of return of 6.8 percent. But this fund has been looking much better recently and scored a nice

17.1 percent gain in the year to June 30, '95. Sold by Savings and Investment Trust (Trust Prêt et Revenu). Available in Quebec and Ontario.

SAXON SMALL CAP FUND $$ ⇑ G NO RSP CSC

Specializes in small Canadian companies, with a market capitalization of less than $150 million. Potentially higher risk than regular stock funds because of small size ($5 million) and type of investments. A solid performer from '91 to '93, but results have slipped recently. Managed by Richard Howson and Robert Tattersall, who use a value investing approach. Available only in Ontario; call (416) 979-1818 for information.

SAXON STOCK FUND $$ ⇒ G NO RSP CE

This tiny fund ($4.3 million) is something of an in-and-outer. It had good years in '92 and '93 but slipped badly relative to the competition in '94. The first half of '95 was exceptionally strong, however, with a 21 percent gain that pulled up all the averages. Portfolio contains more large company stocks than you'll find in the Small Cap Fund (above), although emphasis here is also on growth. See above entry for purchase details.

SCEPTRE EQUITY FUND $$$ ⇒ G NO RSP CE

Allan Jacobs, who took over as manager of this fund in May '93, has breathed new life into it, and investors are delighted. After several years of so-so returns, Jacobs has piloted this fund to an average annual return of 23.2 percent for the two-year period ending June 30, '95. Only one broadly based Canadian equity fund did better. He brings more aggressiveness to the portfolio, taking a stronger position in small cap stocks than his predecessor, but this is not a small cap fund (although some mutual fund surveys show it as such). The portfolio includes several large companies, such as Alcan, Nova, Bombardier, Seagram, and some banks. There is also some exposure to international markets with holdings in the Sceptre Asian Growth and International funds. Rating is upgraded to $$$ this year. No load if purchased directly from the manager (Ontario residents only); phone 1-800-265-1888 for information. Elsewhere, you'll have to buy through a dealer and pay a sales commission of up to 2 percent.

SCOTIA EXCELSIOR BLUE CHIP FUND $ ⇒ G NO RSP CE

A Scotiabank offering. Performance has been below average; annual return for the five years ending June 30, '95, was 7.2 percent. Emphasis is on growth-oriented stocks; there are several other funds that fulfil this goal more effectively. Available through certain branches of the Bank of Nova Scotia in most provinces or from the brokerage firm of ScotiaMcLeod. Note that if you buy through ScotiaMcLeod, you'll pay a $15 fee for each purchase or redemption. Name changed from Scotia Canadian Equity Growth Fund in August '95.

SCOTIA EXCELSIOR CANADIAN GROWTH FUND $$$ ⇒ G NO RSP CE

This is the old Montreal Trust Excelsior Equity Fund. The Montreal Trust family was merged with the Scotia funds in October '95, but this solid performer was left intact, with the same management team. Results have been steadily improving. The managers stick close to home; at the start of '95 the fund was fully invested in Canadian stocks, with no foreign content. Average annual return for the 10 years to June 30, '95, is slightly above the norm, at 8.6 percent. Latest one-year gain was a very strong 19.6 percent. This no-load entry is well worth considering, especially if you're already a Bank of Nova Scotia client. Also available at Montreal Trust branches.

SPECTRUM CANADIAN EQUITY FUND $ ⇒ G #/* RSP CE

A blue-chip, value-oriented fund with a sub-par track record. Portfolio manager is Sun Life of Canada Investment Management (Sun Life owns Spectrum). There was a suggestion that responsibility for this one would move to Kiki Delaney (who is taking over Bullock Growth), but that's not happening. Long-term results are weak, with an average annual gain of 5.8 percent for the five-year period to June 30, '95.

STANDARD LIFE IDEAL EQUITY FUND $$ ⇒ G * RSP S CE

An improving performer from Standard Life Assurance. Don't confuse this (and it's easy to do) with the new Standard Life Equity Mutual Fund, which is not a segregated fund and is still too new to qualify for a rating here. Five-year results are slightly above average; more recent returns are substantially above (one-year return to June 30, '95, was 15.8 percent). Sold by Standard Life reps. Formerly called Standard Life Equity 2000 Fund and before that, Standard Equifund.

STRATA GROWTH FUND $\Rightarrow$ G # RSP CE

This fund family was launched under the sponsorship of Prudential Assurance. However, the funds have since been sold to Mutual Life, which plans to merge them with its own family — which means they're not long for this world. That being the case, there's not much point examining them. Check out the entries for the Mutual Group of funds instead.

TALVEST GROWTH FUND $$ \Rightarrow$ G #/* RSP CE

Manager Philippe Girard looks for value in his stock selections, searching for "the 50 cheapest stocks on the TSE 300." Lately, his approach has started to pay off. The fund gained 18.7 percent in the year to June 30, '95, well above average for this category. That big gain boosted performance numbers across the board; 10-year annual returns have now moved to a better-than-average 8.8 percent. All this merits an upgrade in the rating this year. Front-end load is a maximum of 5 percent. Back-end load is maximum 5.5 percent when you cash in, declining over seven years.

TEMPLETON CANADIAN
STOCK FUND $$ \Rightarrow$ G #/* RSP CE

The Templeton group's only dedicated Canadian equity fund. Was a very poor performer in its first three years. However, it began to look better in '93, with a gain of 36.5 percent and managed to eke out a tiny gain in '94, when many Canadian equity funds were losing money. The first seven months of '95 weren't bad either, with a gain of about 7.5 percent. It looks like a turnaround is taking hold. A glance down the portfolio of this fund may surprise you, however. You'll find companies like Banco Popular Espanol, Banque Nationale de Paris, Deutsche Bank, Telefonos de Mexico, GIO Australia Holdings, British Airways, and many more. Templeton is obviously using its worldwide expertise to make the most of the foreign content allowance of this fund. This is one that should continue to improve (Templeton has acknowledged the need to strengthen their Canadian component). But it's too early yet for an upgrade. Maximum front-end load is 6 percent. There's also a back-end load option (maximum 6 percent). Name changed from Templeton Heritage Retirement Fund.

TOP FIFTY EQUITY FUND $ ⇒ G # RSP CE

Vancouver-based newcomer that originally aimed at outperforming the TSE by investing mainly in senior blue-chip companies. When results came in below average, mandate was changed to allow stocks of medium-sized companies as well. It helped a bit; the fund gained 9.4 percent in the year ending June 30, '95. But that was still well below average for this category. Maximum load of 5 percent. Open to B.C. residents only.

TRANS-CANADA EQUITY FUND $ ⇒ G #/* RSP CE

Sagit Investment Management of Vancouver, which runs the Trans-Canada and Cambridge funds, has established a reputation of taking a go-go, highly aggressive approach to portfolio management. That means you'll usually find a lot of junior VSE issues in their funds. This is one of the company's more conservative portfolios, however. It's a much smaller fund than the companion Cambridge Growth, and there are more recognizable blue-chip names, from Royal Bank to Microsoft. Looking at those holdings, I would expect this fund to be doing a lot better than it is. However, it lost 3.9 percent over the past year, during a period when both Canadian and U.S. markets were strong and the average Canadian equity fund was ahead 12.2 percent. Unfortunately, a few big losers (Advanced Gravis, Journey's End, Pagurian, Royal LePage) pulled everything else down. Not one of my recommendations. See Cambridge Equity Fund for information on the negotiable back-end load.

TRANS-CANADA PENSION FUND $$ ⇒ G #/* RSP CE

A stablemate to the Trans-Canada Equity Fund, specifically intended for pension plans. As a result, the portfolio is the most conservative of the Sagit Canadian equity entries (althought it still has a rating of nine on a scale of 10). Recent returns have been much better than for the companion Equity Fund or Cambridge Growth, so if it's a Sagit Canadian stock fund you want, this may be the best choice. It's a tiny fund, however, with assets of just over $1 million, which is one of the reasons for volatility. Formerly MER Equity Fund, taken over by Sagit Management in '89.

TRIMARK CANADIAN FUND $$$$ ⇒ G # RSP CE

Solid, long-term performer; has one of the best 10-year records in the country with an average annual return of 11.5 percent to June 30, '95. Continues to do well. Gain over the past 12 months was slightly below average for this category, at 11.4 percent, but that's hardly enough to warrant a downgrade after so many solid years. Still, there is a bit of cause for concern here; two top Trimark managers left within the past year and that's always a potential problem. However, Robert Krembil, one of the best in the business, is still around to oversee the portfolio management team. Trimark uses a highly disciplined stock selection approach and is known for strong client service. This is one of the few groups that does not saddle investors with the administration expenses of each fund; except for brokerage charges, these are paid for directly by the management company instead of from fund assets. As a result, this fund has a relatively low management expense ratio (1.55 percent). A favourite of brokers and mutual fund dealers, as well as a profit-maker for clients. Highly recommended. The main difference between this and the other two Trimark Canadian equity funds are the purchase options; this one is strictly front-end load.

TRIMARK RSP EQUITY FUND $$$$ ⇒ G * RSP CE

This is now the largest Canadian equity fund in the country, with almost $2.3 billion in assets. It's a back-end load companion to the Trimark Canadian Fund (see above). Investors pay a higher management fee (2 percent) for the privilege of avoiding upfront sales commissions. Investment team and strategy are the same as for the Canadian Fund and the portfolios are similar, although not identical. Generally, the Canadian Fund tends to outperform this one, at least on a nominal basis, partly because of the lower management fee. However, once you take the front-end load into account (which the mutual fund survey results published in the media don't do), you'll find there's not a lot to choose between the two funds. For example, the Canadian Fund gained an average of 11.4 percent a year over the past five years; the average for this one was 10.7 percent. But if you paid a 3 percent front-end load for the Canadian Fund, your actual five-year return averages out to 10.7 percent — exactly the same. So which fund to choose? All else being equal, the longer you hold a fund, the greater the advantage of a lower annual management fee. Make your decision on that basis. There's a third choice: Trimark Select Canadian Growth Fund, which is an optional front- or back-end load. It's still too new to qualify for a rating, but it has the highest management fee of the three (2.41 percent).

20-20 CANADIAN GROWTH FUND $$ ⇒ G #/* RSP CE

This has been a below-average performer for some time, but there are indications that co-managers Rick Betts (small and mid-cap stocks) and Chuck Roth (large cap) may be finally getting it on track. Profit for the year ending June 30, '95, was 14.5 percent and that was followed with a solid 2.7 percent gain in July — all above-average figures for this category. Focus is on larger companies, but the fund has made some nice gains from smaller firms like Hummingbird, Cinram, and Pallet Pallet. Looking a lot better now, and rating is raised accordingly. Note: if you choose the back-end option, you may redeem up to 10 percent of your units each year without charge. If your RRIF account is over $25,000, trustee fees are free. Formerly the DK Enterprise Fund.

UNITED CANADIAN EQUITY FUND $$$ ⇒ G #/* RSP CE

Oh dear. Manager Catherine (Kiki) Delaney only produced a return of 11.1 percent for the year to June 30, '95. So what's wrong with that? Well, not a lot — except that it was less than the average Canadian stock fund during that period and not up to the level we've come to expect since Ms. Delaney assumed management responsibility for this fund in the fall of '92. Still, this fund's total return for the two-and-a-half years from the start of '93 to mid-'95 is a respectable 24 percent. That was good enough to persuade Sun Life, the owners of the Spectrum Bullock group, to ensure Ms. Delaney was lined up for a five-year contract extension before completing the deal that saw them take over the United funds in mid-'95. This fund will normally hold a larger proportion of blue-chip stocks than the companion Growth Fund (below). Formerly called United Accumulative Retirement Fund. Worth your attention.

UNITED CANADIAN GROWTH
FUND $$$ ⇑ G #/* RSP CSC

Specializes in small and medium-sized companies with
good growth potential, which makes it potentially more
volatile than the companion United Canadian Equity
Fund (above). It has also been much more profitable, however, under the direction of Kiki Delaney. Gain for the 12
months to June 30, '95, was a mouth-watering 20.3 percent. Aggressive investors should take a look. Name
changed from United Venture Retirement Fund in '92.

UNIVERSAL CANADIAN
EQUITY FUND $$$ ⇒ G #/* RSP CE

Managed by Mackenzie Financial for many years for the
old Universal Group (now Canadian International).
Mackenzie bought this and four other Universal funds
early in '93 and this fund's future was in limbo for some
time. But now things have changed with the naming of
former Trimark managers Dina DeGeer and Bill Kanko to
oversee operations here. They come from the highly disciplined Trimark school of investing and their contribution could mean nice profits for investors. Since they
haven't really had an opportunity to take hold yet, I'm
assigning the fund a *$$* rating for now — but I expect it
to do a lot better than that suggests over time. Formerly
known as the Universal Savings Equity Fund.

UNIVERSITY AVENUE CANADIAN
FUND $$ ⇒ G NO RSP CE

Interesting newcomer, with terrific early record. Scored
big gains in each of '91, '92, and '93 before sputtering to
a 9.5 percent loss in '94. The first half of '95 was a little
better, with a 3.4 percent gain, but that was well below
average. So what's the real story on this one — the first
three years, or the past 18 months? Frankly, I don't
know, which is why I'd advise some caution on putting
your money here. The portfolio is an eclectic mix of big
companies (lots of banks) and up-and-coming high-tech
operations. The portfolio is quite small ($18 million),
which means that a couple of big gains or losses can dis-
tort results. One of the other mutual fund guides rated
this among the top funds in the country last year. It may
be, one day — but I think that designation is premature.
New manager Jonathan Baird, who took over in fall '95,

will try to make it happen, however. Available in Ontario, B.C., and Alberta. No sales commission if purchased directly from the manager, but dealers may charge up to 4 percent. Phone 1-800-465-1812 for information.

WESTBURY CANADIAN LIFE EQUITY GROWTH FUND $\Rightarrow$ G NO RSP S CE

Aim is to track the performance of the TSE 35 Index. Had a good year in '93, with a 31.9 percent gain but dropped 4.7 percent in '94. The first half of '95 saw a return to profitability, but only modestly so. Not a strong performer. Tip to Westbury clients: the company also maintains another Canadian stock fund, known as Westbury Fund "A". It's closed to new subscribers, but if you're already in, you can buy more units. It has been by far the better performer in recent years, so if you're eligible for it, I recommend going that route. Sold by Westbury Life representatives.

Canadian Equity Funds (Sector)

Sector funds specialize in a particular area of the economy. In the past, there haven't been many in Canada except for natural resource funds. But several new ones have appeared in recent years, so I've created a special section for them.

Sector funds are notoriously volatile. When the area of the economy in which they specialize gets hot, a given fund can double in value in less than a year. But when the sector falls out of favour, watch out — unit values can plunge! ■

Generally, I suggest using some market timing here — in many cases, especially resource funds, these are not suitable as buy-and-hold vehicles. If you're not confident in your ability to pick the best buy and sell points, consult a professional advisor or choose a more broadly based fund.

RATINGS CHANGES

It was a tough year for resource funds. As a result, several have been downgraded in this edition. Those experiencing the biggest change were the AGF Canadian Resource Fund, the Royal Energy Fund, the AltaFund, and the Altamira Resource Fund, all of which dropped from $$$ to $$.

1996 RATINGS

AGF CANADIAN RESOURCES
FUND $$ ⇑ G #/*/NO RSP SEC

After a dismal '94 (-12.1 percent) this fund rallied smartly in the first half of '95, with an 8.2 percent gain. It might have done better with a different portfolio mix, however — at the end of March, holdings in the surging paper and forest products sector were only 2.2 percent of the portfolio, while oil and gas stocks, which weren't doing much of anything, accounted for almost half the holdings. Over the long term, this fund has been a below-average performer and we're getting to a stage in the business cycle when resource funds can be quite high risk, so I'm downgrading the rating to $$ this year. However, it could be good for one more big profit run before the next downturn.

ALL-CANADIAN CONSUMERFUND $$ ⇒ G # RSP SEC

Here's a switch. This was originally an income fund, operating under the name All-Canadian Revenue Growth Fund. The name was changed in December '92 and so was the direction. It now focuses on consumer-oriented securities; the small portfolio includes such stocks as Canadian Tire, Coca-Cola, George Weston Ltd., Molson, and the like. The goal of the managers is to seek out undervalued stocks in this sector. The fund turned in a gain of 11 percent in the year to June 30, '95, quite respectable by industry standards. A sector fund that concentrates on consumer products doesn't thrill me, but it's holding its own at this stage of the business cycle. Available only in Ontario.

ALL-CANADIAN RESOURCES
CORPORATION $$ ⇑ G # RSP PM

This used to be a broadly based resource fund, but it now concentrates entirely on precious metals. The managers have generated some good returns recently; gain for the

12 months to June 30, '95, was 11.8 percent. Formerly called Natural Resources Growth Fund. Available in Ontario only.

ALTAFUND INVESTMENT
CORPORATION $$ ⇑ G NO RSP SEC

To my knowledge, this Altamira entry is the only fund in the country that focuses on businesses with a significant presence in Western Canada. As such, it's strongly oriented to the resource sector (although not exclusively so) and is therefore likely to be more volatile than more broadly based equity funds. This fund got off to an excellent start, with solid returns in '92 and '93. It suffered a small loss (2.9 percent) in '94, but bounced back smartly with an 8.4 percent gain in the first half of '95. One concern for investors: respected former manager Norman Lamarche has relinquished his responsibilities for what Altamira describes as an "extended sabbatical." His position has been assumed by David Taylor, who formerly managed pension money for a teachers' organization. There hasn't been enough time for him to put his own stamp on this portfolio yet, so it's unclear what effect, if any, this changeover will have. Until we can get a better reading, I'm reducing the rating a notch.

ALTAMIRA RESOURCE FUND $$ ⇑ G NO RSP SEC

This fund was also managed by Norman Lamarche, who has left the post on a leave of absence. Here again, David Taylor is the replacement so we have a new hand at the tiller. The portfolio was dominated by three categories in spring '95: oil and gas (29.5 percent of total assets), gold and precious metals (24.4 percent), and forest products (23.8 percent). Recent results have not been good; the fund dropped 10.8 percent in the year ending June 30, '95. I said in last year's edition that I thought resource stocks had some life left in the current cycle, and I still believe that. But this is a volatile fund with a new manager at the helm, so don't overcommit and make sure you can handle the risk. At this stage, I prefer the AltaFund because of the greater diversification it offers.

BPI CANADIAN RESOURCE FUND $$ ⇑ G #/* RSP SEC

Name changed from BT Landmark Resource Fund as part of the BPI takeover of the Bolton Tremblay Funds.

New manager is Fred Dalley of BPI, who hasn't really had enough time for us to see what he can do. Portfolio has a lot of forestry issues, which began to perform well in mid-'95, but was most heavily weighted to metals and minerals, and the energy sector. Last year, I suggested a wait and see policy here. This year, I'd advise you to wait some more. If you do invest, remember that resource funds are notoriously volatile. Best suited to more aggressive investors.

CAMBRIDGE RESOURCE FUND $ ⇑ G #/* RSP SEC

This is a fund that has lost money in more years than it has turned a profit in this decade. But when it wins, it wins big — 31.9 percent in '92, followed by 85.3 percent in '93. Since then, it's been mostly downhill — the fund dropped 16.5 percent in the year to June 30, '95. There are a lot of junior mines and oils in this portfolio — very few names the average investor will recognize. So this is high-risk stuff, with warrants that can increase in value from $30 to $56,000 (Miramar Mining) and stocks that can plunge from $315,000 to $64,000 (Olympia Energy). Sagit funds are known for volatility and this is a classic example. You might score big, but don't invest unless you can handle the action.

DOMINION EQUITY RESOURCE FUND $$ ⇑ G NO RSP SEC

A Calgary-based resource fund, specializing (as you might expect) in oil and gas stocks. Coming off a poor year, with a 19.2 percent loss in the 12 months to June 30, '95, due in large part to the heavy emphasis on natural gas issues which were hit by declining prices in the industry. This is the type of fund that will roll up huge gains when the energy sector is hot (it gained almost 80 percent in '93) and bomb out when it's not. Sad to say, it's down more often than it's up; unit-holders lost money in six of the nine years between 1986 and 1994. If you'd bought units at the start of '86, you'd have lost an average of 2.1 percent a year to the end of '94. Highly volatile. Open to B.C., Alberta, Quebec, and Ontario residents; minimum initial investment is $20,000. Call (403) 531-2657 for purchase information. There are no load charges, but an administration fee of 0.5 percent is charged when units are redeemed.

DYNAMIC PRECIOUS METALS FUND $ ⇑ G #/* RSP PM

Some precious metals funds (such as Royal Trust) are coming off hot years. However, this isn't one of them — it lost a fractional 0.4 percent for the 12 months to June 30, '95. Lead manager Jonathan Goodman continues to be bullish, however, predicting that the gold price will reach US$700 by the end of the decade, almost double where it has been languishing for some time. His reasoning is simple: gold demand is outstripping supply, which will inevitably drive up the price. Investors hope he's right (although gold bugs tend to be incurable optimists) while at the same time wondering why this, the largest precious metals fund in Canada, has underperformed most of its major competitors by such a wide margin recently. Part of the answer is the portfolio, which was almost 40 percent invested in gold bullion and platinum in mid-'95, neither one of which was showing much strength. Stock focus is currently on small and medium-sized companies, which the manager feels represent better value than larger gold operations. This is a highly volatile fund which has had some great years (unit values almost doubled in '93). So the elevator can go up, or down, at a sometimes sickening pace. I'm concerned about the weak recent showing, so the rating drops a notch this year.

FIRST HERITAGE FUND $ ⇒ G #/* RSP SEC

A small natural resource fund with below-average returns. Gained 6.4 percent a year on average for the five-year period to June 30, '95. That was the lowest return of any fund in this category according to *The Globe and Mail Report on Business*. Although this is billed as a resource fund, the portfolio includes several companies that don't fall into that category, such as Bank of Montreal, Telus, and TD Bank. The result is lower volatility than other resource funds. That's nice, but higher returns would be even better. Available only in Ontario. Name changed from Canadian Natural Resource Fund in June '94. Call 1-800-268-9165 for information.

GOLDFUND $ ⇑ G # £ PM

If you were in this fund in '93, you had the ride of a lifetime. The unit value more than doubled, something that rarely happens in the mutual fund business. That more than made up for the fact the fund had lost value in three of the four previous years. But if you got in after the big run-up, perhaps attracted by the huge gain, you're now probably wondering why. The fund lost 4.1 percent in '94 and was off a touch in the first half of '95. The net result of all this is an average annual compound rate of return of 12.6 percent to June 30, '95 — even though only one of those years was actually profitable. What is it they say about averages? Maybe this fund has another big run in it, but a quick look at the portfolio tells you how speculative it is. Example one: a $7,676 investment in Orvana Minerals had skyrocketed to $126,575 at the end of June '95. Example two: an original investment of $711,447 in Pioneer Metals was worth only $227,808 on that date. If that's the kind of investing you like, then maybe this fund is for you. I could also recommend a trip to Las Vegas.

GOLDTRUST $ ⇑ G # RSP PM

This is an RRSP/RRIF eligible sibling to Goldfund, although its performance record is a little different. It only lost ground in two years from 1988–92, and its '93 gain, at 82.8 percent, was somewhat lower. But the patterns of the two funds are similar (not surprising since they're both run by CSA Management), as are the portfolios. If you're going this route, I recommend Goldfund; I think gold and gold funds are too speculative for retirement plans — especially these gold funds.

MIDDLEFIELD GROWTH FUND $ ⇑ G #/* RSP SEC

Although this fund can technically invest in anything, its focus is primarily on the resource sector, particularly oil and gas, which accounted for almost three-quarters of the portfolio in mid-'95. That heavy energy weighting cost investors in '94, when the fund dropped 10.7 percent. Returns in the first half of '95 were somewhat better. If the oil patch comes back, this fund will be a winner; if it doesn't, it'll be a long winter for investors.

PRUDENTIAL NATURAL RESOURCE FUND OF CANADA $$$ ⇑ G # RSP SEC

One of the better performers in the volatile natural resources sector, this fund consistently places among the leaders for this grouping. Some very astute picks in the mining area, including a huge gain on more than

100,000 shares in Diamond Fields Resources, contributed to a stellar year for the period to June 30, '95. The fund's 18.6 percent return over that time was topped only by the astounding performance of the Royal Trust Precious Metals Fund. One of the better choices you can make in the natural resource sector, but the departure of manager Veronika Hirsch in late '95 was a blow. Maximum load is 5 percent.

PRUDENTIAL PRECIOUS METALS FUND OF CANADA $$ ⇑ G # RSP PM

Caught fire in '93 (+ 97.7 percent) after doing nothing since '89. Bombed in '94 with a 10.6 percent loss. Then more than recovered that with a 13.9 percent gain in the first half of '95. What to make out of all that? Only that this is a volatile fund and you'd better keep your heart pills handy. But with all of those ups and downs, the average annual return over the past five years is 12 percent. By way of comparison, the average broadly based Canadian equity fund returned only 8.4 percent over that time. Portfolio is mostly in small to medium-sized gold and silver mining companies, with some dabbling in the Northwest Territories diamond rush. Loss of manager Veronika Hirsch may hurt. Sold by Prudential Fund Management.

ROYAL ENERGY FUND $$ ⇑ G NO RSP SEC

Fund's performance waxes and wanes with the fortunes of Canadian energy stocks. Had good years in '92 and '93 with gains of 37.1 percent, and 45.6 percent, respectively. But then fell 7.7 percent in '94 and another 11.2 percent in the first half of '95 as energy stocks did nothing. The volatility of this sector makes it higher risk than regular equity funds — it's definitely not for retired people. Portfolio is shifting towards larger firms, which new manager Gordon Zive believes will reduce risk. I said last year I expected to see this sector rebound. It hasn't yet, but I wouldn't sell at this stage. For aggressive investors only. Now available at both Royal Trust and Royal Bank.

ROYAL PRECIOUS METALS FUND $$ ⇑ G NO RSP PM

Here's a turnaround that was totally unexpected. After years of languishing, largely because of the high bullion content of the portfolio, this fund did the skyrocket trick, gaining an amazing 34.1 percent for the year ending

June 30, '95. The key: less gold (only 5 percent of the portfolio was in metals in mid-'95 and most of that was silver) and good stock picking. Investors benefitted from solid gains in stocks like Goldcorp, Kinross, and Franco-Nevada. Every year won't be as good — the precious metals sector is very volatile, after all. But this switch in portfolio direction and the recent good results merit a rating upgrade this year. Now available at both Royal Bank and Royal Trust.

UNIVERSAL CANADIAN RESOURCE FUND $$$ ⇑ G #/* RSP SEC

I keep waiting for this one to have another big year — not as great as '93, perhaps, but gains of almost 90 percent don't happen often. But I've been disappointed up to now. The Canadian resource sector has been doing quite nicely lately — big gains in paper companies, gold mines, some base metals. But this fund hasn't been enjoying the ride — at least not until very recently. It dropped 10.2 percent in value over the 12 months to June 30, '95 — and this after I gave it a $$$ rating last year. But there were signs of a comeback in mid-'95. The fund showed an 8.7 percent advance in the three months to July 31, so maybe it's finally going to start a new run. This is still one of my preferred resource funds, but if you can't stand risk, this isn't the place for you. I'm maintaining the rating this year, but we'd better see results!

U.S. Equity Funds

alk about understatement! In last year's edition, I wrote the following: "I expect U.S. markets to continue to be modestly profitable in 1995, so if you don't have some high-quality U.S. equity funds in your portfolio, I suggest you add some now." ∎

Of course, U.S. stocks were much better than "modestly profitable" in the first half of '95, and U.S. equity funds benefitted accordingly.

Great fun for investors! But, as I warned in the chapter titled "The Year Ahead," be cautious now. Strong market runs are usually followed by a correction and we may see the Dow hit some rough water later in '95 or in the first half of '96. You may want to take some profits and switch some assets into cash for a while.

RATINGS CHANGES

There's a new $$$$ fund this year — the Royal Trust American Stock Fund. It's being promoted to the top rank on the strength of its long, consistent track record, recent excellent returns, quality management, no-load status, and low minimum entry — you can get into this winner for as little as $500.

This is the third U.S. equity fund to receive $$$$ status. The other two, Investors U.S. Growth Fund and Phillips, Hager & North U.S. Fund, retain their position this year, although both turned in slightly sub-par results by their longer-term standards.

Several funds move up to the $$$ level in this edition, including AGF American Growth, Beutel Goodman American Equity, Hyperion Value Line, McLean Budden American Growth, and Scotia Excelsior American Equity. You'll find the background for these changes in the specific fund reviews.

Five funds appear for the first time this year. Three are especially worth your attention: the Royal Zweig Strategic Growth Fund, the RoyFund U.S. Equity Fund (kissing cousin to the $$$$ Royal Trust American Stock Fund), and the Universal U.S. Emerging Growth Fund.

1996 RATINGS

AGF AMERICAN GROWTH
FUND $$$ ⇒ G #/*/NO £ USE

A long-term steady but unspectacular performer that has been looking much better in recent years. This is a blue-chip fund, investing in shares of large, well-established companies with strong fundamentals. Manager Steve Rogers positioned his portfolio to profit from the surge of technology issues in the first half of '95, with major holdings in big movers like Microsoft and Motorola. He has also added to holdings in the health care field. This fund is suitable for more conservative equity investors, because of its emphasis on large companies. One-year return to June 30, '95, was an excellent 24.9 percent. That performance, added to several years of improvement, has earned a rating upgrade.

AGF SPECIAL FUND $$ ⇑ G #/*/NO £ USSC

The first half of '95 wasn't quite as kind to small cap stocks as it was to blue-chip issues. As a result, this fund lagged behind its American Growth Fund stablemate. Still, a 14.6 percent return in six months is not at all bad! This fund is more suited to investors who are prepared to accept the extra risk inherent in small cap stocks, start-ups, and turnaround situations (blue-chip investors should buy the more conservative AGF American Growth Fund). Over the long haul, however, this one has the better record, with a 10-year average annual rate of return of 11.5 percent to June 30, '95, compared to 10.3 percent for American Growth. In last year's *Guide* I downgraded the rating to $$ because of weak performance. The fund bounced back in recent months, but I want another year of evidence before giving it back the third $.

AIC VALUE FUND $$$ ⇒ G #/* £ USE

A U.S. version of the AIC Advantage Fund (see Canadian Equity section), employing the same general approach. Almost half of the fund's portfolio draws on the investing genius of billionaire Warren Buffet, by holding shares in Berkshire Hathaway plus several firms in which that company has large interests (e.g., Coca-Cola). As fund manager Jonathan Wellum points out, Buffet is generally acknowledged as the world's greatest investor, so why not benefit from his wisdom? Since most people can't afford to buy Berkshire Hathaway stock directly (a single share cost over US$24,000 in mid-'95), this is an alternative way to participate (minimum investment is just $500). Other areas of concentration are telecommunications stocks, mutual fund management companies, and other financial services firms. Results have been very good; five-year average annual compound rate of return to June 30, '95, was 15.7 percent. One-year return was 23.7 percent. Worth a look, especially if you're a Warren Buffet fan. Better suited to more aggressive investors. Tip: don't buy into this one at market peaks because of the volatility of telecommunications and financial services stocks. Wait until the price drops and then buy for the long haul.

ADMAX AMERICAN PERFORMANCE FUND

Merged with Admax Global Health Sciences Fund effective July '95.

ALTAMIRA SELECT AMERICAN FUND $$$ ⇑ G NO £ USSC

This fund specializes in small to medium-sized U.S. companies, and manager Ken Abrams of Wellington Management has done an excellent job of fulfilling his mandate so far. Average annual rate of return for the three years to June 30, '95, was 25.6 percent, one of the

best results in this category over that period. This is a
solid choice for aggressive investors willing to accept the
higher risk of a small cap fund.

ATLAS AMERICAN GROWTH FUND $$ ⇒ G NO £ USE

This was originally the Jarislowsky Finsco American
Equity Fund; the name was changed in July '94 when the
Atlas group was created. However, well-known Montreal
investment counsellor Stephen Jarislowsky continues to
manage the fund in its new incarnation. Emphasis is on
larger U.S. companies; portfolio in spring '95 included
holdings such as Phillip Morris, Bristol Myers, Pepsico,
Merck, and Johnson & Johnson. So what you get when
you buy is big corporate America. That was a great place
to be when the Dow was hitting new records in the first
half of '95; this fund jumped 14.7 percent in just six
months. Longer-term results are below average, however.
There are no longer any load charges. Available through
Midland Walwyn.

BPI AMERICAN EQUITY VALUE FUND $$ ⇒ G #/* £ USE

This was formerly the BT Landmark American Fund. It
was acquired by BPI as part of the buyout of Bolton
Tremblay and renamed. The mandate is to invest in
undervalued blue-chip stocks, such as AT&T, Phillip
Morris, and Intel. Fund was not a strong performer in its
previous life but has shown significant improvement
under the direction of new manager Tom Scerbo of
Lazard Frères. Gained 14.2 percent in the first half of
'95, riding the crest of the Dow wave. All BPI funds have
a negotiable back-end load; be sure to get complete
details before making your purchase decision.

BPI AMERICAN SMALL COMPANIES FUND $$$ ⇑ G #/* £ USSC

Started life as the BPI Emerging Growth Fund, then was
the BPI American Equity Growth Fund, now it has yet
another name. You might think all the name changes are
designed to camouflage a lousy fund, but you'd be wrong.
As small cap funds go, this has been one of the best performers, with an average annual return of 21.3 percent
over the past five years. Recent results have continued to
be solid; the fund was up 16.9 percent in the first half of
'95. The mandate is to invest in undervalued small cap
stocks with high growth potential. Managed by Michael

Rome of the highly respected New York house of Lazard Frères. Tends to be more volatile than broadly based U.S. stock funds, but if you're an aggressive investor this is one of the best bets in the BPI stable.

BEUTEL GOODMAN AMERICAN EQUITY FUND $$$ ⇒ G NO £ USE

The most promising of the new fund entries from the investment house of Beutel Goodman, this fund has been racking up big gains for investors since its debut in late '90. Three-year average annual compound rate of return to June 30, '95, was just over 19 percent, compared to an average for this group of 13.7 percent. The managers use a highly disciplined stock selection approach, searching out companies with low debt, a reasonable stock price, and above-average growth potential. The good results so far have earned the fund a $$$ rating this year, but a word of caution: the portfolio is still very small (just $2.6 million at mid-year). Returns can be distorted in a small fund, with one big winner or loser affecting the overall return. Note that the fund is only no load if purchased directly from the manager.

BISSETT AMERICAN EQUITY FUND $$ ⇒ G NO USE

Small fund (under $6 million in assets) with an improving performance record. Emphasis is on growth stocks. Had a solid gain of almost 20 percent for the year to June 30, '95, which has pulled up the averages for previous years. Rating maintained for this edition, but will improve if performance continues strong. See entry for Bissett Canadian Equity Fund for purchase details. Not eligible for RRSPs, even as foreign content.

BULLOCK AMERICAN FUND $$ ⇑ G #/* £ USSC

We're finally starting to see some signs of life from this one-time high-flyer. After several years of excellent returns, this fund began to founder after the departure of guiding genius Barry Fierstein in late '92. His replacement, John Callaghan, had trouble rekindling the magic winning formula and in '94 the fund stumbled to a 9.4 percent loss, ranking it No. 74th out of 78 funds in this category, as measured by Southam's *Mutual Fund SourceBook*. But in '95, the news began to get better. The fund was up 13.2 percent in the first half of the year and then added a fat 6.8 percent gain on top of that in July. The fund invests in small to mid-size U.S. companies, with an emphasis on rapid growth. It tends to be quite volatile, with big price movements up or down — as the July '95 results suggest. A strong half-year performance isn't enough to warrant an increase in the rating, but if Callaghan can keep going at anything like this pace you'll see Bullock American back at $$$ next year.

CIBC U.S. EQUITY FUND $ ⇒ G NO £ USE

The good news is this fund has generated decent profits for its investors — three-year average annual return to June 30, '95, was 10.6 percent. The bad news is the average fund in this category returned 13.7 percent, according to *The Globe and Mail Report on Business,* and many funds topped 15 percent. Portfolio favours blue-chip stocks. There are better choices.

CAMBRIDGE AMERICAN GROWTH FUND $ ⇑ G #/* £ USE

An aggressive U.S. growth stock fund from Sagit Management of Vancouver. Hasn't shown a lot so far; average annual return for the three years to June 30, '95, was just 4.1 percent. The average fund in this category returned 13.7 percent over that time. Not high on my list.

CASSELS BLAIKIE AMERICAN FUND $$ ⇒ G # £ USE

Here's a nice turnaround story for you. This blue-chip stock fund was one of the better performers in this category for many years until it suddenly ran into a brick wall in '92, when it ranked close to the bottom of all U.S. equity funds sold in Canada, according to Southam's *Mutual Fund SourceBook.* That was followed by more losses in '93 and the first half of '94. But then the U.S. market started on a roll and so did this fund. Gain for the year to June 30, '95, was 29 percent, much better than average. Hopefully, this is a sign the managers have got things back on track and I'm raising the rating a notch in recognition of that. Maximum 3 percent load if you buy direct from Cassels Blaikie (Ontario residents only); 5 percent if you purchase through a dealer. Phone (416) 941-7500 for information. Formerly known as the Barrtor American Fund.

CENTURY DJ FUND $ ⇒ G # £ USE

Small fund; specializes in firms which compose the
Dow Jones Industrial Index. But even when the Dow's
been hot, it has not. Not accepting new subscriptions at
this time.

CORNERSTONE U.S. EQUITY FUND $$ ⇒ G NO £ USE

This reincarnation of the old Metropolitan U.S. Fund has
had good results recently. Two-year returns to June 30,
'95, are slightly above average which is significant since
the new managers, Wellington Management Company of
Boston, took over in April '93. I said last year that continued good returns would result in a ratings upgrade, so
the fund moves up a notch this year. Portfolio is oriented to blue-chip stocks. Purchase through North
American Trust (which was taken over by Laurentian
Bank in autumn '95). Not available east of Ontario.

ELLIOTT & PAGE AMERICAN
GROWTH FUND $$ ⇒ G #/* £ USE

Formerly the Metropolitan American Growth Fund,
taken over by E&P in April '93, when Goldman Sachs of
New York was given responsibility for its fortunes.
Manager is James McClure, head of the GS equity management team, who uses a value-oriented style to search
out stocks that are underpriced. He has put together a
well-structured portfolio of 30 – 40 stocks. The fund has
shown considerably better results since McClure took
over; annual two-year return to June 30, '95, was 12.7
percent, above average for this category. As a result, I've
upgraded the rating this year. If you choose the back-end
load option, be prepared for some hard negotiating;
you'll find details in the entry for the Elliott & Page
Equity Fund in the Canadian Equity section.

EVEREST U.S. EQUITY FUND $ ⇒ G NO £ USE

The portfolio of this fund leans strongly towards blue-
chip stocks so, not surprisingly, it performed very well
during the period when the Dow was on a tear. Gain for
the first half of '95 was a healthy 14.5 percent. Longer-
term results are below average, however, with an average
annual rate of return for the three years ending June 30,
'95, of 12.6 percent; average for this category was 13.7
percent. Sold by Canada Trust.

FIDELITY GROWTH AMERICA FUND $$$ ⇒ G #/* £ USE

Boston-based portfolio manager Brad Lewis uses a highly complex screening system to choose stocks, but it obviously works. The fund was very heavily weighted in the technology sector in the spring of '95, and thus rode the big profit wave that swept many stocks in that field to new highs. Gain for the year to June 30, '95, was a resounding 26.8 percent; three-year annual average was 20.9 percent. This is one of the better choices in the Fidelity lineup. See Fidelity Capital Builder Fund in the Canadian Equity section for my comments on the three purchase options.

FIRST AMERICAN FUND $ ⇒ G * RSP USE

A new entry from Jean-Pierre Fruchet of Guardian Timing Services, making its debut in this edition of the *Guide*. This is something of a departure for Fruchet, or "J.P." as he's known on Bay St. His other two funds, Canadian Protected and Protected American, are built on safety-first investment techniques using the principles of portfolio insurance. This is a more aggressive fund launched, as Fruchet tells it, after some of his investors told him they wanted something more exciting. This fund certainly has the potential to be just that. It can be 100 percent long, 100 percent short, it can use leveraging — in other words, it can do all the things that frighten most ordinary investors. So far, however, Fruchet hasn't been as aggressive as he admits he perhaps should have been. As a result, returns have been decidedly sub-par; average annual gain for the three years to June 30, '95, was 9.2 percent (average for this category was 13.7 percent). The manager is clearly still getting a feel for the potential of this fund, so we'll watch future developments with interest. Sold only by offering memorandum, which means you have to have a lot of money ($150,000 for Ontario and Quebec residents) to get in. Call (416) 960-4890 for information.

GENERAL TRUST U.S. EQUITY FUND $$ ⇒ G NO £ USE

A previously average performer that surprised everyone by suddenly catching fire in '91 with a gain of 62 percent, and following that up with a 21.4 percent advance in '92. Momentum seems to be slowing, however; the fund gained a so-so 13.3 percent in '93 and then tumbled 4.8

percent in '94. The first half of '95, was better (plus 7.7 percent), but below average for this category. The portfolio has been trimmed significantly in size over the past year, making it more manageable. Sold by General Trust branches in Quebec only. See additional comments in the entry for the General Trust Canadian Equity Fund in the Canadian Equity section.

GREEN LINE U.S. INDEX FUND $$ ⇒ G NO £ USE

Index funds, by definition, will do no better than the average of the index to which they're tied — in this case, the Standard & Poor's 500. That's been good enough to make this Green Line fund a steady performer in this category since its launch in '86. I prefer an actively managed stock fund but Green Line, surprisingly, doesn't have a U.S. entry that qualifies (their new North American Growth Fund comes closest). So if you're a Green Line client and you want a pure U.S. fund, this is it. Sold at branches of the TD Bank.

GUARDIAN AMERICAN
EQUITY FUND $$$ ⇒ G #/* £ USE

A strong performer in the late '70s but went into a long period of decline around the time of the '81–'82 recession. Changed managers in '87, name in '88 (was Guardian Growth Fund). Results since have been very good; average annual return for the five years to June 30, '95, was just over 15 percent, well above average for U.S. equity funds as a group. Growth-oriented, well-balanced portfolio that focuses on medium-sized companies. Worth considering.

HYPERION VALUE LINE
EQUITY TRUST $$$ ⇒ G #/* £ USE

This fund takes a unique investing approach — in fact, you won't find another like it in Canada. The portfolio advisor is Value Line Inc. of New York, whose analyses of stocks are among the most widely followed in the industry. Shares for the fund are selected on the basis of a high-timeliness ranking under the Value Line system. This ranking takes into account a number of measures, such as earnings, price, and momentum. With this kind of blue-ribbon direction, you'd expect results that would be near the top of this category. Initially, they weren't, but the fund is just coming off a terrific year — a gain of 31.6 percent in the 12 months ending June 30, '95. That pulled up the three-year average annual return to 20 percent, one of the best in this category. I said in last year's edition that I liked the concept of this fund and suggested it might be worth a few of your dollars. I hope you acted on that tip. Rating moves up to $$$ this year.

INDUSTRIAL AMERICAN FUND $$ ⇒ G #/* £ USE

Invests in a diversified portfolio of U.S. stocks, including a large representation of blue-chip issues. Average performer, did not benefit from the recent big run-up in the U.S. market to the same extent as some others in this category.

INVESTORS U.S. GROWTH FUND $$$$ ⇒ G * £ USE

This is an excellent fund that consistently produces above-average returns for investors. It has been one of the star performers for Investors Group for several years and last year was elevated to the top $$$$ status. It has continued to reward investors since, with a gain of 12.8 percent for the year to June 30, '95. That was somewhat below average, but not enough to even consider a downgrade — especially since this fund has shown incredible consistency over time with only one down year since 1984 — a fractional loss in '90. The portfolio, which emphasizes stocks with good growth potential, is managed on a highly disciplined basis, never holding more than about 20 companies. Average annual rate of return for the decade ending June 30, '95, was 12.5 percent, one of the best in this fund category. Sold by Investors Group representatives. Highly recommended. See entry for Investors Canadian Equity Fund in the Canadian Equity section for details on commissions and fees.

JONES HEWARD AMERICAN FUND $ ⇒ G #/* £ USE

This fund invests in a diversified portfolio of mainly U.S. stocks, with the emphasis on firms with good earnings. Portfolio is small (about 25 stocks). Recent results have not been good; the fund gained only 2 percent in the year ending June 30, '95, during a period when most U.S. stock funds were scoring big gains. Optional front-end load (maximum 9 percent) or back-end load (maximum 5 percent, declining to zero after six years).

LONDON LIFE U.S. EQUITY FUND $ ⇒ G * £ S USE

Considering that this is a largely blue-chip portfolio and that the managers entered '95 holding shares in some companies that have been real movers (Motorola, Disney), you'd expect better results. They just aren't there. The fund gained only 7.6 percent in the first half of '95 (12.9 percent was average). Longer-term results are equally disappointing. One of those funds that should do better, but doesn't. Sold by London Life representatives.

MARGIN OF SAFETY FUND $ ⇓ G # USE

Small fund that specializes in value investing by seeking out stocks trading at a discount to the underlying worth of the business (the "margin of safety"). Got off to a good start in '89, but then performance slipped — largely, manager John D. Hillery now admits, because of his conservative style which on average kept almost half the fund's assets in Treasury bills thereby missing out on potential stock market gains. In his latest chatty quarterly report, Hillery includes a *mea culpa* and says he will make some modest adjustment to his approach, especially when it comes to selling winners. But, he adds, "I will continue to do what I have always felt competent and comfortable doing, that is, invest in businesses of acceptable quality, managed by honest and competent people, at very reasonable, if not bargain prices. In other words, once a cheapskate, always a cheapskate." How can you get mad at a manager like that? Minimum initial investment $25,000. Sold in Ontario only; for information call (416) 234-0846. Previously no load but now a front-end sales commission may be charged. Not eligible for RRSPs/RRIFs.

MCLEAN BUDDEN AMERICAN GROWTH FUND $$$ ⇒ G NO £ USE

Uses a conservative approach to investing in the U.S. market. Emphasis is on large companies with good long-term growth potential. Excellent record in first three years, but hit a wall in the early '90s. Has looked much better recently, however, buoyed by a strong performance of U.S. blue chips. Gain for the year ending June 30, '95, was a healthy 23.1 percent. Five-year average annual rate of return is an above-average 13.5 percent. No load if purchased directly from the manager; phone (416) 862-9800 for information.

MUTUAL AMERIFUND $$ ⇒ G # USE

A small fund that invests mainly in U.S. blue-chip stocks.
Returns are respectable but not outstanding; five-year
average annual return to June 30, '95, is 8.5 percent.
Sold by representatives of Mutual Investco. Maximum
load fee of 3.75 percent; less if you invest more than
$100,000. Cannot be held in RRSPs or RRIFs, even
under foreign content rules.

PHILLIPS, HAGER & NORTH
U.S. FUND $$$$ ⇒ G NO £ USE

A solid, long-term performer, which continues to generate good results, although its relative position is slipping
a bit. Average annual return over the past decade is 12.3
percent, still one of the best in this category. But shorter-
term results aren't quite as strong. Three-year average
annual return to June 30, '95, is a very good 16 percent
— but 15 U.S. equity funds did better. I'm maintaining
the $$$$ status for this year because of this fund's excellent long-term record, conservative management style,
and extremely low expense ratio (only 1.07 percent). But
it's on the bubble. Unless results show improvement in
relation to the competition, it may be a candidate for a
downgrade next year. Portfolio is relatively small (about
50 stocks) and is weighted towards blue chips. No sales
charge but a $25,000 minimum initial investment is
required. Buy direct from the managers; phone 1-800-
661-6141 for information.

PROTECTED AMERICAN FUND $$$ ⇓ G #/* RSP D

Began life as the Protected Bond Fund in '85. Mandate
was changed in January '90; the fund now invests mainly in U.S. stock index futures and Treasury bills. Manager
Jean-Pierre Fruchet employs timing systems and portfolio insurance techniques to avoid losses. This is one of
the few mutual funds in Canada that will take short positions. Objective is to outperform the Standard & Poor's
500 Index by at least 6 percent annually in U.S. dollar
terms over a three-year period, while avoiding any down
years. Results are good. The fund gained 10.7 percent in
'90 (the S&P dropped 6.6 percent). In '91, it gained 9.7
percent, compared to a 26.3 percent advance for the S&P
500. In '92, it was ahead 7.6 percent, vs. an S&P gain of
4.5 percent. In '93, the fund had its best year yet, gain-

ing 25.3 percent compared to 7.1 percent for the S&P. In '94, the fund experienced its first-ever down year with a fractional loss of 0.3 percent. But that was better than its target, the S&P 500, which fell 1.5 percent. This fund is best suited to conservative investors who place a high degree of importance on safety. And here's something unusual: this fund is fully RRSP eligible, because of the investment strategies it uses. See Canadian Protected Fund entry in the Canadian equity section for purchase information. Note: no switching is allowed between funds in this group.

PURSUIT AMERICAN FUND $ ⇑ G #/NO USE

This fund must be giving its shareholders fits. It had a huge year in '91, with a 60 percent gain, third best in Canada. Then it lost 12.7 percent in '92, winning the prize for worst performance of the year among funds surveyed by Southam's *Mutual Fund SourceBook*. Results in '93 were marginally profitable, but not good in relation to the competition. That was followed by an 8 percent loss in '94 and a way below-average 4.3 percent gain in the first half of '95. Part of the problem is the fund's tiny portfolio. With assets of only $600,000, gains and losses in individual stock holdings become magnified out of proportion. None of this gives me confidence that this is a good choice at present, and makes me wonder if the fund can continue to be viable. Managed by Nigel Stephens Counsel Inc. of North York, Ontario. See entry for Pursuit Canadian Fund in Canadian Equity section for purchase details, which are somewhat complex. Not eligible for RRSPs/RRIFs.

ROYAL TRUST AMERICAN STOCK FUND $$$$ ⇒ G NO £ USE

This and the companion RoyFund U.S. Equity Fund are among the few no-load U.S. equity funds available in Canada that deliver consistently high returns. They are due to merge shortly, but nothing much is going to change since they're both run by the same manager, Jim Young. This is one of the oldest of the bank U.S. stock funds, dating back to '66. Portfolio has a strong blue-chip flavour. Ten-year average annual rate of return of 12.3 percent. This is not a flashy fund, but it is steady and consistent, year after year — just what a conservative investor wants. As a result, I'm upgrading it to top $$$$

status this year. Available through branches of Royal Trust.

ROYAL ZWEIG STRATEGIC GROWTH FUND $$$ ⇒ G NO £ USSC

Originally launched by Royal Trust during the Paul Starita era, this fund is run by U.S. investment guru Martin Zweig — a household name among American stock watchers but one relatively few Canadians are familiar with. Never mind; he knows what he's doing. This fund invests in smaller U.S. companies with above-average growth potential, which may sound like high-risk stuff at first blush. But Zweig puts a conservative spin on the theme, battening down the hatches and reducing risk if troubles loom on the stock market horizon. Result: a big winner that low-risk investors can comfortably add to their portfolios. Average annual return of 16.5 percent for the three years to June 30, '95. Now available at both Royal Trust and Royal Bank.

ROYFUND U.S. EQUITY $$$ ⇒ G NO £ USE

An excellent performer, one that should be in your portfolio if you're a Royal Bank client (and even if you aren't). Manager Jim Young focuses on mid-size companies, with sales of between US $500 million and $5 billion annually, particularly in the technology, industrial manufacturing, consumer, financial, and energy sectors. Solid, growing cash flow and a clear competitive advantage are two key factors he uses to assess stocks. Portfolio is relatively small, about 50–60 issues. Three-year return to June 30, '95, is an excellent 20.7 percent.

SAVINGS AND INVESTMENT TRUST AMERICAN FUND $$ ⇒ G NO £ USE

Portfolio emphasizes blue-chip stocks, with some growth issues as well. Long-term results are below average but recent performance has been much better. Gained a solid 18.9 percent for the year ending June 30, '95. Sold in Quebec and Ontario by Savings and Investment Trust.

SCOTIA EXCELSIOR AMERICAN EQUITY FUND $$$ ⇒ G NO £ USE

Portfolio emphasis is on mid- to large cap U.S. securities, with a strong blue-chip leaning. Results have been very respectable. Five-year average annual rate of return to June 30, '95, was 11.9 percent. Despite the name, there are some non-U.S. securities in the portfolio, including, at the start of '95, British Airways and Phillips. Sold by branches of the Bank of Nova Scotia, Montreal Trust, and by ScotiaMcLeod. Name changed from Scotia American Equity Growth Fund in August '95.

TALVEST U.S. GROWTH FUND $$ ⇒ G #/* £ USE

This was formerly the NW Equity Fund. It was acquired by Talvest in mid-'92 and renamed. So it's only fair to judge it on the basis of the three-year return to June 30, '95, which is an unspectacular 12 percent. (The average U.S. equity fund gained 13.7 percent over that time.) Despite the name, this is not a small cap fund; the mandate is to invest in stocks with a market capitalization of over $500 million. Portfolio includes stocks like Wal-Mart, General Motors, and Merck. See Talvest Growth Fund entry in Canadian Equity section for purchase details.

TOP FIFTY U.S. EQUITY FUND $ ⇒ G # £ USE

This is essentially a U.S. blue-chip fund, managed out of Vancouver. It's been profitable for investors, with an average annual return of 11.8 percent for the three years to June 30, '95. However, those results are well below average for U.S. funds as a group. Open to B.C. residents only.

UNITED AMERICAN
GROWTH FUND $$$ ⇒ G #/* £ USE

Excellent long-term record. Former managers Gerald Coleman and Jerry Javasky packed their bags in '92 and moved over to competitor Mackenzie Financial. Chicago-based Stein Roe & Farnham is now overseeing things; returns since they took charge have continued to be above average. Gained a terrific 28.9 percent in the year ending June 30, '95. Growth-oriented portfolio may include up to 25 percent non-U.S. shares. Name changed from United American Fund in spring '94.

UNIVERSAL U.S. EMERGING
GROWTH FUND $$$ ⇑ G #/* £ USSC

A dynamite entry from Mackenzie's Universal group, making its debut in the *Guide* this year with a very good $$$ rating. This fund focuses on small cap U.S. companies with high growth potential. That makes it somewhat higher risk by definition, but so far investors haven't minded. That's because the payoff has been great; three-year average annual rate of return to June 30, '95, was a terrific 28.4 percent. Some funds did better — but not many. Lead manager James Broadfoot operates out of Mackenzie's Boca Raton, Florida, office. His portfolio is well diversified, with health care and technology front and centre, as you might expect. This is a good bet for Mackenzie Financial investors who are looking for above-average returns and can accept a higher measure of risk.

UNIVERSITY AVENUE U.S. GROWTH FUND

$ ⇑ G NO £ USE

The original mandate of this fund was to invest in Canadian, U.S., and British issues, but it now focuses exclusively on the States. There are a lot of blue-chip stocks in the portfolio mix but, despite that, the fund underperformed in the first half of '95 when the Dow was hitting record highs. Longer-term results are also weak; over the five years to June 30, '95, the fund *lost* an average of 0.3 percent a year. That's a better five-year result than I reported last year, but it's still on the minus side. No load if purchased directly from the manager, otherwise a commission of up to 4 percent may be charged. See University Avenue Canadian Fund in Canadian Equity section for purchase details.

International and Global Equity Funds

I've always regarded broadly based international funds as the safest way to invest in stocks. That's because the managers have the whole world from which to choose their securities. If they don't like the prospects for, say, Mexico, or if they feel the Hong Kong stock market is overpriced, they can go elsewhere. No restrictions.

In previous editions of this *Guide*, I've put all international funds together, but it's time to change that so as to better compare apples and apples. This year, you'll find several sections on international funds. The funds in this section roam the globe, with no restrictions. Elsewhere, you'll find separate sections on Americas Funds, Far East Funds, European Funds, and Emerging Markets Funds. ■

To illustrate why I consider these distinctions so important, consider this: in the year ending June 30, 1995, almost all broadly based international funds made gains. On the other hand, almost all Far East, Emerging Markets, and Americas funds with strong Latin content lost ground.

Moral: if you're going to buy an international fund, choose carefully.

The two $$$$ funds in this category continue to reward investors. Templeton Growth Fund was ahead 11.5 percent for the 12 months to June 30, 1995. Trimark Fund had a very healthy 20.1 percent gain for the period.

Most funds in this section are eligible for RRSPs and RRIFs, under the foreign content rules. If you aren't making use of them in your registered plan, you should be.

RATINGS CHANGES

Once again this year, no new funds qualified for $$$$ status. But last year's top two, Templeton Growth and Trimark Fund, retain their status. There are three promotions to the $$$ ranks, however: Dynamic International, Saxon World Growth, and Investors Growth Portfolio. They are offset by three demotions from $$$ to $$ — Regent International, Atlas Global Equity, and United Global Growth.

Three funds appear for the first time this year, the most promising being the National Life Global Equity Fund that weighs in with a $$$ rating.

1996 RATINGS

ATLAS GLOBAL EQUITY FUND $$ ⇒ G NO £ IE

This was the star performer of the old Finsco group that was taken over by Midland Walwyn at the end of '93. Management is by IAI International Ltd. (formerly Hill Samuel) of London. Past performance was better than average, but recent results have been weak. The fund gained just 1.3 percent in the year to June 30, '95, in part because of a heavy weighting in Japan of 20 percent. That suggests a downgrade while we wait and see. Available through Midland Walwyn. Formerly the Finsco Global Fund; name changed in July '94.

BPI GLOBAL EQUITY FUND $$ ⟹ G #/* £ IE

Invests throughout the world, in contrast to the International Equity Fund (below) which is excluded from North America. Had a big year in '93 but hasn't shown much since. Was modestly above average in the first half of '95, thanks to a heavy weighting in U.S. blue-chip issues. Managed by John Reinsberg of Lazard Frères. Formerly the Walwyn International Fund.

BPI INTERNATIONAL EQUITY FUND $$ ⟹ G #/* £ IE

Formerly the BT Landmark International Fund and one of the star performers in the now-defunct Bolton Tremblay family. Good long-term results, but hasn't shown much so far under the new leadership of John Reinsberg of Lazard Frères, who also runs the companion Global Equity Fund (above). The difference is that this one is excluded from North America. If you must choose one, take the Global Equity fund.

C.I. GLOBAL FUND $$$ ⟹ G #/* £ IE

This fund had an excellent three-year run from '91 to '93, but has been slipping recently. In '94, there was a 2.1 percent loss and the gain for the first half of '95 was a weak 1.2 percent. These indifferent results were due in part to a heavy weighting in Japan, which was slightly trimmed back in mid-'95. The portfolio is well diversified, with the U.S. (28.6 percent) and Europe (23.9 percent) representing the largest holdings. Managed by BEA Associates of New York. Rating is maintained for this year, but I'll be watching for evidence this one is getting back on track. Formerly known as Universal Global Fund.

C.I. SECTOR FUND $$$ ⟹ G #/* £ IE

This is simply an "umbrella" fund. It allows investors to hold units in a number of Canadian International funds, and to switch between them without incurring any immediate tax liability. (Switches between free-standing mutual funds are considered a sale for tax purposes and may result in a taxable gain.) Eligible for RRSPs as foreign content, but it doesn't make sense to use it there because switches within registered plans don't attract tax. Returns on units held within this fund won't be precisely the same as if the units are held independently because of the timing of purchases. As a result, your profits may be slightly less. So don't go this route unless you're going to make use of the tax-saving strategy.

CIBC GLOBAL EQUITY FUND $\Rightarrow$ G NO £ IE

Offers a well-diversified portfolio, but results haven't been very exciting. Five-year average annual rate of return is just 7.1 percent, well below average for this category. Okay if you're a CIBC client anyway, but it's certainly not worth switching banks for.

CAMBRIDGE GLOBAL FUND $$ ⇑ G #/* £ IE

This fund has travelled a long road to its current position. It started as a Canadian equity fund (called Trans-Canada Shares Series B) and then, more recently, it was known as Cambridge Diversified Fund. Now the transition to an international fund is complete, although Canadian securities still make up a significant part of the portfolio (about 14 percent at the start of '95). All this manoeuvring paid off big for investors when the fund turned in a 44 percent gain in '93. But it took a chunk of that back with a 17 percent loss in '94, due in part to market setbacks in the Far East and Latin America. The first half of '95 has been much better, though, with a 7.7 percent gain. This is anything but your typical global fund. At the start of '95, the largest country in the fund in terms of share value was Indonesia, closely followed by China. So there's a lot of emerging markets in this mix, adding to the potential volatility. Sagit, the company that manages the Cambridge funds, has a history of big performance swings, so anything could happen here. It sure makes life interesting for investors — to paraphrase the old Chinese curse.

CANADA LIFE U.S. AND
INTERNATIONAL EQUITY S-34 $$$ $\Rightarrow$ G * £ S IE

The best performer in the Canada Life stable. Offers a well-diversified portfolio, with broad international representation. In other words, it's not just a U.S. fund with some token foreign holdings. Results have been consistently good; average annual return for the decade to June 30, '95, was a healthy 13.5 percent. Average for all funds in this category was 10.4 percent, so you can see how well this one has done. Redemption fee if cashed within seven years. Sold by Canada Life agents and brokers. See Canada Life listing in Canadian Equity section for an explanation of guarantees.

CAPSTONE INTERNATIONAL
INVESTMENT TRUST $$$ ⇒ G NO £ IE

A small fund with a limited portfolio. Did relatively well in the early '90s, but recent results have been less impressive. However, an above-average return in the first half of '95 preserves the rating for another year. Available only through the managers, Hughes, King & Company; phone (416) 863-0005.

CASSELS BLAIKIE INTERNATIONAL FUND $ ⇑ G # £ IE

A chronic underperformer. Five-year average annual rate of return to June 30, '95, was a tiny 0.1 percent. That wasn't the worst result in this category — but it was close. Maximum 3 percent front-end load if purchased directly from the manager (Ontario residents only). Phone (416) 941-7500 for information.

CHOU ASSOCIATES FUND $$ ⇒ G # IE

Originally started in '81 as an investment club, gained fund status in '86. This fund concentrates on locating stocks trading at a deep discount to their underlying value. Manager Francis Chou professes to ignore exotic selection techniques, preferring the KISS (keep it simple, stupid) approach in choosing securities. Recent results have been quite respectable; the fund's average annual compound rate of return for the five years to June 30, '95, was 12.9 percent. Small portfolio; Chou mainly invests in U.S. stocks although he's not restricted to that country. Sold only in Ontario. Note: not eligible for RRSPs, even as foreign content.

CORNERSTONE GLOBAL FUND $$ ⇒ G NO £ IE

Formerly the Metropolitan Speculators Fund; performance is much improved in this new incarnation. Produced a solid 14.4 percent average annual compound rate of return for the year ending June 30, '95. The assets are well diversified with about a quarter of the portfolio in U.S. issues. A candidate for an upgrade if good results continue. However, its future is uncertain because of the move by parent company to sell its interest in North American Trust, which sponsors this fund to Laurentian Bank of Canada.

CUNDILL VALUE FUND $$$ ⇒ G # £ IE

This is an example of a great fund that became a mediocre fund that's become a great fund again. After some weak results in the early '90s, Peter Cundill and his team have restored this long-time winner as one of the premier international equity funds around. The fund's once-bloated portfolio has been trimmed dramatically, while retaining the value-oriented investing approach of Cundill's guru, Dr. Benjamin Graham. Current emphasis is on seeking value outside North America, with Japan (Fuji Photo Film) and Germany (Bayer, BASF) among Cundill's happy hunting grounds. Cundill himself is something of an oddball, restlessly roaming the world and popping up in the news for unlikely reasons (he recently sued the state of Mississippi over some bonds it defaulted on in 1841, demanding the principal plus 154 years worth of interest!). But while he sometimes does unusual things, he runs a good fund, ably backed up by his VP of investments, Tim McElvaine. Return for the year to June 30, '95, was 11.3 percent; 10-year average annual gain was 12.1 percent. For information, call 1-800-663-0156.

DESJARDINS INTERNATIONAL FUND $$$ ⇒ G NO £ IE

One of the best performers in the Desjardins group. Five-year average annual return to June 30, '95, was 10.8 percent, well above average. Recent returns have slipped, however, due to heavy weighting in Far East markets. Portfolio is broadly diversified internationally. Sold in Quebec by Desjardins Trust and Caisses Desjardins.

DYNAMIC GLOBAL GREEN FUND $ ⇒ G #/* £ IE

This is the old Dynamic Global Fund dressed in a green suit. The fund's mandate is to invest internationally in companies involved in the manufacture of products or in the creation of technologies that will contribute to environmental improvements, or which are recognized as industry leaders in environmentally friendly operations. These include a cross-section of businesses ranging from cosmetics to water treatment. It's a noble idea, but unfortunately the results haven't been good. The fund's average annual rate of return for the five years to June 30, '95, was minus 1 percent, not a fast road to riches. If you feel you'd like to invest anyway because of the objective of the fund, you should resign yourself to more below-average years until something changes. Not recommended.

DYNAMIC INTERNATIONAL FUND $$$ ⇒ G #/* £ IE

This fund was going nowhere until the Dynamic Group took control of all the Allied funds in '91. Since then, things have been looking up. This is Dynamic's broad-based international fund, with a mandate to roam the world. Results have been good in recent years; five-year average annual rate of return to June 30, '95, was 12.4 percent. As of mid-'95, almost half the portfolio was in North American equities, allowing investors to participate in the big run-up in New York. Improving performance earns an upgrade this year. Previously the Allied International Fund; name changed in April '93.

EMPIRE INTERNATIONAL
GROWTH FUND $$$ ⇒ G #/* £ S IE

A solid performer; five-year annual return to June 30, '95, was an above-average 11.9 percent. Has a diversified portfolio that includes a number of Canadian and U.S. issues as well as some closed-end international equity funds (e.g., China Fund). Best bet in the Empire family right now. Available as either a front- or back-end load. Sold by representatives of Empire Life.

EVEREST INTERNATIONAL EQUITY FUND $$ ⇒ G NO £ IE

This fund invests in undervalued companies outside North America. Uses active geographic switching policy in an effort to maximize gains. Portfolio is well diversi-fied, with stocks from more than 20 countries. Got off to a great start after '87 launch, but the '90–'92 period was not good for unit-holders. Came back strong in '93, with a 34 percent gain, but had a weak '94 with an advance of only 2.1 percent. The first half of '95 was even worse, with a 7 percent loss. This deterioration in performance is disappointing and suggests that the '93 results may have been an abberation. Be cautious. Sold by branches of Canada Trust.

FIDELITY INTERNATIONAL PORTFOLIO FUND $$$ ⇒ G #/* £ IE

Generally, a good performer. Annual return for the five years to June 30, '95, was above average at 9.6 percent. There was a managerial change in '94 with Dick Habermann taking over from Bruce Russell. The fund hasn't skipped a beat, however; returns since the change continue to be better than average. This fund uses a classic "bottom-up" strategy, selecting stocks on the basis of the prospects for each individual company. Well-diversified portfolio emphasized U.S., Japan, and Europe in spring '95. Part of the giant U.S.-based Fidelity Group which demands high performance from its managers. See Fidelity Capital Builder Fund in the Canadian Equity section for my comments on the three purchase options.

GBC INTERNATIONAL GROWTH FUND $ ⇑ G NO £ IE

This is the weak link in the otherwise excellent GBC family. If you'd invested five years ago, you'd have gained only 0.2 percent annually to June 30, '95. There are a couple of international funds that did worse, but not many. Perhaps that's why there's been a change at the top; management was taken over recently by Babson-Stewart Ivory International, a joint venture of David L. Babson & Co. of Cambridge, Mass., and Stewart Ivory & Co. Ltd. of Edinburgh, Scotland. First step of the new team was a portfolio shake-up that saw weightings for Latin America and Japan reduced and European holdings increased. Let's hope the new look pays off in results. See GBC entry in Canadian Equity section for purchase details.

GENERAL TRUST INTERNATIONAL FUND $$ ⇒ G NO £ IE

Middle-of-the-road performer offered by branches of General Trust in Quebec. Most recent results have been disappointing, with a loss of 5.3 percent in the year ending June 30, '95, in large part due to a heavy weighting in Japan at a time when share values there were declining. Although its mandate doesn't forbid it specifically, this fund does not invest in North American securities. This lack of exposure to the big gains in the New York stock market also hurt recent returns. See additional comments in the entry for the General Trust Canadian Equity Fund in the Canadian Equity section.

GLOBAL STRATEGY FUND

Merged with Global Strategy World Equity Fund.

GLOBAL STRATEGY WORLD
EQUITY FUND $ ⇒ G #/* £ IE

This is another one of those situations where this is either a brand new fund or a renamed old one, depending how you look at it. In January '95, GS folded their underachieving Global Strategy Fund into this new creation. I won't suggest the change was at least partially motivated by a desire to expunge the returns of the old Global Strategy Fund from the records, but that has been one of the effects. The business press mutual fund listings only show returns for this fund from the start of '95. I suppose that's fair in one sense, since a new multi-manager group has taken over. But, on the other hand, the move makes it appear as though this fund has no prior history — which it does. Playing it by GS's rules, early returns on this one have been uninspiring — a gain of 1.9 percent in the first half of '95. But it's early days for the new managers, so we'll watch and see.

GUARDIAN GLOBAL EQUITY FUND $$ ⇒ G #/* £ IE

A solid performer for many years, but was an underachiever in the early '90s. Has looked better recently, though; two-year average annual rate of return to June 30, '95, was well above average at 14.6 percent. Managed to perform tolerably well in the first half of '95 despite entering the year with a portfolio that was almost 30 percent invested in Japan, an area which has struggled. Note that this fund normally does not invest in any U.S. or Canadian securities.

INVESTORS GLOBAL FUND $$ ⇒ G * £ IE

Investors Group offers a wide range of international funds for its clients. The mandate of this one is far-reaching; the fund can invest anywhere the manager sees opportunities. The fund has performed well recently (average annual return of 13.8 percent for the two years to June 30, '95), but longer-term results are somewhat below average. Sold by Investors Group representatives. See entry for Investors Canadian Equity Fund in the Canadian Equity section for details on commissions and fees.

INVESTORS GROWTH PORTFOLIO FUND $$$ ⇒ G * £ IE

A fund of funds, holding units in several Investors Group growth funds for greater diversification, with an emphasis on foreign stocks. In May '95, holdings were the Global Fund (40 percent), Canadian Equity Fund (20 percent), U.S. Growth Fund (20 percent), Special Fund (10 percent), and North American Growth Fund (10 percent). Results have been above average for this category. Useful for those who prefer a more diversified approach.

LAURENTIAN INTERNATIONAL FUND $$ ⇒ G #/* £ IE

Focus is on growth stocks, with an emphasis on North America, Europe, and the Far East. Portfolio is very large and highly diversified, with stocks selected on a value basis. Results have been improving; average annual return for the three years to June 30, '95, was 13.6 percent. One of the better choices from this company. Formerly the Viking International Fund.

MACKENZIE SENTINEL GLOBAL FUND $$ ⇒ G # £ IE

Owned by Mackenzie Financial as a result of a takeover several years ago, but no longer marketed. Invests exclusively in units of the Universal World Equity Fund. Look for it to be folded into that fund some time in the near future.

MAWER WORLD INVESTMENT FUND $$ ⇒ G NO £ IE

Small, Alberta-based fund that invests in equities outside of North America, specifically Europe, the Pacific Basin, and Latin America. Since North American markets have been strong recently, the lack of exposure to U.S. stocks has hurt this fund's overall performance. Portfolio was heavily weighted towards Europe in spring '95 (about 60 percent of assets). Results have been in and out but five-year average annual returns are above average at 11.6 percent. Minimum investment $25,000. Call (403) 267-1989 for information.

MONTREAL TRUST EXCELSIOR — INTERNATIONAL SECTION

This fund was merged with the Scotia Global Growth Fund in October '95 to form the Scotia Excelsior International Fund.

NAL GLOBAL EQUITY FUND $$ ⇒ G * £ S IE

This international entry from North American Life got off to a poor start with a small loss in '92 but then rang up very decent gains in '93 and '94 (in fact it was one of the top 10 international funds in Canada in '94). But it nosedived in '95, losing 1.7 percent in the first six months. The reason? The portfolio was over one-third in Japan just at the time the Tokyo market went south. That's enough to ruin any manager's day — or half-year. So it's still too soon to tell how good or how bad this one will turn out to be. We need more time for some consistency to develop.

NN GLOBAL FUND

This fund has been closed down.

NATIONAL LIFE GLOBAL EQUITIES FUND $$$ ⇒ G * £ S IE

Another good fund from the National Life stable, but this one's a bit of a cheat. It invests entirely in units of another mutual fund, the Edinburgh, Scotland-based Martin Currie International Fund. Still, you can't argue with the results. The fund has returned 13.4 percent a year for the past five years, one of the best records in this category.

ORBIT WORLD FUND $ ⇒ G # £ IE

A small, broadly diversified, Montreal-based fund that was performing reasonably well until it ran into problems over the past 12 months and lost 7 percent. That pulled all its numbers down to below average. May be a better bet than those performance figures suggest, however. We'll see what happens over the coming year. Sold only in Quebec and Ontario; call (514) 932-3000 for information.

REGENT INTERNATIONAL FUND $$ ⇒ G #/*/NO £ IE

Hong Kong-based manager Peter Everington took over this chronic underperformer in September '92 and turned it around with a 56.8 percent gain in '93. The story since then hasn't been as good, however: the fund gained 5.8 percent in '94 but gave that all back in the first six months of '95. So for a year and a half, it's been essentially a break-even proposition for investors.

Although this is an international fund, the focus is heavily on Asia and Australia, which accounted for more than half of the portfolio in spring '95. This shouldn't be a surprise, considering that Everington is based in Hong Kong. So if you buy, you're essentially getting a Far East fund with some U.S. and European securities added for diversification. I hope that '93 wasn't just a flash in the pan by Everington, but I'm pulling back the rating a notch until we see. The good news here is that the annual "distribution fee" of 0.75 percent on back-end load purchases was discontinued in mid-'95. Call 1-800-667-2369 for information.

SAXON WORLD GROWTH FUND $$$ ⇒ G NO £ IE

Here's a riddle for you. Over the past three years, this has been the top performer among all the broadly based international equity funds sold in Canada. On top of that, it's no load. So why isn't anyone putting any money into it? The fund only has a mere $16 million in assets, a pittance by today's standards. What have you missed by not being there? Just gains of 29.2 percent in '91, 12.2 percent in '92, 44.5 percent in '93, 16.8 percent in '94, and 11 percent in the first half of '95. Has *your* fund manager done as well? Has anybody's? Clearly, the managers, Richard Howson and Robert Tattersall, know what they're doing — no one can be that lucky for that long. The portfolio is well-balanced internationally, with about half the holdings in the U.S. There are also some emerging markets in the mix, such as China and the Czech Republic. This one is definitely worth a look if you're an Ontario resident. See entry for Saxon Small Cap Fund in Canadian Equity section for details on how to purchase.

SCEPTRE INTERNATIONAL FUND $$$ ⇒ G NO £ IE

Continues to be one of the better choices among international equity funds, although the last 12 months have been sub-par due to overexposure in emerging markets. Long-term returns are still good, however, with an average annual gain of 14.3 percent for the five years to June 30, '95. Manager Len McNeely recently increased the weighting in Japan as prices softened there and expects to see a payoff from that move, especially if the yen continues to weaken. Minimum investment for a registered plan is $1,000; for a non-registered plan it is $5,000. Has advantage of being no load if purchased directly from the manager (Ontario residents only). See the entry for the Sceptre Equity Fund in the Canadian Equity section for more purchase details.

SCOTIA EXCELSIOR INTERNATIONAL FUND $$$ ⟹ G NO £ IE

A new fund, formed from the merger in October '95 of the Montreal Trust Excelsior International Fund and the Scotia Global Growth Fund. The Scotia fund was a relatively new entry, but the Montreal Trust fund had been around for many years and its managers will carry on with the new, combined fund. So the rating is based on the performance record of the Montreal Trust fund. That makes this a good bet for those seeking a consistent no-load international fund. The predecessor Montreal Trust fund is coming off a weak year (gained just 2.4 percent in the 12 months to June 30, '95), but the five-year results are above average. Good diversification. About a quarter of the portfolio was in U.S. stocks at the beginning of '95, with Europe and Japan the other major holdings. One of the better choices in the new Scotia Excelsior stable.

SPECIAL OPPORTUNITIES FUND $ ⇑ G # £ IE

The international stablemate of the highly volatile Multiple Opportunities Fund (see Canadian Equity section). Invests in ultra-small companies, with market capitalization of less than $25 million. This quote from the prospectus will give you the flavour: "These companies typically will have no history of earnings and will include natural resource companies in the exploration and development stage and industrial companies in the start-up stage." Results so far have not been anywhere near as exciting as the Multiple Opportunities Fund, although returns have perked up recently. Multiple Opportunities is the better bet if you're a B.C. resident and in a speculative mood. This one is available in all provinces except Quebec and Nova Scotia.

SPECTRUM INTERNATIONAL EQUITY FUND $ ⟹ G #/* £ IE

This is a broadly diversified international fund whose recent performance was dragged down by a heavy weighting (22.3 percent) in Japan in spring '95 and an underweighting in the high-flying U.S. market. Its longer-term record is well below average, with an annual return of 7.6 percent for the five years to June 30, '95. Average for a broadly based international fund, according to *The Globe and Mail*, was 9.3 percent. Not the best choice in this category.

TEMPLETON GLOBAL SMALLER COMPANIES FUND $$$ ⇑ G #/* £ IE

The mandate of this fund is to invest in small companies around the world. The original emphasis was on developing nations but that has changed; over 40 percent of the portfolio was in U.S. stocks in early '95. Emerging markets accounted for barely over 10 percent of the total. That change in direction has been good news for investors. After plunging to a 17 percent loss in its first calendar year ('90), this fund has reeled off four straight years of profits (granted, not a lot in '94, but many funds lost money that year). The pattern continued in the first half of '95, with a gain of almost 12 percent. This fund is now looking a lot better, especially for aggressive investors who don't mind the additional risk associated with small cap stocks. Formerly the Templeton Developing Growth Stock Fund.

TEMPLETON GROWTH FUND $$$$ ⇒ G #/* £ IE

One of the grand-daddies of the mutual fund industry, this giant has grown in size by a billion dollars since last year's edition (it had $3.4 billion in assets in mid-'95). Investors are attracted by the Templeton organization's solid reputation, the fund's stability, and, of course, the many years of above-average returns. Over the past decade, you'd have earned 13.6 percent a year in this fund. A few have done better — but not many. Diversified international portfolio, about 35 percent in U.S. securities as of May '95. In contrast to many other international funds, less than 1 percent of the holdings were in Japan at that point — a testament to the risk-averse approach of the Templeton managers. The fund employs a highly disciplined stock selection process, with a strong value orientation. Stocks are chosen from both developed and emerging countries, to provide a broad mix. Note that although this is classified as a stock fund, it may at times have holdings in bonds and short-term notes. Can be purchased in Canadian or U.S. funds. Maximum front-end load is 6 percent. Still one of my favourites and, yes, I own units in it.

TEMPLETON INTERNATIONAL STOCK FUND $$$ ⇒ G #/* £ IE

Name changed from Templeton Heritage Growth Fund in April '93, and so did the mandate. Previously, the managers could invest worldwide. Under the new objectives, U.S. and Canadian stocks will normally not be held in this portfolio. European stocks were overweighted in this fund in early '95, with Asian holdings at a low 11 percent. The switch in direction is paying off; this was the best performer among these three Templeton funds over the past two years with an average annual return of 19.7 percent. A good choice for investors looking for diversification outside North America. Solid management.

TRIMARK FUND $$$$ ⇒ G # £ IE

How can you argue with success? This fund has the best 10-year record in this category, with an average annual return of 16 percent to June 30, '95. The managers use a highly disciplined stock selection approach that obviously works and has stood the test of time. Although this is an international fund, it has historically concentrated its holdings in the U.S. The portfolio in mid-'95 was over 70 percent in American issues, with Japan the next largest holding at 5.8 percent. Low management expense ratio compared to most of the competition (1.54 percent). Run by committee chaired by well-respected Robert Krembil. Solid and highly recommended.

TRIMARK SELECT GROWTH FUND $$$ ⇒ G * £ IE

A back-end load companion to the front-end Trimark Fund. Same management style, similar portfolio. Nominal returns will generally be slightly below those of the Trimark Fund because this one has a higher management expense ratio (2.28 percent) and a greater percentage of cash assets. It has been growing more rapidly because of the public appeal of back-end load funds, but it may not always be the better choice because of the higher management fee. Example: over the past five years, the Trimark Fund had an average annual return of 18.1 percent. If you paid a 3 percent front-end load, your actual adjusted annual return would be 17.4 percent. The average annual return for this fund over the same period was 16.4 percent — a point less. I know which one I'd choose!

20/20 INTERNATIONAL VALUE FUND $$ ⇒ G #/* £ IE

Here's a strange switch. This fund was a decent performer in its previous guise as the 20/20 U.S. Growth Fund. But in November '94 the company decided to rename it, change the mandate, and bring in a brand new manager, Charles Brandes of San Diego. So if you originally bought units in what you thought was a U.S. fund, you now own a fund that invests around the world. This, of course, means that all previous performance numbers have been rendered meaningless and we start from scratch from the beginning of '95. By that criteria, the revamped fund is off to a good start, with an 8.7 percent gain in the first half of the year. Normally, I don't rate a fund until it has been around for at least three years. This one technically has, although not in this incarnation, so I'll compromise at $$ until we get a better fix on where it's going.

UNITED AMERICAN EQUITY FUND $$ ⇒ G #/* £ IE

This fund has a new name (it was formerly the United Accumulative Fund) that could be somewhat misleading. It is not a pure U.S. stock fund, at least not according to its official mandate. This is a value fund that has no geographic restriction. However, the emphasis is decidedly on U.S. issues for now, with foreign holdings mainly acquired through ADRs (American Depository Receipts) traded on the New York Stock Exchange. The holdings are primarily shares in large corporations, with a market capitalization of at least $500 million. Managers are Stein Roe & Farnham of Chicago. Recent results have shown a great improvement. The fund was up over 20 percent for the year to June 30, '95, buoyed in large part by big gains in the technology sector (Microsoft was the largest single holding in spring '95). Rating is being moved up a notch as a result.

UNITED GLOBAL EQUITY FUND $ ⇒ G #/* £ IE

The mandate here is to take a low-risk approach to international investing. The portfolio is well diversified internationally, but this fund has never seemed to get it all together. The annual return for the three years to June 30, '95, was 7.3 percent, well below average.

UNITED GLOBAL GROWTH FUND $$ ⇒ G #/* £ IE

This well-diversified small to mid-cap fund had been going along nicely until it took a hit in the first half of '95, thanks in part to a very heavy weighting in Japan. It bounced back strongly in July, however, with a 5.7 percent gain. Still, the performance has sputtered since a great run from '91 to '93, so the rating is down a notch this year. Name changed from United Venture Fund in spring '94.

UNIVERSAL WORLD EQUITY FUND $$ ⇒ G #/* £ IE

Does not invest in Canada or the U.S.; main focus is on Europe and the Far East, with a small Latin American holding. The portfolio includes both developed and emerging markets. Three-year record is well above average, but the first half of '95 was weak with a loss of 1.9 percent. That could be attributed largely to the fund's heavy weighting in Japan (32 percent at mid-year). Name changed from Industrial Global Fund in November '93.

Americas Equity Funds

Until recently, most stock funds that invested in this part of the world fell into two clear categories: Canadian funds and U.S. funds. But, as with much else in the mutual fund world, all that has changed. We now have funds that specialize in North American stocks (Canada, U.S., Mexico), funds that invest solely in Latin American stocks, and former U.S. equity funds that jumped on the Latin bandwagon just before it ran off the road by adding Mexican and South American stocks to their portfolios. (Some have since had second thoughts about that move.)

So I've created this new section as a catchall for all funds that invest in this hemisphere and don't limit themselves to one country. The level of risk of the funds here will differ widely, from very conservative to highly speculative, so be careful. ■

RATINGS CHANGES

The most significant development is the loss of $$$ status
by the Universal Americas Fund, where performance has
been hurt by the inclusion of Latin stocks in the portfolio.

1996 RATINGS

CAMBRIDGE AMERICAS FUND $$ ⇒ G #/* £ AE

This used to be strictly a U.S. equity fund, but the mandate has been changed to allow it to invest in Latin
America as well. Fortunately, the Latin holdings were still
very small when the Mexican peso tanked, so the damage
was minimal. As a result, this fund managed a solid 7.5
percent gain for the year to June 30, '95. That may not
seem like a lot, but it was better than many of the other
funds in this category. The Latin holdings are mainly in
closed-end mutual funds traded on New York. U.S. stocks
are a mix of blue chips (Microsoft, McDonalds) and small
growth companies. Note that Sagit has a negotiable back-
end load option; ask for details before you buy.

DYNAMIC AMERICAN FUND $ ⇒ G #/* £ AE

Although this is billed as a U.S. fund, portfolio at the start
of '95 included more than 10 percent Latin American
holdings. The result is to give the fund more of an international flavour. If what you want is a pure U.S. equity
fund, keep that in mind. Results have been deteriorating
in recent years, and long-term averages have fallen below
the norm for this fund category. Part of the reason is the
failure of the managers to get in on the big surge in technology stocks. This one needs a shot of adrenalin which
hopefully will be provided by new manager Anne
MacLean, who moved to Dynamic from Gluskin Sheff in
early '95.

ETHICAL NORTH AMERICAN
EQUITY FUND $$ ⇒ G #/*/NO £ AE

Started out as the Co-operative Trust Growth Fund; purchased from Co-operative Trust Company in September
'92 by the Credit Union Central of Canada to become part
of the new Ethical Funds family. Results since then have

been good; the fund averaged 12.9 percent a year for the two years ending June 30, '95. Although this is billed as a North American Fund, the emphasis is overwhelmingly on U.S. stocks. As of spring '95, the fund held only one Canadian stock, Renaissance Energy, and one Mexican stock, Telefonos de Mexico. So, until management diversifies more, you're really buying a U.S. equity fund here. Can be purchased without load fees at participating credit unions, otherwise a commission will be charged.

EVEREST NORTH AMERICAN FUND $$ ⇒ G NO £ AE

There has been a marked shift in the investment approach of this fund in the past year. At the beginning of '94, about two-thirds of the portfolio was in Canadian stocks. But a year later, that proportion had fallen to just over a quarter of the assets, with U.S. issues forming the major holding and Mexican stocks comprising about 10 percent of the asset base. This fund had a good year in '93 with a 26.4 percent return, largely as a result of the strength of the Canadian market. But it struggled in '94, dropping 9.2 percent. The first half of '95 was better, however. Formerly the Canada Trust North American Fund, sold by branches of Canada Trust.

GBC NORTH AMERICAN
GROWTH FUND $$ ⇒ G NO £ AE

Although the majority of the holdings are in U.S. equities, this fund also holds some Canadian and Mexican stocks. Run by the same people who manage the successful GBC Canadian Growth Fund. Has generally been a solid performer, other than for a terrible year in '90, but got hit pretty hard in the first six months of '94. Has rebounded nicely since, with a gain of 17.9 percent in the year ending June 30, '95, thanks to a heavy weighting in the red-hot technology sector. Another above-average year will push it up a notch in the ratings. $100,000 minimum investment applies (may be spread among several GBC funds). See GBC entry in Canadian Equity section for purchase details.

GLOBAL STRATEGY DIVERSIFIED
AMERICAS FUND $ ⇒ G #/* RSP AE

Whenever you see the word "Diversified" in the name of a Global Strategy fund, it tells you the fund specializes in international markets while being fully RRSP-eligible. Global Strategy was the pioneer in developing funds of this type, an idea which has since been picked up by other companies. Here the goal is to offer an option to RRSP/RRIF investors who want to add additional exposure to the U.S. market beyond the 20 percent foreign content rule. The technique is to invest 80 percent of the portfolio in Canadian T-bills, thus meeting the domestic requirements. This is the passive side of the portfolio. The active portion may be invested in options, futures, and equity positions. In this case, the managers have focused primarily on U.S. stocks (as opposed to derivatives), holding both long and short positions. Unfortunately, results have been very poor; five-year average annual rate of return to June 30, '95, was just 2 percent. Even worse, this fund couldn't make any money in the first six months of '95, when the Dow was going nuts. Avoid; if you're desperate for more RRSP foreign content there are better ways to get it.

IMPERIAL GROWTH NORTH AMERICAN
EQUITY FUND $$ ⇒ G # S AE

Enjoyed many good years in the '80s but struggled in early '90s. Has looked much better recently; one-year return to June 30, '95, was 18.9 percent, well above average. Three-year results are also solid, with an average annual gain of 17.2 percent. I said last year that continued good performance would result in a higher rating, so this one moves up a notch in this edition. Portfolio includes Canadian and U.S. stocks. Note that you can't hold this fund in an Imperial Life RRSP, even as foreign content. There's a 5 percent non-negotiable load charge for purchases under $15,000, reducing to 3.5 percent after that. Sold by representatives of Imperial Life.

INVESTORS NORTH AMERICAN
GROWTH FUND $$$ ⇒ G * £ AE

Invests mainly in Canadian and U.S. stocks, with a strong emphasis on the latter. One of the most reliable performers in this category, both short and long term — average annual gain over the decade to June 30, '95, was 12.5 percent. This fund has also been a model of consistency, with only one down year in the past 10 years — 1990. If you're an Investors Group client, this one should definitely be part of your portfolio.

INVESTORS SPECIAL FUND $$$ ⇒ G * £ AE

Invests in North American stocks, mainly U.S. and Canada. Main difference from North American Growth Fund is the emphasis on small and medium-sized companies with high growth potential. This has been a solid long-term performer, although recent results have slipped a bit. Average annual return of 12 percent over the past decade is nothing to sneeze at. If you like a more aggressive type of fund, this is a good choice. Sold by Investors Group representatives.

LAURENTIAN AMERICAN
EQUITY FUND $$ ⇒ G #/* £ AE

Middle-of-the-road equity fund which invests mainly in the U.S. but with some Canadian and Mexican holdings as well. Long-term results aren't exciting, but this fund has been looking better recently, with a gain of 19.3 percent for the year to June 30, '95. Portfolio is weighted towards medium- and large-sized companies. Name changed from Viking Growth Fund in '93.

UNIVERSAL AMERICAS FUND $$ ⇒ G #/* £ AE

Name changed from Universal American Fund in April '94 to reflect the inclusion of Latin American issues in the portfolio, so previous results are not indicative of the new mandate. The results since the change have not been great (a loss of 1.9 percent for the year to June 30, '95), but considering what happened to some other funds in this category, things could have been worse. As of mid-'95, the portfolio was 60 percent in U.S. and Canadian stocks, 27 percent in Latin countries, and the rest in cash.

Far East Equity Funds

The past couple of years haven't been good ones for investors in the Far East. Everyone agrees this part of the world has tremendous growth potential. But it also has more than its share of risk and volatility, and mutual funds that invest here reflect that.

If you want to minimize risk, your best bet is to select a fund that allows the manager to choose stocks from anywhere in the region. Single country funds, such as pure Japan or China funds, are always a crap-shoot. If the market goes well, you're in clover. If it falls, you can take a big, big hit. ■

One other point. If you plan to invest in this part of the world, take a long-term perspective. I can't tell you how China/Hong Kong-based stocks will do over the next 12 months — there are too many unknown factors. But I *can* tell you that a decade from now I'll be amazed if you don't look back and find you've recorded average annual returns in double digits.

RATINGS CHANGES

One $$$ fund from last year has been demoted to $$ status — the Regent Tiger Fund, which has struggled lately. Three new funds join the list this edition. Regent Korea is Canada's only dedicated South Korea Fund. Fidelity Far East is one of the better broadly based funds in this category and debuts with a $$$ rating, as does the AGF Asian Growth Fund.

1996 RATINGS

AGF ASIAN GROWTH FUND $$$ ⇑ G #/*/NO £ FEE

Good performer, making its debut in this edition. Invests in south-east Asia; no Japanese content. About a third of the portfolio was in Hong Kong in mid-'95. Other significant holdings were in Malaysia (21 percent of the total), Singapore (13 percent), and Thailand (12 percent). Returns so far have been good; average annual return for the three years to June 30, '95 was 23.5 percent, best in this category over that time frame. Worth a look for more aggressive investors.

AGF JAPAN FUND $$$ ⇑ G #/*/NO £ FEE

It appeared the Japanese market might have bottomed out last year, but it didn't work out that way. The combination of the rising yen, the Kobe earthquake, trade disputes with the U.S., and strains in the Japanese banking system all conspired to knock back this fund by 22.3 percent over the year ending June 30, '95. Maybe that was the bottom — Sir John Templeton always suggests buying at times of extreme pessimism. And certainly by late summer '95 there were signs the Japanese banking crisis was easing, the yen was declining to more manageable levels, and the economy was reflating. I moved the rating up a notch last year, thinking the turnaround might have begun. It hadn't, but there were signs in mid-'95 it might be underway — this fund jumped 5.3 percent in July alone. So I'm leaving the rating intact for this edition. But the risks are still higher than I like, so use caution. Note AGF's new purchase options; see the AGF Canadian Equity Fund entry for details.

C.I. PACIFIC FUND $$$ ⇑ G #/* £ FEE

Here's the top-performing mutual fund in Canada over the past 10 years, covering all categories. Average annual rate of return for the decade to June 30, '95, is 18.9 percent. That's an incredible result, especially when you realize that number two (Bullock American at 17.3 percent) is more than a point and a half behind. What's even more amazing is the fact that 10-year return was achieved despite a 3.7 percent loss in the past 12 months. Clearly, this fund was very good for very long. But that's history. Now what? Frankly, there's no reason not to stick with this fund if you're looking for a well-managed, nicely tuned Far East fund. Although the last 12 months ended on the down side, the fund performed better than the average for this category. And the same managers who have been picking winners since '90 are still in place. The fund invests in all Pacific Rim countries, including Japan, thus providing the managers with maximum flexibility. A good bet for aggressive investors who want exposure to the rapid economic growth in that part of the world, but be prepared for some bumps along the way. Southeast Asia is a politically and economically volatile area, especially as we approach China's takeover of Hong Kong in '97. I expect continued fine results over the long term from this one, but you've got to be prepared for the risk. Formerly known as Universal Pacific Fund.

CAMBRIDGE PACIFIC FUND $$ ⇒ G #/* £ FEE

Another example of the big moves to which Sagit funds are prone. If you held the fund in '93, you boasted at cocktail parties about the return of more than 60 percent. If you were still in during '94, you moaned about the 25.6 percent loss. By mid-'95, you were telling folks about how your fund pulled off a solid 7 percent gain while many other Asian funds were taking a bath. A big chunk of this fund is invested directly in the Chinese market, mainly through closed-end mutual funds and ADRs traded in New York. Other major holdings are in Indonesia, the Philippines, and Malaysia. Be prepared for a roller-coaster ride with this one. Not my favourite among Far East funds, but worth a look. If you buy, check out Sagit's negotiable back-end load before you make a purchase commitment.

FIDELITY FAR EAST FUND $$$ ⇑ G #/* £ FEE

One of the better-performing Far East funds, making its debut in the *Guide* this year. Manager K.C. Lee earns a vote of thanks from investors by piloting this fund to a 9 percent gain for the year to June 30, '95, during a period when many other Far East funds were taking big hits. Three-year average annual return is also excellent, at 20.6 percent. But one note of caution. Lee has greatly overweighted this fund in Hong Kong — 55 percent of the portfolio as of May '95. If the Hong Kong market goes sour — which some fund managers expect to happen — this fund will get rocked. So don't overcommit. Suitable for more aggressive investors.

GLOBAL STRATEGY JAPAN FUND $ ⇑ G #/* £ FEE

Let's see if we can follow the genealogy here. The original Global Strategy Far East Fund was renamed the Global Strategy Japan Plus Fund, which was how it appeared in last year's *Guide*. Its mandate was to invest primarily in Japan, with a few securities from other Asian countries tossed in. Then in early '95, the Japan Plus Fund was folded into the new Japan Fund, created as part of Global Strategy's move to a multi-manager approach. So whether this is a new fund with no meaningful track record or an old fund under new management depends entirely on your point of view. Either way, the results aren't impressive. In its old guise, this was a middling Far East fund at best. Since the relaunch, it managed to lose 14.5 percent in the first six months of '95. I suggest you wait a while until the new team sorts itself out and gets on track.

HYPERION ASIAN FUND $$$ ⇑ G #/* £ FEE

This is one of the hot Asia funds that's been turning nice profits for aggressive investors who are prepared to live with risk. Hong Kong-based manager Duncan Mount knows the region well, and the fund has large holdings in countries like Malaysia (about a quarter of the portfolio in spring '95), Thailand, Singapore, and Hong Kong. This part of the world is volatile, however, and the fund's returns show it: a huge 117 percent gain in '93, followed by a big 20.1 percent loss in '94 as the Hong Kong market dropped. The first half of '95 saw a very modest recovery (+1 percent). However, five-year returns are the best in this category, with an average annual gain of

13.4 percent. A good bet for those willing to take some chances in exchange for long-term growth potential. Now owned by Talvest, which bought the Hyperion funds from CIBC Securities in mid-'95. Good news if you want to get in: the previous minimum purchase of $10,000 has been reduced to $2,500, making this and the other Hyperion funds more accessible.

INVESTORS JAPANESE GROWTH FUND $$$ ⇑ G * £ FEE

This one has been on a roller-coaster ride in recent years. Took a beating when the Tokyo market collapsed in the early '90s, but came roaring back in '93 (along with all other Japan funds) with a big 35.3 percent gain. Followed that up with a solid 21.2 percent advance in '94. But then the Japanese market went into the tank again and this fund was down 10.8 percent in the first half of '95. Then in July it popped up 5.8 percent. You'd better have a strong stomach if you have money here! One school of thought has it that Japan has nowhere to go but up, so getting in now could lead to big profits. Maybe — but watch out for high volatility. For more aggressive investors only.

INVESTORS PACIFIC
INTERNATIONAL FUND $$$ ⇒ G * £ FEE

Focuses on the Pacific Rim, excluding Japan. One of the better performers among the new crop of Far East funds; wasn't hit as hard as some of its competitors in the Hong Kong pullback of early '94 and posted a gain of 4.5 percent for the year ending June 30, '95. Not impressed by that? Perhaps you will be when I tell you that the average Far East fund *lost* 5.7 percent over that time. Well-diversified portfolio; lately the managers have been looking for small to medium-sized companies in Taiwan to add to their holdings. A good bet for Investors Group clients seeking to add more growth potential to their portfolios.

REGENT KOREA FUND $$ ⇑ G #/*/NO £ FEE

This is Canada's only dedicated Korea fund. Needless to say, its fortunes will reflect those of the South Korean stock market. That market did well in '93 and '94; lately it's been weak. The fund's returns mirror that: gains of 26.1 percent and 31.3 percent in '93 and '94; a 16 percent loss in the first six months of '95. Over the long term, the

Korean market should produce above-average returns, but it's small and can be volatile. Unless you're a dedicated believer in South Korea's future, I recommend a more broadly based Asian fund. Managed by Peter Everington of Regent Capital Management, Hong Kong.

REGENT TIGER FUND $$ ⇒ G #/*/NO £ FEE

This fund specializes in the "Four Tigers" of Asia: Hong Kong, Taiwan, South Korea, and Singapore. Manager Peter Everington may also hold shares from the "mini-Tigers," Malaysia, Thailand, the Philippines, and Indonesia, as well as from other promising Asian markets like Sri Lanka. This corner of the globe saw some hot stock markets in the early '90s (the fund gained 62.2 percent in '93), but it's been a struggle recently. The fund lost 14.6 percent in the first half of '95, not an encouraging performance. Much of the problem can be traced to the fact that holdings were heavily concentrated in South Korea, Taiwan, and Singapore, all markets that were down (Taiwan by a lot) in the first half of the year. On the other hand, Everington had virtually no holdings in Hong Kong, which he feared was due for a big correction. In fact, Hong Kong was up smartly in the first half of '95. Everington is clearly a hunch manager, and recently the hunches haven't been working — which is not to say they won't in the future.

ROYAL JAPANESE STOCK FUND $$$ ⇑ G NO £ FEE

Boy, I got whipsawed on this one. I raised the rating in last year's edition because I felt economic recovery in North America and Europe would help Japan's exports and, therefore, its stocks. I didn't count on a rising yen, the Kobe earthquake, and a crisis in the Japanese banking industry, all of which sent the market tumbling, along with this fund which fell 25 percent in the year to June 30, '95. I did warn about the risk though — which is about the only positive thing I can say about that bad call. If you got in on the basis of that and are still holding, I wouldn't bail out now. The worst may be over — this fund recovered a whopping 7.4 percent in July '95. Aggressive investors who can handle the risk may even wish to take new positions at this stage. Maybe I'm a glutton for punishment, but I'm leaving the rating intact this year because my innards tell me the battered Japanese market could be heading for a rebound in '96. Don't bet the house on it, though.

European Equity Funds

uropean markets have rebounded recently, after going through some bad times early in the decade. As a result, many mutual fund companies have moved to cash in on the action (and investor interest) by setting up dedicated European funds.

This new section in the *Guide* reflects that trend. You won't find many entries this year, because most of the Europe funds haven't passed their third birthday. But as the years pass, this section will expand; there are currently almost 25 European funds being sold in Canada. ■

Are Europe funds a good buy? Yes, when European markets are buoyant, as they have been recently. But you might want to switch to something else when the continent goes into one of its periodic funks.

RATINGS CHANGES

Three European funds are making their debut in this edition: Fidelity European Growth, C.I. Europe, and Vision Europe. Of the three, the Fidelity fund is your best bet, with a $$$ rating.

Among returnees, Investors European Growth Fund moves up a notch to $$$ status this year.

1996 RATINGS

C.I. EUROPEAN FUND
$ ⇒ G #/* £ EE

All European funds have been making profits for investors lately. Unfortunately, this one has been making less than most. The three-year average annual return of 5.1 percent to June 30, '95, is the lowest for all European entries. So perhaps it's not surprising that new managers took over in October '94 — Robert Rawe and James Burns of London-based TCW Europe. They take a more aggressive position in the emerging European markets than some of the other funds in this category. As of July 31, '95, for example, 5.5 percent of the portfolio was in Portugal, 3.2 percent in Greece, and 3.1 percent in Turkey. So far, we haven't seen a big payoff from the management change, but perhaps another year will bring better results.

DYNAMIC EUROPE FUND
$$ ⇒ G #/* £ EE

When this fund was launched in late '89, it was with the idea of enabling Canadian investors to profit from the bright new future that was to unfold in Europe when trade barriers were eliminated in '92. Unfortunately, the European dream got derailed along the way, amid political and currency turmoil. This fund lost money for investors in each of the first three years of its existence. I maintained its $$ rating, however, with the comment that I thought Europe might be about to turn the corner, and suggested that if you wanted to take a flyer, this might be worth a little money. Europe did indeed turn the corner, and the fund shows an average annual return of 15.1 percent for the two years ending June 30, '95. The portfolio was heavily weighted to France in mid-'95, where the managers saw good value. Name changed from Dynamic Europe 1992 Fund in March '93.

FIDELITY EUROPEAN GROWTH FUND
$$$ ⇒ G #/* £ EE

Boasts the best three-year record of any European fund sold in Canada (average annual gain of 14.7 percent). Manager Sally Walden maintains a well-diversified portfolio, which was most heavily weighted to the U.K., Germany, and France in mid-'95. She uses a bottom-up approach to stock picking, concentrating on company fundamentals. One of the better choices from the Fidelity group. See my comments on purchase options in the listing for the Fidelity Capital Builder Fund in the Canadian Equity section.

GLOBAL STRATEGY EUROPE
PLUS FUND $$ ⇒ G #/* £ EE

The name of this fund was changed from Global Strategy Europe in early '95 and it was given a new team of managers. As a result, GS is presenting this as a brand-new fund — you'll find only short-term performance results in the business press. That's understandable, since the predecessor fund had never been very impressive. The new version, on the other hand, got off to a promising start with a 7.6 percent advance in the first six months of '95. Let's hope this is just the start of better things. Managers are Rothschild Asset Management, Gartmore Capital Management, and UBS International Investment. Each has a different investing style and each is responsible for a specific portion of the fund.

HYPERION EUROPEAN TRUST $$ ⇒ G #/* £ EE

A new entry from Hyperion, managed from London by Bernadotte Attard of Baring International Investment Ltd. In spring '95, portfolio was being restructured to reduce relative weightings in Germany because of the negative export impact of the high Deutschmark and unencouraging labour talks. Holdings in Spain and Switzerland were being increased. Three-year results are slightly below the average for European funds as a group, but more recent returns have been picking up. Fund gained 11.8 percent for the year to June 30, '95.

INVESTORS EUROPEAN GROWTH FUND $$$ ⇒ G * £ EE

Started off somewhat slowly, but Investors' entry into the European equity stakes has come on very strongly recently. Gained 13.2 percent for the year to June 30, '95, one of the better performances in this category. Entering '95, portfolio was about one-third in the U.K., with other significant holdings in France, Germany, and the Netherlands. If you're an Investors Group client, having a little money here isn't a bad idea. See entry for Investors Canadian Equity Fund in the Canadian Equity section for details on commissions and fees.

ROYAL EUROPEAN GROWTH FUND $$$ ⇒ G NO £ EE

This was originally available only to Royal Trust clients; now Royal Bank customers can buy it as well. It's well worth considering, a solid fund that has made some nice profits. Two years ago, I increased the rating on this fund to $$$ with the comment that I was doing so "not because of what this fund has done but because of what I expect it to do." I hope you acted on that advice, because the average annual return for the two years to June 30, '95, was a very handsome 17.3 percent. I think there are still some profits left in Europe, although I don't expect returns of that magnitude in '96. This is one of the few ways to buy into Europe on a no-load basis.

VISION EUROPE FUND $$ ⇒ G * £ EE

A Montreal-based European fund that places special emphasis on privatization issues of previously public companies. Three-year average annual rate of return to June 30, '95, was slightly below average at 8.9 percent, but latest results have been better. Call (514) 879-3624 for purchase details. Formerly known as European Investment and Privatization Fund.

Emerging Markets Equity Funds

W e used to call them "developing countries" or "the Third World." Now they're "emerging markets," and North Americans have been pouring billions of dollars into them — not for altruistic reasons, but in hopes of profiting from the tremendous growth potential of these burgeoning nations.

In the early part of this decade, the cash registers rang merrily and investors who were at the front of the line for this action did very well. Mutual fund companies, seeing what was happening, rushed to get into the game by opening up a bunch of new emerging markets funds. ■

Evidence? At the start of the '90s, there wasn't a single emerging markets fund in Canada. By mid-'95, the number was up to 19, not counting the region-specific Latin funds, and new ones were appearing all the time.

The rapid growth in this category has prompted me to create a special ratings section for broadly based emerging markets funds this year. Included here are funds that invest in these markets around the world. For funds that focus on a single area, see the appropriate ratings section (e.g., Americas Equity Funds for Latin American funds).

This section isn't large now. But as new funds reach their third anniversary over the next few years and become eligible for inclusion in this *Guide*, it will grow substantially. In the meantime, here are the two that have attained that milestone.

1996 RATINGS

C.I. EMERGING MARKETS FUND $ ⇑ G #/* £ EME

Looked at from a three-year perspective, this fund hasn't done too badly, with an average annual gain of 9.7 percent to June 30, '95. But the bulk of that gain was in '93, when this fund zoomed ahead 65 percent. In '94, investors lost just over 12 percent, and that trend continued into the first half of '95, with a 10.8 percent loss (although things were starting to take a turn for the better at mid-year). Part of the problem was this fund's large Latin American weighting entering '95 (over 40 percent of the portfolio). When the Mexican peso went into the tank, that section of the portfolio took a big hit. The fund also had an 8.5 percent weighting (since reduced) in India, where markets have been shocked by growing xenophobia. So, all in all, it's been a rough ride for manager Emilio Bassini of New York-based BEA Associates, and a lesson to investors about the volatility of these markets. As of late summer '95, the portfolio had been rejigged to reduce the Latin emphasis and build positions in countries like South Africa. This fund should get back on the right track, but of the two emerging markets entries in this year's edition, I'd go for the one below.

TEMPLETON EMERGING MARKETS FUND $$$ ⇑ G #/* £ EME

This fund is run by Dr. J. Mark Mobius, a colourful globe-trotter with Templeton's traditional eye for value. The portfolio is broadly diversified, with about 30 countries represented in the first half of '95. No one country dominates; early in '95 Hong Kong was number one with 14.2 percent of the total assets, closely followed by Brazil. Countries not often found in portfolios like this included Bolivia, Botswana, Morocco, and Sri Lanka. That Mobius fellow sure gets around! As with all emerging markets funds, this one is a roller-coaster ride. It suffered small losses in both '92 and '94, but more than made up for those with a gain of almost 83 percent in '93. The early part of '95 was weak, but then emerging markets started to bounce back and the fund showed a nice gain of 10.1 percent for the six months to July 31. I prefer this entry because of Templeton's value-oriented management style, the stock-picking skills of Mobius, and the broad diversification of the portfolio. But never lose sight of the fact that emerging markets are only for investors who are prepared to take risks and stick with their convictions through the down times.

Dividend Income Funds

ividend income funds are supposed to do exactly what the name implies — generate above-average dividends that investors can use to take advantage of the dividend tax credit and improve after-tax returns.

The actual returns on these funds can therefore be somewhat misleading. They reflect changes in the market prices of the underlying securities, as well as the dividend payouts. If you're using these funds properly, market values shouldn't be a significant concern to you. What you want to know is: how much income is the fund generating and is most or all of that in the form of dividends? ■

Not all the funds that follow meet those criteria. They may call themselves dividend funds, but the portfolio says they're something quite different. You'll find such cases noted in the ratings. If it's a true dividend fund you're seeking, be wary.

One other note: dividend funds are especially valuable

to income-oriented investors at times when interest rates are low. Under such conditions, it's quite possible your payouts will match or better those of a GIC in absolute dollars. By the time the dividend tax credit is taken into account, you come out way ahead.

RATINGS CHANGES

One of last year's $$$ entries, and one of my long-term favourites in this category, has been downgraded to $$ status this year. The Guardian Preferred Dividend Fund has taken a change in direction, adding a very large bond component to the portfolio. That seriously dilutes the value of the fund in relation to the dividend tax credit, hence the reduced rating.

The ratings of the 20/20 Dividend Fund and the Prudential Dividend Fund of Canada have both moved up to $$$ this year, but a word of caution is in order. Neither of these is what I would call a true dividend income fund (the 20/20 entry comes closest). But looked at simply as Canadian equity funds, both stand up very well, and I suggest you judge them on that basis and make your purchase decision accordingly.

The CIBC Equity Income Fund debuts this year, with a $$ rating.

1996 RATINGS

BPI INCOME FUND $$ ⇒ FI #/* RSP INC

Name changed from Bolton Tremblay Landmark Income Fund after the BPI takeover. If you're looking for a genuine dividend fund, this one doesn't do it. Over a third of the portfolio is held in cash, mortgages, and convertible debentures, which generate interest income (no tax break there). Returns have picked up significantly since the takeover, however; this fund gained a healthy 16.9 percent in the year ending June 30, '95. Treat it as a balanced fund rather than an income fund and you won't be disappointed.

BISSETT DIVIDEND INCOME FUND $ ⇒ G/FI NO INC

Formerly the Bissett Asset Allocation Fund *and* the Bissett Balanced Fund, which means this fund is both new and old, depending on how you look at it. The original fund has been in existence since 1988, but was a consistent underachiever with little direction. Bissett decided to make major changes. In August '93 the company combined the two funds, reorganized the investment strategy and the portfolio, and launched the revamped fund in this incarnation. The manager is still the same, but everything else is a horse of a different colour. The prospectus says the fund should be of interest to "taxable investors who can utilize the federal dividend tax credit." Unfortunately, the fund's portfolio leaves something to be desired on that score. Entering '95, 23 percent of the holdings were in foreign stocks, which are not eligible for the dividend tax credit. Interest-bearing securities accounted for another 14.5 percent of the assets. If you're looking for a true dividend fund, this doesn't quite fit. Return since the merger has been good, however; the fund gained 16.8 percent in the year to June 30, '95. See Bissett Canadian Equity Fund entry for purchase details. Note that this fund is not eligible for registered plans.

CIBC EQUITY INCOME FUND $$ ⇒ G/FI NO RSP INC

This fund seeks to maximize dividends but also puts some emphasis on growth. As a result, the portfolio is almost entirely made up of shares in blue-chip companies with good dividend records. Unlike most pure dividend funds, there are very few preferred shares in the mix. The net result is likely to be more growth than you might expect from an income fund, but a lower dividend payout. If your goal is to maximize the dividend tax credit, that may not be your preferred combination. Results have been so-so; the fund averaged 9.1 percent a year for the three years to June 30, '95.

DYNAMIC DIVIDEND FUND $$$ ⇒ FI #/* RSP INC

One of the best bets in this category, and one of the few that is a "dividend" fund in the true meaning of the term. Portfolio heavily emphasizes preferred shares, with about a quarter of the holdings in high-yielding common stocks. As a hedge against declines in the Canadian dollar, the fund also holds some U.S. dollar preferreds, issued by Canadian chartered banks. Technically RRSP-eligible but not recommended for registered plans because of the loss of the dividend tax credit. Five-year average annual return to June 30, '95, was a healthy 9 percent. If you're looking for a way to benefit from the dividend tax credit, you won't go far wrong here. Maximum front-end load is 5 percent, less than for most other Dynamic funds.

DYNAMIC DIVIDEND
GROWTH FUND $$$ ⇒ FI #/* RSP INC

Formerly the Allied Dividend Fund; name changed in April '93. Unspectacular performer in previous guise, with below-average results. Has looked much better since being taken over by Dynamic. Holds a higher percentage of its portfolio in common stock than the Dividend Fund (above), so is better suited to those looking for a combination of dividend income and capital gains. Total returns tend to be somewhat higher than those of the Dividend Fund (above) as a result. Which of the two you choose depends on your objectives; if steady dividend income is your priority, stay with the Dividend Fund.

GREEN LINE DIVIDEND FUND $ ⇒ FI NO RSP INC

The mandate of this fund is to invest in quality, high-yielding common and preferred shares so as to maximize use of the dividend tax credit, and to generate some capital gains. The managers, Toronto Dominion Asset Management, may be putting a little too much emphasis on the secondary goal. As of April '95, several of the fund's major holdings were in companies that pay very low dividends, including Nova, Celanese Canada, West Fraser Timber, Teck "B", and Hollinger. Not my idea of a classic dividend fund. Long-term results are above average, but recent returns have been weak. Sold in TD Bank branches.

GUARDIAN PREFERRED
DIVIDEND FUND $$ ⇒ FI #/* RSP INC

This used to be my favourite fund in the dividend income category because it was one of the few that had an almost pure portfolio of preferred shares. But something has changed; in early '95, almost 38 percent of the holdings were in corporate bonds and short-term notes. These pay interest, which is not eligible for the dividend tax credit. As a result, the tax-advantaged status of this fund has been diluted. Guardian says this fixed income component will remain "a permanent feature" of the fund, although not necessarily at this high a level. The reason is to "maximize income generation." True, bonds usually yield more than preferreds. But there are bond funds that do that job. This is supposed to be a dividend fund. That fundamental change in direction, plus generally below-average returns for this category, have led me to knock down the rating this year. RRSP/RRIF-eligible, but not recommended for those plans because you'll lose the benefit of the dividend tax credit, to the extent it applies.

INDUSTRIAL DIVIDEND FUND $$ ⇒ G #/* RSP CBAL

Despite the name, this is not a true dividend income fund, although it's somewhat closer now than before. The new mandate allows up to 75 percent of the assets to be invested in high-yielding common shares, although as of mid-'95 the actual proportion of these shares was just 27.7 percent. The major holding (39.9 percent) was in growth stocks with little or no dividend yield. There is also a relatively large (11.6 percent) foreign stock component and a 20 percent holding in fixed income securities. All of this adds up to a balanced fund in my mind, not a dividend fund at all, despite what Mackenzie says. Certainly, if maximizing use of the dividend tax credit is your goal, this isn't the fund you'd chose. I'm somewhat at a loss as to how to categorize this one, so I'm leaving it in this section for now. But if the portfolio mix doesn't take it closer to a true dividend fund over the next 12 months, I'll have to find another home for it in the '97 *Guide*.

INVESTORS DIVIDEND FUND $$$ ⇒ FI * RSP INC

Mandate is to provide steady income that's eligible for the dividend tax credit, but there's a problem — the managers are having trouble finding things to buy. The company pointed out in its latest annual report they're experiencing difficulty finding good preferred shares. "The redemption of existing issues, along with fewer new issues coming to market and over-aggressive pricing of those that did…all contributed to a shortage of quality issues," the report said. As a result, the weighting of high-yielding common stocks has increased and there has been a slight increase in bond holdings. Results are credible, although the dividend payout is not as high as with some of the other funds in this category. Average annual rate of return for the decade to June 30, '95, was 8.1 percent. This fund is technically eligible for RRSPs/RRIFs, but I wouldn't advise putting it into a registered plan because you'll lose the benefit of the dividend tax credit. See entry for Investors Canadian Equity Fund in the Canadian Equity section for details on commissions and fees.

LAURENTIAN DIVIDEND FUND $$$ ⇒ FI #/* RSP INC

A solid choice in the dividend group. Average annual return of 8.2 percent over the decade ending June 30, '95. Portfolio is made up mainly of high-yielding common stocks and preferreds, thus enabling investors to take advantage of the dividend tax credit. Sold in Eaton's stores by Laurentian Financial Services. Eligible for RRSPs and RRIFs, but not recommended because of loss of the tax credit advantage. Name changed from Viking Dividend fund in '93.

PHILLIPS, HAGER & NORTH
DIVIDEND INCOME FUND $$$ ⇒ FI NO RSP INC

Portfolio concentrates on high-yielding common stocks, rather than preferreds. This suggests a slightly lower income stream, but higher capital gains potential. Good track record; average annual return for the decade to June 30, '95, is 9.6 percent, best in this category. No load, but a minimum investment of $25,000 required. Buy directly from the managers; phone 1-800-661-6141 for information.

PRUDENTIAL DIVIDEND
FUND OF CANADA $$$ ⇒ FI # RSP INC

Take a quick scan of the Dividend Fund section in your newspaper's monthly mutual fund survey and the numbers for this one will pop out at you. Top five-year average annual return to June 30, '95 — 14 percent. Top three-year return — 19.8 percent. Top two-year return — 12.9 percent. Clearly, this is the number one fund in this category. There's just one problem. This isn't a true dividend fund. Sure, the mandate is to invest in securities that will maximize the use of the dividend tax credit. But the composition of the portfolio suggests other factors are influencing the managers — like boosting returns through capital gains, which has the effect of making the numbers look more impressive. How else do you explain the fact the fund was holding several foreign stocks in the spring (G.E., Bristol Myers, Duracell, Glaxo, and more)? They're all good companies, but any dividends they pay aren't eligible for the dividend tax credit. And what are Canadian companies like Corporate Foods (1.5 percent dividend), Ipsco (1.9 percent), Cameco (1.2 percent), and Malette (zero) doing in the mix? Yes, there are some high-yielders — banks, utilities, and some preferreds. But there's too much of the other stuff to make this the best choice for someone whose top priority is tax-advantaged income. Perhaps Prudential should consider changing this fund's mandate to make it an ordinary Canadian equity fund. Ironically, its five-year results are better than Prudential's flagship fund in that category, Growth Fund of Canada. And this fund's returns are much better than the average for all the funds in that group. In the meantime, I suggest you think of this as an ordinary stock fund, with some dividend flow as a bonus. If you judge it from that perspective, it's a good choice. This year's $$$ rating is based on taking that approach — if you want a pure dividend fund, look elsewhere. Sold by Prudential Fund Management.

ROYAL TRUST GROWTH
AND INCOME FUND $ ⇒ FI NO RSP INC

What to do? What to say? This fund has been jacked around so much in recent years that anyone with money in it must be wondering when the revolving door stops. Well, take heart — it's about to. Problem is, it may not be where you want to get off. The investment mandate of this fund has been changed (again!) to make it a dividend fund (which, ironically, is where it started out). Reason: it is soon to merge with the RoyFund Dividend Fund and the managers wanted to align both portfolios to make the transition as flawless as possible. All well and good, but if you weren't looking for a dividend fund when you originally got in, or if you're holding this one in an RRSP or RRIF, you should exit now. There's no way to put a meaningful rating on this, since the strategy keeps changing, but RoyFund Dividend has looked pretty good so far (it's too new for a formal rating here). Formerly called the RT Preferred Blue Chip Fund.

SCOTIA EXCELSIOR DIVIDEND FUND $$$ ⇒ FI NO RSP INC

Formerly the Montreal Trust Dividend Fund, this was merged into the Scotia Fund group in August '95. It's a solid dividend fund with a portfolio that's well designed to take maximum advantage of the dividend tax credit. Gained 10.4 percent in the year to June 30, '95. If you're looking for a pure dividend fund, this is one of the few around. Technically eligible for RRSPs/RRIFs, but not recommended for that purpose because of the loss of the tax credit. Sold by Scotiabank branches.

SPECTRUM DIVIDEND FUND $$ ⇒ G/FI #/* RSP INC

Spectrum has made a strong effort to make this into more of a true dividend fund. In the past, a large percentage of the assets were held in interest-bearing securities, diluting the value of the dividend tax credit. But that has been changing since Stuart Pomfrey of Sun Life Investment Management rejoined the management team in March '94. He has raised the preferred share component of the portfolio to the 30–40 percent range. Another 40 percent of the holdings are in high-yielding common stocks. There is an 18 percent Canadian bond component to offset the fund's fees and expenses with interest income. This move ensures that maximum dividend income can be distributed out to investors. Dividend yield as of spring '95 was a healthy 6.6 percent. A decent choice for income-oriented investors seeking to make use of the dividend tax credit. RRSP/RRIF-eligible, but better held outside such plans for the tax breaks.

20/20 DIVIDEND FUND $$$ ⇒ G/FI #/* RSP INC

The returns on this fund are quite healthy and the portfolio is conservatively managed by Gord MacDougall of Connor, Clark and Lunn. However, this is not a classic dividend fund. The portfolio is heavily weighted to high-yielding blue-chip common stocks; preferreds make up only a tiny percentage of the holdings. As well, there were some significant U.S. bond holdings in the early part of '95. All this means that dividend payouts will be less than from funds with a large percentage of higher-yielding preferreds; keep that in mind if maximizing the dividend tax credit is your main goal. Also, the cash distributions from this fund show considerable variance from year to year, which is not helpful if you're relying on the income to fund your retirement. I suggest you treat this fund as a solid blue-chip entry for risk-averse investors, and make your purchase judgment on that basis. Using that criteria, its performance would be above average for Canadian equity funds generally. Formerly known as the Sunset Convertible Preferred and Dividend Fund.

Canadian Bond Funds

W e saw a strong recovery in bond funds in the first half of '95, but there could be some turbulent times in store for '96 as we get closer to the end of this growth cycle. Patient investors should hang tough, as long as their portfolios aren't overweighted in fixed income securities. Defensive investors may wish to switch some holdings into short-term bond funds and mortgage funds. ■

RATINGS CHANGES

Last year, I downgraded the two $$$$ funds in this category because of the bond market turbulence that was swirling at the time. This year I'm happy to report the Altamira Income Fund and the Phillips, Hager & North Bond Fund have both been restored to their previous top-level status. They've been joined on that lofty perch by a newcomer — the little-known and unheralded National Life Fixed Income Fund. National Life has emerged as the top segregated fund company in Canada, and this solid entry is just one example of that.

Seven other bond funds have been upgraded this year. Those attaining $$$ standing are the First Canadian Bond Fund, Green Line Canadian Bond Fund, Standard Life Ideal Bond Fund, and Talvest Bond Fund.

Three funds appear in this edition for the first time, with the Colonia Bond Fund enjoying a *$$$* rating in its initial year.

1996 RATINGS

AGF CANADIAN BOND FUND $$$ ⇓ FI #/*/NO RSP CB

This fund has been a dependable performer for many years. It was hard hit by the bond market tumble of early '94, losing 13 percent of its unit value in the first six months. But it more than made up that ground over the next 12 months, gaining 16.9 percent for the year to June 30, '95. This is a conservative fund from a portfolio safety perspective, investing only in government issues. As of April '95, 89 percent of the assets were in federal government bonds, with 11 percent in provincial issues. The fund has had only one down year in the past two decades, losing 8.5 percent in '94.

AMI PRIVATE CAPITAL INCOME FUND $$ ⇒ FI NO RSP CB

This fund invests in a mix of federal, provincial, and municipal bonds, with some high-quality corporates as well. Longer-term results are slightly above average. No load if purchased through the fund manager (Quebec, B.C., Nova Scotia, and Ontario residents only), otherwise a 2 percent commission may be applied. Minimum investment is $50,000, which can be spread over several funds in the group ($10,000 minimum per fund). Formerly the Church Street Income Fund.

ADMAX CANADIAN INCOME FUND

Merged with Regent World Income Fund.

ALTAMIRA BOND FUND $$$ ⇒ FI NO RSP CB

How wrong I was on this one! In last year's edition, I said I didn't feel a bond fund with an aggressive management style, like this one has, would perform well in the current economic environment. That statement was written at a time when bond markets were experiencing their worst turbulence in a decade. Well, the markets rallied and the style of manager Robert Marcus paid off big time. This fund surged to a 24.8 percent gain for the year to June

30, '95, the best performance of any Canadian bond fund over that time. *Mea culpa,* and the $$$ rating is restored.

ALTAMIRA INCOME FUND $$$$ ⇒ FI NO RSP CB

I dropped the rating of this fund a notch last year because of the tough bond markets we were experiencing and the possibility there would be more turbulence ahead. As it turned out, the bond market snapped back more strongly than most people thought possible and this fund gained an excellent 21.9 percent for the year to June 30, '95. Only the companion Altamira Bond Fund, which is more aggressively positioned, did better. Over the long haul, this is one of the top-performing bond funds in Canada, with an average annual return of just under 12 percent over the past decade. Manager Will Sutherland does a solid, consistent job. If you're looking for a good bond fund, this should be way up on your list. There is a small ($40) one-time setup fee when you open a new account. Purchase directly from Altamira Investment Services, 1-800-263-2824.

ATLAS CANADIAN BOND FUND $$ ⇒ FI NO RSP CB

This fund has gone through so many incarnations that I'm losing track. It started out as the AMD Fixed Income Fund, became the Finsco Bond Fund, evolved to the Jarislowsky Finsco Bond Fund, and now is the Atlas Canadian Bond Fund. You can't tell the players without a program! A decent performer; was hit in the '94 bond market drop like everyone else, but rebounded well in '95 with a first-half gain of 11.1 percent. Available through Midland Walwyn brokers.

BPI CANADIAN BOND FUND $ ⇒ FI #/* RSP CB

Formed out of the merger of the BPI Canadian Bond Fund, the BT Landmark Bond Fund, and the Bolton Tremblay Bond Fund. The Bolton Tremblay Funds had a better track record; since the merger this one has been a below-average performer.

BEUTEL GOODMAN INCOME FUND $$ ⇒ FI NO RSP CB

Another new entry from the Beutel Goodman group, this fund maintains a mix of high-quality government and corporate bonds. It turned in above-average results in its first two years (11.3 percent in '92; 17.2 percent in '93).

But it nosedived in '94, dropping 7.2 percent. Recovered nicely in the first half of '95, however, with an 11.3 percent gain. Needs more time before it's clear whether this will be a consistent above-average performer. No sales commission if purchased directly from Beutel Goodman.

BISSETT BOND FUND $$$ ⇒ FI NO RSP CB

This Alberta-based fund has turned in a respectable record since its launch in '86. It showed some signs of weakness in the early '90s, but has picked up nicely since. Although it recorded a small loss, it held up relatively well in the rough bond market of '94, and recorded a smart 10.6 percent gain in the first half of '95. Minimum investment is $5,000. See entry for Bissett Canadian Equity Fund for purchase details.

CIBC CANADIAN BOND FUND $$ ⇒ FI NO RSP CB

Has been one of the better entries from this big bank, but took a big loss of 9.2 percent in '94 when bond markets plunged. Came back well in '95, however, with a 10.4 percent gain in the first six months. Very conservative portfolio; most of the assets are in Government of Canada bonds. Available through branches of the Bank of Commerce. Formerly known as the CIBC Fixed Income Fund.

CANADA LIFE FIXED INCOME FUND S-19 $ ⇒ FI * RSP S CB

Performance about average for this group. Like most other bond funds, it took a big hit in '94, losing 7 percent. Portfolio is a mix of government and corporate issues. Rebounded in the first half of '95, but 10-year results are well below average. Redemption fee applies if cashed within seven years. If held more than 10 years, you are guaranteed a return of not less than 75 percent of your contributions, which puts a floor under any possible losses (unlikely in a bond fund over the long term, despite short-term gyrations). If you die, the guarantee goes to 100 percent. Sold by Canada Life reps.

CANADA TRUST INVESTMENT FUND — INCOME $$ ⇒ FI NO RSP CB

Average income fund. No longer actively marketed but still available through Canada Trust if you ask. Likely to be merged with the Everest Bond Fund.

COLONIA BOND FUND $$$ ⇓ FI * RSP S CB

Solid little entry from Colonia Life. Portfolio was exclusively in Government of Canada bonds as of spring '95,
although the managers can add corporates and provin-
cials if they wish. Performance has been above average
so far, although the fund has only been operating since
'92. Sold by Colonia reps.

CONCORDE INCOME FUND $ ⇒ FI #/* RSP CB

Underachieving fixed income fund offered by the
Quebec City-based Concorde Financial Group. Portfolio
includes a significant percentage of Quebec-based debt
issues, which may concern some investors. Three-year
annual return to June 30, '95, was 6.2 percent, well
below average for this category. Call 1-800-363-0598 for
information.

CONFEDERATION LIFE FUND C

Sold to Maritime Life in May '95. Future plans uncertain.

CORNERSTONE BOND FUND $$ ⇓ FI NO RSP CB

High safety level; at least 75 percent of the assets are to
be invested in government or government-guaranteed
securities. Actual government bond holdings at the start
of '95 was over 90 percent. Results have moved to above
average, thanks to a strong first half of '95. Continued
improvement will lead to a higher rating. Sold at branches of North American Trust. Formed by a merger between
the North American Income Fund (formerly First City
Income Fund) and the Metropolitan Bond Fund. Future is
uncertain due to the take-over of North American Trust
by Laurentian Bank in fall, '95.

DESJARDINS BOND FUND $$ ⇒ FI NO RSP CB

A solid, average performer. Heading into '94, 77 percent
of the assets were in Government of Canada bonds, with
only 13 percent in Quebec government and municipal
issues. Considering this is one of Quebec's premier financial institutions, that mix is interesting! Sold by offices of
the Quebec-based Desjardins Trust and Caisses
Desjardins. Quebec residents can call toll-free for details
at 1-800-361-6840.

DYNAMIC INCOME FUND $$$ ⇓ FI #/* RSP CB

A steady performer for many years, this fund enjoys a
special distinction: it was one of the few Canadian bond
funds to finish '94 in the black, with a gain of 6.7 percent. Just about everyone else lost money, thanks to
the debacle in the bond market in the early part of the
year. That result earned the fund the number one ranking for '94 among all bond funds in Southam's *Mutual
Fund SourceBook*, a huge rebound from the previous
year when it was number 99 out of 100, even though
the actual return that year was higher. Manager Norm
Bengough has a conservative style (one of the main reasons for those results). For example, he was quick to
take profits when the bond market rallied in early '95,
increasing cash holdings to more than 50 percent of the
portfolio by May. This approach will sometimes result in
below-average returns, but it minimizes downside risk
as well. This is the only bond fund in Canada with a
long-term record that did not record a single losing year
in the decade from 1985–94. Well worth a look.

ELLIOTT & PAGE BOND FUND $$ ⇒ FI #/* RSP CB

A steady but unexciting performer. Took an 8.3 percent
hit in '94, but bounced back with an 8.5 percent gain in
the first half of '95. Portfolio quality is good, with most
of the assets invested in Government of Canada bonds.
Watch out for the unusual back-end load option; see
entry for Elliott & Page Equity Fund in Canadian Equity
section for more details.

EMPIRE BOND FUND #2 $$ ⇒ FI #/* RSP S CB

Usually a solid if unexciting performer, but has slipped a
bit lately compared to the competition. Portfolio is heavily weighted to government issues and includes some
mortgage-backed securities. Available as either a front-
or back-end load. Sold by representatives of Empire Life.

EQUITABLE LIFE SEGREGATED
ACCUMULATIVE INCOME FUND $$$ ⇒ FI * RSP S CB

Solid performer, both short and long term. This is an
annuity-type plan that is only available to existing
Equitable policy-holders.

ETHICAL INCOME FUND $$ ⇒ FI #/*/NO RSP CB

Performance has been steadily improving since this fund was acquired from Co-operative Trust for the Ethical Funds family. Solid one-year return of 17 percent to June 30, '95. Portfolio is heavily weighted to government bonds. You can get it without any sales commissions at participating credit unions; otherwise a fee will be charged.

EVEREST BOND FUND $$ ⇒ FI NO RSP CB

Has been a steady performer. Results relative to other bond funds showed signs of slipping, resulting in a rating cutback last year. But the managers turned things around in the first half of '95, with a solid 10.7 percent gain. Another good year will see the $$$ rating restored. High-quality portfolio; more than half the assets are in Government of Canada bonds and mortgage-backed securities. Sold by branches of Canada Trust.

FICADRE BOND FUND $ ⇒ FI * RSP CB

Small Quebec-based fund with improving returns, although longer-term results are sub-par. Portfolio is heavily invested in Quebec-based issues. Formerly the SNF Bond Fund.

FIDELITY CANADIAN BOND FUND $$ ⇒ FI #/* RSP CB

This fund started out as a balanced fund, under the name Fidelity Capital Conservation Fund, then was called Fidelity Government Bond Fund for a while. Still invests mainly in government bonds but now has some corporate issues in the mix. Results have been uninspiring and the shift in portfolio emphasis hasn't helped much. Same purchase options as Fidelity Capital Builder Fund (see section on Canadian Equity Funds).

FIRST CANADIAN BOND FUND $$$ ⇒ FI NO RSP CB

Steady performer from the Bank of Montreal. Never flashy, but consistent above-average returns merit an upgrade in the rating this year. A respectable no-load alternative for bond fund investors.

GBC CANADIAN BOND FUND $$$ ⇓ FI NO RSP CB

A solid performer which has posted above-average returns over the years, although it got hit like just about everyone else in '94, losing 5.6 percent. Rebounded well in the first half of '95, however, with an 11.4 percent gain. Invests mainly in government securities; there were no corporate bonds in the portfolio in spring '95. No load if purchased directly from the manager, otherwise a commission of up to 3 percent may apply. For the super-rich only: you'll need $100,000 to get in. See GBC entry in Canadian Equity section for purchase details.

GENERAL TRUST BOND FUND $$ ⇒ FI NO RSP CB

This fund hadn't experienced a down year for at least two decades, until it took a 7.1 percent hit in '94. Like most funds in this category, it recovered in the first half of '95, with a 9.6 percent gain. Longer-term results are about average. The portfolio composition has changed significantly in the past year. Most of the assets were in Government of Canada bonds and T-bills in mid-'95. Interestingly, there were no Quebec provincial government holdings at all, a complete reversal from the previous year. That's especially significant because General Trust is owned by Quebec-based National Bank and this fund is sold only in Quebec. See additional comments in the entry for the General Trust Canadian Equity Fund in the Canadian Equity section.

GREAT-WEST LIFE CANADIAN BOND FUND $ ⇒ FI */NO RSP S CB

Managers specialize in high-quality bonds with an emphasis on government issues, although some corporates are also included in the portfolio. Long-term performance has fallen to below average for this category; 10-year average annual rate of return to June 30, '95, was 8.9 percent — a full point below average. Sold by Great-West Life reps.

GREEN LINE CANADIAN BOND FUND $$$ ⇒ FI NO RSP CB

After taking a big hit in the first half of '94, this fund has come roaring back with a stellar performance. Gain for the year ending June 30, '95, was 18 percent, one of the best in this category. That result pulled up the long-term averages as well, making this Green Line's number one bond fund performer. Invests in a combination of government and corporate bonds. Has advantage of being no load and widely available.

GREEN LINE CANADIAN
GOVERNMENT BOND FUND $$ ⇓ FI NO RSP CB

Differs from the Canadian Bond Fund (above) only in that the mandate here is to invest only in bonds issued or guaranteed by the various levels of government (including municipal) and their agencies. This should make it somewhat safer than an ordinary bond fund. Record in previous incarnation wasn't impressive, but it's looking better under the direction of Toronto Dominion Asset Management, which has done well by investors in Green Line's other fixed income funds. Returns are somewhat lower than those of the Canadian Bond Fund. Sold at TD Bank branches and through Green Line. Formerly the FuturLink Government Bond Fund.

GREEN LINE SHORT TERM
INCOME FUND $$$ ⇓ C NO RSP CB

This is a short-term bond fund that can invest in securities with a maturity of up to three years. In a time of low interest rates, this should result in a higher return than you'll receive from a money market fund, but at slightly more risk because unit values may fluctuate. When rates are rising, this fund offers more protection because of the short maturities. This was proven in the first half of '94 when the loss here was less than half that of Green Line's other bond funds. However, predictably, this fund did not perform as well when the bond market snapped back, gaining a modest 10.3 percent for the year ending June 30, '95. This investment strategy makes this fund appropriate for fixed income investors who want to limit risk but earn better returns than offered by money market funds. Available at branches of the TD Bank.

GUARDIAN CANADIAN
INCOME FUND $$ ⇓ FI #/* RSP B/M

This fund adopts a very conservative approach to fixed income investing. The bulk of the assets are held in short-term securities, which minimizes risk during times when interest rates are rising. The strategy looked pretty smart when interest rates rose in the first half of '94; this fund was hit less hard than most. When rates fall, however, this fund won't get the capital gains benefits. Portfolio also includes mortgage-backed securities. Safety factor is good, so this is a reasonable choice for conservative investors. Just don't expect high returns. Previously known as Guardian Canada Bond Fund.

HODGSON ROBERTON LAING
BOND FUND $$ ⇒ FI NO RSP CB

Long-term performance to date has been slightly below average, but returns showed improvement in the first half of '95. Portfolio is a fairly even mix of government and corporate bonds. Sold directly by the managers; phone 1-800-268-9622. Formerly the Waltaine Bond Fund.

HYPERION FIXED INCOME FUND

Sold to Talvest in mid-'95 and is being merged into one of their funds.

INDUSTRIAL ALLIANCE BOND FUND $$ ⇒ FI * RSP S CB

Not part of the Mackenzie Financial group, but rather an offering from a Quebec-based insurance company. Returns have been slightly above average.

INDUSTRIAL BOND FUND $$ ⇒ FI #/* RSP CB

Surprisingly, there was no dedicated bond fund in the sprawling Mackenzie empire until this one was created in '89. Portfolio consists mainly, but not exclusively, of Government of Canada issues. Was heavily overweighted in longer-term bonds (maturities over 10 years) in mid-'95, which could spell problems if interest rates rise. Expense ratio is on the high side for a bond fund (2.12 percent), but returns are slightly above average nonetheless.

INVESNAT SHORT-TERM
GOVERNMENT BOND FUND $$ ⇓ FI NO RSP CB

Switched from a regular bond fund to a short-term fund just in time to avoid being badly mauled in the downturn of '94, although the fund did suffer a small 2.3 percent loss. Good choice for defensive investors during periods of rising rates, but will tend to underperform when rates are declining. A large percentage of the portfolio is held in short-term notes issued by Quebec municipalities, hospitals, and community colleges. Available through branches of the National Bank.

INVESTORS GOVERNMENT BOND FUND $$ ⇒ FI * RSP CB

Solid performer, had never had a down year until '94, when just about every bond fund took a hit. Despite the name change (it was previously the Investors Bond Fund), there were still some corporate issues in the portfolio entering '95. However, the new mandate is to stick to government issues only — federal, provincial, and municipal. Recent returns have been above average, with a gain of 15.8 percent for the year to June 30, '95. No load, but there is a 3 percent redemption fee if cashed within five years. Sold only by Investors Group representatives.

INVESTORS INCOME PORTFOLIO FUND $$ ⇒ FI * RSP B/M

This is a "fund of funds" that invests one-third of its assets in the Investors Government Bond Fund, one-third in the Mortgage Fund, and one-third in the Corporate Bond Fund. Five-year results show an average annual return of 9.6 percent — which is somewhat misleading because the mix has changed recently. Still, this should perform somewhere between the low-risk mortgage fund and the higher-risk bond funds.

JONES HEWARD BOND FUND $$ ⇒ FI #/* RSP CB

A small fund with assets of just $4.3 million. Portfolio is now much better balanced (at one point, three-quarters of the assets were in Ontario Hydro bonds; they're now all gone). Routine performance, took a hard hit in '94 losing 7.6 percent. Formerly the Burns Fry Bond Fund.

LAURENTIAN GOVERNMENT BOND FUND $$ ⇓ FI #/* RSP CB

Invests primarily in short- to medium-term securities (not exceeding five years) issued or guaranteed by various levels of government. This strategy will make the portfolio less vulnerable to losses when interest rates rise, and in fact that's what happened in early '94 when the loss was about half that of most Canadian bond funds. Returns in good bond years will tend to be lower than for other funds, but conservative investors may like the extra safety this fund offers. Name changed from Endurance Government Bond Fund in '93.

LAURENTIAN INCOME FUND $ ⇒ FI #/* RSP CB

A more conventional bond fund than the companion Government Bond Fund (above). Invests in a range of debt issues, with the emphasis on medium- to longer-term securities. Had a tough year in '94 but came back well in the first half of '95 with a solid 9.2 percent gain. Longer-term record is somewhat below average, however. Previously known as the Viking Income Fund. Sold through Eaton's and member companies of Laurentian Financial.

LONDON LIFE BOND FUND $$ ⇒ FI * RSP S CB

Diversified portfolio, about 75 percent invested in federal and provincial government issues with some corporate bonds also in the mix. Like most bond funds, this one struggled in '94, losing 6.9 percent. Also like most bond funds, it snapped back in the first half of '95, gaining 10.5 percent. Long-term results are below average, however. This one's okay if you're a London Life client, but I wouldn't buy it otherwise.

MACKENZIE SENTINEL CANADA BOND FUND

Closed down in mid-'95.

MANULIFE VISTAFUND
BOND FUND $$ ⇒ FI #/* RSP S CB

Conservative portfolio consisting mainly of Government of Canada bonds. Took a big hit in '94, losing 9.4 percent. First half of '95 was above average, though. Long-term results slightly above average, if you used the Option 1 purchase plan. See entry for Manulife VistaFund Capital Gains Growth Fund in Canadian Equity section for purchase details. Sold by reps of Manufacturers Life. Managed by Altamira.

MARITIME LIFE BOND FUND $$ ⇒ FI NO RSP S CB

Average performance, but took a big hit in '94 with a loss of more than 6 percent. First half of '95 was better, with a 9.8 percent gain. Managed by T.A.L. Investment Counsel of Montreal, who also run several other Canadian bond funds, including Talvest. Most of the assets are in federal, provincial, and municipal government bonds, but corporate holdings represent about 15 percent of the portfolio. Sold by representatives of Maritime Life.

MAWER CANADIAN BOND FUND $$ ⇒ FI NO RSP CB

Routine bond fund from this Calgary-based company. Portfolio is a mixture of government and corporate issues. Three-year average annual return is just a tick above average. Call (403) 267-1989 for information.

MCLEAN BUDDEN FIXED INCOME FUND $$$ ⇒ FI NO RSP CB

Specializes in high-quality government and corporate bonds. Returns have been better than average despite taking a hit in '94, with a loss of 6.2 percent. Five-year average annual return to June 30, '95, was 11.4 percent. Small fund; assets of about $8 million. Call (416) 862-9800 for information.

METLIFE MVP BOND FUND $ ⇒ FI * RSP S CB

Indifferent performer with below-average returns. Maximum redemption fee of 2.5 percent, declining to zero after four years. Sold by MetLife reps.

MONTREAL TRUST EXCELSIOR — INCOME SECTION

Merged with the Scotia Income Fund to form the new Scotia Excelsior Income Fund in October '95.

MUTUAL BOND FUND $$ ⇒ FI # RSP CB

Average-performing fund from The Mutual Group. Portfolio is a mix of government and corporate bonds and mortgage-backed securities.

NAL CANADIAN BOND FUND $$ ⇒ FI * RSP S CB

Most of the portfolio is in federal and provincial government bonds, with about 10 percent corporate holdings. Results have shown definite improvement in recent years. Gain for the 12 months to June 30, '95, was a solid 15.2 percent. Management is by Elliott & Page. Sold by representatives of North American Life.

NN BOND FUND $$ ⇒ FI * RSP S CB

Returns have been steadily improving. Gained an above-average 14.6 percent in the 12 months to June 30, '95. Longer-term results are about average. Portfolio is mainly invested in federal and provincial bonds, with a few corporates mixed in. There's a 6 percent redemption fee, declining to zero after five years. Sold by representatives of NN Life.

NATIONAL LIFE FIXED INCOME FUND $$$$ ⇒ FI * RSP S CB

Superior-performing segregated fund, with an excellent long-term record (average 10-year annual gain to June 30, '95, was 11.8 percent, second only to the much better known Altamira Income Fund). What's more amazing is that those returns have been earned despite a high management expense fee (2 percent). Portfolio is a mix of government and corporate bonds. This is a top-notch entry, the best fixed income fund offered by an insurance company. As a result, I'm moving it up to $$$$ status. Sold by representatives of National Life.

NATIONAL TRUST CANADIAN BOND FUND $$ ⇒ FI NO RSP CB

A steady performer. It took a big hit in the first half of '94, as did most bond funds, but came back well with a gain of 16 percent in the year to June 30, '95. Portfolio composition is mainly federal and provincial bonds, with a small holding of corporate issues. Sold by National Trust. Name changed from National Trust Income Fund in June '94.

OPTIMUM BOND FUND $$ ⇒ FI NO RSP CB

Tiny ($2.5 million) Quebec-based fund with good returns, including a big 18 percent gain for the year ending June 30, '95. Most assets are in bonds issued or guaranteed by the Quebec government. May be purchased without load directly from the manager, Placements Optimum du St.-Laurent. Phone 1-800-363-7675 for details. Available in Quebec only. Formerly St. Laurent Optimum Bond Fund.

PHILLIPS, HAGER & NORTH BOND FUND $$$$ ⇒ FI NO RSP CB

No one was immune to the bond market crash of '94, not even this consistently good performer which lost 4.1 percent. But '94 was the worst year for bonds in a generation and, hopefully, we won't see its like again in our lifetime. Fund came back strongly in first half of '95 with a 10.7 percent gain. Despite the '94 setback, the long-term results of this well-run fund are still well above average, with an annual return of 11.6 percent for the decade to June 30, '95. High-quality portfolio, heavily weighted to government securities. An extra benefit is the very low management expense ratio — just 0.58 percent, making this one of the best values you'll find in bond funds. Top $$$$ rating is restored this year. Minimum initial investment of $25,000 required, except when held in an RRSP.

PRUDENTIAL INCOME FUND OF CANADA $$ ⇒ FI # RSP CB

Portfolio is a blend of federal government and blue-chip corporate bonds, with a small number of mortgages tossed in. Long-term track record slightly below average, but the fund is coming off a solid year with a gain of 17.2 percent in the 12 months to June 30, '95. Good safety record; never had a losing year until '94, when it dropped 6.7 percent. Maximum front-end load is 5 percent. Sold by Prudential Fund Management.

PURSUIT INCOME FUND $$ ⇓ FI #/NO RSP CB

Nigel Stephens Counsel Inc. of North York, Ontario, took over the four Pursuit funds in early '90. The performance of this fund has been respectable since. A timely move into cash in early '94 sheltered investors from the worst of the bond market fall; value declined just under 3 percent for the year. The safety factor is good; at the start of '95 all the assets were in securities issued by the Canadian government. See Pursuit Canadian Equity Fund for purchase details.

ROYAL LIFE INCOME FUND $ ⇒ FI * RSP S CB

Uses a two-pronged investment approach. Two-thirds of the portfolio is structured to mirror the ScotiaMcLeod Universe Bond Index. The other third uses an "interest rate anticipation" approach — which simply means the managers trade actively to attempt to benefit from moves in the bond/interest rate market. Below-average long-term performer, with an annual return of 8.9 percent for the five years to June 30, '95. Most recent results show improvement. Sold by Royal Life reps.

ROYAL TRUST BOND FUND $$ ⇒ FI NO RSP CB

Good no-load performer. Results are generally slightly above average for this category, although it got socked like everyone else in '94. Solid portfolio is weighted in favour of government and government-guaranteed issues. A decent choice among financial institution bond funds.

ROYFUND BOND FUND $$ ⇒ FI NO RSP CB

A solid, conservatively managed fund investing in high-quality government and corporate bonds. Pattern is very similar to the Royal Trust Bond, with which it will eventually merge. Available through Royal Bank branches.

SAVINGS AND INVESTMENT TRUST BOND FUND $$ ⇒ FI NO RSP CB

Portfolio has large holdings of Quebec-based bonds and debentures, which is hardly surprising since this is an offering from a Quebec-based financial institution. Performance has been improving recently; fund gained a solid 15.1 percent in the year to June 30, '95. Sold at branches of Savings and Investment Trust (Trust Prêt et Revenu).

SCEPTRE BOND FUND $$ ⇒ FI NO RSP CB

A solid performer, with improving results. Most of the portfolio is in government or government-guaranteed issues. Manager Bill Malouin tends to be conservative in his style, keeping the fund fairly short term to cut volatility. Despite this cautious approach, returns over the longer term are slightly above average. See Sceptre Equity Fund in Canadian Equity section for purchase details.

SCOTIA EXCELSIOR DEFENSIVE INCOME FUND $$ ⇓ FI NO RSP CB

Invests in high-grade bonds and notes, primarily government or government-guaranteed, with relatively short maturities (maximum five years). The fund has a longer time horizon than a money market fund, but a shorter one than most bond funds, thus reducing its volatility during times of sharp interest rate movements (hence the word "defensive" in the name). Target average term to maturity of the portfolio is two years. During a period of falling interest rates, a fund like this will underperform most conventional bond funds. But when rates are rising, it will do much better. That's exactly what's happened recently. When interest rates rose in the first half of '94, this fund held its ground better than most. But when the bond market rallied in '95, returns here were lower — 8.2 percent for the first six months of the year compared to 11.5 percent for the companion Income Fund (below). This is a fund to move your money into if you're a cautious investor and/or it looks like rates are heading up. Available through branches of the Bank of Nova Scotia and Montreal Trust. May also be acquired through the brokerage firm of ScotiaMcLeod, but there's a $15 fee for each purchase or redemption.

SCOTIA EXCELSIOR INCOME FUND $$ ⇒ FI NO RSP CB

This fund was formed in August '95 by the merger of the Montreal Trust Excelsior Income Section and the Scotia Income Fund. The portfolio of the Scotia fund (the larger of the two) tends to be somewhat longer term than that of the Defensive Income Fund (see above). The fund may also hold stocks (no more than 10 percent) and mortgages (maximum 30 percent), but there were no such holdings entering '95. Results have been showing improvement recently.

SPECTRUM GOVERNMENT
BOND FUND $$ ⇒ FI #/* RSP CB

Invests primarily in Canadian government and government-guaranteed issues. Was going along nicely, producing decent returns, when — wham! It got clobbered in the first half of '94, losing almost 14 percent. Manager Stuart Pomphrey engineered a quick recovery, however; the fund gained a fat 17.5 percent in the year ending June 30, '95. High-quality portfolio, rated AAAi (Superior) by the Canadian Bond Rating Service. However, the risk inherent in this fund is higher than in the companion Interest Fund (below) because of the longer term-to-maturity of the portfolio (17.8 years in April '95).

SPECTRUM INTEREST FUND $$ ⇒ FI #/* RSP CB

Invests in a mix of government and corporate debt securities. Returns have tended to be somewhat below those of the Government Bond Fund (above), but because of a shorter term-to-maturity of the portfolio, the risk factor is somewhat lower as well. Quality of assets is good; the Canadian Bond Rating Service gives the fund a top AAAi rating and reports that it has never incurred a loss due to default since its inception. Managed by Stuart Pomphrey, who also runs the companion Government Bond Fund.

STANDARD LIFE IDEAL
BOND FUND $$$ ⇒ FI * RSP S CB

Good entry from Standard Life Assurance Co. Solid long-term record. Was hard hit in the market fall of early '94, losing 10.4 percent in six months, but has come back well with a gain of 15.4 percent in the year to June 30, '95. Sold by Standard Life Assurance agents and brokers. Formerly known as Standard Life Bond 2000 Fund. Don't confuse this with the newer Standard Life Bond Mutual Fund, which is not a segregated fund. It's too new for inclusion in these ratings.

STRATA INCOME FUND $$ ⇒ FI # RSP CB

The Strata funds have been sold to Mutual Life and are scheduled to be merged into the Mutual fund family by the end of '95.

TALVEST BOND FUND $$$ ⇒ FI #/* RSP CB

Good performer over long term, from one of the companies best liked by mutual funds sales professionals. Until '94, had an excellent safety record, never losing money over a calendar year since it was set up in the early '70s. But that streak came to an end with a 6.1 percent loss last year. The fund bounced back nicely in the first half of '95, however, with a nice 10.2 percent gain. Manager John Braive had overweighted the portfolio in corporate securities in mid-'95 to improve yields. This is a solid, well-managed fund. See Talvest Growth Fund entry in Canadian Equity section for purchase details.

TALVEST INCOME FUND $$ ⇓ FI #/* RSP CB

Invests in a mixture of short- to mid-term bonds, with a very small percentage of the portfolio in mortgages. As a result, this fund wasn't hit as hard as the companion Bond Fund in '94, losing just 2.9 percent. This one is more appropriate for defensive investors, because the shorter term of the securities makes it less vulnerable to interest rate movements. Maximum front-end load is 2 percent (the Bond Fund charges up to 5 percent); maximum redemption fee is 2.5 percent (Bond Fund is 4.5 percent).

TEMPLETON CANADIAN BOND FUND $$ ⇓ FI #/* RSP CB

This is a conservatively managed bond fund which will at times switch a large chunk of assets into Treasury bills, as it did in early '95 when over 40 percent of the portfolio was in short-term notes. This approach reduces risk, but it also means investors won't enjoy the full benefits of big bond market rallies. Case in point: this fund only gained 4.6 percent in the first half of '95, compared to an average of 9.6 percent for all Canadian bond funds. So this fund is really best suited for defensive investors. If you want more potential profit from your bond fund, look elsewhere. Manager Neil Devlin invests mainly in government issues. Portfolio also contains mortgage-backed securities and a small amount of foreign bonds. Name changed from Templeton Heritage Bond Fund.

TOP FIFTY T-BILL/BOND FUND $ ⇒ FI/C # RSP CB

This fund uses a most unusual investment strategy. The managers place most or all of the assets in T-Bills when interest rates are rising, switching into bonds when interest rates are falling. This defensive approach is designed to protect capital while providing decent rates of return in all economic climates. At least, that's the theory. In practice, it isn't working, proving how difficult it is to time markets and judge interest rate direction. The fund started off well and, in fact, was the number two performer in this category in '90, according to Southam's *Mutual Fund SourceBook*. But results have been steadily deteriorating since and in '94 — a year when the capital protection technique should have come to the fore — the unit value fell a whopping 9.3 percent. The fund recovered some ground in the first half of '95, but performance was nowhere near the average for this category. It appears the managers have some serious fine-tuning to do. Maximum 5 percent front-end load. Sold in B.C. only. For purchase information call (604) 682-6446.

TRANS-CANADA BOND FUND $$ ⇓ FI #/* RSP CB

This fund invests exclusively in bonds and T-bills issued or guaranteed by the Government of Canada. This gives it a high degree of safety in terms of investment quality, which is the fund's main advantage. But returns have tended to be below average for this category, in part because the managers concentrate their holdings in short- to mid-term bonds. That approach paid off in '94 with a much smaller-than-average loss, but the fund missed out on the big gains in the market rally of early '95. Worth a look if safety, not return, is your main concern.

20/20 INCOME FUND $ ⇒ FI #/* RSP CB

Took a larger-than-average hit when bond prices fell in early '94, and the '95 bounce-back wasn't quite up to the standards of the competition. Manager Phillip Falls of Connor, Clark & Lunn takes a conservative approach. Portfolio at mid-year had an average term-to-maturity of seven years, a relatively defensive position. Formerly the Sunset Convertible Debenture & Income Fund.

UNITED CANADIAN BOND FUND $$ ⇒ FI #/* RSP B/M

Long-term results are about average, but this fund has looked much better lately with a nice 17.5 percent gain in the year to June 30, '95. Portfolio is a mix of government and corporate bonds with some mortgage-backed securities. Name changed from United Security Fixed Income Fund in spring '94.

WESTBURY CANADIAN LIFE BOND FUND $ ⇒ FI NO RSP S CB

Started off well, but recent performance has been below average for this category. Special tip to Westbury clients: ask if you're eligible for the company's "B" Fund, a closed bond fund that's been doing much better than this one. New clients can't buy it, but if you're already in you can add to your holdings. It's the better bet. Sold by representatives of Westbury Canadian Life.

Canadian Mortgage Funds

Mortgage Funds are the ideal safe haven for conservative investors who want slightly better returns than they'll get from GICs. They produce steady returns year after year and rarely fall in value over a 12-month period (1994 being an exception in some cases). In short, if you're looking for a fund you can invest in and forget about, mortgage funds come about as close to filling the bill as you'll find.

Most of these funds invest almost exclusively in residential first mortgages. However, a few go beyond that to include mortgage-backed securities and, occasionally, commercial mortgages. The latter can be higher risk, so be sure you check out the fund's policy before putting in your money. ■

RATINGS CHANGES

The most important development is the awarding of the first $$$$ ranking to a mortgage mutual fund. The recipient is the Bank of Montreal's First Canadian Mortgage Fund, a steady performer with the best results of any fund in this category over the past decade. Two funds have been elevated a notch to $$$ status: the entries from Canada Trust's Everest group and the Scotia Excelsior fund.

Three new funds are debuting this year. The most significant is the Royal Bank's RoyFund Mortgage Fund, with a $$$ rating.

1996 RATINGS

CIBC MORTGAGE INVESTMENT FUND $$$ ⇓ FI NO RSP M

A solid performer with better-than-average returns. This fund has gone two decades without recording a loss in any calendar year — it managed to break even in '94 when many mortgage funds were down. Has the advantage of being no load and readily available through most CIBC branches. A good bet, especially for conservative investors looking for a slightly better return than a GIC will normally provide. AAA-rated for safety by Dominion Bond Rating Service.

COLONIA MORTGAGE FUND $ ⇒ FI * RSP S M

Small fund, below-average returns so far. Sold by reps of Colonia Life.

CONCORDE MORTGAGE FUND $$ ⇓ FI #/* RSP M

Average performer offered by the Quebec-based Concorde Financial Group. Sold only in Quebec and Ontario.

CONFED MORTGAGE FUND

Sold to Burgeonvest Ltd. in mid-'95 after the collapse of Confederation Life. Future plans are uncertain.

DESJARDINS MORTGAGE FUND $$ ⇒ FI NO RSP M

An average performer with improving results. The annual return to June 30, '95, was a healthy 11.7 percent, better than average for mortgage funds generally. Most of the investments are Quebec-based. Sold by offices of Desjardins Trust and Caisses Desjardins.

EVEREST MORTGAGE FUND $$$ ⇒ FI NO RSP M

This was one of the few mortgage funds to emerge from '94 with a gain. It wasn't much, a modest 1.2 percent, but that was a lot better than most other mortgage funds did. As a result, this was one of the few mortgage funds in Canada that completed the decade 1985–94 without a single down year. Long-term results are slightly above average for this category. A solid performer; sold by Canada Trust.

FIRST CANADIAN MORTGAGE FUND $$$$ ⇓ FI NO RSP M

One of the better long-term performers in the mortgage fund group, with consistently above-average returns. Never had a losing year prior to '94, when it dropped a fractional 0.5 percent. Sold by branches of the Bank of Montreal. Recommended for conservative investors. AAA-rated for safety by Dominion Bond Rating Service and Canadian Bond Rating Service. (This, of course, does not mean the fund can't lose money; the rating relates to the quality of the securities held in the portfolio.) As an added guarantee, the Bank of Montreal has undertaken to repurchase any defaulting mortgages from the fund, at no penalty to unit-holders. This is the best no-load mortgage fund in Canada and its solid long-term record earns it promotion to the *$$$$* class this year.

GENERAL TRUST MORTGAGE FUND $$$ ⇓ FI NO RSP M

Fine safety record. One of the few mortgage funds to stay in the black in '94, with a gain of 3 percent. That was enough to make this the number two performing mortgage fund in the country that year, according to Southam's *Mutual Fund SourceBook*. Long-term returns are about average for mortgage funds. Sold by branches of General Trust in Quebec. A better choice than the companion Bond Fund for more conservative investors.

GREAT-WEST LIFE MORTGAGE FUND $ ⇒ FI */NO RSP S M

Invests mainly in apartment building and commercial mortgages, unlike most mortgage funds, which concentrate on single-family residential first mortgages. Commercial mortgages typically have a longer term than residential mortgages, which makes them vulnerable to bigger losses when interest rates rise. That's what happened in '94, when the fund lost 2.8 percent, the second-largest drop in the mortgage fund group. So this fund should be considered as slightly higher risk in the mortgage category. Long-term performance is a little below average. See the entry for Great-West Life Canadian Equity Fund in the Canadian Equity section for purchase details and recommendations. Sold by Great-West Life reps.

GREEN LINE MORTGAGE FUND $$$ ⇓ FI NO RSP M

One of the better funds in this category. Great safety record; had never had an annual return below 6.8 percent since its launch in '73 until it suffered a fractional 0.7 percent drop in '94. More than made up for that with a first-half gain of 7.7 percent in '95, however. No load and widely available through TD Bank.

GREEN LINE MORTGAGE-BACKED FUND $$ ⇓ FI NO RSP M

One of the benefits to investors of the integration of the old Central-Guaranty FuturLink funds into Green Line has been the creation of the most diversified range of fixed income funds within any single group. This one was formerly the FuturLink Mortgage Fund. Under its new mandate, it specializes in mortgage-backed securities. These are guaranteed for both principal and interest by CMHC (in effect, by the federal government). As well, the fund may also invest in first mortgages and short-term notes. Recorded a small 1.1 percent loss in '94, but recovered with a 6.9 percent gain in the first half of '95. Until events prove differently, I suggest sticking with the original Mortgage Fund (above). Sold at TD Bank branches.

INDUSTRIAL ALLIANCE MORTGAGE FUND $$ ⇒ FI/G * RSP S M

Not part of the Mackenzie Financial group, but rather an offering from a Quebec-based insurance company. Routine performance record.

INVESNAT MORTGAGE FUND $$ ⇒ FI NO RSP M

One of the few Canadian mortgage funds that managed to stay in the black during tough '94, with a gain of 1.7

percent. As a result, its three-year average annual rate of return is nicely above average, at 7.6 percent. Worthwhile option for customers of National Bank looking for a low-risk fund.

INVESTORS MORTGAGE FUND $$ ⇓ FI * RSP M

One of the largest mutual funds in Canada, with assets of more than $3 billion! The attraction doesn't seem to be performance, since long-term results have been slightly sub-par as mortgage funds go (although recent returns are better). The appeal appears to be the combination of safety and steady returns; until '94 this fund had never had a losing year. It only lost 1.7 percent during that tough period, but even that modest setback was apparently enough to send some investors scurrying; assets are down significantly from a year ago. The fund continues to enjoy an AA (High) safety rating from Canadian Bond Rating Service — not quite as good as the AAA status accorded the Bank of Montreal and CIBC Mortgage funds, but very respectable nonetheless. A portion of the assets are held in industrial and commercial mortgages (most mortgage funds are exclusively made up of residential mortgages), mortgage-backed securities, and bonds. Back-end load of 3 percent applies if redeemed within five years.

LONDON LIFE MORTGAGE FUND $$$ ⇓ FI * RSP S M

How about a mutual fund that hasn't had a losing year going all the way back to 1975! Will that help you sleep at night? This one managed to keep its record intact by escaping a loss (by the skin of its teeth) in '94, when many other mortgage funds were hitting the red ink. It wasn't much of a gain — just 0.6 percent. But hey, if you're an investor, don't complain. This is a solid performer, and is less vulnerable than the companion Bond Fund to movements in interest rates. So it's better suited to conservative investors. Returns are usually above average for this category. Sold by London Life reps.

MONTREAL TRUST EXCELSIOR — MORTGAGE SECTION

See Scotia Excelsior Mortgage Fund

ROYAL TRUST MORTGAGE FUND $ ⇒ FI NO RSP M

The performance of this fund relative to others in this category has been steadily slipping in recent years. It still makes half-decent profits for investors, but there are better alternatives, including the cousin RoyFund Mortgage Fund, with which this will likely eventually be merged. Useful for RRSP investors seeking steady income or, when interest rates are stable or declining, as a way to hold short-term cash. Limit purchases when rates are rising.

ROYFUND MORTGAGE FUND $$$ ⇓ FI NO RSP M

A new entry from Royal Bank, making its debut in this year's edition. One of the top-performing mortgage funds over the past three years, mainly due to the fact it was one of the few to stay in the black during the turbulent times of '94. Three-year average annual rate of return to June 30, '95, was 8.2 percent.

SAVINGS AND INVESTMENT TRUST
H FUND $$ ⇒ FI NO RSP M

Good no-load mortgage fund, although it took a small 2 percent hit in '94. Sold through Quebec-based Savings and Investment Trust.

SCOTIA EXCELSIOR
MORTGAGE FUND $$$ ⇓ FI NO RSP M

This fund was created in October '95 by the merger of the Montreal Trust Excelsior Mortgage Section and the Scotia Mortgage Fund. The latter was quite new, but the Montreal Trust entry had been around for a long time. Its big attraction was that it hadn't had a losing year in at least two decades. It even managed to scrape through '94 with a small gain, something only a few mortgage funds were able to achieve. Long-term results were about average, but more recent returns were well above the norm for this category. The rating is based on that performance, but the Scotia Fund it merged with was no slouch either. Available through branches of Scotiabank.

UNITED CANADIAN
MORTGAGE FUND $ ⇓ FI #/* RSP M

Returns have tended to be sub-par for a mortgage fund, although things have perked up a bit recently. Good safety record; never had a down year until '94 broke the string. Besides mediocre performance, load charge is big drawback — maximum front-end load is 5 percent, with a back-end option available. There are too many good no-load mortgage funds around to make this one attractive at those commissions, unless you are simply switching money from another United fund.

International Bond Funds

Many people have used international bond funds as a safe haven from the volatile Canadian dollar, and they've filled that role well. During the '90s, the average international bond fund has returned about 10 percent a year, a decent performance during a turbulent period.

In last year's *Guide* I said I didn't expect international bond funds to perform as well in '94-'95 as they have in the recent past because the economies of most developed nations had now moved into the recovery phase, leaving little room for interest rate cuts. But I said these funds were still useful for investors worried about the Canadian deficit and the future of our dollar. ∎

In fact, international bond funds had a respectable year, gaining 9.7 percent on average for the 12 months to June 30, '95, according to *The Financial Post*. Best of the bunch was the new First Canadian International Fund, with a 16.6 percent gain. You won't find it in this section because it's still too new to be rated.

I'm not high on international bond funds for '96, for two reasons. First, the second phase of the economic recovery could drive interest rates higher, which will be bad news for bond funds.

Second, the Canadian dollar is seriously undervalued by comparison to such currencies as the Swiss franc, German mark, and Japanese yen. As it moves up towards more realistic levels, the effect on international bond funds won't be good. Of course, a lot will depend on the outcome of the Quebec referendum, which is unknown as this is written. But I'm an eternal optimist.

So don't load up on these funds this year. Having a few dollars in them is fine, but don't overdo it.

RATINGS CHANGES

The major change this year is the debut of two $$$ additions to this category.

The Royal Trust International Bond Fund was the best-performing fund in this group over the three years to June 30, '95, but a word of warning — the manager was recently changed. Whether that will have an impact on performance remains to be seen.

The Scotia CanAm Income Fund takes a somewhat different approach than most others in this category, investing exclusively in Canadian securities denominated in U.S. dollars.

1996 RATINGS

AGF GLOBAL GOVERNMENT
BOND FUND $$ ⇒ FI #/*/NO £ IB

AGF now offers two international bond funds: this one, which invests directly in foreign bonds and can therefore only be held as foreign content in RRSPs, and the repositioned Strategic Income Fund (see below), which is fully RRSP-eligible. This has been the better performer so far, with a gain of 8.3 percent for the year to June 30, '95. As of spring '95, the fund's portfolio was heavily weighted towards the U.S. dollar, with 52 percent of the portfolio denominated in that currency. Deutschmark-denominated bonds were also strongly represented (21 percent). The fund managers missed out on the big gains made by the Japanese yen in early

'95, having sold off the entire yen position in mid-'94. Note: this fund pays interest monthly. If you have opted for automatic reinvestment, and hold the fund in an RRSP, the additional units you receive could push you over the foreign content limit. Be careful.

AGF STRATEGIC INCOME FUND $$ ⇒ FI #/*/NO RSP IB

This fund has the same management team (Warren Goldring and Clive Coombs) as the Global Government Bond Fund, so it shouldn't come as a great surprise that the broad strategies are similar. The difference is that this fund invests only in RRSP-eligible government bonds to minimize risk and make the fund fully eligible for registered plans. That's a different direction for this fund, which was previously known as the AGF Convertible Income Fund. For that reason, any results prior to the mandate change (which took effect in late '93) are not relevant. Gain for the year ending June 30, '95, was 6.7 percent. As of spring '95, 60 percent of the portfolio was in U.S. dollar denominated bonds, with deutschmark bonds accounting for 24 percent.

DYNAMIC GLOBAL BOND FUND $$$ ⇒ FI #/* RSP IB

Invests in bonds issued by Canadian governments and corporations which are denominated in foreign currencies. This gives the fund full RRSP/RRIF-eligibility. A solid, steady performer; five-year annual return to June 30, '95, was 11.5 percent, well above average for this category. As of mid-'95, portfolio emphasis was strongly on bonds denominated in European currencies.

GLOBAL STRATEGY DIVERSIFIED
BOND FUND $ ⇒ FI #/* RSP IB

A fully RRSP-eligible bond fund, for those wishing to increase the foreign exposure in their registered plans. Invests directly in RRSP-eligible bonds from Canadian and approved international institutions (e.g., the World Bank), as well as in bond futures and foreign issues within the 20 percent foreign content limit. Bonds are limited to those with a AA rating or better, for added safety. In fact, most of the portfolio is in AA+ and AAA securities. This is the largest international bond fund in Canada (assets of more than $860 million in mid-'95). Frankly, it's hard to figure out why, unless it's the mystical name of Rothschild on the management marquee. Returns have been decidedly sub-par for this category. Three-year average annual rate of return to June 30, '95, was just 5.3 percent, making this the worst-performing international bond fund over that period according to figures compiled by *The Globe and Mail Report on Business*.

GLOBAL STRATEGY WORLD
BOND FUND $ ⇒ FI #/* £ IB

Had been one of the better performers in this category but started to slump in '93 and took an 8.8 percent hit in '94. Return of 3 percent in the first half of '95 was also well below average for international bond funds as a group. Part of the reason for weak '95 results appears to be the fund's heavy weighting towards the U.S. dollar and away from the Japanese yen entering the year. The yen gained sharply in value against the greenback during the winter and spring. Managed by N.M. Rothschild, who should know something about this business, having had nearly 200 years of experience (although not with this particular fund, of course). But recent results force a drop in the rating this year.

GUARDIAN INTERNATIONAL
INCOME FUND $$ ⇒ FI #/* RSP IB

This is an international bond fund which is fully RRSP/RRIF-eligible. It achieves this by investing mainly in the securities of international financial institutions, such as the World Bank, that have been granted special RRSP/RRIF eligibility status by the Canadian government. As well, the portfolio holds bonds issued directly by foreign governments and banks, and invests in forward and option currency contracts. It does not invest in Canadian government bond issues. Long-term returns have slid to below average, although the first half of '95 looked better. The fund employs a conservative management style and provides protection when the Canadian dollar is under pressure. Since it's fully RRSP-eligible, owning it won't infringe on your foreign content.

REGENT WORLD
INCOME FUND $$ ⇒ FI #/*/NO RSP IB

Invests in a portfolio of Canadian and World Bank interest-bearing securities as well as some more exotic foreign bond holdings (e.g., Pakistan, Australia, South Korea). Three-year results to June 30, '95, were slightly better than average. Fully eligible for RRSPs/RRIFs. Admax Regent funds now offer a no-load option which you should inquire about if you're buying.

ROYAL TRUST INTERNATIONAL BOND FUND $$$ ⇒ FI NO RSP IB

This was the top-performing international bond fund in Canada for the three years to June 30, '95, with an average annual gain of 12.9 percent. Add to that the fact this is a no-load fund and 100 percent RRSP-eligible and you have a pretty potent combination. However, this fund had a recent managerial change. It's now being run by Barry Edwards, who also handles the RoyFund International Income Fund, which is too new to be rated here. He's done a fine job with that fund, but a managerial change on a top-performing fund is always a cause for some concern. Funds like this do best when two conditions are in place: a weakening Canadian dollar and falling international interest rates. I think the prospects are for a stronger dollar (depending on Quebec) and somewhat higher rates later in '96. But if you're in the market for an international bond fund, this is a good choice.

SCOTIA EXCELSIOR CANAM INCOME FUND $$$ ⇒ FI NO RSP IB

The portfolio of this fund is made up mainly of fixed income securities issued by Canadian governments and corporations that are denominated in U.S. dollars. As a result, it offers RRSP/RRIF investors full U.S. dollar exposure, while still retaining 100 percent registered plan status. The unit value is expressed in U.S. dollars, so the performance figures do not reflect any currency fluctuation between Canadian and U.S. money. So when the Canadian dollar is falling, this fund is actually doing better than the numbers indicate, and vice-versa. Three-year average annual return to June 30, '95, was a solid 10.7 percent. Recommended for investors who want more U.S. dollar exposure in their retirement plans without sacrificing foreign content room.

TEMPLETON GLOBAL BOND FUND $$ ⇒ FI #/* £ IB

This is a true global bond fund, investing directly in securities issued by foreign governments and corporations. As a result, it may only be held in RRSPs and RRIFs as foreign content. Manager Neil Devlin has built a broadly based portfolio, including bonds and T-bills from some emerging market countries like Indonesia, India, and Hungary. He may hedge currencies to reduce the risk of volatile price movements. Recent results have been sub-par compared to other funds in this category. Recorded a gain of 9.3 percent in the year ending June 30, '95, (average was 9.7 percent according to figures published by *The Globe and Mail*). Name has been changed from Templeton Global Income Fund.

UNIVERSAL WORLD INCOME RRSP FUND $$ ⇒ FI #/* RSP IB

Formerly the Universal Canadian Bond Fund, this Mackenzie Financial entry has been converted into an RRSP-eligible international bond fund, investing in foreign bonds and bond index futures. Needless to say, that makes the long-term track record of the old fund obsolete, although this new version still carries it like a worn-out coat in the business press mutual fund surveys. As a result, it's hard to give it a meaningful rating. The fund scored a 5.3 percent return in the first half of '95, but that was well below average for the international bond fund category. We'll leave the rating at $$ for now and see what happens.

Canadian Balanced and Asset Allocation Funds

A "balanced" fund can mean many different things, depending on the investment approach of the manager. These funds normally hold a mix of stocks, bonds, and cash-type investments in their portfolio, but the relative percentage of each will vary depending on economic conditions and the aggressiveness of the managers. Usually, funds that hold a higher percentage of equities will tend to be somewhat more volatile and higher risk than those that give priority to preservation of capital through fixed income investments.

This fund category took a beating in 1994 when both stock and bond prices were weak. But the first half of 1995 brought happier times. With both bond and stock

322

prices climbing, the average Canadian balanced fund gained 8.4 percent, according to *The Financial Post.* ∎

I've never been a big fan of balanced funds, although some of the new asset allocation entries, like Dynamic Partners Fund, have shown good results. If you do decide to go this route, read the chapter titled "Asset Allocation Services" first.

RATINGS CHANGES

Ten funds have been upgraded this year, three of them to $$$ status — the Elliott & Page Balanced Fund, the Leith Wheeler Balanced Fund, and the ICM Balanced Fund. Five funds have had their rating cut back, the most notable being the Cambridge Balanced Fund, which falls all the way from $$$ to $.

There are no new $$$$ funds this year, but last year's two top-ranked funds, ABC Fully-Managed Fund and Altamira Growth and Income, have retained their status despite sub-par performances over the past 12 months.

A total of eight funds appear for the first time this year, and this has to be the classiest freshman group we've seen in a long time. Six of the eight start off with $$$ status — Bissett Retirement, Global Strategy Income Plus, National Life Balanced, PH&N Balanced, Industrial Alliance Diversified, and Clean Environment Balanced.

Among the departures this year are the two Montreal Trust balanced funds, which have been folded into the Scotia family.

1996 RATINGS

ABC FULLY-MANAGED FUND $$$$ ⇒ G NO RSP CBAL

Despite an indifferent year (gain of 7.8 percent for the 12 months to June 30, '95), this remains the top-performing balanced fund in Canada over the past five years with an average annual compound rate of return of 15.8 percent to June 30, '95. That compares with an average for this category of 9.4 percent, which shows you just how far ahead of the competition manager Irwin Michael has been. His defensive stance may have cost the fund some profits in early '95, but Michael, while an aggressive manager, tries to keep risk within tolerable limits. Both ABC funds are still an excellent choice for patient investors with lots of money — minimum investment required is $150,000. Call (416) 365-9696 for information.

AGF GROWTH AND INCOME FUND $ ⇒ G/FI #/*/NO RSP CBAL

This was formerly Corporate Investors Ltd. I had included it with the dividend funds in the past because the main objective was to generate above-average dividend income. However, that's changed, along with the name. AGF has converted it to a true balanced fund, which means that results prior to '94 are meaningless, although you'll still find them in the monthly fund surveys in the business press. The mandate now is to achieve a combination of long-term capital appreciation and current income, with moderate risk. As of spring '95, the portfolio was almost equally divided among bonds (35 percent), cash (35 percent), and stocks (30 percent). The fund lost the manager of its equity component in mid-'95, when Steve Uzielli left AGF. I'm taking the rating down a notch this year, while we await developments. Note: all AGF funds are now offered with three purchase options; see the entry for AGF Canadian Equity Fund for details.

AGF HIGH INCOME FUND $ ⇓ FI #/*/NO RSP CBAL

This was formerly known as the AGF Preferred Income Fund, and operated as a dividend fund with the goal of enabling investors to take maximum advantage of the dividend tax credit. Although it still holds some high-yielding stocks and preferred shares, about two-thirds of the portfolio is now in bonds and other types of interest-bearing securities. For that reason, I've shifted it into the balanced fund category (although you may find it still listed as a dividend fund in the business press). But it's not like most of the other balanced funds in this group; in this case the main emphasis is on income generation. If you're looking for a conservatively managed balanced fund, this would be one to consider, although its returns haven't been particularly impressive. If you want to maximize use of the dividend tax credit, this isn't the right fund for you; there are better bets around. Note: ignore returns prior to '94, since the fund was operating under its old mandate before then.

AMI PRIVATE CAPITAL
OPTIMIX FUND $$ ⇒ G/FI NO RSP CBAL

This fund's historic track record is weak, but it has been doing better recently. The portfolio is fairly evenly balanced between stocks and bonds, although the total number of securities held seems way out of proportion to its small size (only $3.5 million in assets). Return for the year to June 30, '95, was a respectable 12.3 percent. No load if purchased through the fund manager (Quebec, B.C., Nova Scotia, and Ontario residents only), otherwise a 2 percent commission may be applied. Minimum investment is $50,000, which can be spread over several funds in the group ($10,000 minimum per fund). Formerly the Church Street Balanced Fund.

ADMAX CANADIAN SELECT
GROWTH FUND $ ⇒ G #/*/NO RSP CBAL

There have been a lot of changes with this one. First the name: this was formerly the Polymetric Performance Fund; the name was changed in July '95. Next, the portfolio: this used to be a Canadian equity fund; now it blends a lot of bonds into the portfolio (over 80 percent as of spring '95!). As a result, I've switched it to this section, which more accurately reflects the portfolio. The management of this fund is based on the investment principles developed by J. Picton Davies, editor and publisher of the Polymetric Report newsletter. The methodology involves adjusting security holdings to reflect current market conditions. The fund may hold large amounts of cash when indicators suggest a market correction is in the offing. When markets are strong, the cash component may be reduced to zero, as it was in spring '95. Over the longer term, the fund's performance has been disappointing, with a 5.7 percent annual gain for the three years to June 30, '95. Most recent results have been somewhat better, but I'm not prepared to raise the rating yet. Let's wait a while and see how it does under the revised mandate. Note: this group offers both a no-load option and a negotiable back-end load. See the entry for the Admax Canadian Performance Fund in the Canadian Equity section for details.

ALTAMIRA BALANCED FUND $$ ⇒ G/FI NO RSP CBAL

This began life in '85 as one of the much-publicized Hume funds. Was a disappointment to investors for many years.

It was taken over by Altamira Investment Services in '88, but the magic of some of their other funds was slow to rub off, despite strong efforts by portfolio managers Will Sutherland (bonds) and Normand Lamarche (equities) to turn things around. (Lamarche is now gone, replaced by Sue Coleman, whose Special Growth Fund has struggled lately.) There are some signs this one may finally be picking up steam, though. It managed a gain of 10.6 percent for the year to June 30, '95. While that was below average for this category, it was better than the performance of the Growth and Income Fund (below), which has traditionally outperformed it. We'll have to wait and see whether that was a flash in the pan, or if this fund is going to emerge as Altamira's number one balanced choice.

ALTAMIRA GROWTH & INCOME FUND $$$$ ⇓ G NO RSP CBAL

This has been one of my favourite Altamira funds for several years, and it has rewarded investors well. Average annual return for the five years to June 30, '95, was 12.5 percent, among the best in this category. Veteran manager Cedric Rabin has pulled off the neat trick of combining good returns with an ability to allow his investors to rest easy at night. This fund has not had a single losing calendar year since its launch in 1986, a remarkable achievement considering the turbulent markets we've experienced over that time. The most recent results don't merit a continued $$$$ rating — the fund gained just 6.6 percent in the year to June 30, '95. But the longer-term performance and the safety record cannot be minimized. The rating is maintained for this year, but I'll be watching for an improvement in returns.

ATLAS CANADIAN BALANCED FUND $ ⇒ G/FI NO RSP CBAL

Name changed from Jarislowsky Finsco Balanced Fund in July '94; however, Montreal-based investment firm Jarislowsky Fraser continues to run the show. The solid portfolio of blue-chip stocks and high-quality bonds has finally started to produce results for investors —— gain for the year to June 30, '95, was a healthy 15.6 percent. Long-term results are still sub-par, however. Current strategy is to emphasize companies that earn much of their revenues in U.S. dollars. Sold on a no-load basis through Midland Walwyn.

BPI CANADIAN
BALANCED FUND $\Rightarrow$ G/FI #/* RSP CBAL

This fund was created from the merger of the BT Landmark Balanced Fund and the BPI One Decision Balanced Fund, as part of the BPI takeover of Bolton Tremblay. Both funds had similar track records, with performance a little below average for this category. BPI has appointed two new managers, Michael Labanowich and Fred Dalley, to make a silk purse out of this one. It's going to take them some time to reposition the portfolio to their liking, so this is a shakedown period. Early returns are ho-hum: the fund gained a below-average 6.7 percent for the year to June 30, '95.

BEUTEL GOODMAN
BALANCED FUND $$ \Rightarrow$ G/FI NO RSP CBAL

A conservatively managed entry, this fund got off to a rocky start. However, it has recovered well and now shows a slightly better-than-average three-year rate of return of 10.1 percent for the period to June 30, '95. The fund will normally be invested in the range of 60 percent equities, 40 percent fixed income, but this can vary depending on conditions. The managers make maximum use of the foreign content allowance. No load only if purchased directly from the manager.

BISSETT RETIREMENT FUND $$$ \Rightarrow$ G/FI NO RSP CBAL

A solid little balanced fund, making its first appearance in the *Guide* this year. This is a fund of funds, investing in other Bissett funds. Manager Michael Quinn actively juggled the portfolio in the first half of '95 to take advantage of rising bond and stock prices; at mid-year it was 41 percent in the Bissett Bond Fund, 34 percent Canadian Equity Fund, 20 percent American Equity Fund, and 6 percent Small Cap Fund. The happy result was a healthy 10.8 percent gain in the first half of the year. Longer-term results are also good; this fund showed a 12.1 percent average annual return for the three years to June 30. See Bissett Canadian Equity Fund entry for purchase details.

BULLOCK ASSET
STRATEGY FUND $ ⇒ G/FI #/* RSP CBAL

This previously was the Bullock Balanced Fund. The new name reflects a more aggressive asset allocation management strategy than in the past. Fund manager Lynne Boivin of AMI Partners maximizes the allowable foreign content holdings and invests 10–15 percent of the assets in foreign pay bonds. Derivatives, such as TIPs, may also be used. Results since the strategy change, while improved, are still below average for this category. This continues to be a wait-and-see situation.

CIBC BALANCED INCOME &
GROWTH FUND $$ ⇒ G/FI NO RSP CBAL

This fund has a strange performance pattern. It does well in odd years ('89, '91, '93, '95), poorly in even years ('90, '92, '94). Now the question is, will '96 continue this trend? The fund employs a conservative investment approach, with extensive diversification in its stock portfolio. Overall results have been below average. Five-year average annual compound rate of return to June 30, '95, was just 7.5 percent (average was 9.4 percent). But the fund staged a comeback in the first half of '95, with a 7.9 percent gain. Still, more consistency is needed. This fund needs to do better or another downgrade will be in order.

CAMBRIDGE BALANCED FUND $ ⇑ G/FI #/* RSP CBAL

This fund still shows one of the best long-term records in the balanced category, but the more aggressive management style introduced after former manager Tony Massie left the Vancouver-based Sagit group in '92 is starting to take a toll. After a strong year in '93, the fund lost 15.2 percent in '94. Only one Canadian balanced fund out of the 139 surveyed for Southam's *Mutual Fund SourceBook* did worse. The first half of '95 was better, but only slightly with a 1.6 percent gain. The average balanced fund gained 8.3 percent during that time. Normally, we think of balanced funds as being conservatively managed, but not in this case. There are some blue-chip names on the stock list, like Royal Bank and Seagram. But there are a lot more junior growth companies. On the bond side, there are some reassuring Canadas. But there are also bond issues from companies such as Williston Wildcat Oil, not exactly a household name in the bond world. This is not a fund I think most balanced investors would be comfortable with and I'm adjusting the rating accordingly.

CANADA LIFE MANAGED
FUND S-35 $$ ⇒ G/FI * RSP S CBAL

This is an average long-term performer. It invests in a combination of bonds and Canadian and international stocks. Gained a solid 13.3 percent for the year ending June 30, '95, but longer-term results are less impressive. Redemption fee payable if cashed before seven years. See Canada Life Canadian Equity Fund listing in Canadian Equity section for details on plan guarantees. Sold by Canada Life agents and brokers.

CAPSTONE INVESTMENT
TRUST $$ ⇒ G/FI NO RSP CBAL

An erratic performer that usually manages to end each year with a modest profit, although '94 was an exception. Stock portfolio favours blue chips (Bank of Montreal, BCE) with a few small growth companies blended in. Annual rate of return for the decade ending June 30, '95, was 7.6 percent, slightly below average for balanced funds generally. Adequate would be the best description of this small fund. Sold by Hughes, King and Co. of Toronto; phone (416) 863-0005 for information.

CASSELS BLAIKIE
CANADIAN FUND $$ ⇒ G/FI # RSP CBAL

After going through a lull that caused the rating to drop last year, this small fund has bounced back nicely with a solid gain of 15.5 percent for the year ending June 30, '95. Long-term record is also good, with an average annual return of 9.3 percent over the past decade. Rating will be restored to $$$ level with another solid year of returns. Maximum 3 percent load if purchased directly from the manager (Ontario residents only). For information phone (416) 941-7500.

CLEAN ENVIRONMENT
BALANCED FUND $$$ ⇒ G/FI #/* RSP CBAL

The Clean Environment Funds have emerged as one of the best bets for socially conscious investors looking for some profits to go with their conscience. This entry, making its appearance in the *Guide* for the first time this year, shows a solid average annual return of 15.4 percent for the three years to June 30, '95. That's well above the average of 9.9 percent for this category. The portfolio was split 60-40 in favour of equities in mid-'95, with a strong foreign component. These funds are available in all provinces except Quebec; phone 1-800-461-4570 for information.

CORNERSTONE
BALANCED FUND $$ ⇒ G/FI NO RSP CBAL

A long-time underachiever as the Metropolitan Balanced Growth Fund, but more recent results have been good. The fund gained 14.8 percent for the year ending June 30, '95, well above average for this category. Conservative portfolio blends government bonds and blue-chip stocks. Available through branches of North American Trust (which has been sold to Laurentian Bank by parent North American Life). Not available east of Ontario.

DESJARDINS BALANCED FUND $$ ⇒ G/FI NO RSP CBAL

Below-average long-term results, but performance has picked up lately. Portfolio was about equally divided between stocks and bonds with a good chunk of foreign holdings entering '95. There are a lot of securities in the portfolio, which can sometimes be hard to manage. Sold by Quebec-based Desjardins Trust and Caisses Desjardins.

DYNAMIC MANAGED
PORTFOLIO $$ ⇒ G/FI #/* RSP CBAL

A fund of funds, investing in units of other mutual funds managed by Dynamic. It's a way to buy a piece of the entire Dynamic group, rather than buying funds individually. When the other funds are going well, so will this one; when they're experiencing problems, this one will too. If you're looking to Dynamic for a balanced fund, the Partners Fund (below) has been a consistently stronger performer.

DYNAMIC PARTNERS FUND $$$ ⇒ G/FI #/* RSP CBAL

This fund uses asset allocation principles and they are clearly working. Results have been very good, with a five-year average annual rate of return of 14.8 percent to June 30, '95. Only one other balanced fund (ABC Fully-Managed) did better over that time. Portfolio in mid-'95 was weighted towards stocks, with fixed income manager Norm Bengough having pocketed some solid gains from the bond market rally. A good performer, worth your attention and your money.

ELLIOTT & PAGE BALANCED FUND $$$ ⇒ G/FI #/* RSP CBAL

Steadily improving; posted a fine 14.3 percent gain for the year ending June 30, '95. This fund uses a multi-manager approach, employing the services of E&P's in-house team, Goldman Sachs of New York, Jardine Fleming of Hong Kong, and the Fleming Group of London — a pretty potent lineup. Foreign content use is maximized. I like the look of this one, so I'm raising the rating this year. Note: be aware of the back-end load purchase option with all funds offered by this group; see the entry on the Elliott & Page Equity Fund in the Canadian Equity section for a detailed explanation. Phone 1-800-363-6647 for information.

EMPIRE BALANCED FUND $ ⇒ G/FI #/* RSP S CBAL

Aims for a balance between long-term growth and preservation of capital with a fund that invests in stocks, bonds, mortgages, and short-term notes. Performance has tailed off to below average. Five-year average annual return to June 30, '95, was 8.6 percent, compared to an industry average of 9.4 percent. Sold by Empire Life representatives.

ETHICAL BALANCED FUND $$ ⇒ G/FI #/*/NO RSP CBAL

A long-time underperformer as the Classic I-Plan Balanced Fund, but has been coming along well since being acquired by the Credit Union Central of Canada in September '92 as part of their new Ethical Funds family. Portfolio is well balanced, with a strong U.S. equity component. Gained a nice 16.6 percent in the year ending June 30, '95. Management is by Co-operators Investment Counselling. Worth a rating increase this year. May be purchased without load charges at participating credit unions, otherwise sales commissions will apply.

EVEREST BALANCED FUND $$ ⇒ G/FI NO RSP CBAL

Invests in a well-diversified portfolio of blue-chip stocks, high-grade bonds, and T-bills, with some U.S. and international stocks added for foreign content. Suited for investors looking for a conservatively managed balanced fund. Returns are about average for this type of fund. Sold by branches of Canada Trust.

FIDELITY GROWTH AND
INCOME FUND $ ⇒ G #/* RSP CBAL

A so-so performer with below-average five-year returns. The stocks are chosen by George Domolky who also runs the Capital Builder Fund. The bond department is in the hands of Ford O'Neil, who took over that responsibility in '94 just as the bond market was going south. Asset mix in spring '95 heavily favoured stocks, which were doing well at that stage. Despite that, returns for the first half of the year, while in the black, lagged behind the competition. This fund seems to be having trouble sorting itself out. I suggest holding off until it starts proving itself. Three purchase options; see the entry for the Fidelity Capital Builder Fund in the Canadian Equity section for details and a recommendation. Formerly the Fidelity Capital Balanced Fund.

FIRST CANADIAN ASSET
ALLOCATION FUND $ ⇒ G/FI NO RSP CBAL

A truly balanced fund with a solid mix of quality bonds and blue-chip stocks. Advantages are no load, easy availability through Bank of Montreal branches, and conservative portfolio. Disadvantage is that longer-term results have been below average. However, recent performance has improved — the fund gained an above-average 15 percent in the year to June 30, '95. Continued solid results will produce an upgrade in the rating. Formerly called First Canadian Balanced Fund.

FICADRE BALANCED FUND $ ⇒ G/FI * RSP CBAL

Long-term results are below average for this category, but some improvement has been noted recently. Stock portion of the portfolio is blue chip in nature. Bond segment includes many Quebec-based issues. Formerly known as the SNF Balanced Fund.

GENERAL TRUST
BALANCED FUND $ ⇒ G/FI NO RSP CBAL

A broadly based portfolio that was tilted slightly towards stocks in mid-'95. Returns have been below average for this category, although the fund returned a decent 12.4 percent for the year to June 30, '95. Sold by General Trust in Quebec only. See additional comments in the entry for the General Trust Canadian Equity Fund in the Canadian Equity section.

GLOBAL STRATEGY INCOME
PLUS FUND $$$ ⇒ G/FI #/* RSP CBAL

The second part of the one-two punch manager Tony Massie launched when he moved over to Global Strategy (see Canada Growth Fund write-up in Canadian Equity section). This one has been much the better of the two, with an average annual return of 11.5 percent for the three years to June 30, '95. That's much better than most Canadian balanced funds did over that time. Portfolio is a mix of high-quality bonds, T-bills, common stocks, and preferred shares. One of Global Strategy's stronger entries.

GREAT-WEST LIFE
DIVERSIFIED RS FUND $$ ⇒ G/FI */NO RSP S CBAL

Performance is a bit below average for this category. Average annual return for the decade to June 30, '95, was 7.9 percent — average for this category was 8.4 percent. Highly diversified portfolio; fund holds a wide range of assets, including stocks, bonds, mortgages, real estate, and short-term notes. More conservative in its approach than the Equity/Bond Fund (below). This fund has a huge portfolio, in contrast to the approach used by the same company's Canadian Equity Investment Fund, which is more than twice as big in asset terms yet holds only a limited number of securities. Sold by Great-West Life agents and brokers.

GREAT-WEST LIFE
EQUITY/BOND FUND $$$ ⇒ G/FI */NO RSP S CBAL

Another balanced entry from Great-West Life. May hold up to 80 percent of the portfolio in stocks, depending on the situation, but recently equities have only represented about 50 percent of assets. Generally outperforms the

Diversified Fund (see above), so would appear to be the better choice for investors who want maximum growth. See the entry for Great-West Life Canadian Equity Investment Fund in the Canadian Equity section for purchase details and recommendations. Sold by Great-West Life reps.

GREEN LINE BALANCED GROWTH FUND $ ⇒ G/FI NO RSP CBAL

The main difference between this and the Balanced Income Fund (see below) is a greater emphasis on stocks for enhanced growth potential. This fund also makes more use of foreign content, with almost 18 percent of the portfolio in U.S. equities as of April '95. That helped to boost returns to an above-average 14.2 percent for the year to June 30, '95 — a definite improvement over past results and an indication that, under the new management of McLean Budden, this fund is on the upswing. Another solid year will result in a rating upgrade. Sold at branches of TD Bank. Formerly the FuturLink Select Fund.

GREEN LINE BALANCED INCOME FUND $ ⇒ FI/G NO RSP CBAL

Formerly the Green Line Canadian Balanced Fund, now has a different mandate. The main goal is to generate income through a combination of high-quality fixed income securities, money market instruments, and stocks. As of April '95, the portfolio was 55 percent stocks, with the balance in bonds and short-term notes. Results have not kept pace with the improvements in the Balanced Growth Fund (above). Management is by Sceptre Investment Counsel. Sold through branches of TD Bank.

GUARDIAN CANADIAN BALANCED FUND $$$ ⇓ G/FI #/* RSP CBAL

This fund has a unique record: it is the only major Canadian balanced fund to have gone for more than a decade without losing money in a single calendar year ('81 was the last time it suffered a loss, and then only a small one). Plus, it's an above-average performer over the long haul, with an annual return of a tick under 10 percent for the decade ending June 30, '95. Cautious management emphasizes safety of principal and income — manager Larry Kennedy believes in sticking to fundamentals and avoiding higher-risk situations. As a result, this fund fared better than most in the stock and bond market downturns of early '94. Portfolio is well diversified but has grown substantially in size with the addition of a wide range of foreign stocks. This is a good choice for investors more concerned about security of principal than with aspirations for big returns.

HODGSON ROBERTON LAING BALANCED FUND $\Rightarrow$ G/FI NO RSP CBAL

Steady but somewhat sub-par performer; average annual rate of return for the decade to June 30, '95, was 7.5 percent (average for this category was 8.4 percent). Uses a value-investing approach; portfolio was heavily weighted to stocks entering '95. But despite the strong performances of the U.S. and Canadian markets, returns continued below average. Sold by the managers; call 1-800-268-9622. Formerly Waltaine Balanced Fund.

HONGKONG BANK BALANCED FUND $$ $\Rightarrow$ G/FI NO RSP CBAL

Longer-term returns on this fund are above average, but it hasn't shown a lot since a managerial change to M.K. Wong and Associates was made in late '92. Average annual return for the two years to June 30, '95, was 5.3 percent, compared to an average of 6.9 percent for this category. Entering '95, the portfolio was slightly weighted towards bonds. Stocks are well diversified, with a lot of small and mid-size companies included. Note that with all Hongkong Bank funds, there is a $15 annual service fee if units are held in an RRSP.

HYPERION MANAGED FUND

CIBC Securities sold the Hyperion funds to Talvest in mid-'95. This fund is to be merged into the Talvest Diversified Fund.

ICM BALANCED FUND $$$ $\Rightarrow$ G/FI #/NO RSP CBAL

Unusual management structure. Run by two organizations with years of experience in the pension management field, Gryphon Investment Counsel and Lincluden

Management, each of which handles half the fund's $47 million portfolio. Each uses a different investment management style; Lincluden takes a value-investing approach while Gryphon uses a top-down strategy, over-weighting the sectors that are expected to perform best. Results are steadily improving. The fund had an annual return of 10.7 percent for the five years to June 30, '95, above average for this category. No load if purchased directly from the manager; phone 1-800-363-2480 for information. Maximum front-end load of 5 percent if you buy through a broker. Minimum investment is $10,000. Formerly known as the Integra Balanced Fund.

IMPERIAL GROWTH
DIVERSIFIED FUND $ ⇒ FI # RSP S CBAL

The mandate of this fund is to combine long-term capital growth with stable income. The large portfolio is well balanced between stocks and bonds. Results have been slipping compared to competitors. Average annual rate of return for the five years to June 30, '95, was 8.4 percent. There are several funds with worse results, but that performance is below average for balanced funds as a group. Sold by Imperial Life reps.

INDUSTRIAL ALLIANCE
DIVERSIFIED FUND $$$ ⇒ FI/G * RSP S CBAL

Not part of the Mackenzie Financial group, but rather an offering from a Quebec-based insurance company. Very good results over the long term. The large portfolio was fairly evenly divided between stocks and bonds entering '95.

INDUSTRIAL
BALANCED FUND $$ ⇒ FI/G #/* RSP CBAL

Mackenzie Financial now offers four balanced funds, each with a different investment emphasis. This one comes the closest to a true balanced fund, with fixed income securities representing 40 to 60 percent of the portfolio at any given time. In mid-'95, the blend was 46 percent fixed income, 43 percent Canadian stocks, and small amounts of cash and foreign equities. Portfolio is small and solid. Returns to date have been slightly above average.

INDUSTRIAL INCOME FUND $$ ⇒ FI/G #/* RSP CBAL

Not a true fixed income fund, despite the name, hence its inclusion in the balanced section. Federal government bonds are the core holding, but the managers may also invest up to 30 percent of the fund's assets in stocks. The fund's portfolio was about two-thirds in fixed income securities in mid-'95. That plus the equity holdings helped boost the return to a fine 15.7 percent for the year to June 30, '95. That's great, but this fund needs to show more consistency to get a better rating.

INDUSTRIAL MORTGAGE
SECURITIES FUND $$ ⇒ FI/G #/* RSP CBAL

This is essentially a fixed income fund with some equity exposure (maximum 30 percent) to provide extra growth potential. Mackenzie Financial ranks this as the most conservative of their four balanced funds. At least half the portfolio is in mortgage-backed securities, which are guaranteed for principal and interest by Canada Mortgage and Housing Corporation (so, in effect, by the federal government). A steady performer, although the companion Income Fund (above) has looked better recently. Name changed from Mackenzie Income Fund in December '92.

INDUSTRIAL PENSION FUND $$ ⇒ G/FI #/* RSP CBAL

For years, this was yet another in the seemingly endless series of similar Mackenzie equity funds. The only thing distinctive about it was that it qualified for pension plans. That changed in January '94. In an effort to give this fund its own niche, the mandate was amended to allow up to 30 percent of the portfolio to be held in bonds. This doesn't make it a full balanced fund, but it certainly nudges it in that direction. This is the fund to choose if you're looking for a Mackenzie entry that emphasizes stocks but offers some fixed income exposure as well. Managerial responsibilities have been taken over by the veteran Bill Procter, a well-respected figure in the Canadian mutual funds industry. As of mid-'95, the asset mix was 25 percent bonds and 73 percent stocks, with a tiny amount of cash. Because of the strategy change, long-term performance isn't relevant, but it's worth noting that this fund outperformed both Industrial Growth and Industrial Horizon by a wide margin in the year to June 30, '95. If you own some Mackenzie funds, you might consider adding this one to the list.

INVESNAT RETIREMENT
BALANCED FUND $ ⇒ G/FI NO RSP CBAL

Well-diversified entry from National Bank. Fixed income side holds a lot of Quebec-based issues. Quite a large fund with about $250 million in assets, but results until recently have been sub-par.

INVESTORS INCOME PLUS
PORTFOLIO $ ⇒ FI/G * RSP CBAL

A fund of funds from Investors Group. The emphasis is on income, with some growth potential thrown in. As of spring '95, units in six Investors funds were held, with the main weighting being the Dividend Fund and the Government Bond Fund, each with 25 percent of the total portfolio. Results have been mediocre; five-year average annual return to June 30, '95, was 8.5 percent. If it's a balanced investment approach you're looking for, Investors Mutual (below) is a better bet.

INVESTORS MUTUAL
OF CANADA $$ ⇒ G/FI * RSP CBAL

This was the fund that got Investors Group started in the mutual fund business back in 1950, so it has a proud history attached to it. Returns are steadily improving, in large part due to a heavy weighting towards stocks recently. The 10-year annual return has now moved to slightly above average, at 8.6 percent. Portfolio is well diversified. Stocks tend towards the blue-chip variety, but there are enough growth companies included to make things interesting. This is a candidate for an upgrade if returns continue to look better. Sold by representatives of Investors Group.

INVESTORS RETIREMENT PLUS
PORTFOLIO $ ⇒ G/FI * RSP CBAL

This fund of funds is more diversified than the Income Plus Portfolio (above). It held units in eight Investors Group funds in spring '95, with no single fund having more than a 20 percent weighting. Balance is the key word here; this fund was 50 percent in stocks, 50 percent in fixed income in '95. It's made money for unit-holders, but returns have been below average and not up to the level of Investors Mutual.

JONES HEWARD CANADIAN
BALANCED FUND $$ ⇒ G/FI #/* RSP CBAL

Middle-of-the-road balanced fund, neither particularly good nor bad. Produced solid returns from '91 to '93 before suffering a setback in '94. Bounced back with a nice 9.8 percent gain in the first half of '95, however. Large, well-diversified portfolio. Formerly the Burns Fry Canadian Fund.

LAURENTIAN CANADIAN
BALANCED FUND $ ⇒ G/FI #/* RSP CBAL

Mandate is to invest in a mix of shares of medium to large companies and high-quality government and corporate bonds. Performance continues to be weak compared to many of its competitors. Average annual return for the five years to June 30, '95, was only 7.2 percent, compared to an industry average of 9.4 percent. Recent results aren't much better. Originally called Endurance Canadian Balanced Fund. See Laurentian Canadian Equity Fund entry for purchase details.

LEITH WHEELER
BALANCED FUND $$$ ⇒ G/FI NO RSP CBAL

A small B.C.-based fund, managed by partners Murray Leith and Bill Wheeler, who are doing their darnedest to get a new fund group going. Portfolio is well constructed and makes good use of U.S. stocks to add foreign content and boost returns. Results have been good; fund gained 14.7 percent for the year ending June 30, '95, well above average. Five-year average annual gain is 11.3 percent, also above average. Worth a look if you're a B.C. or Alberta resident with $50,000 in your pocket (the minimum investment required). Now completely no load. Company added four new funds to the group in early '94, but they're still too young for inclusion in this *Guide*. Phone (604) 683-3391 for information. Name changed from Leith Wheeler All-Value Balanced Fund in '94.

LONDON LIFE
DIVERSIFIED FUND $$ ⇒ G/FI * RSP S CBAL

A fund of funds, investing in units of other funds in the London Life family. Asset mix will vary, depending on the economic climate. Since none of the other London Life funds are particularly exciting, you can't expect this one to be either. Five-year results to June 30, '95, are just slightly below average at 9.2 percent a year. To add some juice to this one, London Life introduced a global component in mid-'95. We'll see. No front-end sales commission, but there is a redemption charge if you cash in before six years (maximum 5 percent). Sold by London Life reps.

LOTUS BALANCED FUND $$ ⇒ G/FI NO RSP CBAL

This entry from Vancouver-based M.K. Wong Management has been around for a decade, with indifferent results. The bond section of the portfolio is conservatively managed, with a mix of Government of Canada, provincial, municipal, and high-grade corporate bonds, along with some mortgage-backed securities. The stock section is much more aggressive — focus is on companies with high growth potential. This fund had been showing improving results, but the past year was disappointing — a gain of just 7.5 percent to June 30, '95, well below average for this category. Purchase through M.K. Wong Management; phone 1-800-665-9360 for details. Sold in all provinces west of the Ontario–Quebec border. Minimum investment is $10,000. Name changed from Lotus Fund in April '94.

MANULIFE VISTAFUND DIVERSIFIED
INVESTMENT FUND $$ ⇒ G/FI #/* RSP S CBAL

Results have generally been below average but have started to pick up recently. Invests in a broad mix of securities, including stocks, bonds, T-bills, and mortgages. Bond section is about as conservative as you'll find; the stock portfolio tends to be more aggressive. If you buy this one, choose Option 1 (you'll be offered two purchase choices). See entry for Manulife VistaFund Capital Gains Growth Fund in Canadian Equity section for purchase details. Sold by representatives of Manulife.

MARITIME LIFE
BALANCED FUND $$ ⟹ G NO RSP S CBAL

Unusual system, employing four money management companies. Fund is divided into three segments — fixed income, stocks, and balanced. The fund uses an active asset allocation strategy, overweighting the portfolio in the asset class expected to perform best. However, stocks may not exceed two-thirds of the total. The managers make maximum use of their foreign content allotment by adding a wide range of U.S. blue-chip issues to the total mix. That move has helped recent performance perk up considerably; the fund gained 13.9 percent for the year ending June 30, '95. Rating moves up a notch this year.

MAWER CANADIAN BALANCED
RETIREMENT SAVINGS FUND $$ ⟹ G/FI NO RSP CBAL

This Alberta-based fund has had generally respectable results. It ran into tough going in the first half of '94, but rebounded strongly with a 15.1 percent gain for the year to June 30, '95. Five-year average annual return was 10.2 percent, somewhat better than average. But here's a mystery for you. This fund is fully RRSP eligible while the companion Canadian Diversified Investment Fund (below) is not. Yet they both have almost exactly the same stock portfolio and the foreign content element of both funds is similar. So why two funds? Maybe the folks at Mawer should take another look at this situation. Minimum investment $25,000. Phone (403) 267-1989 for information.

MAWER CANADIAN DIVERSIFIED
INVESTMENT FUND $$ ⟹ G/FI NO £ CBAL

Conservatively managed fund, designed to maximize income for unit holders through a portfolio of bonds, pre-ferreds, and high-yielding common stocks. Results similar to Retirement Savings Fund (above) and portfolio is much the same except that this one has a little more foreign content. There's too much Canadian content in this fund for it to fit comfortably in the international category. If the managers want to make this into an international balanced fund, some portfolio changes are needed; otherwise why not just merge these two funds? See purchase details above.

MCLEAN BUDDEN BALANCED FUND $$ ⇒ G/FI NO RSP CBAL

This fund employs a conservative investment strategy, combining stocks of large companies with bonds and debentures with at least an "A" safety rating. Maintains a truly balanced portfolio with equity component between 40 and 60 percent. Recent results have shown improvement; gain for the year to June 30, '95, was a solid 15.3 percent. Longer-term performance is slightly above average. See entry for McLean Budden Equity Growth Fund in Canadian Equity section for purchase details.

METLIFE MVP BALANCED FUND $ ⇒ G/FI * RSP S CBAL

Uninspired performer since '86 launch. Five-year average annual return to June 30, '95, is a very weak 6.4 percent. Not your best choice among segregated funds. Redemption fee payable if cashed within four years of purchase. Sold by Met Life reps.

MONTREAL TRUST EXCELSIOR — BALANCED SECTION

Combined with the Scotia Stock and Bond Fund to form the new Scotia Excelsior Balanced Fund.

MONTREAL TRUST EXCELSIOR — TOTAL RETURN SECTION

See Scotia Excelsior Total Return Fund.

MUTUAL DIVERSIFUND 25 $ ⇒ FI/G # RSP CBAL

One of three balanced funds from the Mutual Life group. The percentage of stocks in each portfolio is the main difference between them; the number of the fund represents the approximate proportion of equities it will hold. This is the most conservative of the three, emphasizing preservation of capital. Equity holdings will range between 15 and 35 percent of assets. This and Diversifund 40 have the best long-term records, but they're nothing to get excited about — average annual return of 7.7 percent over the decade to June 30, '95 (average for this category is 8.4 percent). Maximum sales charge is 3.75 percent, applicable on all three funds. Sold by representatives of Mutual Investco.

MUTUAL DIVERSIFUND 40 $ ⟹ G/FI # RSP CBAL

Most balanced portfolio of the three funds in this family. Stocks may make up between 25 and 55 percent of the portfolio, depending on conditions. Did better than Diversifund 25 in rising Canadian stock market over the past year, but long-term results are exactly the same and below average for balanced funds as a group.

MUTUAL DIVERSIFUND 55 $ ⟹ G/FI # RSP CBAL

The most aggressive of the Diversifunds. Has the highest mix of equities in its portfolio (between 35 and 75 percent), making it a somewhat greater risk. This has been the best performer of the three Mutual Diversifunds in recent years, thanks to a rising stock market. Long-term results still lag behind the other two, however.

NAL CANADIAN DIVERSIFIED FUND $ ⟹ G/FI * RSP S CBAL

Recent results have been much better than the long-term average because of a heavy portfolio weighting in stocks (57 percent) as the market ran up in '95. Longer-term returns are still below average, however. Management is by Elliott & Page, who have run this fund since its inception. Redemption fee if cashed within five years. Sold by licensed insurance agents and brokers.

NN BALANCED FUND $ ⟹ G/FI * RSP S CBAL

Invests primarily in a mix of TSE 300 issues and high-quality bonds. Below-average performer with a five-year average annual return of 8.2 percent to June 30, '95. Sold by representatives of NN Life.

NATIONAL LIFE BALANCED FUND $$$ ⟹ G/FI * RSP CBAL

A true balanced fund from National Life Assurance, making its debut appearance in the *Guide* this year. Portfolio offers a solid blend of Canadian stocks, foreign mutual funds, bonds, mortgages, and T-bills. Excellent performance record, with a three-year average annual rate of return of 11.7 percent to June 30, '95. The National Life family is one of the top segregated fund groups in the country, and this is one worthy example. Sold by National Life representatives.

NATIONAL TRUST
BALANCED FUND $ ⇒ G/FI NO RSP CBAL

The equity portion of this portfolio has a strong blue-chip flavour. The bond portion invests only in issues with a safety rating of "A" or higher. The result is an okay fund if you don't want a lot of risk or excitement. Long-term results are sub-par, but recent returns are better. Sold by branches of National Trust.

OPTIMUM BALANCED FUND $$ ⇒ G/FI NO RSP CBAL

Decent performer, with a slightly above-average long-term record. Stock portion of the portfolio is heavily invested in blue-chip issues. The bond section is comprised mainly of federal government and Quebec provincial issues. No sales fee if purchased directly from the manager; phone 1-800-363-7675 for details. Sold only in Quebec. Formerly known as St. Laurent Optimum Balanced Fund.

PHILLIPS, HAGER & NORTH
BALANCED FUND $$$ ⇒ G/FI NO RSP CBAL

A well-diversified fund from this solid, Vancouver-based money manager, making its debut in the *Guide* this year. The portfolio is made up of a carefully chosen mix of Canadian, U.S., and international stocks, federal and provincial bonds, and corporate paper. Three-year average annual return to June 30, '95, was 11.1 percent, well above average. Another winner from this fine house.

PRUDENTIAL DIVERSIFIED
INVESTMENT FUND $$$ ⇒ FI # RSP CBAL

Had a rough time in the first half of '94, but has rebounded strongly. Gained 15.8 percent for the year to June 30, '95. Well-balanced portfolio. Mike Weir took over as manager in September '94. The uncertainty created by that move caused me to temporarily drop the rating a notch, but it is now restored. Sold by Prudential Fund Management. Maximum load of 5 percent.

ROYAL LIFE BALANCED FUND $ ⇒ G/FI * RSP S CBAL

A solid portfolio that has turned in profits for investors. Long-term results have been below average compared to other funds in this category, but it has looked better recently with a gain of 13.1 percent for the year ending June 30, '95. Sold by Royal Life representatives. Maximum back-end load of 4.5 percent.

ROYAL TRUST ADVANTAGE BALANCED FUND $$ ⇒ G/FI NO RSP CBAL

A fund of funds that invests in other Royal Trust mutual funds using asset mix principles. Equity holdings normally represent 40 to 60 percent of fund assets. Strikes a middle ground between the conservative Advantage Income Fund and the more aggressive Advantage Growth Fund. No load. Available through branches of Royal Trust.

ROYAL TRUST ADVANTAGE GROWTH FUND $$ ⇒ G/FI NO RSP CBAL

Uses the same techniques as the company's Advantage Balanced Fund but puts a greater emphasis on stocks (usually 60 to 80 percent of the portfolio). This makes it higher risk than the other Advantage funds, but it also means it will do better when stock markets are strong. It should come as no surprise, therefore, that this was the best performer of these three funds for the year to June 30, '95, with a gain of 17.4 percent.

ROYAL TRUST ADVANTAGE INCOME FUND $$ ⇒ FI/G NO RSP CBAL

Emphasis is on fixed income investments, with stocks normally limited to 15 to 30 percent of the portfolio. As a result, this fund holds up better when stock markets are weak, but underperforms when they're strong. Has the best long-term record of the three Advantage funds, with a five-year average annual compound rate of return of 9.5 percent.

ROYFUND BALANCED FUND $$$ ⇒ G/FI NO RSP CBAL

Conservatively managed portfolio, focusing on high-grade fixed income securities and stocks of companies with a proven track record. Results have been good but not spectacular. Average annual return for the decade to June 30, '95, was an even 10 percent, not bad at all. Sold by Royal Bank Mutual Fund Services, through Royal Bank branches.

SAVINGS AND INVESTMENT TRUST RETIREMENT FUND $$ ⇒ G/FI NO RSP CBAL

Results of this long-time average performer are starting to look a lot better. Gained 16 percent for the year to June 30, '95, well above average. Well-balanced portfolio. Worth your attention if you're a client of Savings and Investment Trust (Trust Prêt et Revenu) in Quebec or eastern Ontario.

SAXON BALANCED FUND $$ ⇒ G/FI NO RSP CBAL

Hadn't done much of anything until '92, when it scored an 11.5 percent gain to rank in the top 10 among all funds in this category. Followed that with a 34.4 percent gain in '93, for another top-10 finish. But then it slumped in '94, losing 3.2 percent. Things turned positive again in '95, however, with a big 19 percent gain in the first half. I'd like to think '94 was an aberration, but let's see what happens over the next year before raising the rating. This is a small fund, with assets of only $3.2 million, so it could experience more volatility than the average balanced fund. As of mid-'95, the portfolio was heavily weighted to equities (67 percent), with a mix of blue chips (Alcan, Nova, banks), and small growth stocks. Bonds were only 21 percent of the holdings, with the rest in cash. See Saxon Small Cap Fund in Canadian Equity section for details on how to purchase.

SCEPTRE BALANCED FUND $$$ ⇒ G/FI NO RSP CBAL

One of the better long-term performers in this category with an average annual return of 10 percent over the past decade. Manager Lyle Stein has constructed a well-balanced portfolio that takes maximum advantage of the foreign content allowance. Stock holdings tend to be of the blue-chip variety (Seagram, Moore Corp., Nova, Telus). No load charge if purchased directly from the manager (Ontario residents only). See entry for Sceptre Equity Fund in Canadian Equity section for more purchase details.

SCOTIA EXCELSIOR BALANCED FUND $$ ⇒ G/FI NO RSP CBAL

This fund was created in October '95 by combining two underperforming entries — the Scotia Stock and Bond

Fund and the Montreal Trust Excelsior Balanced section. The result is a middle-of-the-road balanced fund that's designed for more conservative investors. It invests in a combination of bonds, short-term securities, common stocks, and foreign issues. Results of both funds have been below average for this category, but maybe the combined version will fare better. The holdings are solid and several of the stocks have performed well. But for some reason, it all hasn't jelled so far. Sold in branches of the Bank of Nova Scotia and Montreal Trust as well as by ScotiaMcLeod.

SCOTIA EXCELSIOR TOTAL RETURN FUND $$$ ⇒ G/FI NO RSP CBAL

Another balanced entry from Scotiabank, but this one adopts a more aggressive investment approach. That means pursuing capital gains more vigorously, with a potentially higher degree of risk — although that has not been evident so far. Results to date have been very impressive; the fund had a five-year average annual compound rate of return of 13 percent to June 30, '95, well above average for this category of fund. More recent returns have slipped a bit, however; the fund gained a below-average 9.5 percent in the year ending June 30, '95. Still, this appears to be a better bet than the companion Balanced Fund for investors who want higher returns and are prepared to accept a little more risk. If you're looking for something a little different from the usual ho-hum trust company balanced fund, here it is. Recommended. Formerly the Montreal Trust Total Return Section; renamed in October '95 as part of the merger of the Scotia and Montreal Trust funds. Available at both Scotiabank and Montreal Trust branches.

SPECTRUM DIVERSIFIED FUND $$ ⇒ G/FI #/* RSP CBAL

A conservatively managed fund that invests mainly in blue-chip stocks and government bonds. Performance has started to pick up after going through some rough times. Gain for the year ending June 30, '95, was 13.2 percent. The managers have added a foreign content component (14 percent in spring '95) to improve performance and add more diversity to the portfolio.

STANDARD LIFE IDEAL
BALANCED FUND $$ \Rightarrow$ G * RSP S CBAL

One of the funds in the renamed "Ideal" series, offered by Standard Life Assurance Co. Don't confuse this one with the newer Standard Life Balanced Mutual Fund, which is not tied to any life insurance purchase (it's not included in these listings because it hasn't been operating for three years). This fund aims to provide capital appreciation and income while limiting risk. After going through a difficult period, returns have begun to improve significantly — the fund gained 16.3 percent for the year to June 30, '95. This fund is a candidate for an upgrade with another year of good performance. Sold by Standard Life agents and brokers. Formerly called the Standard Life Balanced 2000 Fund and before that known as the Standard Diversifund.

STRATAFUND 40 $$ \Rightarrow$ G/FI # RSP CBAL

The Strata funds have been sold to Mutual Life and are scheduled to be merged into the Mutual fund family by the end of '95.

STRATAFUND 60 $$ \Rightarrow$ G/FI # RSP CBAL

See comments above.

TALVEST DIVERSIFIED FUND $ \Downarrow$ G/FI #/* RSP CBAL

Never had a losing year prior to '94, and even then the drop was a minuscule 0.5 percent. So from a safety perspective, this fund's not bad. It's just not making a lot of money for investors. Average annual return for the five years to June 30, '95, was 8.4 percent — a full percentage point below the norm for this category. This is one of those funds that should be performing better. Talvest is a solid money manager and the fund is well diversified, with some sound holdings. But it's just not cutting it — at least, not to the extent it should be. See Talvest Growth Fund entry in Canadian Equity section for purchase details.

TEMPLETON
BALANCED FUND $$ \Rightarrow$ G/FI #/* RSP CBAL

This was a poor performer in its original guise as a pure stock fund under the name Templeton Canadian Fund.

Now, however, it's a balanced entry with a strong foreign component, and it's showing much better. The portfolio was heavily weighted to stocks in the first half of '95, with the banking sector the most strongly represented. The result was a slightly better-than-average gain of 8.6 percent for the first half of the year. Three-year average annual returns to June 30, '95, were 10.3 percent, again slightly better than average for this category. This isn't the top balanced fund available by any means, but if you're a Templeton client and you want some diversification in your holdings, this one shouldn't let you down.

TRANS-CANADA INCOME FUND $$ ⇒ G/FI #/* RSP CBAL

It's hard to know where to slot this fund. The portfolio is heavily weighted to common stocks (about 73 percent at the start of '95), but there are enough bonds in the mix to push it over here. But a dividend fund it definitely is not, although you'll find it listed there in business press mutual fund surveys. As a balanced fund, recent returns are quite good; longer-term results are slightly below average. There's a negotiable back-end load on all Sagit funds that you should look into before you buy. Formerly known as Trans-Canada Shares Series C.

TRIMARK INCOME GROWTH FUND $$$ ⇒ G/FI # RSP CBAL

Above-average performer since '87 launch except for an off-year in '90. Five-year average annual compound rate of return to June 30, '95, was an excellent 12 percent. Well-balanced portfolio with a strong foreign content component (21.3 percent of market value as of mid-'95). Fixed income component includes mortgage-backed securities, government bonds, and corporate issues. If a pure stock fund worries you, this is an excellent compromise. The main difference between this and the Select Balanced Fund (below) is the purchase option.

TRIMARK SELECT BALANCED FUND $$$ ⇒ G/FI * RSP CBAL

The back-end load companion to the Income Growth Fund (above). Similar portfolio; nominal results will usually be a little lower due to higher management fees (2.28 percent vs. 1.75 percent). However, once adjustment is made for the front-end load on the Income Growth Fund, there's very little difference in actual total return until you get out beyond five years.

20-20 CANADIAN ASSET
ALLOCATION FUND $$ ⇒ G/FI #/* RSP CBAL

Uses asset allocation techniques to minimize risk and enhance return. This strategy hasn't been particularly successful thus far; fund has made some money for investors, but long-term returns have been slightly below average for this category. Manager Larry Lunn has built up the foreign stock component to close to the limit. The fund was about two-thirds in stocks in mid-'95. An okay performer, but there are better.

UNITED CANADIAN
PORTFOLIO OF FUNDS $$$ ⇒ G/FI #/* RSP CBAL

A fund of funds that invests in other United funds, thus offering investors a mix. Portfolio is structured so as to ensure full RRSP eligibility. Results are somewhat better than the average for Canadian balanced funds as a group. Name changed from United Portfolio of RSP Funds in spring '94.

WESTBURY CANADIAN LIFE
BALANCED FUND $ ⇒ G/FI NO RSP S CBAL

Three-year results are sub-par, but this insurance company entry has shown better recently with a gain of 14.3 percent for the year to June 30, '95. Sold by representatives of Westbury Canadian Life.

U.S. and International Balanced and Asset Allocation Funds

nother new category this year, reflecting the growth of balanced funds that invest mainly outside of Canada. The parameters of these funds will differ considerably, so be sure you know exactly what you're buying before plunging ahead. ■

RATINGS CHANGES

Just one of significance. The 20/20 World Fund, which had been doing very well, ran into some problems in the first half of '95, resulting in a significant loss. The fund appears to have rallied, but the rating has been dropped from the $$$ category for the time being.

1996 RATINGS

ADMAX AMERICAN SELECT GROWTH FUND
$$ ⇒ G/FI #/* £ IBAL

Formerly the U.S. Polymetric Performance Fund, this entry uses the market timing principles of Picton Davies (see Admax Canadian Select Growth Fund for details). Invests in a blend of U.S. stocks, cash, and U.S.-dollar denominated bonds, including Canadian issues. Goal is long-term capital gains, while minimizing risk. Results have been respectable; fund gained an above-average 18.7 percent in the year ending June 30, '95. Three-year average annual return for the period was 10 percent.

ALTAMIRA GLOBAL DIVERSIFIED FUND
$ ⇒ G/FI NO £ IBAL

This has been one of the weak links in the Altamira chain. Started as the Hume Growth & Income Fund, it was purchased by Altamira in '88. Results since then have been below average for this category. Five-year average annual rate of return to June 30, '95, was just 5.1 percent. Average for this category was 8.7 percent. The fund is managed for Altamira by Marie-Claude Bernal and Robert Rands of Wellington Management. Although it's a diversified fund, the portfolio tends to be heavily weighted towards stocks. If you want an international balanced fund, there are much better choices available. Formerly known as Altamira Diversified Fund.

BPI GLOBAL BALANCED RSP FUND
$$$ ⇒ G/FI #/* RSP IBAL

A balanced fund for Canadians who want extensive foreign exposure within an RRSP-eligible fund. Stocks focus on Canadian corporations that do a lot of business abroad (e.g., Alcan, Thomson Corp., Sherritt). Bonds are split between Canadian and foreign currency issues, although portfolio favoured Canadian-dollar issues in June '95. I raised the rating a notch last year and manager Mark Bonham (BPI president) didn't disappoint; the fund returned an above-average 8.1 percent for the year ending June 30, '95. Worth a look if you want a fund with lots of foreign exposure for your RRIF or RRSP.

GLOBAL STRATEGY DIVERSIFIED
GROWTH FUND $ ⇒ G/FI #/* RSP IBAL

This is another of Global Strategy's many foreign funds
that are fully RRSP-eligible. This one invests in a mix of
equities, fixed income securities, and derivatives, plus a
core holding of Government of Canada T-bills for the
required 80 percent domestic content. Despite the fancy
portfolio, this fund has trouble making a buck; average
annual rate of return for the five years to June 30, '95,
was a paltry 2.3 percent. Recent results haven't given
much cause for optimism; the fund lost 0.9 percent in
the past year. Not the best place for your RRSP money.

INVESTORS GROWTH PLUS
PORTFOLIO $$$ ⇒ G/FI * £ IBAL

Investors Group offers several "portfolio" funds, which
invest in units of other funds for more diversification.
This has been one of the most successful. It holds units
in six Investor funds: Government Bond, Corporate
Bond, Canadian Equity, Global, Real Property, and U.S.
Growth Fund. If you want a balanced fund that really
covers the investment horizon, this is it. Good results
too; average annual rate of return for the five years ending June 30, '95, was a very respectable 9.8 percent.
See entry for Investors Canadian Equity Fund in the
Canadian Equity section for details on commissions
and fees.

LAURENTIAN COMMONWEALTH
FUND $$ ⇒ G #/* £ IBAL

Respectable long-term performer under its old name of
Viking Commonwealth Fund. Had been in a bit of a
decline but appears to be coming back again. Although
this fund holds some bonds (hence its inclusion in the
balanced category), the main emphasis is on stocks,
specifically large companies with good growth potential. Well diversified internationally; not limited to
Commonwealth countries despite the rather misleading
name. Generally turns in solid but not sensational
results; suited for more conservative investors. Now eligible for RRIFs and RRSPs, as foreign content. Results
tend to be better than for the sister Global Balanced
Fund (below).

LAURENTIAN GLOBAL BALANCED FUND $$ ⇒ G/FI #/* £ IBAL

Invests in a portfolio of large international companies and high-quality foreign currency bonds. This is a switch in direction; previously, the fund was primarily a stock fund, operating under the name Endurance Global Equity Fund. This is much more of a true international balanced fund than the companion Commonwealth Fund (above), which is more top-heavy in stocks. This makes this fund the better choice for conservative investors. The Commonwealth Fund tends to have better returns, however.

TALVEST GLOBAL DIVERSIFIED FUND $$ ⇒ G/FI #/* £ IBAL

This fund is run by Christian Wignall of G.T. Capital Management, who uses a top-down approach to decide on geographic weightings. As of mid-'95, stocks made up about 57 percent of the portfolio, with fairly even distribution between the Far East, Europe, and North America. Bonds were about 40 percent of the mix. This fund had been going along quite nicely until the first half of '95, when it stumbled to a 2 percent loss. It more than made that back in July, however, with a 3.1 percent advance, so things may be back on track. Worth a look.

TALVEST U.S. DIVERSIFIED FUND $$ ⇒ G/FI #/* £ IBAL

The stock component of this U.S. balanced fund was heavily into blue-chip stocks in mid-'95. So the gain of almost 10 percent in the first seven months of the year was no surprise. Longer-term results aren't as impressive, however; the average annual return for the three years to June 30, '95, was slightly below average at 9.9 percent. Manager is Jean-Guy Desjardins, Talvest's chairman and CEO.

20/20 AMERICAN TACTICAL ASSET ALLOCATION FUND $$$ ⇒ G/FI #/* £ IBAL

Manager Kathy Taylor of Wells Fargo in San Francisco adjusts the portfolio of this fund between U.S. bonds, stocks, and short-term notes according to the dictates of a computerized asset, allocation formula developed by her company. Results have been very good; fund averaged 13.3 percent a year for the five years to June 30,

'95. That was better (substantially) than the average for pure U.S. equity funds sold in Canada, much less a balanced fund. If you're interested in an asset allocation approach for your U.S. holdings, this one is well worth looking at.

20/20 WORLD FUND $$ ⇒ G/FI #/* £ IBAL

This fund had been sailing along quite nicely until it ran into a double-whammy in the first half of '95 that produced a big 8.4 percent loss and knocked all its performance numbers for a loop. Hit number one was a heavy (24 percent) weighting in Japan at the start of '95, where manager Keith Brown expected to see rising profits. Instead, a rising yen, concerns about the banking industry, and the Kobe earthquake hurt the Japanese stock market. Hit number two was the Mexican peso devaluation. Brown was holding a 10 percent stake in Latin America, which was roughed up badly. This fund, at the core, is better than its recent numbers would lead you to believe, as shown by the fact it bounded back with a big 8 percent gain in July '95. But I've reduced the rating a notch until we see sustained evidence that Brown has got this one pointed in the right direction again.

UNITED GLOBAL PORTFOLIO OF FUNDS $$ ⇒ G/FI #/* £ IBAL

Invests primarily in units of other United funds, but also has a significant bond position. Decent long-term results. Addition of the new United Global Telecommunications Fund to the mix has spiced up returns. Hovering on the brink of an upgrade. Name changed from United Portfolio of Funds in spring '94.

Specialty Funds

This is something of a catch-all category, designed as a slot for funds that don't really fit in well anywhere else. Included in this mixed bag you'll find real estate funds, labour-sponsored venture capital funds, international sector funds, derivative funds, and more. In short, if the fund you're looking for has been around at least three years and you can't find it anywhere else, it's probably here. ∎

RATINGS CHANGES

As more labour-sponsored venture capital funds appear on the scene, investor interest in them is increasing. As a result, two new funds in this category have been added to the ratings this year: Quebec's Solidarity Fund, which has been around for many years but has been difficult to get information about, and B.C.'s Working Opportunity Fund, which has reached the three-year qualifying mark.

As well, the rating of the Working Ventures Canadian Fund is being upgraded this year, in recognition of the fact that, as the fund matures, returns are starting to show some improvement.

1996 RATINGS

EXAR REAL ESTATE FUND $ ⇑ G # RSP RE

If you're unhappy with the performance of your mutual funds, look on the bright side. You might have had money in this one (if you did, I'm sorry for you). The net asset value per unit of this small, Quebec-based real estate fund dropped — hold on now — 69.4 percent in '94! That's the largest one-year decline I can ever recall in a Canadian mutual fund. It's hardly surprising that fund president Jean Boisvert writes in his annual report: "The real estate sector is the area of the economy worst hit by the recession and it's not over yet." The holdings in the portfolio are exclusively Quebec-based. Maybe it will turn around, but the main concern of the managers right now is just to stay afloat. Phone (819) 758-0669 for information.

GLOBAL STRATEGY REAL ESTATE SECURITIES FUND $ ⇑ G #/* £ SEC

The mandate of this fund is to invest for long-term growth through stocks in real estate and development companies throughout the world. Unlike most other real estate funds, this one does not invest directly in land and buildings. The distinction hasn't made much difference, though — the fund is down an average of 3.5 percent a year over the five-year period to June 30, '95. Recent results don't give much hope for an imminent turn-around. Avoid.

GREAT-WEST LIFE REAL ESTATE FUND $ ⇑ G */NO RSP S RE

These are hard times for real estate funds — so tough, in fact, that Great-West Life has stopped publishing the returns for this fund in the business press. But we have them. To June 30, '95, one-year return was -0.5 percent; three-year average annual compound rate of return was -6.6 percent; five-year annual return was -5.7 percent; and 10-year annual results were +1.8 percent. Pretty sorry results if you're an investor, but indicative of the problems the Canadian real estate industry has been experiencing. Hopefully, the worst has passed — but I said that last year! See the entry for Great-West Life Canadian Equity Fund in the Canadian Equity section for purchase details and recommendations. Sold by Great-West Life reps. Not available in Ontario.

INVESTORS REAL PROPERTY FUND $$ ⇒ G * RSP RE

Held up better than most during the assault on commercial and office real estate in the past few years. This is

357

due in part to the fact that a large number of the fund's
properties are located in western Canada, which was not
as hard hit by the economic downturn. The managers
seem to think the worst is over because they've been
snapping up properties right and left in the depressed
Ontario market — 40 new ones in '94 alone. Gained a
modest 2.6 percent for the year to June 30, '95, but that
was better than some of its competitors. RRSP/RRIF-eli-
gible, but you'll lose the tax breaks if you hold units in
registered plans (see the section on "Tax-Advantaged
Funds"). Sold by Investors Group representatives. See
entry for Investors Canadian Equity Fund in the
Canadian Equity section for details on new fee policy.

ROYAL LEPAGE COMMERCIAL REAL ESTATE FUND

Closed down, despite being one of the better performers
in this category in recent years.

ROYCOM-SUMMIT REALTY FUND $ ⇒ G * RE

This small, Halifax-based group still boasts the best five-
year record in the embattled real estate fund business,
but lately things have been rough — this fund dropped
6.2 percent in the year ending June 30, '95. That sparked
a bunch of redemption requests, which in turn prompted the managers to introduce a "stabilization process" in
mid-'95. That means limiting redemptions so that properties don't have to be sold off at distress prices. Several
other real estate funds have been forced into a similar
position, and this is just the latest sign that the crisis in
this business isn't over. This is the only Canadian real
estate fund with significant U.S. property holdings and,
in fact, the fund recently sold a North Carolina building
for a good profit. But it's a tough time for real estate and
you have to be a believer to buy in. Note that this fund
may not be held in registered plans. The companion TDF
Fund can. Phone 1-800-565-1979 for purchase details.
Flash: Just as we were going to press, the managers
announced they would seek unitholder approval to turn
this and the companion TDF Fund into a closed-end real
estate investment trust (REIT).

ROYCOM-SUMMIT TDF FUND $ ⇒ G * RSP RE

RRSP-eligible twin to the Roycom-Summit Realty Fund.
Wasn't hit quite as badly last year.

SOLIDARITY FUND $$ ⇑ G * RSP LAB

The oldest and biggest of the labour-sponsored venture capital funds, with assets of more than $1.1 billion in mid-'95. Open only to Quebecers. Investments can at times be politically motivated. Average annual rate of return for the decade to June 30, '95, was a modest 5 percent, but of course you get tax breaks on top of that.

WORKING OPPORTUNITY FUND $ ⇑ G * RSP LAB

A labour-sponsored venture capital fund for British Columbia residents. Like all such funds, it's just finding its feet. Returns have been modest so far, because most of the assets have been in short-term securities. However, the managers are now starting to find homes for some of their money, especially in the high-tech and tourism sectors. Has promise.

WORKING VENTURES CANADIAN
FUND $$ ⇑ G * RSP LAB

The largest labour-sponsored venture capital fund in Canada, after Quebec's gigantic Solidarity Fund. Like all funds of this type, the mandate is to invest in fledgling Canadian companies. The big initial attraction is the tax break you get when you invest (see section on Labour-Sponsored Funds). Returns to date have been low (average annual return of 4.7 percent for the five years ending June 30, '95), but are gradually improving. Until now, most of the assets have been in T-bills and short-term bonds, awaiting investment decisions. However, the investment pace is starting to pick up and some of the early deals are coming to maturity with favourable results for unit-holders. Potentially high risk because of venture capital nature of the investments. If you decide to put money in, remember you'll be locked in for several years, in most cases. I'm moving up the rating a notch this year in recognition of the fact this fund is starting to mature and we're getting a better feel for where president Ron Begg and his people are heading.

Canadian Money Market Funds

s I predicted in last year's edition, yields on Canadian money market funds rose through the second half of '94 and into early '95. During the 12 months ending June 30, 1995, the average Canadian money market fund returned 5.8 percent, about two percentage points more than during the same period the previous year. This made money market funds a more attractive parking spot for cash. ■

The drop in short-term rates that occurred in mid-'95 had an impact on yields, and that trend could continue into early 1996. But we could see a rise in rates as the year progresses.

With stock markets having hit record highs in '95, some profit-taking may be in order. These funds are a good place to stash some cash while you wait to see what comes next. Certainly, they beat the returns being offered for deposit accounts at most banks and trust companies.

When you purchase a money market fund, be aware that the yields you see quoted are not guaranteed for the future. They're merely a projection, based on the fund's most recent performance. If short-term interest rates are rising, you'll very likely receive more income than you expect over the next 12 months. If they're falling, the opposite is true.

RATINGS CHANGES

A total of nine funds in this category have been downgraded a notch this year. However, none of last year's top *$$$$* performers were affected. One fund, Trans-Canada Money Market, moved up a notch to *$$$*.

Five funds appear for the first time in this edition, the most notable being the National Life Money Market Fund which weighs in with a solid *$$$* rating.

1996 RATINGS

AGF MONEY MARKET ACCOUNT $$ ⇓ C #/*/NO RSP CMM

This fund comes about as close to the statistical averages as you'll find. It's never great, never poor, just dull and steady. Invests only in Canadian T-bills, which gives it a high safety quotient. Of the three purchase options, only the no-load choice should be considered. Do not, under any circumstances, choose the back-end load. You'll be assessed a redemption fee of as high as 5.5 percent if you cash in before eight years, and you'll pay a higher annual management fee. Money market funds are short-term holdings by nature, so a redemption fee of that magnitude is out of line. Your redemption fee could exceed an entire year's worth of profits!

AMI PRIVATE CAPITAL MONEY MARKET FUND $$$ ⇒ C NO RSP CMM

Good performer from this new group; returns have been above average thanks in part to a relatively low management fee (0.75 percent). If you live in B.C., Ontario, Nova Scotia, or Quebec, buy directly from the manager (call 416-865-3006), otherwise a 2 percent sales charge may apply. Minimum investment is $50,000, which may be spread among other funds in the group. Formerly the Church Street Money Market Fund.

ATLAS CANADIAN MONEY MARKET FUND $$ ⇒ C NO RSP CMM

Name changed from Finsco Canadian Money Market Fund in July '94 and management responsibilities were handed to the well-known international house of

Salomon Brothers. This is a middle-of-the-road money fund, with an average performance record. Portfolio is a mix of federal, provincial, and corporate notes. Available on a no-load basis through Midland Walwyn representatives.

ATLAS CANADIAN T-BILL FUND $$ ⇓ C NO RSP CMM

Brother to the Atlas Canadian Money Market Fund (above) with the same managers. Only difference is that this one invests primarily in Government of Canada Treasury bills, for slightly better safety. Returns tend to be slightly lower than for the Money Market Fund. You'll have to decide if it's worth it; personally, I'd go for the higher yield.

BPI T-BILL FUND $$ ⇒ C NO RSP CMM

This was formerly the BPI Money Market Fund. It has been beefed up by the addition of two funds from the now-dead Bolton Tremblay family: the BT Landmark Money Market Fund and the BT Landmark Short-Term Interest Fund. Returns are average. BPI's only no-load fund.

BEUTEL GOODMAN MONEY MARKET FUND $$$ ⇒ C NO RSP CMM

A solid entry from the Beutel Goodman investment management house. Returns have been well above average for this category. Portfolio is very high quality, a combination of Treasury bills and banker's acceptances with some corporate short-term bonds added for good measure. Recommended.

BISSETT MONEY MARKET FUND $$$ ⇒ C NO RSP CMM

Steady performer from this Calgary-based company. Returns have been above average. Three-year average annual return to June 30, '95, was 5.5 percent (average of all Canadian money market funds was 4.9 percent). See Bissett Canadian Equity Fund entry for purchase details.

C.I. MONEY MARKET FUND $$$ ⇓ C #/* RSP CMM

Good performer from Canadian International Group. Invests almost exclusively in Government of Canada T-bills. Useful as a temporary place to park cash while you're deciding which part of the world to invest in next.

Tip: don't buy this or any other money market fund on a back-end load basis. Try to get the front-end load waived as well.

CIBC CANADIAN T-BILL FUND $ ⇓ C NO RSP CMM

Safe, solid performer from one of Canada's big banks. Nothing unusual, just steady return with little risk. Results are somewhat below average for this category, however.

CIBC MONEY MARKET FUND $ ⇒ C NO RSP CMM

The Bank of Commerce has a large family of money market funds (four as of mid-'95). This is the original one. It's a steady performer, but results tend to be below average for this category. It is best suited to CIBC clients who want to get a better return on the money they've been holding in deposit accounts. The bank's T-Bill Fund offers slightly more safety and, oddly, its returns have been almost the same. But your best bet, if you have the minimum amount required, is the Premium Canadian T-Bill Fund (see below).

CIBC PREMIUM CANADIAN
T-BILL FUND $$$ ⇓ C NO RSP CMM

The Bank of Commerce's money fund for the rich. Minimum investment is $250,000, in case you have the loose change around the house. Investment strategy is the same as for the Canadian T-Bill Fund, which you only need $5,000 to buy. The difference is that the management expense ratio on this fund is less than half (0.55 percent versus 1.2 percent), boosting return accordingly.

CANADA LIFE MONEY
MARKET FUND S-29 $ ⇒ C * RSP S CMM

A below-average performer. Canada Life boasts about the fact that 1994 was the 14th straight year this fund had a higher rate of return than the increase in the CPI, but that's hardly a proper criterion for measuring mutual fund results. I don't like the redemption fees of up to 4.5 percent that apply for up to seven years if you cash in. Money market funds should be viewed as short-term investments; you shouldn't have to pay a fee to withdraw cash. The good news is that transfers to other Canada

Life funds are exempt from this charge, as long as you don't switch your money more than four times a year.

CAPSTONE CASH MANAGEMENT FUND $$ ⇓ C NO RSP CMM

A dependable performer with a high safety factor. Invests mainly in Government of Canada T-bills. Note that no management fee is assessed directly against the fund; however, investors are directly charged a fee of 1 percent a year (diminishing if you have more than $500,000 in the fund). That's a lot when interest rates are low. The result of this unusual method of management compensation is to make the returns published in the business press appear significantly higher than they actually are. Keep that in mind if you're contemplating a purchase. Call (416) 863-0005 for information.

COLONIA MONEY MARKET FUND $$ ⇓ C NO RSP S CMM

Very small portfolio, invested entirely in Canada T-bills as of spring '95. Average returns. Sold by Colonia Life reps.

CONCORDE MONEY MARKET FUND $$ ⇒ C #/* RSP CMM

Routine money market fund from the Quebec-based Concorde Financial Group. Watch out for the sales commissions on this one! If you can't get it no load, look elsewhere.

CORNERSTONE GOVERNMENT MONEY FUND $$ ⇓ C NO RSP CMM

An amalgamation of the former First City Government Money Fund and the Metropolitan Protection Fund. Assets are invested almost exclusively in Canada T-bills, providing a high measure of safety. Performance is average. Sold at branches of North American Trust (which was sold to Laurentian Bank in fall, '95).

DESJARDINS MONEY MARKET FUND $$ ⇒ C NO RSP CMM

Bulk of the portfolio is in corporate notes, with Canada and Quebec T-bills mixed in. Returns tend to be slightly below average. Offered by Desjardins Trust and Caisses Desjardins.

DYNAMIC MONEY MARKET
FUND $$ ⇓ C #/* RSP CMM

Steady performer. Was invested entirely in Government of Canada T-bills in spring '95. Optional front-end load of up to 2 percent or back-end load starting at 6 percent. For heaven's sake, don't choose the back-end option; if you cash in early it could cost you more than a year's worth of returns. In fact, if you can't get all load charges waived, look elsewhere.

ELLIOTT & PAGE MONEY FUND $$$ ⇓ C # RSP CMM

The nominal returns of this fund have been consistently above average (but with a caveat, see below). Conservatively managed portfolio is another plus. However, acquiring units could be expensive. The fund is subject to a front-end load charge of up to 1.5 percent. As well, there's a negotiable annual management fee of up to 1 percent, which Elliott & Page splits with the sales person. This may have been acceptable when money market funds were earning double-digit returns, but it's much too pricey in the current interest rate environment. Another problem: the published returns on this fund are net of a 0.5 percent management fee. If you agree to pay more than that (1 percent is the maximum, remember), you won't receive the returns reported in the business press. To put this in perspective, *The Globe and Mail Report on Business* shows the returns on this fund to be well above average over the years. But if you subtract an additional 0.5 percent from those returns, the numbers come in much closer to average. One other wrinkle to watch for if you move cash in and out of money funds frequently: E&P allows two free redemptions a month from this fund but reserves the right to charge a $10 fee for each transaction beyond that. Bottom line: if you can't acquire this fund free of all charges, look for a no-load alternative elsewhere.

EMPIRE MONEY MARKET FUND $ ⇒ C NO RSP S CMM

Steady money fund from Empire Life, but returns are somewhat below average. Invests primarily in T-bills and banker's acceptances. Sold by Empire Life reps.

ETHICAL MONEY MARKET FUND $$ ⇒ C #/*/NO RSP CMM

Started out as the Co-operative Trust Interest Fund, now part of the Ethical Funds group offered by the credit unions of Canada. Average returns. In the past, invested mainly in federal government T-bills, but now the portfolio is slightly weighted in favour of corporate notes. Average results. Don't pay a load charge for this one; you can get it free through participating credit unions everywhere except Quebec.

EVEREST MONEY MARKET FUND $$ ⇓ C NO RSP CMM

Steady income earner, but relative performance has slipped recently. High safety standard; most of the portfolio is invested in government T-bills. Available through branches of Canada Trust.

FICADRE MONEY MARKET FUND $$ ⇒ C * RSP CMM

Small Quebec-based fund; long-term results have been slightly above average.

FIDELITY CANADIAN SHORT TERM ASSET FUND $$ ⇒ C #/* RSP CMM

Invests almost exclusively in short-term corporate paper — no T-bills. As a result, you'd expect returns to be somewhat above average, but they're not. Part of the reason is the management expense ratio of 1.25 percent, high by money market fund standards. If you're not already a Fidelity investor, this is no reason to switch to them. If you do buy, try to acquire this one without any load fee.

FIRST CANADIAN MONEY MARKET FUND $$ ⇓ C NO RSP CMM

Solid performer from the Bank of Montreal. Nothing flashy, but safe; most of the assets are in government or government-guaranteed notes. Sold by Bank of Montreal branches.

GBC MONEY MARKET FUND $$$ ⇓ C NO RSP CMM

Solid performer. Conservative investment approach; the fund invests primarily in federal government T-bills and other government-guaranteed securities. Unfortunately, you'll need $100,000 before the company will look at you. See GBC entry in Canadian Equity section for purchase details.

GENERAL TRUST MONEY MARKET FUND $$ ⇒ C NO RSP CMM

Average performer, but has looked better recently. The portfolio, which was heavily weighted to Quebec provincial T-bills in the past, was rebalanced in mid-'95 to include substantial federal T-bill holdings. Sold by General Trust in Quebec only. See additional comments in the entry for the General Trust Canadian Equity Fund in the Canadian Equity section.

GLOBAL STRATEGY T-BILL SAVINGS FUND $$ ⇓ C #/* RSP CMM

Invests in mix of government T-bills and banker's acceptances, so safety element is good. Recent results slightly above average for this category. All load charges are negotiable with your dealer; aim for zero in this case.

GREAT-WEST LIFE MONEY MARKET FUND $ ⇒ C */NO RSP S CMM

Portfolio is a mix of Canada T-bills, banker's acceptances, high-quality corporate notes, and short-term bank bonds. The management fee on this fund is way too high, no matter which purchase option you select — 1.74 percent a year on the no-load option, 1.62 percent if you choose the back-end load. Those high fees are the main reason this fund's results are consistently below average. See the entry for Great-West Life Canadian Equity Fund in the Canadian Equity section for purchase details and recommendations. Sold by Great-West Life representatives.

GREEN LINE CANADIAN MONEY MARKET FUND $$$ ⇒ C NO RSP CMM

Excellent performance since '88 launch, with consistently above-average returns. Invests mainly in commercial paper and short-term (less than one year) government bonds. No load, easily available through branches of Toronto Dominion Bank.

GREEN LINE CANADIAN
T-BILL FUND $$ ⇓ C NO RSP CMM

Another Green Line money market offering. The only difference is that this one invests solely in Government of Canada Treasury bills, giving you a slightly higher level of safety. Returns tend to be a bit less than for the Canadian Money Market Fund. For the small safety difference, I'd go for the Money Market Fund and the higher return.

GUARDIAN CANADIAN MONEY
MARKET FUND $$$ ⇒ C #/* RSP CMM

Usually produces slightly above-average returns in the money market category, but there's a reason for it. The portfolio is made up entirely of short-term, high-grade corporate notes. There wasn't a single government security in it at the beginning of '95. This makes the fund slightly higher risk than one that invests mainly in Treasury bills; you have to decide if you're prepared to accept that small extra risk in exchange for a higher return. How much better can you do here? Well, over the past decade the annual average return for Canadian money market funds as a group was 8 percent. This one returned 8.3 percent. But beware. That apparent advantage can be wiped out by commissions and other charges. If you buy on a front-end load basis, you could be hit for up to 2 percent. The back-end load is even worse: you'll be assessed a redemption fee if you cash in within seven years of purchase. That's silly, especially during times when interest rates are down. Unless you can obtain the fund on a completely no-load basis, look for another option. Previously called Guardian Short Term Money Fund.

HODGSON ROBERTON LAING
INSTANT $$ FUND $$$$ ⇓ C NO RSP CMM

Very good results, the convenience of chequing privileges, plus a high degree of safety all translate into a fund you should look at. What's the secret of this little fund's ability to generate above-average returns year after year? Very low management fees — at 0.5 percent, it's one of the cheapest money market funds to operate in Canada. Government of Canada T-bills are the largest single holding in the portfolio; the balance is in high-quality corporate notes. The average maturity for all securities in the fund is kept well below 90 days to reduce interest rate risk. A useful feature (and an unusual one in Canadian money market funds) is the chequing privileges for unit-holders. All cheques over $500 are processed free; there's a $3 service charge for cheques under that amount. Minimum for new accounts: $2,500. Buy directly from the managers; phone 1-800-268-9622. Formerly known as the Waltaine Instant $$ Fund.

HONGKONG BANK MONEY MARKET FUND $$ ⇓ C NO RSP CMM

Returns have been slightly below average, but safety factor is good — fund invests primarily in Treasury bills. Five-year average annual return to June 30, '95, was 6.3 percent. Available at branches of the Hongkong Bank of Canada.

IMPERIAL GROWTH MONEY MARKET FUND $ ⇓ C # RSP S CMM

Invests primarily in Government of Canada T-bills, so safety record is good. Results have been below average, however, weighed down by a very high (1.5 percent) management fee. Compounding the sub-par performance is the fact you're charged a commission to buy in. Look elsewhere.

INDUSTRIAL ALLIANCE MONEY MARKET FUND $ ⇒ C * RSP S CMM

Don't confuse this or any other fund with the Industrial Alliance name with the more widely known Industrial group run by Mackenzie Financial. Industrial Alliance is a Quebec City-based insurance company, and this is part of their segregated fund family. Performance has been below average, due in large part to a hefty management expense fee of 1.5 percent.

INDUSTRIAL CASH MANAGEMENT FUND $$$$ ⇓ C # RSP CMM

One of the better money market funds in the country. Combines above-average returns with a high degree of safety (as of mid-'95, the entire portfolio was in Government of Canada T-bills). Returns are well above average, thanks in part to a very low management expense ratio of 0.5 percent. (Compare that to the MER of 1.42 percent for the sister Short-Term Fund below and you can immediately see why this one consistently outperforms it.) As a bonus, this fund offers good chequing privileges for non-registered accounts over $3,000. Maximum front-end load of 2 percent, but you should be able to get it without charge. Minimum investment is $1,500. Available to investors who buy Mackenzie funds on a front-end load basis.

INDUSTRIAL SHORT-TERM FUND $$ ⇓ C #/* RSP CMM

Investment objectives and portfolio are similar to companion Cash Management Fund (above). However, there are three big differences. (1) This fund has no chequing privileges. (2) Sales charge is on a back-end load basis. (3) Management fee is much higher, reducing return accordingly. The Cash Management Fund is by far the better choice.

INVESNAT MONEY MARKET FUND $$ ⇒ C NO RSP CMM

This money market fund invests heavily in short-term notes issued by the Province of Quebec and Quebec-based municipalities and institutions. Average returns. Available through National Bank.

INVESTORS MONEY MARKET FUND $$ ⇓ C NO RSP CMM

Average performer. Mix has been shifting away from corporate notes, because of scarcity of supply, to government T-bills. Rated AAA for safety by the Canadian Bond Rating Service. The only no-load fund offered by Investors Group; sold by their reps.

LAURENTIAN MONEY MARKET FUND $$ ⇓ C NO RSP CMM

Laurentian's only no-load fund. Results have been about average. Managers take a conservative approach, with most assets held in federal and provincial government T-bills, including some Quebec issues at times. Sold at Eaton's and member companies of the Laurentian Financial group. Formerly known as the Viking Money Market Fund.

LONDON LIFE MONEY MARKET FUND $$\Rightarrow$ C * RSP S CMM

Above-average long-term results, although recently it's been only average, due in part to high management fees. Invests mainly in federal T-bills, with some banker's acceptances tossed in. Was no-load but now subject to a redemption fee if you cash in within six years. Sold by London Life reps.

LOTUS INCOME FUND $$$ $\Rightarrow$ C NO RSP CMM

It's hard to know where to put this fund. Its mandate suggests it's a short-term bond fund — the portfolio may have an average term-to-maturity of not more than five years, and may hold securities with maturities up to seven years out. In practice, however, the managers (M.K. Wong Management) have been running it as a money market fund, investing primarily in Canada T-bills. Before you invest any money, you may wish to obtain clarification from them as to their future plans. Good results; five-year average annual rate of return is slightly above average at 6.9 percent. Residents of Ontario and the western provinces may purchase directly from the manager; phone 1-800-665-9360. Not available in other parts of Canada. Minimum initial investment has been increased to $10,000. Name changed from MKW Income Fund in April '94.

MACKENZIE SENTINEL CANADA MONEY MARKET FUND

Closed down in early '95.

MANULIFE VISTAFUND SHORT TERM SECURITIES FUND $ ⇓ C #/* RSP S CMM

Average results, but this isn't a money market fund you really want to own. Reason: a complex fee structure that requires you to either pay a high (some might say exorbitant) front-end load of 4 percent (Option one) or choose a back-end load plan (Option two) with a much higher management fee (a base 2.375 percent on a money market fund!). Published performance results suggest the front-end load is better, but they don't discount the 4 percent, which is almost a year's worth of returns at current interest rates. With the front-end load taken into account, the return over five years is more or less the same between the two purchase options. The longer you hold the fund, the less the advantage of the back-end option because of the higher management fee. But frankly, this is not a good way to buy a money market fund. Sold by Manulife reps.

MARITIME LIFE MONEY MARKET
FUND $ ⇒ C NO RSP S CMM

Solid portfolio, consisting of T-bills and banker's acceptances. But this isn't a fund you want to stay in for any length of time. Returns are consistently well below average, in large part because of the onerous management fee of 1.75 percent — far too high for a money fund. Sold by Maritime Life reps.

MAWER CANADIAN MONEY
MARKET FUND $$ ⇒ C NO RSP CMM

Part of growing Alberta-based fund group. Average results so far. Holds a combination of T-bills and corporate notes with a small amount of short-term mortgage-backed securities. Returns are helped by relatively low management fee of 0.7 percent.

MCLEAN BUDDEN MONEY
MARKET FUND $$ ⇒ C NO RSP CMM

Small fund with average returns that invests mainly in Canadian T-bills. See entry for McLean Budden Equity Growth Fund in Canadian Equity section for purchase details.

METLIFE MVP MONEY MARKET
FUND $ ⇒ FI * RSP S CMM

Very weak results, in part due to high management fee (1.5 percent). There are many better families of segregated funds out there. Maximum redemption fee of 2.5 percent, declining to zero after four years. Sold by MetLife reps.

MONTREAL TRUST EXCELSIOR - MONEY MARKET
SECTION

See Scotia Excelsior Money Market Fund.

MUTUAL MONEY MARKET FUND $$ ⇒ C NO RSP CMM

Routine performer although recent returns have been better. Portfolio is a blend of government and corporate notes. Available through Mutual Investco.

NAL CANADIAN MONEY MARKET
FUND $$ ⇓ C * RSP S CMM

An average-performing money market fund from North American Life. May invest in any type of short-term note but was exclusively in federal government T-bills at the start of '95. Be careful how you use this one; there's a redemption fee (maximum 4.5 percent) if you cash in within five years. You may switch to other NAL funds without charge, however (up to four free transfers a year).

NN MONEY MARKET FUND $$$ ⇒ C * RSP S CMM

Solid entry from NN Life Insurance. Portfolio is weighted towards corporate notes but also contains banker's acceptances and T-bills. Better returns than the T-bill Fund (below). Note there is a hefty back-end load on this fund (maximum 6 percent), so don't put money in it for the short term.

NN T-BILL FUND $$ ⇓ C * RSP S CMM

Invests only in Government of Canada T-bills, giving it a high degree of safety. Returns are slightly below average, however, and are much below the companion Money Market Fund (above), which has a lower management fee. Sold by representatives of NN Life Insurance.

NATCAN TREASURY BILL FUND $$ ⇒ C NO RSP CMM

The NatCan funds are the blue-ribbon line offered by National Bank. Minimum initial investment is $50,000. This one invests only in federal and provincial Treasury bills (particularly Province of Quebec T-bills, which made up almost two-thirds of the portfolio entering '95). Average returns.

NATIONAL LIFE MONEY
MARKET FUND $$$ ⇒ C NO RSP S CMM

Small fund offered by National Life, invests mainly in Government of Canada T-bills. Has managed to generate above-average returns despite high management fee.

NATIONAL TRUST MONEY
MARKET FUND $$ ⇒ C NO RSP CMM

Routine money market entry available through National Trust branches. Invests mainly in Canada T-bills, but there are some corporate notes in the mix as well. Returns are slightly below average.

OPTIMUM SAVINGS
FUND $$ fi C NO RSP CMM

Good results from this small Quebec-based fund. Invests mainly in Government of Canada T-bills. No load if bought directly from manager; see entry for Optimum Stock Fund in Canadian Equity section for purchase details. Formerly known as St. Laurent Optimum Savings Fund.

PHILLIPS, HAGER & NORTH
MONEY MARKET FUND $$$$ ⇒ C NO RSP CMM

Solid performer from Vancouver-based PH&N. Invests mainly in high-grade corporate notes, which enhances return with slightly more risk. Major advantage: one of the lowest management fees in the business (0.51 percent). Consistently good returns, timeliness, and no-load status earn it top $$$$ rating. Minimum initial investment of $25,000 required, except for RRSP purchases.

PRUDENTIAL MONEY MARKET
FUND OF CANADA $$$ ⇒ C NO RSP CMM

Solid performer, consistently among the leaders in this field. Composition of the portfolio is a mixture of short-term corporate notes and Canadian T-bills. The only no-load fund in the Prudential family.

PURSUIT MONEY MARKET
FUND $$$ ⇓ C NO RSP CMM

Good results plus safety from a portfolio exclusively made up of federal government T-bills (although the managers may invest in corporate notes, they haven't done so to date). The only totally no-load entry from Pursuit. However, if you buy through a dealer, you may be assessed an annual "service fee" of up to 0.5 percent. Try to avoid that.

ROYAL TRUST CANADIAN MONEY MARKET FUND $$ ⇒ C NO RSP CMM

Steady performer, although returns have slipped to slightly below average. Most of the portfolio is in T-bills with some short-term corporate notes mixed in to boost returns. Benefits from being part of the largest no-load group in the country in terms of total funds available, thus providing unit-holders with a wide range of switching options. Big bonus is chequing privileges — one of the few money market funds to offer this service.

ROYAL TRUST CANADIAN TREASURY BILL FUND $ ⇓ C NO RSP CMM

Brother to the RT Canadian Money Market Fund; invests only in Government of Canada T-bills. That provides a small additional measure of safety, but that's more than offset by the lower returns and the higher management expense ratio of this fund, which results from the fact that it's very small (about $13 million in assets). Things aren't going to get any better over the next year, until it's merged into the huge RoyFund Canadian T-Bill Fund. If you're investing in a Royal Trust fund in the meantime, the Money Market Fund is the better choice.

ROYFUND CANADIAN T-BILL FUND $$ ⇓ C NO RSP CMM

Behemoth fund ($1.6 billion in assets) from Royal Bank that invests only in Government of Canada Treasury bills. Routine performance record.

ROYFUND MONEY MARKET FUND $ ⇒ C NO RSP CMM

Companion to T-Bill Fund (above). A portion of the portfolio is in commercial paper, but most of the assets are in government or government-guaranteed securities. Should provide better returns than the T-Bill Fund but hasn't to date because of higher management expense ratio (1.22 percent vs. 0.86 percent). So take the T-Bill Fund instead. Sold by branches of the Royal Bank.

SAVINGS AND INVESTMENT TRUST MONEY MARKET FUND $$ ⇒ C NO RSP CMM

Average-performing money market fund from this Quebec-based trust company. Sold through branches of Savings and Investment Trust (Trust Prêt et Revenu) in Quebec and Ontario.

SCEPTRE MONEY MARKET FUND $$$$ ⇓ C NO RSP CMM

Very good, consistent performer. Safety-oriented portfolio; invests primarily in government or government-guaranteed notes. Returns are consistently above average. Manager is Bill Malouin, who also directs the Sceptre Bond Fund. No-load; phone 1-800-265-1888 for purchase details.

SCOTIA EXCELSIOR T-BILL FUND $$ ⇓ C NO RSP CMM

Invests exclusively in federal T-bills, giving it a slight safety edge over the companion Money Market Fund (below). Returns have also been slightly better.

SCOTIA EXCELSIOR MONEY MARKET FUND $$ ⇒ C NO RSP CMM

Formed from the merger of the Montreal Trust Excelsior Money Market Section and the Scotia Money Market Fund in October '95. Both funds had been routine performers, so the combined entry gets a routine rating. Portfolio holds a combination of T-bills and corporate notes. Returns of the old Scotia fund, the larger of the two that merged, had been marginally below those of the companion Government of Canada Treasury Bill Fund.

SPECTRUM CASH RESERVE FUND $$ ⇓ C #/* RSP CMM

A dependable performer. Average return, but above-average safety; portfolio is mainly in Treasury bills. Asset quality of the fund has received a top AAA*i* rating from the Canadian Bond Rating Service. Optional front- or back-end load, but don't agree to any load charge at all — the returns aren't high enough to justify paying a sales commission. If you can't get the charges waived, look elsewhere. You can transfer into any other Spectrum fund without cost.

SPECTRUM SAVINGS FUND $$$ ⇓ C NO CMM

Another good entry from Spectrum, this one no-load. High-quality portfolio, mainly invested in Government of Canada T-bills. If all you're looking for is a pure money market fund and you have no desire to switch between the other Spectrum funds, this is the preferred choice. Results tend to be slightly better than for the Cash Reserve Fund. Not eligible for RRSPs.

STRATA MONEY MARKET FUND $ ⇒ C NO RSP CMM

The Strata funds have been sold to Mutual Life and are scheduled to be merged into the Mutual fund family by the end of '95.

TALVEST MONEY FUND $$$ ⇒ C # RSP CMM

Quality portfolio made up mainly of government securities. Results have been above average. Maximum front-end load of 2 percent; try to get it without charge.

TEMPLETON TREASURY BILL
FUND $$$ ⇓ C NO RSP CMM

A solid performer. The name could be misleading, however; the fund managers are allowed to invest up to 30 percent of the assets in short-term corporate notes and banker's acceptances. So far, however, the portfolio has been entirely in federal government T-bills. Templeton's only no-load entry.

TRANS-CANADA MONEY
MARKET FUND $$$ ⇓ C #/* RSP CMM

A steady performer from Sagit Management, with a high degree of safety — all the assets are normally held in Government of Canada Treasury bills. Don't bother if you can't get the sales commission waived, however; there are no-load entries that are just as good.

TRIMARK INTEREST FUND $$$ ⇒ C # RSP CMM

This fund invests entirely in commercial paper (no government T-bills). This boosts return, but adds a slightly higher degree of risk. The extra profit isn't substantial, however. Average annual return over the past five years is 6.8 percent. The average fund in this category returned a shade less, at 6.7 percent. You may be charged a front-end load of up to 2 percent or, alternatively, a semi-annual commission of 0.25 percent (half a percent annually). Try to obtain the fund without any of these charges; otherwise you may want to check out other options. There are plenty to choose from.

20/20 MONEY MARKET FUND $$ ⇒ C #/* RSP CMM

A decent entry from 20/20, with slightly above-average returns. Most of the assets are in T-bills, with some corporate notes and short-term bonds. However, the load charges are way too high; you could be hit with a front-end load of up to 9 percent or a back-end load of up to 6 percent. Those are absurd numbers for a money market fund; to put them in perspective, this fund gained 5.2 percent in the year ending June 30, '95. 20/20 didn't listen last year when I suggested they should rethink this one and make it no-load, the way many other groups do with their money market entries. If not that, then reduce the maximum charge to, say, 2 percent. So I'll offer this advice again, gratis. And my advice to you, dear reader, is not to buy this fund unless you can pick it up on a no-load basis, or 20/20 changes its terms.

UNITED CANADIAN INTEREST FUND $$$ ⇒ C #/* RSP CMM

Good performer. Portfolio is a mix of government issues, short-term mortgage-backed securities and high-grade corporate notes. Maximum 2 percent front-end load; avoid the back-end option. Better still, try to acquire this one without any commission. Formerly called United Canadian Money Market Fund.

International Money Market Funds

As Canadians become more interested in international investing, a wider range of products is being offered. A few years ago, it was almost impossible to find an international money market fund in this country. Now there are more than a dozen of them, and the number is growing.

Most of these funds specialize in U.S. dollar denominated short-term notes. However, a few more diversified funds have started to appear and I expect more in the future. ■

As is the case with international bond funds, many of these new money market funds haven't been around long enough to qualify for inclusion in this *Guide*. But this section will grow larger every year, as more funds reach their third birthday.

RATINGS CHANGES

Two $$$ funds from last year's edition have been downgraded this year — the AGF U.S. Dollar Money Market Account and the Altamira Short Term Income Fund, both of which drop to $$.

New this year is the InvesNat U.S. Money Market Fund, which debuts with a $$ rating.

1996 RATINGS

AGF U.S. DOLLAR MONEY
MARKET ACCOUNT $$ ⇓ C # £ IMM

U.S. money market funds are a good hedge at times when the Canadian dollar is falling. When it's rising, they work against you in two ways: currency exchange and the lower rates paid on U.S. securities. So keep a close eye on Canadian dollar movements if you have money here. This fund invests mainly in U.S.-pay Canada T-bills. Return for the year to June 30, '95, was 4.5 percent. That does not reflect changes in the currency rate, which is not factored into U.S. money market fund returns for reasons that escape me. Note that this is the only AGF fund that is not affected by the company's new three-tier purchase system. You can only buy it on the front-end load basis (maximum 2 percent). But don't pay any commission; the low return isn't worth it. If the sales rep won't provide it without charge, look for a no-load alternative.

ALTAMIRA SHORT TERM GLOBAL
INCOME FUND $$ ⇑ C NO RSP IMM

One of the new breed of international money funds, this one invests in a basket of short-term notes, denominated in foreign currencies. This makes it fully RRSP-eligible. Unlike Canadian and U.S. dollar money market funds, the unit value is not fixed and will fluctuate with exchange rate and interest rate movements. That's why it receives a higher risk rating. Over the past three years, this is the top-performing international money market fund in Canada, with an average annual gain of 7.3 percent. Lately, however, a strengthening Canadian dollar has been cutting into returns; the fund was ahead just 1.7 percent for the year to June 30, '95. If the dollar looks like it's going to continue to gain strength, this won't be a good place for your money. But if the dollar is falling, switch some money here.

ATLAS AMERICAN MONEY MARKET FUND $$ ⇒ C NO £ IMM

Name changed from Finsco U.S. Dollar Money Market Fund in July '94, and management responsibilities were given to the well-known firm of Salomon Brothers. An average performer, good choice if you want to diversify out of the Canadian dollar. Now available on a no-load basis. Sold through Midland Walwyn.

CIBC U.S. DOLLAR MONEY MARKET FUND $$ ⇒ C NO RSP IMM

The distinguishing feature about this U.S. dollar fund is that it's fully RRSP-eligible. The fund invests mainly in short-term Canadian securities, such as Canadian Wheat Board Discount Notes, that are denominated in U.S. currency. This makes it especially useful if you want to increase U.S. dollar assets in a registered plan. Performance is about average.

GLOBAL STRATEGY DIVERSIFIED SHORT-TERM INCOME FUND $$$ ⇒ C #/* RSP IMM

Here's a way to hold a range of international currencies in your RRSP without running afoul of foreign content rules. This fund invests in Canadian short-term securities denominated in various currencies. This provides some currency protection in the event our dollar weakens. Recent returns have been better than those from most other money market funds; annual gain for the five years to June 30, '95, was 6.9 percent. Fund was primarily holding U.S. dollar issues in early '95. The expense ratio on this one tends to be quite high, which depresses returns. Beware of the back-end purchase option — you'll pay a redemption fee of up to 4.5 percent if units are cashed within six years. Formerly known as the Global Strategy World Money Fund.

GLOBAL STRATEGY U.S. SAVINGS FUND $$ ⇒ C #/* RSP IMM

Invests in U.S. dollar denominated short-term securities issued by Canadian governments, banks, or corporations, thus providing full RRSP eligibility. Expect a lower return than on Canadian money market funds because of interest rate differentials. Formerly known as the Global Strategy U.S. Money Fund.

GREEN LINE U.S. MONEY
MARKET FUND $$ ⇒ C NO RSP IMM

Invests in short-term securities denominated in U.S. dollars but issued by Canadian governments and corporations. This makes it fully RRSP/RRIF-eligible, which is useful if you want to reduce Canadian currency risk in a retirement plan. You won't get rich here, though — average annual rate of return for the five years to June 30, '95, was just 3.9 percent. Sold by Green Line Investor Services and through selected branches of the TD Bank.

GUARDIAN U.S. MONEY
MARKET FUND $$ ⇒ C #/* RSP IMM

Invests in short-term securities issued by Canadian corporations that are denominated in U.S. dollars. This allows full RRSP/RRIF eligibility, an advantage for investors who want to hold more U.S. dollars in their retirement plans without running afoul of foreign content rules. Useful option at times when Canadian dollar is weak. Watch out for back-end load option (see entry for Guardian Short Term Money Fund in Canadian Money Market Funds section).

INVESNAT U.S. MONEY
MARKET FUND $$ ⇓ C NO RSP IMM

Fully RRSP-eligible fund that invests in Canadian securities (mainly Government of Canada T-bills) denominated in U.S. dollars. Good quality portfolio, but below-average returns. Available through National Bank.

PHILLIPS, HAGER & NORTH
$U.S. MONEY MARKET FUND $$$ ⇒ C NO RSP IMM

Solid U.S. money fund with full RRSP eligibility. Invests in short-term notes issued by Canadian governments and corporations but denominated in U.S. currency. Offers one of the lowest management fees in this category. A good choice, especially for those who want to hold U.S. dollars in their RRSPs or RRIFs.

ROYAL TRUST $U.S. MONEY
MARKET FUND $$ ⇒ C NO £ IMM

Average-performing U.S. dollar fund from this big no-load family. Foreign content in an RRSP.

ROYFUND U.S. DOLLAR MONEY
MARKET FUND $$ ⇒ C NO RSP IMM

Invests in Canadian short-term notes (both government and corporate) denominated in U.S. currency. This gives it full RRSP eligibility. Average results. Sold through Royal Bank branches.

UNITED U.S. DOLLAR MONEY
MARKET FUND $$ ⇒ C #/* IMM

Invests in U.S. dollar denominated short-term securities. Recent results have been among the best in this category, thanks to a low management expense ratio (0.43 percent). Use as a hedge if you're worried about a decline in the value of the Canadian dollar. Not eligible for RRSPs/RRIFs.

FUNDLISTS

Every year people ask me questions like:

"If I can only buy one fund, which do you recommend?"

"What are the best funds for an RRSP?"

"I'm just starting to invest in mutual funds. Which funds should I use as a base?"

"I don't want to take a lot of risk. Which funds are best for me?"

"Which funds should I avoid?" ■

If these are the kinds of questions you've found yourself asking, this new section of the *Guide* should be helpful. I've compiled a series of lists to cover those and a lot of other questions I receive. While I was at it, I also tossed in some lists that I thought were interesting, or just fun.

The numerical ranking within the lists isn't significant. For example, don't interpret the fact that Trimark Fund appears ahead of Templeton Growth on the first list to mean it's the superior fund. All that list is showing you is the top 10 funds in the country. They're *all* good.

I hope you enjoy glancing through these lists and that you find some useful tips. If you have any ideas for other lists I should include in this section in the future, drop me a line in care of my publishers, Prentice Hall Canada.

The Top 10 Mutual Funds in Canada — Period!

1. Trimark Fund. *Profits just roll and roll. Bob Krembil must have a magic lamp!*

2. Templeton Growth. *Sir John's hand is off the tiller, but his philosophy still guides the ship.*

3. Phillips, Hager & North Bond. *Conservative style, low fees, solid returns.*

4. Altamira Income. *Best-performing Canadian fixed income fund over the past 10 years. '94 loss was the first in two decades and should be considered an aberration.*

5. Trimark Canadian. *Manages to look good even in off years. Only one losing year ('90) since launch in '81.*

6. Trimark RSP Equity. *A twin to Trimark Canadian except this one is purchased on a back-end load basis.*

7. Investors U.S. Growth. *When a stock fund manager can produce nine winning years out of 10, you have to pay attention. Not only that, this fund has made good profits too!*

8. Industrial Cash Management. *Everything you could want in a money market fund — safety, good returns, and chequing privileges too!*

9. First Canadian Mortgage. *Solid returns, a long track record, and low risk make this one a core holding for any RRSP or RRIF.*

10. Royal Trust American Stock. *Excellent performance and no load charges. The best of the financial institution U.S. stock funds.*

10 Funds I Don't Own — and Don't Want to

1. 20/20 India Fund. *Lost almost 40 percent in the first nine months — and, if you want to get out, they hit you with another 10 percent as a penalty! Plus, management expenses are a high 3.4 percent. Spare me!*

2. Dominion Equity Resource Fund. *If you'd invested money way back in 1985, you'd actually have less today than you started with. Not my idea of a good result!*

3. Dynamic Global Green. *The mandate is noble — make money by investing in socially responsible companies worldwide. The results are awful. Dynamic just can't seem to make this one fly.*

4. GBC International Growth. *It costs $100,000 to get in. For that you would have received a piddling 0.2 percent annual profit for the past five years. You can do much better for much less.*

5. Global Strategy Diversified Americas Fund. *Couldn't even make a buck in the first six months of '95, when U.S. stocks were going bananas.*

6. Global Strategy Real Estate Securities Fund. *Dropped an average of 3.5 percent a year over the past five years. Real estate will come back someday, but you can go broke waiting.*

7. Cambridge Special Equity. *Turned in a great performance in '93 but has been on the losing side every other year in this decade.*

8. Great-West Life Real Estate. *Things have gotten so bad they don't even publish the returns anymore. If they did, they'd reveal an average annual loss of 5.7 percent a year for the past five years — the worst performance over that time of any fund rated in this* Guide.

9. Cassels Blaikie International. *You would be showing a profit if you'd invested five years ago. Let's see — it works out to 0.1 percent a year to June 30, '95. I think even my savings account manages more.*

10. Exar Real Estate. *This Quebec-based real estate fund suffered a drop in unit value of 69.4 percent in '94. That has to be a record. Be thankful that you weren't one of the investors — or the manager. Condolences if you were.*

10 Bank Equity Funds You'd Like to Own

1. Green Line Science and Technology. *Proved that bank funds don't have to be stodgy underperformers by turning in a dynamite year.*

2. RoyFund U.S. Equity. *Solid, long-term performance record; run by a top-notch manager with a clearly defined investing strategy. Its kissing cousin, the*

Royal Trust American Stock Fund, would also be on this list except that it's not available through Royal Bank and so is technically not a bank fund.

3. Royal European Growth. *Simply the best no-load Europe fund around.*

4. Green Line North American Growth. *Promising debut, with big first-year gain.*

5. Royal Zweig Strategic Growth. *Small cap, low risk — a unique combination under the direction of Wall Street guru Martin Zweig.*

6. First Canadian NAFTA Advantage Fund. *Survived peso devaluation well; will look better as time progresses.*

7. Scotia Excelsior American Equity. *Solid, unassuming U.S. stock fund that produces decent returns year after year.*

8. Scotia Excelsior International. *A solid performer in the Montreal Trust family for years, it now adds strength to the Scotia camp.*

9. Scotia Excelsior Canadian Growth. *Another former Montreal Trust winner that now graces the much-improved Scotia family.*

10. Royal Asian Growth. *After a rocky start, it was coming on like gangbusters in mid-'95.*

Five Bank Equity Funds to Be Glad You Don't Own

1. CIBC Canadian Equity. *A mediocre performer for so long that it can't be an accident.*

2. First Canadian International Growth. *Off to a poor start with a 5.6 percent loss in the year ending June 30.*

3. Green Line Latin American Growth. *A 13.3 percent loss in the first six months of '95. Ouch!*

4. Scotia Precious Metals. *Somehow managed only a 3.3 percent gain for the year ending June 30, 1995. Royal Precious Metals Fund was up 34.1 percent during that same period!*

5. First Canadian Japanese Growth. *Launched just as the Japanese market went into the tank. Down 12.7 percent for the first half of '95.*

A Half-Dozen Bank Fixed Income Funds That Will Let You Sleep at Night

1. Green Line Canadian Bond. *Always above average in performance, solid and dependable.*

2. Royal Trust Bond. *Not quite up to Green Line's standards, but doesn't miss by much.*

3. RoyFund Bond. *Ditto.*

4. First Canadian Mortgage. *Best of the bank mortgage funds; almost always generates decent returns.*

5. CIBC Mortgage. *Two decades without a loss. Throw away the sleeping pills!*

6. Scotia Excelsior Mortgage. *Essentially, the old Montreal Trust Mortgage Fund with a new name. In its old guise, it hadn't had a losing year in at least two decades.*

Five Bank Funds That Show Promise

1. First Canadian International Bond. *Made number one on the international bond fund hit parade with a 16.6 percent gain in the year to June 30, '95.*

2. First Canadian Asset Allocation. *Long-term results have been below average, but it's been showing much better recently and the portfolio is solid.*

3. Royal Zweig Global Managed Assets. *Sure it's brand new, but Martin Zweig has already shown what he can do with his Strategic Growth Fund so why not give this one a try?*

4. Royal Precious Metals. *It did nothing for years, but now a totally new management approach has brought it to life in a big way.*

5. RoyFund International Income. *It's too new for a rating, but results so far have been very good. Will be merged with the Royal Trust version in '96.*

Five Funds With a Brilliant Future

1. Global Strategy Small Cap. *Manager John Sartz is a whiz when it comes to picking winning juniors. Fund gained 15.5 percent in its first six months!*

2. 20/20 Aggressive Growth. *Chicago-based Richard Dreihaus is one of America's small cap geniuses. This fund's early performance (17.6 percent average annual return for the two years to June 30, '95) reflects his stock-picking skill.*

3. Universal Canadian Equity. *With Trimark-trained managers Dina DeGeer and Bill Kanko now calling the shots, this previously moribund fund looks to be heading onwards and upwards.*

4. Trimark Indo-Pacific. *Trimark never does anything by halves and this newcomer is no exception. It reeled off a gain of 15.5 percent in the six months to July 31, '95.*

5. Universal U.S. Emerging Growth. *The U.S. is so big there are inevitably all sorts of hidden gems on the stock lists. This fund's job is to root them out. So far, it's found all sorts of buried treasures for investors.*

10 Funds to Own If You're Very Rich

1. ABC Fundamental Value. *Profit pace has slowed recently, but five-year average return of 25.3 percent is the best among Canadian stock funds over that time.*

2. Phillips, Hager & North Bond. *You won't find a better bond fund than this for good returns and sound management, but if you're investing outside a registered plan you'll need $25,000 to get in.*

3. BPI Global Opportunities. *An action fund — lots of trading, shorts, leveraging. Got off to an incredibly fast start. But you'll need as much as $150,000 to get in, depending on where you live. They have an instalment plan, though!*

4. CIBC Premium Canadian T-Bill. *Returns are nicely above average and all you need is $250,000 in spare change to participate. Wins the award for the most exclusive fund in Canada.*

5. Scotia Excelsior Premium T-Bill. *If you can't afford the CIBC version, try this one. It's just about as good and they'll let you in for a mere 100 grand.*

6. GBC Canadian Growth. *One of the better performing small cap funds in the country. All it takes is $100,000 for a ticket.*

7. GBC North American Growth. *On a good run, thanks to strong technology holdings, but you'll need $100,000 for this one too.*

8. Protected Canadian Fund. *Manager Jean-Pierre Fruchet successfully employs market timing techniques to protect your assets against major losses. All it costs to use his services is $25,000 to $150,000, depending on where you live.*

9. Leith Wheeler Balanced Fund. *A mere $50,000 buys a ticket to this small but promising Vancouver-based entry.*

10. AMI Private Capital Money Market. *Good returns, a low management fee, and all you need is $50,000.*

Five Funds to Build Education Savings

1. Templeton Growth. *Dependable capital gains year after year make this an ideal choice for a child's future. They have a monthly savings plan too.*

2. Trimark Fund. *Just about as good as Templeton for this purpose; make your own call.*

3. First Canadian Mortgage. *If you're saving for college in an RESP and you want to keep risk to an absolute minimum, you won't go far wrong with this $$$$ winner.*

4. Altamira Income. *Another good candidate for an RESP, with the likelihood of somewhat better returns than a mortgage fund.*

5. Industrial Cash Management. *Provides the ultimate in safety for those education dollars, but returns will be less than the others. Use in a self-directed RESP.*

A Baker's Dozen of Funds That Made a Dynamite Debut

1. Global Strategy World Emerging Companies. *Invests in small companies with great growth potential. Gained over 28 percent in first six months!*

2. Fidelity Emerging Markets Portfolio. *A big bet on Malaysia paid off as this fund gained 17.1 percent for investors in its first six months.*

3. Green Line Precious Metals. *Scored a big 20 percent gain in the first half of '95, thanks in part to a major position in Diamond Field Resources — which, despite the name, isn't a precious metals play at all! Investors weren't complaining, however.*

4. Green Line Science & Technology. *A 70 percent gain for the year ending June 30, '95 — you don't get off to a better start than that!*

5. Manulife Cabot Canadian Equity. *Altamira spins its management magic for parent company Manulife with a 23.9 percent gain in the first year for this flagship of a new fund line.*

6. Maritime Life S&P 500 Fund. *Talk about great timing! Maritime Life launched this RRSP-eligible fund that trades in S&P 500 futures contracts in January '95. Then the U.S. market took off. Early-bird investors saw profits of almost 19 percent in just six months. All right!*

7. Prudential American Equity. *Launched just at the time the U.S. market was getting set to take off. Result: a 16 percent gain in just three months!*

8. Royal Life Canadian Growth. *Aggressive small cap fund that only got rolling in October '94 and surprised almost everyone (except, presumably, the managers) with a 15.6 percent gain in the first half of '95. Only a handful of funds did better.*

9. Altamira U.S. Larger Company. *Got rolling just in time to catch the Dow wave, which it rode to a 31 percent gain for the year to June 30, '95.*

10. Altamira Precious and Strategic Metal. *Some timely stock picks like Goldcorp and Euro-Nevada*

propelled this new entry to a 19 percent gain in the first half of '95.

11. Cambridge China. *A bunch of China funds have appeared recently. This one got the least attention and turned in the best result, with a 12.4 percent gain for the year to June 30, '95.*

12. G.T. America Growth. *A new small to mid-cap entry that had the good fortune to launch just about the time the U.S. market took off. Result: a gain of almost 28 percent in the first seven months of '95.*

13. Scotia CanAm Growth. *One of the best debuts of the new breed of RRSP-eligible derivative funds. Uses futures to track the S&P 500; gained 25 percent in the year to June 30, '95.*

Five Funds That Got Off on the Wrong Foot

1. Global Strategy Japan. *Got started just as the Japanese market hit the skids again. Lost 14.5 percent in first six months.*

2. Green Line Latin American Growth. *Had the misfortune to launch just before the peso dived. Result: a 13.3 percent loss in the first half of '95.*

3. Altamira Japanese Opportunity. *A small cap Japan fund that debuted just before the Nikkei staged its latest swan dive. Dropped 20 percent in the first half of '95.*

4. National Trust Emerging Markets. *Came out just as the bloom was coming off the emerging markets rose. Result was a 12 percent drop in the first half of '95.*

5. Universal Japan. *Another fund that got going just about the time the Nikkei was falling on its face. Lost 24.3 percent in the year to June 30, '95.*

Five Funds for Tax-Advantaged Income

1. Phillips, Hager & North Dividend Income. *The top-performing dividend fund in Canada over the past decade, with an annual gain of 9.6 percent.*

2. Dynamic Dividend Fund. *Solid performer that maximizes your ability to use the dividend tax credit. Great way to beat the folks at RevCan!*

3. Dynamic Dividend Growth. *Not as pure a dividend fund as its stablemate, but delivers more on the capital gains side. The tax breaks aren't as big there, but they'll do.*

4. Prudential Dividend Fund of Canada. *Not a true dividend fund by any stretch of the imagination, but if you don't mind a healthy dose of tax-advantaged capital gains in your profit mix, this will do the job nicely.*

5. 20/20 Dividend. *A solid performer with a blue-chip portfolio. Perfect for risk-averse investors looking for a nice combination of dividends and capital gains.*

Seven Funds to Substitute for a Trip to Vegas

1. Marathon Equity. *Best five-year record of all Canadian stock funds, but the dips and doodles can shake you to your boots.*

2. Multiple Opportunities. *Unabashed speculator's fund that sniffs out winners on the free-wheeling Vancouver Stock Exchange — and gets it right more often than not.*

3. Prudential Natural Resource. *Resource funds are notoriously volatile, but this one manages to limit the downside risk while churning out great returns.*

4. Royal Precious Metals. *Top-performing precious metals fund in Canada over the past year, thanks to some inspired stock picking.*

5. Friedberg Currency. *The only Canadian fund that invests solely in the often wild international currency markets. Can pay off big — but there will be nosedives along the way.*

---

6. Goldfund. *The managers of this one do a lot of speculating in small mining companies. Sometimes the bets pay off big, as in '93. More often than not, they don't.*

7. Cambridge Special Equity. *Huge gains in good years, big losses in bad years. Roll the dice with a lot of junior companies you never heard of and see what comes up. Whoops — was that snake eyes?*

Five Funds I'd Want in My RRIF

1. First Canadian Mortgage. *This should be a core holding for retired Canadians because of the combination of income and safety it provides.*

2. Altamira Income. *Steady returns, long-term consistency, regular income, no-load charges. What more could you want for your retirement years?*

3. Phillips, Hager & North Bond. *I can't think of any fund I'd be more content to depend on for conservative management and steady income.*

4. Trimark Fund. *Some growth potential in a retirement portfolio is always a good idea.*

5. Industrial Cash Management. *An RRIF needs liquid assets to generate cash flow. This one will handle the job nicely.*

Five Funds for Nervous Investors

1. Trimark Canadian. *Only one down year since inception in 1981. Plus top-notch returns as well!*

2. London Life Mortgage. *Hasn't had a losing year in at least two decades. What more could you ask?*

3. Scotia Excelsior Mortgage. *In its former Montreal Trust version, another fund with a 20-year unblemished win record.*

4. GTS Canadian Protected. *Never a big gainer, but strategy is to keep risk to an absolute minimum. Succeeds admirably.*

5. Dynamic Income. *Not a down year in the past decade. No other bond fund can make that statement!*

Five Exciting New Funds

1. Green Line Science and Technology. *Gained a blazing 70 percent in its first year!*

2. Trimark Indo-Pacific. *Trimark's venture into the tricky, risky Far East got off to a solid start with a gain of better than 10 percent in the first seven months of '95.*

3. Hyperion Aurora. *Value-oriented small cap fund managed by Montreal's Sebastian van Berkom, a first-rate stock-picker. Gained 9.1 percent in first year in a tough market.*

4. Universal European Opportunities. *A Europe fund with a difference — small companies, emerging markets, turnarounds, and privatizations are the spice here. So far, this unusual mix has worked; the fund gained over 14 percent in the first half of '95.*

5. Trimark Advantage Bond. *A high-yield bond fund that hit the market just as bonds were emerging from their '94 slump. Gained 12.5 percent in the first half of '95.*

10 Disappointments

1. Cambridge Pacific. *The only mutual fund in Canada with a 10-year negative return (-2.3 percent per year). It's great to be patient, but...*

2. Cambridge Special Equity. *Want a high-risk fund that loses money? Then this is for you. Average return of -1.1 percent a year for past five years.*

3. Fidelity Capital Builder Fund. *The flagship fund of a major company should be able to do better than this!*

4. Fidelity North American Income. *Supposedly a low-risk way to earn good interest returns. Then the peso went south!*

5. Global Strategy Real Estate. *You lost 3.5 percent a year over the last five years if you had money in this turkey.*

6. University Avenue Growth. *Mandate is to invest in successful U.S. companies. It hasn't been very successful in finding them!*

7. Dynamic Global Green. *A global fund given an environmental spin, it's never managed to get off the ground.*

8. Global Strategy Canadian Growth. *A lot was expected when big-name manager Tony Massie launched his own fund for Global Strategy, but results have been mediocre, at best.*

9. Royal LePage Commercial Real Estate Fund. *Launched just as the Toronto real estate market collapsed. Never did much for investors. Ironically, was just starting to look better when LePage announced it was pulling out its money and the fund folded.*

10. Templeton Canadian Stock. *Their international funds are terrific. But when it comes to Canada, the magic touch still eludes them, although this one is starting to show improvement.*

10 Good Funds for International Investors

1. Canada Life U.S. and International Equity. *It's almost a good enough reason to switch your insurance business to Canada Life.*

2. Cundill Value. *If value-investment guru Benjamin Graham were alive today, this is the kind of fund he'd be running.*

3. C.I. Pacific. *Best-performing Canadian fund over the long term; proven management team. Will be front and centre when Asian stocks rebound.*

4. 20/20 American Tactical Asset Allocation. *A computer-driven balanced fund that has turned in some excellent results. It's even outperformed many pure U.S. equity funds over the past five years.*

5. Fidelity European Growth. *Manager Sally Walden has piloted this to the top of its class with an average annual gain of 14.7 percent in the three years to June 30, '95.*

6. Fidelity Growth America. *No one can figure out the complex formulae manager Brad Lewis uses to select stocks, but they sure work well.*

7. Fidelity International Portfolio. *Fidelity's Canadian funds aren't so hot, but their international funds are just fine, thanks. This is just one more example.*

8. Templeton Growth. *How could you think of starting an international portfolio without it?*

9. Trimark Fund. *Ditto.*

10. Templeton Smaller Companies. *Higher risk than Templeton Growth, but if you don't mind that, the returns have been terrific.*

The 10 Best Canadian Equity Funds

1. Trimark Canadian. *How can you argue with a 10-year annual return of more than 11 percent?*

2. Trimark RSP Equity. *The biggest Canadian stock fund around and without question one of the best. The only real difference between these two funds is how you buy them.*

3. Altamira Equity. *Returns have fallen off from the heady days of the early '90s, but this is still a sound, well-managed fund.*

4. ABC Fundamental Value. *Let hotshot manager Irwin Michael manage your money to profits. All it takes is $150,000 and his personal approval to let you in.*

5. Altamira Capital Growth. *For Altamira investors who prefer a more conservative management style.*

6. Cundill Security. *The wallflower becomes the belle of the ball.*

7. Sceptre Equity. *Nobody's noticed, but this one is burning up the performance charts.*

8. United Canadian Growth. *Kiki Delaney is working wonders with this small cap entry. No wonder Spectrum insisted on a five-year contract extension before they concluded the United deal.*

9. National Life Equities. *The best Canadian fund from a life insurance company.*

10. Scotia Excelsior Canadian Growth. *One of the best no-load choices around; just moved over from the Montreal Trust stable.*

10 Good Alternatives to the Mattress

1. Dynamic Income. *The only long-established bond fund in Canada that didn't have a single losing year over the decade 1985–94.*

2. Protected American Fund. *Primary goal is to prevent serious losses when markets plunge. Only time manager Jean-Pierre Fruchet missed the mark was in '94 when the fund dropped — hold on! — 0.3 percent. Otherwise every year since '86 has been in the black.*

3. Phillips, Hager & North Short Term Bond and Mortgage. *A sound defensive portfolio to protect your assets when bond markets go haywire, as they did in '94.*

4. Guardian Canadian Balanced. *It's been 15 years (1981) since this fund last experienced a losing year. Plus, it's been a solid money-maker. Can your mattress say the same?*

5. Altamira Growth and Income. *Hasn't gone as long as Guardian Balanced without a losing year, but only because it's a newer fund. Unblemished safety record dates all the way back to '87 — yes, it even turned a profit in the Crash year.*

6. First Canadian Mortgage. *Simply the best, most dependable mortgage fund in the country. If this one runs into serious problems, we might as well shut down Canada.*

7. Industrial Cash Management. *One of the best money market funds available with excellent returns, hardly any risk, and chequing privileges to boot!*

8. Phillips, Hager & North Money Market. *Low management fees and solid returns make this one a perennial winner.*

9. Scotia Excelsior Defensive Income. *A no-load short-term bond fund that protects your assets when interest rates are on the rise.*

10. Trimark Canadian. *Not as low risk as the others because it invests in the stock market, but it's only had one losing year in the past decade.*

The 10 Best Pure No-Load Funds

1. Phillips, Hager & North Bond. *When you can get one of the best bond funds in Canada with no-load charges plus an absurdly low management fee, you'd be a fool to pass it up. Yes, I own it.*

2. First Canadian Mortgage. *Bank of Montreal will sell you this top-flight mortgage entry with no charges, front or back.*

3. Royal Trust American Stock. *Consistent, long-term performer that continues to churn out above-average returns.*

4. Phillips, Hager & North Balanced. *Solid portfolio, good managers, fine returns, no-load — what else is there?*

5. Altamira Income. *The top-performing fixed income fund over the past decade, and there's no admission fee.*

6. Altamira Equity. *Returns aren't what they were but still a good place for dedicated no-load investors.*

7. Royal Zweig Strategic Growth. *You won't find many funds around that successfully combine small cap investing with conservative management — and no-load fees too.*

8. Scotia Excelsior International. *A great example of how the merger with Montreal Trust strengthened this formerly lacklustre family.*

9. Green Line Science & Technology. *It will have its ups and downs along the way, but it looks like a winner for more aggressive investors.*

10. Phillips, Hager & North U.S. *I know their name keeps popping up, but they're good. What else can I say?*

Five Funds for Starting a Portfolio

1. Trimark Canadian. *You won't find a better Canadian stock fund around. A core holding for anyone just starting out.*

2. Templeton Growth. *Make this your core international holding and you'll never live to regret it — I hope.*

3. Altamira Income. *You'll need a good fixed income fund in your mix. Here it is.*

4. First Canadian Mortgage. *A sound mortgage fund should be a central holding in a beginning portfolio.*

5. Altamira Growth & Income. *Here's a dependable balanced fund to round out your list.*

Five Funds for People Who Want to Forget About Their Money

1. CIBC Mortgage Investment Fund. *Steady returns, never loses money. Invest it and forget it!*

2. Everest Mortgage Fund. *Hasn't had a down year in the past decade. Not many funds can make that statement.*

3. Green Line Short Term Income. *A perfect choice for anyone who wants to keep risk low but get better returns than are normally produced by money market funds.*

4. Scotia Excelsior Defensive Income. *Scotiabank's equivalent to the Green Line entry. Will protect your money during bad bond markets, but returns will be lower when bonds are on the rise.*

5. Phillips, Hager & North Bond. *No need to worry. The money will be there with decent profits when you need it.*

10 Funds on the Way Up

1. Admax Global Health Sciences. *Got off to a rocky start, but setting a hot pace now.*

2. Cundill Security. *Was so bad for so long that no one noticed when it started to turn around. Take a look at it now, baby!*

3. Elliott & Page Equity Fund. *Making big headway under new lead manager Nereo Pittico.*

4. Bullock Growth. *With Kiki Delaney now at the helm, the future of this fund suddenly looks a whole lot brighter.*

5. Bullock American. *Went into a tailspin after the departure of its hot shot manager a few years back, but now appears to be in a strong recovery mode, gaining 20 percent in the first seven months of '95.*

6. Ivy Canadian. *Got off to a slow start after the two Jerrys (Coleman and Javasky) left United to launch this group for Mackenzie. But this one is now gathering steam; gained a solid 15.7 percent in the year to June 30, '95.*

7. Sceptre Equity. *New manager Allan Jacobs has this one really rolling. Average annual gain of 23.2 percent over the past two years is among the best in the business.*

8. Templeton International Stock. *Amazing what a change in mandate will do. This fund was recently excluded from the hot North American market and responded by turning in the best performance of the three Templeton international stock funds over the past couple of years. Yes, it even did better than Templeton Growth!*

9. Global Strategy Income Plus. *Tony Massie's much-publicized move to GS is finally starting to produce good returns for faithful investors.*

10. United American Equity. *Has really come on strong since management was assumed by Stein Roe & Farnham of Chicago. The mandate allows it to invest internationally, but so far it's stuck to U.S. shores — with good results.*

Five Funds on the Way Down

1. Cambridge Balanced. *The high-risk investment strategies of Sagit Management are starting to take their toll on this one-time good performer.*

2. Imperial Growth Canadian. *Still sports a great 10-year record, but recent returns have been decidedly sub-par.*

3. Altamira Special Growth. *Manager Sue Coleman is having all kinds of problems getting this one back on track.*

4. Industrial Growth. *The glory days seem to be behind for this one unless Alex Christ and team can rediscover the magic touch.*

5. Dynamic Precious Metals. *Long-time leader among precious metals funds, but results are tailing off compared to the up-and-coming competition.*

10 Funds That Should Be Doing Better But Aren't

1. Fidelity Capital Builder. *With all the resources of the giant Fidelity organization behind it, this flagship fund of the Canadian subsidiary should be a big winner. It isn't.*

2. Global Strategy Canada Growth. *Tony Massie has proven his ability as a top-flight manager. So why is this fund lagging so far behind in the averages?*

3. Green Line Blue Chip Equity. *A good manager. A solid investment philosophy. So why does this fund continue to disappoint?*

4. London Life U.S. Equity. *U.S. blue-chip stocks soared in the first half of '95. This fund has a blue-chip portfolio. Did it soar too? No.*

5. C.I. European. *European funds have been money-spinners recently. This one has made profits too — but it's been eating the competition's dust. Perhaps that's why they changed the managers.*

6. Trans-Canada Equity. *The portfolio tends towards the blue-chip, but a few big losers have pulled everything else down.*

7. Fidelity Growth & Income. *Another Fidelity entry that can't seem to cut the mustard. If they don't start doing better with their Canadian funds, it's going to cost them a lot of business.*

8. Talvest Diversified. *All the ingredients seem to be present, but the chefs can't make this one into a gourmet meal.*

9. Dynamic Global Green. *You'd think a fund with a mandate to make money from the world's obsession with the environment would do well. It isn't.*

10. GBC International Growth. *If they're going to charge a $100,000 admission fee, you expect outstanding results for your money. This one turned in a measly 0.2 percent a year for the past five years. No wonder new managers are on the case.*

Five Funds With Exceptionally Low Management Fees

1. Phillips, Hager & North Bond. *They only charge 0.58 percent? For a fund of this quality? If a department store had comparable bargains, they'd sell out!*

2. Phillips, Hager & North Money Market. *This one only gets dinged 0.51 percent a year. That's one of the reasons its returns have been consistently above average.*

3. Phillips, Hager & North U.S. *Most U.S. equity funds ding their investors for management expenses in the 2.5 percent range. This one comes in at just over 1 percent. No wonder returns are consistently so good!*

4. Mawer Canadian Balanced Retirement Savings. *This small Alberta fund manager has figured out a way to keep expenses below 1 percent, while many of its competitors are in the 2 percent range.*

5. Trimark Fund. *Most international stock funds hit their investors for well over 2 percent. This one only collects 1.5 percent, and it's been the best of the bunch over the past decade.*

Five Funds That Better Outperform Because Their Management Fees Are Out of Sight

1. Regent Korea. *The fund pays 3.4 percent in management fees before you see a cent!*

2. Manulife VistaFund Short Term Securities. *A management expense fee of 2.375 percent? On a money market fund? That's so far out of sight it's silly. Don't buy it!*

3. Elliott & Page T-Bill. *With a management expense ratio of 2.36 percent, it's small wonder the returns are way, way below those of the companion Money Fund.*

4. Royal Trust Canadian T-Bill. *Even Royal funds people admit the 1.56 percent management fee is way too high. This one is just marking time until it can be merged with its much more efficient RoyFund counterpart.*

5. Integrated Growth Fund. *Labour-sponsored venture capital funds all have high management expenses, but this one is in the stratosphere. Ask them to explain it; I can't.*

Five Promising Labour-Sponsored Funds

1. Working Ventures Canadian. *It's taken time, but the patience shown by president Ron Begg and his group is now starting to reap returns for investors.*

2. Canadian Medical Discoveries. *If I had to place a bet on which of the new labour-sponsored funds is most likely to score a big gain, this would be the one. Medical technology is going to be hot, hot, hot.*

3. C.I. Covington. *A solid management team headed by Grant Brown makes this one a contender.*

4. VenGrowth Investment. *Made the strongest debut of all the new venture capital funds that launched in early '95. Solid management team.*

5. Capital Alliance Ventures. *This one invests in high-tech companies in Ottawa's Silicon Valley North. It only needs to pick one winner for a blockbuster return.*

A Half-Dozen Funds for Socially Conscious Investors

1. Desjardins Environment. *Sound stock portfolio, above-average returns for past two years.*

2. Investors Summa. *Outperformed all other Investors Canadian funds for the year to June 30, '95.*

3. Clean Environment Equity. *Top-performing social fund in the Canadian equity category over the past three years with an average annual gain of 15.7 percent. So you can be kind to the environment and get rich too!*

4. Clean Environment Balanced. *If a pure stock fund is too risky for you, try this one. It has a chunk of bonds in the portfolio, but the total return is almost as good as the companion Equity Fund.*

5. Ethical North American Equity. *Improving results. Invests mainly in the U.S., with a little bit of Canada and Mexico added for zest.*

6. First Ontario. *The only labour-sponsored venture capital fund to employ ethical and environmental screening criteria. So you can enjoy your tax breaks with a clear conscience!*

10 Funds for the 21st Century

1. Green Line Science and Technology. *The 21st century will be technology driven.*

2. Talvest New Economy. *Nuala Beck's theories are in tune with the changing times and this fund is starting to show nice profits.*

3. Admax Global Health Sciences. *If there's one thing an aging population will spend money on, it's health care.*

4. United Global Telecommunications. *Half the people in the world have never made a phone call! Growth potential a-plenty here.*

5. GT Global Telecommunications. *Ditto.*

6. GT Global Infrastructure. *Everyone needs new roads, airports, ports, bridges — even the U.S.*

7. First Canadian NAFTA Advantage. *The big NAFTA free-trade payoff will come in the next century. This fund is positioned to take advantage of it.*

8. AGF China Focus. *If the 21st century is to belong to China, you may as well profit from it.*

9. Industrial Future. *Focuses on high-tech, but not exclusively so there's some balance. Excellent recent returns; gained over 20 percent last year.*

10. Fidelity Far East. *If Asia shows anything like the kind of growth everyone expects in the 21st century, this fund will be an excellent way to be part of the profits.*

10 Funds for Your RRSP

1. London Life Mortgage. *Good returns; nary a losing year since at least '75. That's the stuff good retirement plans are built on.*

2. Phillips, Hager & North Bond. *Sound management, conservative style, excellent returns, low management fees. Your RRSP will thank you, year after year.*

3. BPI Global Balanced RSP. *A good way to add extra international stocks and bonds to your registered plan without running afoul of the foreign content rules.*

4. First Canadian Mortgage. *Best-performing mortgage fund over the past decade, and a high degree of safety too.*

5. Altamira Income. *The top-performing fixed income fund in Canada over the past 10 years, and it's no-load too.*

6. Dynamic Income. *A conservative management style and excellent numbers make this a solid candidate for your retirement savings.*

7. National Life Fixed Income. *If you're saving for retirement through an insurance company plan, this is the place to be.*

8. Templeton Growth. *For your core foreign content holding.*

9. Trimark Fund. *Pair it up with Templeton Growth for an awesome one-two international punch.*

10. Trimark RSP Equity. *If you have only one Canadian stock fund in your retirement savings plan, this should be it.*

10 Funds You Don't Want in Your RRSP

1. Global Strategy Diversified Japan Plus. *A Japan fund that's fully RRSP-eligible — but Japan is a high-risk place to be right now and the fund lost 19 percent in the year to June 30, '95. Too risky for your retirement nest egg.*

2. Goldtrust. *CSA Management specifically offers this fund for retirement plans. Unless you like to gamble with your retirement dollars, don't take them up on it.*

3. Cambridge Growth. *There's too much of the casino mentality in this fund's portfolio to make me comfortable putting retirement dollars into it.*

4. Top Fifty T-Bill/Bond. *Supposedly a defensive fund that switches assets into T-bills when the bond market looks rough. Unfortunately, the tactic doesn't work — the unit value dropped 9.3 percent in '94, one of the worst results among fixed income funds.*

5. Global Strategy Diversified Americas. *Won't count against your foreign content, but average annual returns over the past five years have been only 2 percent. You won't build much of a retirement nest egg that way.*

6. University Avenue U.S. Growth. *Not only does it eat up foreign content room, but returns over the five years to June 30, '95, were actually negative — the only U.S. equity fund in that unfortunate position.*

7. Multiple Opportunities. *Speculating in junior VSE companies is not my idea of building a retirement nest egg, even though the results have been sensational on occasion.*

8. Great-West Life Real Estate. *It's been going through such a rough period they're uncomfortable publishing the results. But even when things pick up, you won't want it in an RRSP because you'll lose the tax breaks. The same goes for all other real estate funds.*

9. Phillips, Hager & North Dividend. *Sure, it's got a great record. But you don't want it in your RRSP because you'll lose the benefit of all that tax-advantaged dividend income.*

10. Altamira Global Diversified. *You'd have gained only 3.4 percent a year over the past decade. The average money market fund did better.*

Five Funds That Probably Have Nowhere to Go But Up

1. Regent Dragon 888. *A China fund that lost 12.8 percent in its first year. China's growth potential should turn it around.*

2. University Avenue U.S. Growth. *Any fund that can manage to show an average annual loss in the U.S. market over the past five years has to do better in the next five. Doesn't it?*

3. AGF Canadian Resource. *This is a lot better fund than the past two years suggest. Look for a rebound soon.*

4. Royal Japanese Stock. *A 25 percent loss in the year to June 30, '95, is pretty awful, but this one should start recovering soon.*

5. Industrial Equity. *This small cap fund simply can't be as bad as the most recent numbers suggest. At least, I don't think it can.*

Five Funds That Are Doing So Well It's Scary

1. BPI Global Opportunities Fund. *A trader's fund that uses leveraging and takes short positions. Gained 12.8 percent in its first month!*

2. Universal U.S. Emerging Growth. *28.4 percent a year, over the past three years! Wow, I wish I'd been there. The only question is, how long can manager James Broadfoot keep up the pace?*

3. Green Line Science & Technology. *It's not going to continue to gain 70 percent a year. You can bet on it.*

4. Multiple Opportunities. *A 54 percent gain in the first half of '95 is sensational, but how long can this keep going on?*

5. Royal Precious Metals. *Outperformed the competition by such a wide margin over the past year that it was unreal. No one can keep up that pace — but it would be nice if they could.*

A Half-Dozen Good Segregated Funds

1. Canada Life U.S. and International Equity. *Great returns — 13.5 percent a year over the past decade. That's almost as good as Templeton!*

2. Empire International Growth. *A solid performer, best bet in the Empire family.*

3. Great-West Life Equity/Bond. *Consistent results and a well-structured portfolio make this the best bet in the GWL stable.*

4. London Life Mortgage. *Solid returns, plus no losing years in at least two decades. Mortgage funds don't come much better.*

5. National Life Fixed Income. *Excellent long-term record, consistent performance, plus guarantees to protect you on the downside. As a plus, all the other funds in this group are good too.*

6. NN Can-Am. *A derivative fund that invests in S&P 500 futures. So far, it's been a great success, with an annual return of 11.5 percent over the past two years. Use it to add foreign content to an RRSP without coming under the 20 percent restriction.*

Five Not-So-Good Segregated Funds

1. MetLife MVP Equity. *A chronically weak performer, average five-year return of just 3.7 percent. The only reason more MetLife funds didn't make this particular list was that I decided it would be overkill. This group needs a huge shot in the arm.*

2. NN Canadian Growth. *If you'd had money in this one over the past decade, it would have only grown at a rate of 4.5 percent a year. Not good enough, by a long shot.*

3. Great-West Life Real Estate. *This hasn't been a good place to be for the past five years or so.*

4. Manulife Equity. *Not only are returns sub-par, but you also face a Hobson's Choice of purchase options.*

5. Empire Elite Equity. *Not a disaster by any means, but just not very good. There are several other funds in the company's own stable that beat it in performance terms.*

10 Good Funds You've Probably Never Heard Of

1. AIC Advantage Fund. *Great returns from an unusual mix of mutual fund shares and technology stocks.*

2. BPI American Small Companies. *Eye-popping results — gained over 21 percent a year for the past five years!*

3. Beutel Goodman American Equity. *Hardly anyone has yet discovered this gem, which has been beating the averages by a wide margin.*

4. Bissett Canadian Equity. *If you live in Alberta and don't have some money in this one, you're missing a good bet. It's no-load too.*

5. Cundill Security. *A former ugly duckling that's turned into a beautiful swan. How's 20.5 percent a year for the past three years?*

6. Canadian Protected Fund. *Manager uses market timing techniques to keep investors out of trouble in tough markets. It works — and you get decent returns too.*

7. National Life Equities. *Very good returns and consistent too — only one losing year in the past decade. If you want to stash some insurance money somewhere, try this one.*

8. Sceptre Equity. *Only one of the best-performing Canadian equity funds over the past couple of years. Plus it's no-load if you live in Ontario.*

9. Saxon World Growth. *The top-performing international equity fund in Canada over the past three years, and hardly anyone knows it exists! And it's no-load too. Ontario residents, listen up! Unfortunately, other Canadians can only watch with envy.*

10. Hyperion Value Line Equity. *Bases investment decisions on the calls of highly respected Value Line Inc. of New York. That's really putting stock-picking theory to the test — and so far Value Line is passing with flying colours.*

Five Funds That May Provide an Unpleasant Surprise

1. Capstone Cash Management. *No management fee is assessed against the assets. Instead, you're hit with a direct charge of up to 1 percent a year. Result: performance figures appear better than they really are.*

2. Elliott & Page Money. *Sales person can negotiate a higher annual management fee than is calculated when reporting fund returns. Result: you don't get as much as the papers say you do.*

3. BPI Canadian Equity value. *Choose the back-end load option and you may discover down the road that you could have gotten a much better deal. Your sales person just "forgot" to mention the redemption fee schedule was negotiable. A similar surprise lurks in other BPI funds as well as those offered by Admax Regent, Elliot & Page, Global Strategy and Sagit.*

4. Prudential Dividend. *A good fund with good returns. But if maximizing the dividend tax credit is your goal, you may start wondering what all those foreign stocks and low-yielding common shares are doing in the portfolio.*

5. General Trust Canadian Equity. *Yes, this is a no-load group. But if you cash out within the first three months, they'll hit you with a 2 percent penalty.*

Five Funds Whose Managers Bucked the Trend

1. AGF Asian Growth "A". *While most other Far East funds were on the skids, this one managed a 12 percent gain for the year.*

2. Dynamic Precious Metals. *Most gold funds gained ground in the year to June 30, '95, this one slid slightly backwards.*

3. Fidelity Far East. *Many Asian funds took a beating last year. K.C. Lee managed to pilot this one to a 9 percent gain, to the delight of investors.*

4. Cambridge China. *China was not a happy place for mutual fund companies last year. But Sagit*

loved it — their new fund racked up a 12.4 percent gain, best by far for China-watchers.

5. Global Strategy U.S. Growth. *It was almost impossible for a U.S. stock fund to lose money in the 12 months to June 30, '95. But this was one of only two that managed to turn the trick. Unhappily for Global Strategy, the other one was also one of theirs.*

Seven Funds You're Lucky If You Own

1. AIC Value Fund. *Manager Jonathan Wellum hit on a great idea — just do what billionaire Warren Buffet does. Guess what? It works! Investors in this fund are delighted.*

2. Fidelity Small Cap America. *Nobody paid much attention when this one was launched, and not a lot of money flowed in by Fidelity standards. Too bad — it only gained 25.6 percent in the year to June 30, '95.*

3. Leith Wheeler U.S. Equity. *Hardly anyone has money in this one. Maybe more will come when people discover it gained 22 percent last year.*

4. Altamira Bond. *Most people are in the companion Altamira Income Fund, which is five times bigger. But this one turned in the top performance of any Canadian bond fund in the year to June 30, '95, with a gain of almost 25 percent.*

5. 20/20 American Tactical Asset Allocation. *Computer programs can figure out the markets! This fund proves it, using a program developed by Wells Fargo. Excellent returns; this isn't a flash in the pan.*

6. Dynamic Partners. *Turned in the second-best results of all the balanced funds in Canada for the five years to June 30, '95. The managers have got asset allocation down to a fine art.*

7. Saxon World Growth. *It's returned almost 18 percent a year for the past five years. So why is there less than $16 million in it?*

Five Funds With Interesting Managers

1. Cundill Value. *Globe-trotting manager Peter Cundill keeps buying dollars for 40¢ and his investors prosper. Now he's trying to get Mississippi to pay up on some old 1830 bonds!*

2. United Canadian Equity. *More women are showing up among the money managerial elite. Kiki Delaney is the best of the bunch.*

3. Margin of Safety. *The performance isn't very good, but manager John Hillery writes great newsletters.*

4. Canadian Protected Fund. *Jean-Pierre Fruchet ("J.P." to his friends) employs his unique market timing strategies to protect investors' capital and give good returns too.*

5. Templeton Emerging Markets. *Sit and listen to Dr. Mark Mobius spin some of his world-traveller adventure yarns for a while. Fascinating!*

The One Fund to Buy If You're Buying Only One

Templeton Growth. *The Ol' Man River of the Canadian mutual funds industry, it just keeps rolling out the profits year after year after year.*

Fund Index

A

ABC Fully-Managed Fund, 323, 323-24

ABC Fundamental Value Fund, 177, 389, 397

Abrams, Ken, 231

Admax American Performance Fund, 231

Admax American Select Growth Fund (formerly U.S. Polymetric Performance Fund), 352

Admax Canadian Income Fund, 290

Admax Canadian Select Growth Fund (formerly Polymetric Performance Fund), 325

Admax Global Health Sciences, 400, 405

Admax Regent Group, 111, 167

Aetna Capital Management, 191

AGF American Growth Fund, 230

AGF Asian Growth Fund "A," 65, 87, 411

AGF Canadian Bond Fund, 54, 290

AGF Canadian Equity Fund, 54, 178

AGF Canadian Resources Fund, 83, 222, 408

AGF China Focus Fund "A," 67, 405

AGF Global Government Bond Fund, 317-18

AGF Group, 111-12

AGF Growth Equity Fund, 178

AGF Growth and Income Fund (formerly Corporate Investors Ltd.), 324

AGF High Income Fund (formerly AGF Preferred Income Fund), 324

AGF Japan Fund, 87, 268

AGF Money Market Account, 54, 361

AGF Special Fund, 230-31

AGF Strategic Income Fund, 318

AGF U.S. Dollar Money Market Account, 104, 105, 380

AIC Advantage Fund, 178-79, 410

AIC Group, 112

AIC Value Fund, 231, 412

All-Canadian Capitalfund (formerly All-Canadian Dividend Fund), 180

All-Canadian Compound Fund. See All-Canadian CapitalFund

All-Canadian Consumerfund (formerly All-Canadian Revenue Growth Fund), 222

All-Canadian Resources, 83

All-Canadian Resources Corporation (formerly Natural Resources Growth Fund), 222-23

Allan Jacobs, 213

Allied Canadian Fund. See Dynamic Canadian Growth Fund

Allied Dividend Fund. See Dynamic Growth Fund

AltaFund Investment Corporation, 222, 223

Altamira Balanced Fund, 325-26

Altamira Bond Fund, 166, 290-91, 412

Altamira Capital Growth Fund, 107, 180-81, 397

Altamira Equity Fund, 103, 104, 107, 177, 180, 181, 397, 399

Altamira Global Diversified Fund (formerly Altamira Diversified Fund), 168, 352, 408

Altamira Growth and Income Fund, 105, 323, 326, 398, 400

Altamira Income Fund, 104, 105, 106, 107, 108, 289, 291, 385, 390, 394, 399, 406

Altamira Investment Services, 152-54, 167
fund family, 112-13

Altamira Japanese Opportunity, 392

Altamira Precious and Strategic Metal, 391

Altamira Resource Fund, 222, 223

Altamira Science and Technology Fund, 153

Altamira Select American Fund, 103, 231-32

Altamira Short Term Income Fund, 380
Altamira Short-Term Global Income Fund, 103, 107, 380-81
Altamira Special Growth Fund, 181, 401
Altamira Speculative High-Yield fund, 153
Altamira U.S. Larger Company, 391
AMD Fixed Income Fund *see* Atlas Canadian Bond Fund
AMI Partners, 328
AMI Private Capital Equity Fund (formerly Church Street Equity Fund), 179
AMI Private Capital funds, 113
AMI Private Capital Income Fund (formerly Church Street Income Fund), 290
AMI Private Capital Money Market Fund (formerly Church Street Money Market Fund), 361, 390
AMI Private Capital Optimix Fund (formerly Church Street Balanced Fund), 325
Apex, fund family, 113-14
Associate Investors Ltd., 182
Atlas American Growth Fund, 232
Atlas American Money Market Fund (formerly Finsco U.S. Dollar Money Market Fund), 381
Atlas Canadian Balanced Fund (formerly Jarislowsky Finsco Balanced Fund), 326-27
Atlas Canadian Bond Fund (formerly Jarislowsky Finsco Bond Fund), 291
Atlas Canadian Growth Fund (formerly Jarislowsky Finsco Canadian Equity Fund), 182
Atlas Canadian Money Market Fund (formerly Finsco Canadian Money Market Fund), 362
Atlas Canadian T-Bill Fund, 362
Atlas funds, 114
Atlas Global Equity Fund (formerly Finsco Global Fund), 246
Attard, Bernadotte, 275

B
Babson-Stewart Ivory International, 252
Bank of Montreal, 115, 310, 311
Baring International Investment Ltd., 275

Barrtor American Fund. *See* Cassels Blaikie American Fund
Bassini, Emilio, 278
Bay, Greg, 199
BEA Associates, 247, 278
Beck, Nuala, 97, 98, 405
Begg, Ron, 359
Bengough, Norm, 294, 331
Bernal, Marie-Claude, 353
Bernardo, Robert J., 187
Betts, Rick, 218
Beutel, Austin, 44
Beutel Goodman, 183
    funds, 116
Beutel Goodman American Equity, 230, 233, 410
Beutel Goodman Balanced Fund, 327
Beutel Goodman Canadian Equity Fund, 183-84
Beutel Goodman Income Fund, 291-92
Beutel Goodman Money Market Fund, 362
Biard, Jonathan, 190, 191
Bissett American Equity Fund, 233, 327
Bissett Asset Allocation Fund. *See* Bissett Dividend Income Fund
Bissett and Associates, 94, 182
Bissett Balanced Fund. *See* Bissett Dividend Income Fund
Bissett Bond Fund, 292, 327
Bissett Canadian Equity Fund, 184, 327, 409
Bissett, David, 94
Bissett Dividend Income Fund, 281-82
Bissett funds, 116
Bissett Money Market Fund, 362
Bissett Multinational Fund, 94-95
Bissett Retirement Fund, 323, 327
Bissett Small Cap Fund, 184
Boisvert, Jean, 357
Boivin, Lynne, 328
Bolton Tremblay, 182, 183, 232, 327, 362
Bolton Tremblay Bond Fund. *See* BPI Canadian Bond Fund
Bolton Tremblay and Landmark funds, 182-83
Bolton Tremblay Landmark Income fund. *See* BPI Income Fund
Bonham, Mark, 352
BPI, 167

BPI American Equity Value Fund (BT Landmark American Fund), 232

BPI American Small Companies Fund (formerly BPI American Equity Growth Fund), 232-33, 410

BPI Canadian Balanced Fund, 327

BPI Canadian Bond Fund, 291

BPI Canadian Equity Fund, 183

BPI Canadian Equity Value Fund, 182-83

BPI Canadian Resource Fund (formerly BT Landmark Resource Fund), 83-84, 223-24

BPI Canadian Small Companies Fund (formerly BPI Canadian Small Cap Fund), 73, 183

BPI Capital, 114-15

BPI Emerging Growth Fund, 232

BPI Global Balanced RSP Fund, 352, 406

BPI Global Equity Fund (formerly Walwyn International Fund), 247

BPI Global Opportunities, 389, 408

BPI Income Fund (formerly Bolton Tremblay Landmark Income Fund), 281

BPI International Equity Fund (formerly BT Landmark International Fund), 247

BPI One Decision Balanced Fund, 327

BPI T-Bill Fund (formerly BPI Money Market Fund), 362

Braive, John, 306

Brandes, Charles, 260

Broadfoot, James, 244

Brown, Grant, 43, 46, 404

Brown, Keith, 355

BT Landmark American Fund. See BPI American Equity Value Fund

BT Landmark Balanced Fund, 327

BT Landmark Bond Fund. See BPI Canadian Bond Fund

BT Landmark Canadian Fund, 182

BT Landmark International Equity Fund. See BPI International Equity Fund

BT Landmark Money Market Fund, 362

BT Landmark Resource Fund. See BPI Canadian Resource Fund

BT Landmark Short-Term Interest Fund, 362

BT Landmark Small Cap Fund, 183

Bullock American Fund, 184, 233-34, 269, 401

Bullock Asset Strategy (formerly Bullock Balanced Fund), 328

Bullock Growth Fund, 184-85, 214, 400

Burgeonvest Ltd., 189, 310

Burns Fry Bond Fund. See Jones Heward Bond Fund

Burns Fry Canadian Fund. See Jones Heward Canadian Balanced Fund

Burns, James, 274

C

C.I. Covington, 404

C.I. Emerging Markets Fund, 278

C.I. European Fund, 273, 274, 402

C.I. Global Fund (formerly Universal Global Fund), 247

C.I. Money Market Fund, 363

C.I. Pacific Fund (formerly Universal Pacific Fund), 66, 88, 104, 168, 269, 396

C.I. Sector Fund, 247-48

C.I.—C.P.A. Business Ventures Fund Inc., 43, 48

Callaghan, John, 233, 234

CAMAF, 187

Cambridge American Growth Fund, 234

Cambridge Americas Fund, 263

Cambridge Balanced Fund, 323, 328-29, 401

Cambridge China, 391, 411

Cambridge Global Fund (formerly Cambridge Diversified Fund), 248

Cambridge Growth Fund, 185-86, 407

Cambridge Pacific Fund, 88, 269, 395

Cambridge Resource Fund, 84, 224

Cambridge Special Equity Fund, 81, 186, 386, 393, 395

Campbell, Richard, 98

Canada Life Assurance Co., 116-17

Canada Life Canadian Equity S-9, 186

Canada Life Fixed Income Fund S-19, 292

Canada Life Investment Management, 187

Canada Life Managed Fund S-35, 329

Canada Life Money Market Fund
S-29, 363-64
Canada Life U.S. and International
Equity Fund, 187, 396, 409
Canada Life U.S. and International
Equity Fund S-34, 248-49
Canada North American Fund. *See*
Everest North American Fund
Canada Trust, 310
Canada Trust Investment Income
Fund—Income, 292
Canadian Anaesthetists Mutual
Accumulating Fund, 187
Canadian Imperial Bank of
Commerce. *See* CIBC
Canadian International Group,
117-18, 363
Canadian Investment Fund, 187
Canadian Medical Discoveries
Fund, 43, 48, 404
Canadian Natural Resource Fund.
See First Heritage Fund
Canadian Protected Fund, 187-88,
236, 410, 413
Capital Alliance Ventures Inc., 43,
404
Capstone Cash Management Fund,
364, 411
Capstone International Investment
Trust, 249
Capstone Investment Trust, 329
Cassells Blaikie American Fund
(formerly Barrtor American
Fund), 234, 334
Cassells Blaikie Canadian Fund,
329
Cassels Blaikie International Fund,
249, 386
Central Guaranty Trust, 197
Central-Guaranty FuturLink funds,
312
Century DJ Fund, 235
Charlebois, L. Richard, 43
Chou Associates Fund, 188, 249
Chou, Francis, 188, 249
Chou RRSP Fund, 188
Christ, Alex, 201, 401
Church Street Balanced Fund. *See*
AMI Private Capital Optimix
Fund
Church Street Equity Fund. *See*
AMI Private Capital Equity
Fund
Church Street Income Fund. *See*
AMI Private Capital Income
Fund

Church Street Money Market Fund.
See AMI Private Capital Money
Market Fund
CIBC
fund family, 117
funds, 76-77
CIBC Balanced Income & Growth
Fund, 328
CIBC Canadian Equity Fund, 72,
185, 387
CIBC Canadian Bond Fund, 292
CIBC Canadian T-Bill Fund, 363
CIBC Capital Appreciation Fund,
72, 185
CIBC Equity Income Fund, 281,
282
CIBC Global Equity Fund, 248
CIBC Money Market Fund, 363
CIBC Mortgage Investment Fund,
106, 107, 108, 109, 310, 388,
400
CIBC Premium Canadian T-Bill
Fund, 167, 363, 389
CIBC Securities, 168, 335
CIBC U.S. Dollar Money Market
Fund, 381
CIBC U.S. Equity Fund, 234
Clean Environment Balanced Fund,
323, 329-30, 404
Clean Environment Equity Fund,
177, 188, 404
Clean Environment Funds, 118
Co-operative Trust Company, 263
Co-operative Trust for Ethical
Funds, 295
Co-operative Trust Growth Fund.
See Ethical North American
Equity Fund
Co-operative Trust Interest Fund.
See Ethical Money Market Fund
Co-operators Investment
Counselling, 331
Coleman, Gerald, 161, 243, 400
Coleman, Sue, 181, 326, 401
Colonia Bond Fund, 290, 293
Colonia Equity Fund, 189
Colonia Life, 189
funds, 118-119
Colonia Money Market Fund, 364
Colonia Mortgage Fund, 310
Concorde funds, 119
Concorde Growth Fund, 189
Concorde Income Fund, 293
Concorde Mortgage Fund, 310
Confed Growth Fund, 189
Confed Mortgage Fund, 310

Confederation Life B Fund, 189
Confederation Life Fund C, 293
Connor, Clark and Lunn, 193, 287, 308
Contrarian Strategy Futures Limited Partnership, 90
Coombs, Clive, 318
Cornerstone Balanced Fund (formerly Metropolitan Balanced Growth Fund), 330
Cornerstone Bond Fund, 293
Cornerstone Canadian Growth Fund, 189
Cornerstone funds, 119
Cornerstone Global Fund (formerly Metropolitan Speculators Fund), 249
Cornerstone Government Money Fund, 364
Cornerstone U.S. Equity Fund (formerly Metropolitan U.S. Fund), 235
Corporate Investment Associates, 209
Corporate Investors Ltd. See AGF Growth and Income Fund
Corporate investors Stock Fund. See AGF Growth Equity Fund
Credit Union Central of Canada, 193, 263, 331
Crocus Fund, 43-44
CSA Management, 226
Cundill, Peter, 166, 250, 413
Cundill Security Fund, 166, 176, 190, 397, 400, 410
Cundill Value Fund, 103, 250, 396, 413

D
Dalley, Fred, 83, 224, 327
David L. Babson & Co., 252
Davies, J. Picton, 325, 352
Deans Knight Capital Management, 206
Deans, Wayne, 206
DeGreer, Dina, 101, 389
Delaney, Ken, 45
Delaney, Kiki, 185, 214, 218, 219, 397, 400, 413
Desjardins Balanced Fund, 330
Desjardins Bond Fund, 293
Desjardins Environment Fund, 190, 404
Desjardins Equity Fund, 190
Desjardins funds, 120
Desjardins International Fund, 250

Desjardins, Jean-Guy, 354
Desjardins Money Market Fund, 365
Desjardins Mortgage Fund, 310
Devlin, Neil, 307, 321
DGC Entertainment Ventures Corp., 44
Disbrow, Robert, 206
DK Enterprises Fund. See 20-20 Canadian Growth Fund
Dominion Equity Resource Fund, 84, 224, 385
Domolky, George, 194, 332
Driehaus, Richard, 389
Dunn, Alastair, 193
Dynamic American Fund, 263
Dynamic Canadian Growth Fund (formerly Allied Canadian Fund), 81, 190-91
Dynamic Dividend Fund, 105, 282-83, 393
Dynamic Dividend Growth Fund, 393
Dynamic Europe Fund (formerly Dynamic Europe 1992 Fund), 274
Dynamic Fund of Canada, 191
Dynamic Funds Management, 164
fund family, 120
Dynamic Global Bond Fund, 107, 108, 109, 318
Dynamic Global Green Fund (formerly Dynamic Global Fund), 250-51, 386, 396, 402
Dynamic Growth Dividend Fund (formerly Allied Dividend Fund), 283
Dynamic Income Fund, 109, 294, 394, 398, 406
Dynamic International Fund (formerly Allied International Fund), 246, 251
Dynamic Managed Portfolio, 330
Dynamic Money Market Fund, 365
Dynamic Partners Fund, 52, 105, 106, 107, 108, 109, 323, 330-31, 412
Dynamic Precious Metals Fund, 86, 225, 402, 411

E
Edwards, Barry, 320
Elliott & Page American Growth Fund (formerly Metropolitan American Growth Fund), 235
Elliott & Page Balanced Fund, 323, 331

Elliott & Page Bond Fund, 294

Elliott & Page Equity Fund, 191-92, 400

Elliott & Page Investment Management, 121, 167, 208, 301, 331, 343

Elliott & Page Money Market Fund, 365, 411

Elliott & Page T-Bill, 403

Empire Balanced fund, 331

Empire Elite Equity Fund, 192, 409

Empire Equity Growth Fund (formerly Equity Growth Fund #1), 192

Empire Fund #2, 294

Empire Funds, 121-22

Empire International Growth Fund, 251, 409

Empire Money Market Fund, 366

Endurance Canadian Balanced Fund. See Laurentian Canadian Balanced Fund

Endurance Canadian Equity Fund. See Laurentian Special Equity Fund

Endurance Global Equity Fund. See Laurentian Global Balanced Fund

Endurance Government Bond Fund. See Laurentian Government Bond Fund

Enterprise Fund, 44

Equitable Life funds, 122

Equitable Life Segregated Accumulative Income Fund, 294

Equitable Life Segregated Common Stock Fund, 193

Ethical Balanced Fund (Classic I-Plan Balanced fund), 331

Ethical fund family, 122-23, 193

Ethical Income Fund, 295

Ethical Money Market Fund (Co-operative Trust Interest Fund), 366

Ethical North American Equity Fund (formerly Co-operative Trust Growth Fund), 263-64, 405

European Investment and Privitization Fund. See Vision Europe Fund

Everest
fund family, 123
group, 310

Everest Balanced Fund, 332

Everest Bond Fund, 292, 295

Everest Emerging Markets Fund, 64

Everest Money Market Fund, 366

Everest Mortgage Fund, 311, 400

Everest North American Fund (formerly Canada Trust North American Fund), 264

Everest Special Equity Fund, 193-94

Everest Stock Fund (formerly Everest Growth Fund), 194

Everest U.S. Equity Fund, 335

Everington, Peter, 68, 255-56, 272

Exar Real Estate Fund, 168, 356-57, 386

Excelsior group, 310

F

Falls, Phillip, 308

Farmer, Patrick, 99

Ficadre Balanced Fund (formerly SNF Balanced Fund), 332

Ficadre Bond Fund (formerly SNF Bond Fund), 295

Ficadre Money Market Fund, 366

Ficadre Stock Fund (SNF Stock Fund), 194

Fidelity, 164
fund family, 123-24

Fidelity Canadian Bond Fund (formerly Fidelity Government Bond Fund), 295

Fidelity Canadian Short Term Asset Fund, 366

Fidelity Capital Builder Fund, 194-95, 395, 402

Fidelity Capital Conservation Fund. See Fidelity Canadian Bond Fund

Fidelity Emerging Markets Portfolio, 64, 391

Fidelity European Growth Fund, 104, 273, 274-75, 396

Fidelity Far East Fund, 66, 88, 268, 270, 405, 411

Fidelity Growth America Fund, 103, 236, 396

Fidelity Growth and Income Fund (formerly Fidelity Capital Balanced Fund), 332, 402

Fidelity International Portfolio Fund, 252, 397

Fidelity Japanese Growth, 104

Fidelity North American Income, 395

Fidelity Small Cap America, 412

Fierstein, Barry, 233

Finsco Bond Fund. *See* Atlas
Canadian Bond Fund
Finsco Global Fund. *See* Atlas
Global Equity Fund
Finsco and Jarislowsky Finsco
funds, 182
Finsco Money Market Fund. *See*
Atlas Canadian Money Market
Fund
Finsco U.S. Dollar Money Market
Fund. *See* Atlas American
Money Market Fund
First American Fund, 236
First Canadian Asset Allocation
Fund (First Canadian Balanced
Fund), 332, 388
First Canadian Bond Fund, 289, 295
First Canadian Equity Index Fund,
72, 195
First Canadian funds, 75-76
First Canadian International Bond
Fund, 316
First Canadian International
Growth, 387
First Canadian Japanese Growth,
387
First Canadian Money Market
Fund, 104, 105, 106, 107, 108,
366
First Canadian Mortgage Fund,
106, 107, 108, 109, 310, 311,
385, 388, 390, 394, 398, 399,
406
First Canadian NAFTA Advantage
Fund, 387, 405
First Canadian Special Growth
Fund, 72
First City Government Money
Fund. *See* Cornerstone
Government Money Fund
First Heritage Fund (formerly
Canadian Natural Resource
Fund), 225
First Ontario Fund, 44-45, 405
Fleming Group, 331
Friedberg Currency Fund, 90, 393
Fruchet, Jean-Pierre, 187-88, 236,
240, 390, 398, 413
FuturLink Canadian Growth Fund,
197
FuturLink Mortgage Fund. *See*
Green Line Mortgage-Backed
Fund
FuturLink Select Fund. *See* Green
Line Balanced and Growth
Fund

G

G.T., 168
funds, 124-25
G.T. America Growth, 392
G.T. Capital Management, 354
Garmaise, Gordon, 57
Gartmore Capital Management,
275
GBC Canadian Bond Fund, 295-96
GBC Canadian Growth Fund, 195,
390
GBC Group, fund family, 124
GBC International Growth Fund,
252, 386, 402
GBC Money Market Fund, 367
GBC North American Growth, 390
GBC North American Growth
Fund, 264
General Trust Balanced Fund, 333
General Trust Bond Fund, 296
General Trust Canadian Equity
Fund, 195-96, 411
General Trust Growth Fund, 196
General Trust International Fund,
252
General Trust Investment, fund
family, 125
General Trust Money Market Fund,
367
General Trust Mortgage Fund, 311
General Trust U.S. Equity Fund,
236-37
Girard, Philippe, 215
Global Strategy, 167, 185
fund family, 125-26
Global Strategy World Bond Fund,
319
Global Strategy Canada Growth
Fund, 196, 402
Global Strategy Canadian Growth,
396
Global Strategy Canadian Small
Cap Fund, 96-97
Global Strategy Diversified
Americas Fund, 264-65, 386,
407
Global Strategy Diversified Bond
Fund, 318-19
Global Strategy Diversified Growth
Fund, 353
Global Strategy Diversified Japan
Plus, 407
Global Strategy Diversified Savings,
103, 107
Global Strategy Diversified Short-
Term Income Fund (formerly

Global Strategy World Money Fund), 381

Global Strategy Europe Plus Fund (formerly Global Strategy Europe), 275

Global Strategy Far East Fund. *See* Global Strategy Japan Fund

Global Strategy Fund, 253

Global Strategy Income Plus Fund, 323, 333, 401

Global Strategy Japan Fund (formerly Global Strategy Japan Plus Fund), 270, 392

Global Strategy Real Estate Securities Fund, 357, 386, 395

Global Strategy Small Cap, 389

Global Strategy T-Bill Savings Fund, 367

Global Strategy U.S. Growth, 412

Global Strategy U.S. Savings Fund (formerly Global Strategy U.S. Money Fund), 381-82

Global Strategy World Emerging Companies, 391

Global Strategy World Equity Fund, 253

Gluskin Sheff, 263

Goldfund, 86, 225-26, 394

Goldman Sachs, 235, 331

Goldring, Warren, 318

Goldtrust, 226, 406

Goodman, Jonathan, 225

Graham, Benjamin, 250, 396

Great West Life, fund family, 126

Great-West Life Canadian Bond Fund, 296

Great-West Life Canadian Equity Fund, 196-97

Great-West Life Diversified RS Fund, 333

Great-West Life Equity Index Fund, 197

Great-West Life Equity/Bond Fund, 333-34, 409

Great-West Life Money Market Fund, 367

Great-West Life Mortgage Fund, 311-12

Great-West Life Real Estate, 357, 386, 407, 409

Green Line, 75

Green Line Balanced Growth Fund (formerly FuturLink Select Fund), 334

Green Line Balanced Income Fund, 334

Green Line Blue Chip Equity Fund, 72, 197-78, 402

Green Line Canadian Bond Fund, 289, 296, 388

Green Line Canadian Equity Fund, 198

Green Line Canadian Government Bond Fund, 297

Green Line Canadian Index Fund, 72, 198

Green Line Canadian Money Market Fund, 367-68

Green Line Canadian T-Bill Fund, 368

Green Line Dividend Fund, 283

Green Line Emerging Markets Fund, 65

Green Line Latin American Growth, 387, 392

Green Line Mortgage Fund, 312

Green Line Mortgage-Backed Fund (formerly FuturLink Mortgage Fund), 312

Green Line North American Growth, 387

Green Line Precious Metals, 391

Green Line Science and Technology Fund, 71, 96, 166, 386, 391, 395, 399, 405, 408

Green Line Short Term Income Fund, 297, 400

Green Line U.S. Index Fund, 237

Green Line U.S. Money Market Fund, 107, 108, 282

Group Investment Ltd., 204

Gryphon Investment Counsel, 335-36

GT Global Infrastructure Class, 95, 405

GT United Global Telecommunications Class, 95, 405

GTS Canadian Protected, 394

Guardian American Equity Fund (formerly Guardian Growth Fund), 237

Guardian Canadian Balanced Fund, 334-35, 398

Guardian Canadian Equity Fund, 198

Guardian Canadian Income Fund (formerly Guardian Canada Bond Fund), 297-98

Guardian Canadian Money Market Fund (formerly Guardian Short Term Money Fund), 368

Guardian Emerging Markets Fund, 65
Guardian Enterprise Fund, 198
Guardian Global Equity Fund, 253
Guardian Group, fund family, 127
Guardian Growth Equity Fund, 198-99
Guardian International Income Fund, 319
Guardian Preferred Dividend Fund, 283-84
Guardian Timing Services, 236
Guardian U.S. Money Market Fund, 382

H

Habermann, Dick, 252
Hazlewood, Richard, 64
Hercules, fund family, 127-28
Hill and Samuel, 246
Hillery, John D., 239, 413
Hirsch, Veronika, 85
Hodgson Roberton Laing, fund family, 128
Hodgson Roberton Laing Balanced Fund, 335
Hodgson Roberton Laing Bond Fund (formerly Waltaine Bond Fund), 298
Hodgson Roberton Laing Canadian Fund (formerly Waltaine Canadian Fund), 199
Hodgson Roberton Laing Instant $$ Fund (formerly Waltaine Instant $$ Fund), 368-69
Hongkong Bank, fund family, 128
Hongkong Bank Balanced Fund, 335
Hongkong Bank Equity Fund, 199-200
Hongkong Bank Money Market Fund, 369
Howson, Richard, 256
Hughes, King & Company, 249
Hume Growth & Income Fund. See Altamira Global Diversified Fund
Hyperion Asian Trust, 66, 88
Hyperion Aurora, 73, 394
Hyperion European Trust, 275
Hyperion Fixed Income Fund, 298
Hyperion Managed Fund, 335
Hyperion Value Line Equity Trust, 230, 237-38, 410

I

IAI International Ltd., 246

ICM Balanced Fund (formerly Integra Balanced Fund), 323, 335-36
Ihnatowyez, Ian, 188
Imperial Growth Canadian Equity Fund, 200, 401
Imperial Growth Diversified Fund, 336
Imperial Growth Money Market Fund, 369
Imperial Growth North American Equity Fund, 265
Imperial Life, fund family, 128-29, 200
Industrial Alliance, 200
fund family, 129
Industrial Alliance Diversified Fund, 336
Industrial Alliance Money Market Fund, 369
Industrial Alliance Mortgage Fund, 312
Industrial Alliance Stocks Fund, 200
Industrial American Fund, 238
Industrial Balanced Fund, 336
Industrial Bond Fund, 298
Industrial Cash Management Fund, 163, 369-70, 385, 390, 394, 398
Industrial Dividend Fund, 284
Industrial Equity Fund, 200-201, 408
Industrial funds (Mackenzie), 162, 163
Industrial Future Fund, 210, 405
Industrial Global Fund. See Universal World Equity Fund
Industrial Growth Fund, 177, 201, 337, 401
Industrial Horizon Fund, 177, 201-202, 337
Industrial Income Fund, 337
Industrial Mortgage Securities Fund (formerly Mackenzie Income Fund), 106, 107, 108, 109, 337
Industrial Pension Fund, 337-38
Industrial Short-Term Fund, 370
Integra Balanced Fund. See ICM Balanced Fund
Integrated Growth Fund, 45, 404
Invesco Trust, 94
Invesnat Canadian Equity Fund, 202
Invesnat Money Market Fund, 370
Invesnat Mortgage Fund, 312-13
Invesnat Retirement Balanced Fund, 338

Invesnat Short-Term Government
    Bond Fund, 298-99
InvesNat U.S. Money Market Fund,
    380, 382
Investors Canadian Equity Fund,
    202, 254, 353
Investors Dividend Fund, 284
Investors European Growth Fund,
    274, 275-76
Investors Global Fund, 203, 253,
    254, 353
Investors Government Bond Fund
    (formerly Investors Bond Fund),
    299, 353
Investors Group, 160-62
    fund family, 129-30
Investors Growth Plus Portfolio, 353
Investors Growth Portfolio Fund,
    246, 254
Investors Income Plus Portfolio, 338
Investors Income Portfolio Fund,
    299
Investors Japanese Growth Fund,
    89, 271
Investors Mortgage Fund, 313
Investors Mutual of Canada, 338
Investors North American Growth
    Fund, 254, 265
Investors Pacific International Fund,
    66, 89, 271
Investors Real Property Fund, 353,
    357-58
Investors Retirement Growth
    Portfolio, 202-03
Investors Retirement Mutual Fund,
    203
Investors Retirement Plus Portfolio,
    338-39
Investors Special Fund, 254, 266
Investors Summa Fund, 203, 404
Investors U.S. Growth Fund, 229,
    238, 254, 353, 385
Ivy Canadian, 162, 401
Ivy Enterprise Fund, 203

J
Jacobs, Allan, 401
Jardine Fleming, 331
Jarislowsky Finsco Balanced Fund.
    See Atlas Canadian Balanced
    Fund
Jarislowsky Finsco Bond Fund. *See*
    Atlas Canadian Bond Fund
Jarislowsky Finsco Canadian
    Equity Fund. *See* Atlas
    Canadian Growth Fund

Jarislowsky Fraser, 326
Javasky, Jerry, 161, 203, 243, 401
Jones Heward, fund family, 130
Jones Heward American Fund, 238
Jones Heward Bond Fund (formerly
    Burns Fry Bond Fund), 299
Jones Heward Canadian Balanced
    Fund (formerly Burns Fry
    Canadian Fund), 339
Jones Heward Fund, 203-04
Jones Heward Group, 203, 208

K
Kanko, Bill, 100-101, 389
Kennedy, Larry, 325
Kinlough, Richard, 46
Kleinwort Guardian Overseas Ltd.,
    65
Knight, Bain, Seath & Holbrook
    Capital Management, 198
Krembil, Robert, 217, 259

L
Labanowich, Michael, 327
Laketon Investment Management,
    187
Lamarche, Normand, 223, 326
Large Cap Canadian Growth Fund,
    182
Laurentian American Equity Fund,
    266
Laurentian Canadian Balanced
    Fund (formerly Endurance
    Canadian
Balanced Fund), 339
Laurentian Canadian Equity Fund
    (formerly Viking Canadian
    Fund), 204
Laurentian Commonwealth Fund
    (formerly Viking
    Commonwealth Fund), 353
Laurentian Dividend Fund (formerly
    Viking Dividend fund), 285
Laurentian Financial Services,
    285
Laurentian Funds Mananagement,
    fund family, 130-31
Laurentian Global Balanced Fund
    (formerly Endurance Global
    Equity Fund), 354
Laurentian Government Bond
    Fund (formerly Endurance
    Government Bond Fund),
    299-300
Laurentian Income Fund (formerly
    Viking Income Fund), 300

Laurentian International Fund (formerly Viking International Fund), 254

Laurentian Money Market Fund, 370-71

Laurentian Special Equity Fund (formerly Endurance Canadian Equity Fund), 204

Lazard Frères, 232, 233, 247

Lee, K.C., 66, 88, 270, 411

Leith, Murray, 339

Leith Wheeler, fund family, 131

Leith Wheeler Balanced Fund (formerly Leith Wheeler All-Value Balanced Fund), 239, 323, 390

Leith Wheeler U.S. Equity, 412

Leon Frazer and Associates, 182

Lewis, Brad, 396

Lewis, Simon, 70

Lincluden Management, 336

LLoyd George Management, 99

LLoyd George, Robert, 67

London Life, fund family, 131-32

London Life Bond Fund, 300

London Life Canadian Equity Fund, 204-205

London Life Diversified Fund, 340

London Life Money Market Fund, 371

London Life Mortgage Fund, 313, 394, 406, 409

London Life U.S. Equity Fund, 239, 402

Lotus Balanced Fund (formerly Lotus Fund), 340

Lotus Income Fund (formerly MKW Income Fund), 371

Lovatt, Neil, 201

Lunn, Larry, 350

M

M.K. Wong and Associates, 199, 335

M.K. Wong Management, 340

McClure, James, 235

MacDougall, Gord, 287

McElvaine, Tim, 165, 176, 190, 250

Mackenzie Equity Fund, 203, 205

Mackenzie Financial Corporation, 100-101, 161-63, 166, 177, 200-201, 202, 205, 243-44, 254, 269, 284, 298, 321, 336, 337, 401
fund family, 131-32

Mackenzie Income Fund. *See* Industrial Mortgage Securities Fund

Mackenzie Sentinel Canada Bond Fund, 300

Mackenzie Sentinel Canada Equity Fund, 205

Mackenzie Sentinel Canada Money Market Fund, 371

Mackenzie Sentinel Global Fund, 254

MacLean, Anne, 263

McLean Budden, 334
fund family, 134-35

McLean Budden American Growth Fund, 230, 239

McLean Budden Balanced Fund, 342

McLean Budden Equity Growth, 207

McLean Budden Fixed Income Fund, 301

McLean Budden Money Market Fund, 372

McLeod, Curt, 100

McNeely, Len, 256

Mahoney, Michael, 95

Malouin, Bill, 304, 376

Manulife Cabot Canadian Equity, 391

Manulife Cabot Funds, fund family, 132-33

Manulife Capital Gains Fund, 205

Manulife Equity, 409

Manulife VistaFund Bond Fund, 300

Manulife VistaFund Diversified Investment Fund, 340

Manulife VistaFund Equity Fund, 205-206

Manulife VistaFund Short Term Securities Fund, 371-72, 403

Manulife-Vista Funds, fund family, 133, 205

Marathon Equity Fund, 81-82, 206, 393

Marcus, Robert, 290

Margin of Safety Fund, 239, 412

Maritime Life, 189
fund family, 133-34

Maritime Life Balanced Fund, 340

Maritime Life Bond Fund, 300-301

Maritime Life Growth Fund, 206

Maritime Life Money Market Fund, 372

Maritime Life S&P 500 Fund, 391

Martin Currie International Fund, 255

Massie, Tony, 185, 196, 328, 333, 396, 402

Mawer Canadian Balanced Retirement Savings Fund, 340, 403

Mawer Canadian Bond Fund, 301

Mawer Canadian Diversified Investment Fund, 340

Mawer Canadian Equity Fund, 206-207

Mawer Canadian Money Market Fund, 372

Mawer Investment Management, fund family, 134

Mawer New Canadian Fund (formerly Mawer North American Shares Fund), 207

Mawer World Investment Fund, 254

MDS Ventures, 43

MER Equity Fund. See Trans-Canada Pension Fund

Mersch, Frank, 153, 181

Met Life, 167

MetLife MVP Balanced Fund, 342

MetLife MVP Bond Income Fund, 301

MetLife MVP Equity Fund, 207, 409

MetLife MVP Money Market fund, 372

Metropolitan American Growth Fund. See Elliott & Page American Growth Fund

Metropolitan Balanced Growth Fund. See Cornerstone Balanced Fund

Metropolitan Life, fund family, 135

Metropolitan Protection Fund. See Cornerstone Government Money Fund

Metropolitan Speculators Fund. See Cornerstone Global Fund

Metropolitan U.S. Equity Fund. See Cornerstone U.S. Equity Fund

Michael, Irwin, 177, 323-24, 397

Middlefield Growth Fund, 226

Midland Walwyn, 182, 246, 291

Misener, Steven, 183

MKW Income Fund. See Lotus Income Fund

MM Canadian 35 Index Fund, 209

Mobius, Mark, 63, 278-79, 413

Montgomery Asset Management, 64

Montreal Trust, 177, 310

Montreal Trust Dividend Fund. See Scotia Excelsior Dividend Fund

Montreal Trust Excelsior Equity Fund, 214

Montreal Trust Excelsior Money Market Section, 376

Montreal Trust Excelsior—Balanced Section, 342

Montreal Trust Excelsior—Dividend, 105

Montreal Trust Excelsior—Income Section, 301

Montreal Trust Excelsior—International Section, 254

Montreal Trust Excelsior—Mortgage Section, 313, 314

Montreal Trust Excelsior—Total Return Section, 342, 347

Morgan Stanley Asset Management, 65

Mount, Duncan, 270

Multiple Opportunities Fund, 82, 207-208, 257, 393, 407, 408

Mutual Amerifund, 240

Mutual Bond Fund, 301

Mutual Canadian Indexfund, 208

Mutual Diversified 25, 342

Mutual Diversified 40, 343

Mutual Diversified 55, 343

Mutual Equifund, 208

Mutual Investco Inc., fund family, 135-36

Mutual Money Market Fund, 373

N

NAL Canadian Bond Fund, 301

NAL Canadian Diversified Fund, 343

NAL Canadian Equity Fund, 208

NAL Canadian Money Market Fund, 373

NAL Global Equity Fund, 255

NatCan Treasury Bill Fund, 373

National Bank, 202, 328
fund family, 136

National Life, 165
fund family, 136-37

National Life Balanced Fund, 323, 343

National Life Equities Fund, 209, 397, 410

National Life Fixed Income Fund, 289, 302, 406, 409

National Life Global Equities Fund, 255

National Life Money Market Fund, 361, 374

National Trust Balanced Fund, 344

National Trust Canadian Bond Fund (formerly National Trust Income Fund), 302

National Trust Canadian Equity Fund, 209

National Trust Emerging Markets, 392

Natural Resources Growth Fund. *See* All-Canadian Resources Corporation

Natural Trust, fund family, 137

Nigel Stephens Counsel Inc., 211, 251, 303

NN Balanced Fund, 343

NN Bond Fund, 302

NN Can-Am, 409

NN Canadian Growth Fund, 209, 409

NN Fund Management Ltd., fund family, 137

NN Global Fund, 255

NN Money Market Fund, 373

NN T-Bill Fund, 373

North American Life, 208
fund family, 138

O

O'Neil, Ford, 332

Optimum Balanced Fund, 344

Optimum Bond Fund (formerly St. Laurent Optimum Bond Fund), 302

Optimum Funds, fund family, 138

Optimum Savings Fund (formerly St. Laurent Optimum Savings Fund), 374

Optimum Stock Fund, 210

Orbit World Fund, 255

P

Pembroke Management Ltd., 195

Penman, Scott, 202

Phillips, Hager & North, 153-55
fund family, 138-39

Phillips, Hager & North $U.S. Money Market Fund, 382, 399, 403

Phillips, Hager & North Balanced Fund, 323, 344, 399

Phillips, Hager & North Bond Fund, 289, 303, 385, 389, 394, 399, 400, 403, 406

Phillips, Hager & North Canadian Equity Fund, 210

Phillips, Hager & North Dividend, 407

Phillips, Hager & North Dividend Income Fund, 285, 393

Phillips, Hager & North Money Market, 374, 398, 403

Phillips, Hager & North RSP/RIF Equity Fund, 210

Phillips, Hager & North Short Term Bond and Mortgage, 398

Phillips, Hager & North U.S. Fund, 230, 240, 399

Phillips, Hager & North Vintage Fund, 210-11

Pittico, Nereo, 191

Placements Optimum du St.-Laurent, 302

Polymetric Performance Fund. *See* Admax Canadian Select Growth Fund

Pomfrey, Stuart, 287

Pomphrey, Stuart, 305, 306

Premier Capital Management, 45

Proctor, Bill, 337

Protected American Fund, 236, 240-41, 398

Protected Canadian Fund, 390

Prudential American Equity, 391

Prudential Assurance, 215

Prudential Diversified Investment Fund, 344

Prudential Dividend Fund of Canada, 281, 285-86, 393, 411

Prudential Group, fund family, 139

Prudential Growth Fund Canada Ltd., 211

Prudential Income Fund of Canada, 303

Prudential Money Market Fund of Canada, 374

Prudential Natural Resource Fund of Canada, 84-85, 226-27, 393

Prudential Precious Metals Fund of Canada, 86, 227

Pursuit American Fund, 241

Pursuit Canadian Equity Fund, 211-12

Pursuit Group, fund family, 139-40

Pursuit Income Fund, 303

Pursuit Money Market Fund, 374-75

Q

Quinn, Michael, 184, 327

R

Rabin, Cedric, 326

Rands, Robert, 352

Rawe, Robert, 274

Regent Capital Management, 271

Regent Dragon 888, 408

Regent International Fund, 246, 255-56
Regent Korea Fund, 68, 268, 271, 403
Regent Tiger Fund, 268, 271-72
Regent World Income Fund, 290, 319-20
Reinsberg, John, 247
Rogers, Steve, 230
Rome, Michael, 233
Roth, Chuck, 218
Rothschild Asset Management, 275
Rothschild, N.M., 319
Royal Asian Growth, 387
Royal Canadian Small Cap Fund (formerly Royal Trust Canadian Special Growth Fund), 55, 72
Royal Energy Fund, 74-75, 222, 227
Royal European Growth Fund, 74, 104, 276, 387
Royal Funds, 73-75, 155-57, 167
fund family, 140-41
Royal Japanese Stock Fund, 89, 272, 408
Royal LePage Commercial Real Estate Fund, 358, 396
Royal Life, fund family, 141
Royal Life Balanced Fund, 344-45
Royal Life Canadian Growth, 391
Royal Life Equity Fund, 212
Royal Life Income Fund, 303-304
Royal Precious Metals Fund, 86-87, 227-28, 388, 393, 408
Royal Trust Advantage Balanced Fund, 345
Royal Trust Advantage Income Fund, 52, 345
Royal Trust American Stock Fund, 73, 229, 241-42, 385, 387, 399
Royal Trust Bond Fund, 55, 304, 388
Royal Trust Canadian Equity Fund, 55
Royal Trust Canadian Money Market Fund, 55, 375
Royal Trust Canadian Stock Fund, 212
Royal Trust Canadian Treasury Bill Fund, 375, 403
Royal Trust Energy Fund, 85
Royal Trust Growth and Income Fund (formerly RT Preferred Blue Chip Fund), 286

Royal Trust International Bond Fund, 104, 105, 106, 107, 108, 109, 317, 320
Royal Trust Mortgage Fund, 313-14
Royal Trust $U.S. Money Market Fund, 383
Royal Zweig Global Managed Assets, 388
Royal Zweig Strategic Growth Fund, 75, 230, 242, 387, 399
Roycom-Summit Realty Fund, 358
Roycom-Summit TDF Fund, 358
RoyFund Balanced Fund, 345
RoyFund Bond Fund, 304, 388
RoyFund Canadian Equity, 212
RoyFund Canadian Growth, 72
RoyFund Canadian T-Bill Fund, 104, 105, 106, 107, 108, 375
RoyFund Dividend Fund, 286
RoyFund Equity, 72
RoyFund International Income, 388
RoyFund Money Market Fund, 375-76
RoyFund Mortgage Fund, 310, 314
RoyFund U.S. Dollar Money Market Fund, 107, 108, 383
RoyFund U.S. Equity Fund, 73, 103, 230, 242, 386-87
RT Preferred Blue Chip Fund. See Royal Trust Growth and Income Fund
Russell, Bruce, 252

S
Sagit Management, 185, 186, 216-17, 324, 328, 377, 401, 411
fund family, 141-42
Sartz, John, 96-97, 183, 389
Satterhwaite, Patti, 64
Savings and Investment Trust American Fund, 242
Savings and Investment Trust Bond Fund, 304
Savings and Investment Trust Canadian Fund, 212-13
Savings and Investment Trust H Fund, 314
Savings and Investment Trust Money Market Fund, 376
Savings and Investment Trust Retirement Fund, 346
Savings and Investment Trust/Prêt et Revenue, fund family, 142
Saxon Balanced Fund, 346
Saxon International Fund, 256-57
Saxon Small Cap Fund, 213

Saxon Stock Fund, 213
Saxon World Growth, 246, 410, 412
Sceptre Asian Groth and
    International funds, 213
Sceptre Balanced Fund, 346
Sceptre Bond Fund, 304
Sceptre Equity Fund, 213, 397,
    401, 410
Sceptre Funds, 166
    fund family, 142
Sceptre Investment Counsel, 187,
    197, 334
Sceptre Money Market Fund, 376
Scerbo, Tom, 232
Scotia CanAm Growth, 392
Scotia Defensive Income Fund, 109
Scotia Excelsior American Equity
    Fund (formerly Scotia
    American Equity Growth
    Fund), 242-43, 387
Scotia Excelsior Balanced Fund,
    346-47
Scotia Excelsior Blue Chip Fund
    (formerly Scotia Canadian
    Equity Growth Fund), 214
Scotia Excelsior Canadian Growth
    Fund (formerly Montreal Trust
    Excelsior Equity Fund), 214,
    387, 397
Scotia Excelsior CanAm Income
    Fund, 317, 320
Scotia Excelsior Defensive Income
    Fund, 304-305, 398, 400
Scotia Excelsior Dividend Fund
    (Montreal Trust Dividend
    Fund), 287
Scotia Excelsior Funds, fund fami-
    ly, 143
Scotia Excelsior Income Fund
    (formerly Scotia Income Fund),
    305
Scotia Excelsior International
    Fund, 254, 257, 387, 399
Scotia Excelsior Money Market
    Fund, 376
Scotia Excelsior Mortgage Fund,
    314, 388, 394
Scotia Excelsior Premium T-Bill,
    390
Scotia Excelsior T-Bill Fund, 376
Scotia Excelsior Total Return Fund
    (formerly Montreal Trust Total
    Return Section), 347
Scotia Funds, 76, 177
Scotia Global Growth Fund, 254
Scotia Money Market Fund, 376

Scotia Precious Metals, 387
Scotia Stock and Bond Fund,
    346-47
Sherry, David, 95
Shrewsbury, Sandra, 100
Sjogren, Keith, 76
SNF Balanced Fund. See Ficadre
    Balanced Fund
SNF Bond Fund. See Ficadre Bond
    Fund
SNF Stock Fund. See Ficadre Stock
    Fund
Solidarity Fund, 356, 358-59
Solomon Brothers, 362, 381
Special Opportunities Fund, 73, 257
Spectrum Bullock, 185, 218
    See also Spectrum/Bullock,
    fund family
Spectrum Canadian Equity Fund,
    214
Spectrum Cash Reserve Fund,
    376-77
Spectrum Diversified Fund, 347
Spectrum Dividend Fund, 287
Spectrum Government Bond Fund,
    305
Spectrum Interest Fund, 306
Spectrum International Equity
    Fund, 257-58
Spectrum Savings Fund, 377
Spectrum/Bullock, fund family,
    143-44
Sportfund, 45-46
Sprung, Michael, 190-91
Stamdard Life Ideal Equity Fund,
    214-15
Standard Diversifund. See Standard
    Life Ideal Balanced Fund
Standard Life Bond Mutual Fund,
    306
Standard Life Ideal Balanced Fund
    (formerly Standard Life
    Balanced 2000 Fund), 348
Standard Life Ideal Bond Fund
    (formerly Standard Life Bond
    2000 Fund), 289, 306
Standard Life Ideal Equity Fund
    (formerly Standard Life Equity
    2000 Fund), 214-15
Starita, Paul, 70
Stein, Lyle, 346
Stein Roe & Farnham, 243, 260,
    401
Stewart Ivory & Co. Ltd., 252
Storie, Earl, 46
Strata Growth Fund, 215

Strata Income Fund, 306
Strata Money Market Fund, 377
Stratafund 40, 348
Stratafund 60, 348
St. Laurent Optimum Bond Fund. *See* Optimum Bond Fund
St. Laurent Optimum Savings Fund. *See* Optimum Savings Fund
Sun Life of Canada Investment Management, 214
Sun Life Investment Management, 287
Sunset Convertible Debenture and Income Fund. *See* 20/20 Income Fund
Sunset Convertible Preferred and Dividend Fund. *See* 20/20 Dividend Fund
Sutherland, Will, 291, 326
Swan, Robert, 188

T

T.A.L. Investment Counsel, 300-301
Talvest Bond Fund, 104, 105, 106, 107, 108, 289, 306
Talvest Diversified Fund, 325, 348, 402
Talvest Foreign Pay, 104, 105, 106
Talvest Funds, 270
  fund family, 144-45
Talvest Global Diversified Fund, 354
Talvest Growth Fund, 215
Talvest Income Fund, 306-307
Talvest Money Fund, 377
Talvest New Economy, 73, 97-98, 405
Talvest U.S. Diversified Fund, 354
Talvest U.S. Growth Fund, 243
Tattersall, Robert, 256
Taylor, David, 223
Taylor, Kathy, 354
TCW Europe, 274
TD Capital Group, 46
Templeton Balanced Fund (formerly Templeton Canadian Fund),348-49
Templeton Canadian Bond Fund (formerly Templeton Heritage Bond Fund), 307
Templeton Canadian Stock Fund (formerly Templeton Heritage Retirement Fund), 215-16, 396
Templeton Emerging Markets Fund, 63-64, 278-79, 413

Templeton Global Bond Fund, 320-21
Templeton Global Smaller Companies Fund (formerly Templeton Developing Growth Stock Fund), 258
Templeton Growth Fund, 103, 104, 106, 107, 108, 109, 246, 258-59, 385, 390, 397, 399, 406, 413
Templeton International Stock Fund (formerly Templeton Heritage Growth Fund), 259, 401
Templeton Management Ltd., fund family, 145-46
Templeton, Sir John, 268
Templeton Smaller Companies, 397
Templeton Treasury Bill Fund, 377
Top Fifty Equity Fund, 216
Top Fifty T-Bill/Bond Bond Fund, 307-308, 407
Top Fifty U.S. Equity Fund, 243
Toronto Dominion Asset Management, 283, 297
Toronto Dominion Securities (Green Line), 157
  fund family, 146
  See also Green Line
Trans-Canada Bond Fund, 308
Trans-Canada Equity Fund, 216, 402
Trans-Canada Income Fund (Trans-Canada Shares Series C), 349
Trans-Canada Money Market Fund, 361, 377
Trans-Canada Pension Fund (formerly MER Equity Fund), 82, 216-17
Trans-Canada Shares Series B, 248
TransAmerica's Growsafe Funds, fund family, 147
Trimark Advantage Bond, 98-99, 395
Trimark Canadian Fund, 103, 104, 106, 109, 177, 217, 385, 394, 397, 398, 399
Trimark Financial, 178
Trimark Fund, 103, 104, 106, 107, 108, 109, 165, 246, 259, 385, 390, 394, 397, 403, 406
Trimark Income Growth Fund, 349
Trimark Indo-Pacific Fund, 67, 99-100, 389, 395
Trimark Interest Fund, 377-78

Trimark Investment Management,
157-59, 162, 165
fund family, 147-48
Trimark RSP Equity Fund, 107,
176, 217-18, 385, 397, 406
Trimark Select Balanced Fund,
349-50
Trimark Select Canadian Growth
Fund, 218
Trimark Select Growth Fund,
259-60
Trimark—the Americas Fund, 67
20/20 Aggressive Growth, 389
20/20 American Tactical Asset
Allocation Fund, 354-55, 396,
412
20/20 Canadian Asset Allocation
Fund, 350
20/20 Canadian Growth Fund (formerly DK Enterprises Fund), 218
20/20 Dividend Fund (formerly
Sunset Convertible
Preferred and Dividend Fund),
106, 109, 281, 287-86, 393
20/20 Group, fund family, 148
20/20 India Fund, 166, 385
20/20 International Value Fund
(formerly 20/20 U.S.
Growth Fund), 260
20/20 Managed Futures Fund, 91-92
20/20 Money Market Fund, 378
20/20 World Fund, 351, 355
20/20 Income Fund (formerly
Sunset Convertible
Debenture & Income Fund), 308

U
U.S. Polymetric Performance Fund.
See Admax American Select
Growth Fund
UBS International Investment, 275
United American Equity Fund Ltd.
(formerly United Accumulative
Fund), 401 260
United American Growth Fund
(formerly United American
Fund), 243
United Canadian Bond Fund (for-
merly United Security Fixed
Income Fund), 308
United Canadian Equity Fund (for-
merly United Accumulative
Retirement Fund), 104, 218,
413
United Canadian Growth Fund
(formerly United Venture

Retirement Fund), 72-73, 103,
219, 397
United Canadian Interest Fund
(formerly United Canadian
Money Market Fund), 378
United Canadian Mortgage Fund,
314-15
United Canadian Portfolio of Funds
(formerly United Portfolio of
RSP Funds), 350
United Financial Management, fund
family, 148-49
United Global Equity Fund, 260-61
United Global Growth Fund Ltd.
(formerly United Venture
Fund), 246, 261
United Global Portfolio of Funds
(formerly United Portfolio of
Funds), 355
United Global Telecommunications
Fund, 100, 355, 405
United Security Fixed Income
Fund. See United Canadian
Bond Fund
United U.S. Dollar Money Market
Equity, 104, 105, 383
Universal Americas Fund (formerly
Universal American Fund), 263,
266
Universal Canadian Equity Fund
(formerly Universal Savings
Equity Fund), 219, 389
Universal Canadian Resource
Fund, 85, 228
Universal European Opportunities,
395
Universal Global Fund. See C.I.
Global Fund
Universal Group, 161-62
funds, 162
Universal Growth Fund, 100-101
Universal Japan, 392
Universal Pacific Fund. See C.I.
Pacific Fund
Universal U.S. Emerging Growth
Fund, 230, 243-44, 389, 408
Universal World Equity Fund (for-
merly Industrial Global Fund),
254, 261
Universal World Income RRSP
Fund, 321
University Avenue Canadian Fund,
219-20
University Avenue Growth, 395
University Avenue U.S. Growth
Fund, 244, 408

Uzielli, Steve, 178, 324

V

Value Line Inc., 237
van Berkom, Sebastian, 294
Vancouver City Savings Credit
    Union, 193
VenGrowth Investment Fund Ltd.,
    46, 48, 404
Viking Canadian Fund. *See*
    Laurentian Canadian Equity
    Fund
Viking Commonwealth Fund. *See*
    Laurentian Commonwealth
    Fund
Viking Dividend Fund. *See*
    Laurentian Dividend Fund
Viking Income Fund. *See*
    Laurentian Income Fund
Viking International Fund. *See*
    Laurentian International Fund
Vision Europe Fund (formerly
    European Investment and
    Privitization Fund), 273, 276
Vivash, John, 76

W

Walden, Sally, 274-75, 396
Waltaine Balanced Fund. *See*
    Hodson Roberton Laing
    Balanced Fund
Waltaine Bond Fund. *See* Hodson
    Roberton Laing Bond Fund
Waltaine Canadian Fund. *See*
    Hodgson Robertson Laing
    Canadian Fund

Waltaine Instant $$ Fund. *See*
    Hodson Roberton Laing Instant
    $$ Fund
Walwyn International Fund. *See*
    BPI global Equity Fund
Wellington Management, 231, 235,
    352
Wells Fargo, 354
Wellum, Jonathan, 178, 231, 412
Westbury Canadian Life Balanced
    Fund, 350
Westbury Canadian Life Bond
    Fund, 308
Westbury Canadian Life Equity
    Growth Fund (formerly
    Westbury Fund "A"), 220
Westbury Life Funds, fund family,
    149
Wheeler, Bill, 339
Wignall, Christian, 354
Wong, M.K. *See* M.K. Wong and
    Associates; M.K. Wong
    Management
Working Opportunity Fund, 46,
    356, 359
Working Ventures Canadian Fund,
    46, 48, 356, 359, 404

Y

Young, Jim, 73-74, 241, 242

Z

Zechner, John, 191
Zive, Gordon, 74-75, 227
Zweig, Martin, 73, 75, 242, 387,
    388

Subject Index

A

AGF MAP (Maximum Asset Plan), 58

asset allocation, 50-60
    do-it-yourself, 51-52
    mutual funds, 52-53
    non-personalized services, 53-56
    personalized services, 56-60

B

back-end load, 11-17
    negotiable, 15

balanced funds
    Canadian, 322-33
    international, 351

bank funds, 69-77

bond funds
    Canadian, 289-90
    international, 316-17
    marginal tax rate, 30

bond market movements, 7-8

C

Canadian dollar, 7, 317

capital cost allowance (CCA), 21, 29

capital gains, 19-20, 29

computer-driven asset allocation programs, 51-52

D

deferred sales charge, negotiable, 15

deferred-load option, 14

deferred sales charge. See back-end load

disposition costs, 20

dividend income funds, 280-81
    and registered plans, 40
    shopper's guide, 39-40
    tax advantages, 30-31, 38

dividend income mutual funds, 38-39

dividend tax credit, 19, 20, 29

dividends
    Canadian, 20-21, 29
    foreign, 21

E

economy, North American, 6

emerging markets funds, 8-9
    market timing, 63
    share value inflation, 62

equity funds
    Americas, 262
    broadly based, 81-82
    Canadian, 176
    Canadian sector, 221
    emerging markets, 277-78
    European, 8, 273-74
    Far East, 8, 87-89, 267
    international, 245-46
    U.S., 229-30

F

front-end load, 11-15

Fund companies
    load, 157-63
    no load, 151-56

I

inflation, 8

interest income, 21, 28-29

interest rates, 7, 8

L

labour-sponsored venture capital funds
    investment considerations, 47
    and registered plans, 47-49
    tax-advantaged income, 41-42

load charges, 10-17

load costs, 20

M

management fee, 11-14

money market funds, 9
    Canadian, 360-61
    international, 379
    marginal tax rate, 30

mortgage funds, 309
    commercial mortgages, 311-12
    marginal tax rate, 30

mutual fund
    profits, 19-21
    structures, 19

volitility, 78-80
mutual fund corporations, 19
mutual fund trusts, 19

N
no-load funds, no-load option, 10-15

P
portfolio mix
    aggressive growth, 103-104
    conservative growth, 104-105
    RIFs, 107-108
    self-directed RRSPs, 106-107
    short term, 108-109
precious metals funds, 85-87

Q
Quebec referendum, 7

R
real estate bust, 32-33
real estate funds
    open-ended, 34-35
    and registered portfolio, 35
    tax-advantaged income, 30-31, 34
Real Estate Investment Trusts

(REITs), 33-34
    dividend error, 35-36
registered retirement income plan (RRIP), 18
registered retirement savings plan (RRSP), 18
reinvested distributions, 20
rental income, 21, 29, 34
resource funds, 83-85, 176

S
sales commissions, 11, 14-16
STAR (Strategic Asset Allocation) program, 57-58, 60
stock market movements, 5-7

T
tax liability, mutual fund switches, 26, 50
tax rates, 21-25
tax shelters, 18

U
"umbrella" funds, 26

Y
year-end fund purchases, 26-27